Petra Grell · Winfried Marotzki · Heidi Schelhowe (Hrsg.)

Neue digitale Kultur- und Bildungsräume

Medienbildung und Gesellschaft
Band 12

Herausgegeben von

Winfried Marotzki
Norbert Meder
Dorothee M. Meister
Uwe Sander
Johannes Fromme

Petra Grell · Winfried Marotzki
Heidi Schelhowe (Hrsg.)

Neue digitale Kultur- und Bildungsräume

VS VERLAG FÜR SOZIALWISSENSCHAFTEN

Bibliografische Information der Deutschen Nationalbibliothek
Die Deutsche Nationalbibliothek verzeichnet diese Publikation in der Deutschen Nationalbibliografie; detaillierte bibliografische Daten sind im Internet über <http://dnb.d-nb.de> abrufbar.

1. Auflage 2010

Lektorat: Stefanie Laux

VS Verlag für Sozialwissenschaften ist Teil der Fachverlagsgruppe Springer Science+Business Media.
www.vs-verlag.de

Umschlaggestaltung: KünkelLopka Medienentwicklung, Heidelberg
Druck und buchbinderische Verarbeitung: Ten Brink, Meppel
Gedruckt auf säurefreiem und chlorfrei gebleichtem Papier
Printed in the Netherlands

ISBN 978-3-531-16958-3

Inhalt

Einleitung

von Petra Grell, Winfried Marotzki, Heidi Schelhowe

Um den Wandel und die Integration digitaler Medien in die Alltagswelt zu dokumentieren, ist ein Blick auf aktuelle Zahlen hilfreich. Sprunghaft gestiegen ist die Nutzung von Online-Medien in der Bevölkerung laut ARD-ZDF-Online-Studie von 6,5 % im Jahr 1997 auf 65,8 % im Jahr 2008. Die Internetnutzung der 14 bis 19 jährigen ist laut (N)Onliner Atlas von 63,4 % im Jahr 2001 auf 91,3 % gestiegen ([N]onliner Atlas 2008, 10). Nach der JIM-Studie nutzen aktuell 97 % der 12 bis 19-Jährigen zumindest gelegentlich das Internet. Starke Unterschiede zwischen den Geschlechtern oder bezüglich des formalen Bildungshintergrunds sind nur noch wenig erkennbar (JIM 2008, 46). Erkennbar ist dagegen, dass Online-Medien längst keine Tummelplätze für eine kleine Gruppe Technikbegeisterter sind, sondern zur Normalität des Alltags gehören. Im Alltag vermischen sich real-materielle, real-soziale und virtuelle Räume. Häufig ist es für uns irrelevant, ob wir Informationen offline oder online erhalten. Konvergenz findet nicht nur innerhalb der Medienwelt statt, sondern auch zwischen Medien- und Sozialwelten. Wir können in der Regel keinen systematischen Unterschied mehr zwischen Lebens- und Medienwelten machen. Das Schlagwort der Hybridisierung der Alltagswelt bezeichnet genau diesen Sachverhalt.

Für die Erforschung digitaler Kulturräume sind offensichtlich andere Forschungsansätze notwendig als für Mediennutzungsuntersuchungen. Mit Hilfe solcher Studien ist es in der Regel nur schwer möglich, differenzierter zu beschreiben, was beispielsweise Jugendliche im multifunktionalen Raum Internet tun und welche Bedeutung dies für den Wandel von Jugend hat. Aus der JIM-Studie wissen wir etwa, dass bei Jugendlichen die Nutzung von Suchmaschinen mit 73 % die häufigste Nennung erhält. Vielfach wird auch der Online-Raum exploriert: „einfach drauf los zu surfen (44 %) zählt bei knapp der Hälfte der Jugendlichen zu den regelmäßig ausgeübten Tätigkeiten“ (JIM 2008, 48). Was bedeutet „einfach drauf los zu surfen“? De facto steht durch das Internet eine nahezu unbegrenzte Zahl von Daten unterschiedlichster Qualität und Aktualität zur Verfügung, die – sofern man über hinreichende Kenntnisse verfügt – mit minimalem Aufwand visuell oder audiovisuell aufgerufen und zu Informationen oder auch zu Wissen werden können. Aber nicht alle Aktivitäten im Internet lassen sich mit „Informationen abrufen“ beschreiben. Social networking, Mitglied in einer Community sein sind Formen sozialer Interaktion, die eher Fragen der Anerkennung betreffen als Fragen der Wissensgenerierung. Von neuen methodischen Ansätzen wie Online-Ethnographie oder strukturaler Ethnographie, Weblog-Analyse, wisssenssoziologisch orientierter Diskursanalyse u.ä ist die Rede (vgl. Jörissen/Marotzki 2009).

Die Möglichkeit, differierende Sichtweisen zu nahezu jedem Aspekt des Lebens zu finden, ist mit keiner Bibliothek oder Mediathek aus der Vor-Internet-Zeit vergleichbar. Jeder Gegenstand und jedes Thema, unabhängig davon, ob es gesellschaftlich tabuisiert oder im eigenen sozialen Milieu verpönt ist, ist in seiner digitalen Repräsentation prinzipiell zugänglich, kann mit allen digital dokumentierten Widersprüchen und Alltagsfacetten „ergriffen" und sinnhaft mit der eigenen Person verbunden werden. Ob und wie Jugendliche in diese Diskurse einsteigen und welche Konsequenzen dies für ihr Selbst- und Weltverhältnis hat, darüber wissen wir bislang eher wenig.

Eine der zentralen Formen der Online-Nutzung ist unter Jugendlichen die Kommunikation: „73 Prozent nutzen regelmäßig (mind. mehrmals pro Woche) Instant Messenger, Online-Communities (57 %), E-Mails (49 %) oder Chats (29 %)." (JIM 2008, 48) Neben dem Aspekt Kommunikation spielt gerade die Vermischung von symbolischer Selbstinszenierung und Kommunikation in den Online-Communities eine entscheidende Rolle (vgl. Schelhowe 2007). Mehr ins Detail gehende Untersuchungen zum Social Web, wie etwa aktuell von Jan Schmidt et al. (2009) aus dem Hans-Bredow-Institut, verdeutlichen den hohen Stellenwert, den Online-Communities unter Jugendlichen und jungen Erwachsenen haben. „Die sich eröffnenden Möglichkeiten zur Selbstdarstellung, Partizipation, Vernetzung und Beziehungspflege nutzen sie dabei je nach Bedürfnis und Anliegen auf ganz unterschiedliche Art und Weise. Die Faszination der Angebote sowie die Art der Selbstdarstellung und -inszenierung sind für Außenstehende und Unbeteiligte oftmals nicht nachvollziehbar und werden eher skeptisch betrachtet" (Schmidt et al 2009, S. 19). Die von Schmidt et al. beschriebene Differenz der Erfahrungen – für die einen sind je spezifische digitale Räume sinnhaft in den Alltag integriert, anderen ist das Agieren in diesen Räumen fremd und unverständlich – wiederholt sich auf verschiedenen Ebenen. Es ist sicher kein Wunder, dass vielfach immer noch „Second Life" als Synonym für virtuelle Räume herhalten muss, obwohl eine Vielzahl unterschiedlicher Entwürfe nebeneinander zu finden sind, denn Second Lifes visuelle und dreidimensionale Strukturen erscheint einem real-materiellen Raum am ähnlichsten. Das Neue und Fremde am Bekannten zu messen, ist eine gängige Strategie, verfehlt aber dort den Gegenstand, wo das Fremde gänzlich neue Strukturen schafft.

Um eine Aufmerksamkeit für diese neuen Strukturen und deren erziehungswissenschaftliche Reflexion geht es in diesem Band. In welcher Weise entstehen neue kulturelle Räume und soziale Vergemeinschaftungen im Kontext neuer Informationstechnologien und was bedeuten diese veränderten Optionen, sich zu inszenieren, zu kommunizieren und zu kooperieren, im Hinblick auf das Selbst- und Weltverständnis der (jungen) Menschen? Die in diesem Sammelband publizierten Beiträge akzentuieren unterschiedliche Facetten der Thematik. Ausgangspunkt sind Vorträge, die im Rahmen einer digital übertragenen Ringvorlesung (Videokonferenz) an den Universitäten Magdeburg, Bremen und Potsdam gehalten worden sind. Hinzugenommen wurden Vorträge, die während eines Symposium auf dem Kongress der Deutschen Gesellschaft für Erziehungswissenschaft 2008 in Dresden gehalten wurden. Im Folgenden sollen die Beiträge kurz charakterisiert werden:

Neil Selwyn durchleuchtet die Debatte um Digitale Medien bezogen auf den schulischen Kontext und entfaltet ein Spektrum kritischer Fragen – „A new education for a new digital age? Towards a critical analysis of young people, education and the contemporary digital landscape". Selwyn prüft dabei die Verheißungen des Einsatzes von Web 2.0 Technologien und markiert, vor dem Hintergrund der Aufgaben eines staatlichen Bildungssystems, deutliche Problemstellungen. Gegen einen anti-schulischen Impetus angehend plädiert Selwyn dafür, die Potenziale des Lehrens und Lernens mit Digitalen Medien erziehungswissenschaftlich zu kontextualisieren, d.h. in der Auseinandersetzung mit schulischen Realitäten und Diskursen zu betrachten.

Christina Schwalbe und Torsten Meyer betrachten den Bildungsraum Universität und thematisieren den Zusammenhang von Medientechnologien, Kommunikationsstrukturen und Bildungssystem – „Umbauten im und am Bildungsraum. Zum medieninduzierten Wandel der Kommunikationsstrukturen in der Hochschulbildung". Das Eindringen dialog- und vernetzungsorientierter digitaler Medien in einen linear und hierarchisch strukturierten Bildungsraum wird theoretisch-mediologisch problematisiert und am Beispiel des Hochschulentwicklungsprojekts ePush der Universität Hamburg konkretisiert.

Udo Thiedeke erarbeitet Charakteristika der Internetkultur und analysiert die Strukturentwicklung des Internets – „Von der ‚kalifornischen Ideologie' zur ‚Folksonomy' - die Entwicklung der Internetkultur". Er unterscheidet die Expansionsphase in den 1990er Jahren von der Konsolidierungsphase seit dem Jahr 2000. Transparent wird durch Thiedekes differenzierte Analyse das Nebeneinander von utopischen und dystopischen Überzeichnungen der Internetkultur. Eine Besonderheit der Entwicklung der Internetkultur liegt für Thiedeke in der Entgrenzung physischer, physikalischer und sozialer Beschränkungen und der „Vermöglichung" der Wirklichkeit durch die individuelle Verfügbarkeit eines kybernetischen Interaktionsmediums.

Christina Schachtner beleuchtet die Möglichkeit virtueller Netzwerke sowohl Raum für interkulturelle Kommunikation zu schaffen als auch, durch die ihnen innewohnende Architektur des Übergangs, Transkulturalität zu befördern – „Digitale Medien und Transkulturalität". Wie Digitale Medien Transkulturalität befördern können, veranschaulicht Schachtner exemplarisch an Hand der Netzwerke „Global Modules" und „Mideast Youth".

Kai-Uwe Hugger analysiert, wie Jugendliche mit Migrationshintergrund Online-Communities zur Vergewisserung sozialer Zugehörigkeit und bei der Suche nach Anerkennung nutzen – „Anerkennung und Zugehörigkeit im Social Web. Tendenzen der Identitätsbildung am Beispiel junger Migranten". Hugger bezieht sich auf die Online-

Communities Vaybee.de, Aleviler.de und Bizimalem.de und verdeutlicht, dass diese Online-Communities Bildungsräume darstellen, die von den jugendlichen Türken zur orientierenden Reflexion genutzt werden. Sie konkretisieren sich als natio-ethno-kulturelle Hybrid-Umgebungen identitätsorientierter Vergewisserung.

Alexander Unger thematisiert Formen der Verbindung real-materieller und virtuell-softwarebasierter Räume und daraus entstehende Erfahrungs- und Handlungssphären – „Virtuelle Räume und die Hybridisierung der Alltagswelt". Unger verdeutlicht, dass Hybridisierungen sowohl technisch induziert sind als auch individuelle Integrations- und Sinnstiftungsleistungen erfordern. Materielle und virtuelle Anteile verbinden sich zu einer hybriden Alltagswelt, die sinnhaft erschlossen werden und Erfahrungsräume öffnen kann.

Benjamin Jörissen analysiert systematisch die strukturelle Komplexität virtueller Welten und markiert daran anschließend bildungstheoretische Anknüpfungspunkte – „Strukturale Ethnografie Virtueller Welten". Jörissen unterscheidet drei Strukturbereiche virtueller Welten: die virtuelle Umgebung, die Avatar-Technologie und die Community-Umgebung und Community-Funktionalität. Mithilfe seiner kategoriengeleiteten Analyse erschließen sich ganz unterschiedliche Potenziale virtueller Welten, Selbst- und Weltbezüge in einem alternativen Raum tentativ zu erfahren und zu erweitern.

Jörn Lamla untersucht Handlungspraktiken von Verbraucherinnen und Verbrauchern in den Konsumwelten des Internets und er fragt nach deren Bedeutung für Bildungsprozesse in Richtung einer bürgerschaftlichen Mobilisierung und Consumer Citizenship – „Digitale Konsumwelten als politische Bildungsräume? Zur Typologisierung der Online-Praktiken von Verbrauchern". Typologisierend dargestellte Fallanalysen aus dem DFG-Projekt „CyberCash" geben Einblick in unterschiedliche Handlungspraktiken und deren Einwirkung auf die Aushandlungsarenen digitaler Konsumwelten.

Daniela Küllertz verdeutlicht am Beispiel des medienkünstlerischen Umgangs mit Wissenschaft, welche Artikulations- und Reflexionsoptionen in einem künstlerischen Medienbildungsraum eröffnet werden – „Medienkunst als Medienbildungsraum an der Schnittstelle von Wissenschaft und Öffentlichkeit". Küllertz stellt drei Medienkunstprojekte vor – Bio Art, Nanomandala und Six Appartments – und verdeutlicht, wie durch eine medienspezifische „prägnanzbildende Unbestimmtheit" eine Basis für Dialog und veränderte selbst- und weltkonstitutive Sinnbezüge geschaffen werden kann.

Wir danken Wolfgang Ruge für seine Hilfe bei der Editionsarbeit.

Literatur

ARD/ZDF-Online Studie (2008) http://www.ard-zdf-onlinestudie.de/index.php?id=116 (8.5.2009).

Fischli, Martin/Gescheidle, Christoph (2008): Mitmachnetz Web 2.0: Rege Beteiligung nur in Communitys. In: Media Perspektiven 7/2008, 356-364.

Jörissen, Benjamin/Marotzki, Winfried (2009): Medienbildung – Eine Einführung. Bad Heilbrunn: UTB.

Medienpädagogischer Forschungsverbund Südwest (Hrsg) (2008): JIM 2008. Jugend, Information, (Multi) Media. Basisstudie zum Medienumgang 12- bis 19-Jähriger in Deutschland. Stuttgart: VERLAG.

(N)Onliner-Atlas (2009): Eine Topographie des digitalen Grabens durch Deutschland. Eine Studie der Initiative D21. Online: http://old.initiatived21.de/fileadmin/files/08_NOA/NONLINER2008.pdf [8.5.2009].

Schelhowe, Heidi (2007): Technologie, Imagination und Lernen: Grundlagen für Bildungsprozesse mit Digitalen Medien. Münster: Waxmann.

Schmidt, Jan-Hinrik/Paus-Hasebrink, Ingrid/Hasebrink, Uwe/Lampert, Claudia (2009): Heranwachsen mit dem Social Web. Zur Rolle von Web 2.0-Angeboten im Alltag von Jugendlichen und jungen Erwachsenen. Kurzfassung des Endberichts für die Landesanstalt für Medien Nordrhein-Westfalen (LfM), Hamburg/Salzburg, April 2009. Online: http://www.hans-bredow-institut.de/webfm_send/367 [8.5.2009].

A new education for a new digital age?
Towards a critical analysis of young people, education and the contemporary digital landscape

by Neil Selwyn

Introduction

These are exciting yet uncertain times in which to be studying education and technology, with rapid developments in digital media entwined with contemporary education change. In particular, growing numbers of writers and researchers are portraying the emergence of so-called 'web 2.0' internet technologies in transformatory terms. There has been much discussion, for instance, of a general recasting of education provision along more fluid and democratic lines. Some commentators have heralded the emergence of an 'Education 2.0' built around the re-engagement and empowerment of learners (Fumero 2006, Rosenfeld 2007). Yet these enthusiasms are tempered by pessimistic predictions of heightened dis-engagement and disconnection of learners from their studies, or else an imminent decline in 'traditional' skills and literacies amongst upcoming generations of digitally dependent young people (Brabazon 2007). Education researchers are therefore left facing a long-standing question - i.e. can the changes associated with this new wave of education innovation be said to be enhancing *or* harming learners and the forms of learning in which they are engaged?

Whilst debate over the nature of future forms of teaching and learning can only be speculative, there is a clear need for the education research community to engage in sustained scrutiny of the *present* realities of the digital education landscape. This chapter offers a critical framework through which to view the educational opportunities associated with the emergence of web 2.0 technologies. The chapter starts by reviewing the educational promises and potential benefits assumed to accrue from web 2.0 use. In contrast, a number of problems arising from the idealised nature of these discourses are then identified. This allows us to highlight some critical - yet often unvoiced - issues that lie at the heart of understanding the situated nature of web 2.0 uses within educational settings. The chapter concludes by suggesting some empirical, theoretical and methodological priorities for education researchers seeking to produce relevant and rigorous analyses of these ostensibly 'new' forms of digital education.

It should be stressed from the outset that the arguments presented in this chapter are not intended to bolster the current 'counter-orthodoxy of pessimism' amongst some critical scholars "where nothing good can be said about information technology" (Wresch 2004, 71). Instead, the starting point for this chapter is that digital media undeniably matter in contemporary education. However there is a pressing need for education researchers to move beyond polarised debates of either "rejecting or embracing new media" (Lovink 2004, 4) and allow themselves to think positively *and* negatively about digital technologies as the situation demands. In this sense the chapter merely presents a case for looking at the socially situated nature of web 2.0 use and asking critical questions which are concerned with both the social *and* technical aspects of education technology. Rather than adding an antagonistic voice to current debate, it is hoped that focussing on the problematic realities of education technology *in situ* will serve to strengthen and improve the quality of research and discussion in the field. In this spirit we can now go on to consider the promises, problems *and* practicalities of the new digital education.

Considerdering the Promises of Digital Education

Discussion of digital media in education is dominated currently by web 2.0 internet applications. Although often used in an imprecise and uncertain manner, 'web 2.0' can be seen as an umbrella term for a host of internet applications such as social networking, wikis, folksonomies, virtual societies, blogging, multiplayer online gaming and 'mash-ups'. Much of the current educational enthusiasm for web 2.0 stems from the impressive capabilities of these new digital media to support the generation and sharing of content, and subsequent communication and collaboration amongst communities of users. Web 2.0 is therefore seen to encourage 'interactive' rather than 'broadcast' forms of exchange, with information shared between 'many-to-many' rather than transmitted from 'one-to-many' (Shirky 2003, O'Reilly 2005). Yet it is not the technical capabilities of web 2.0 that are perhaps of most interest here, but how and why the *idea* of web 2.0 has come so quickly to be valorised in contemporary discussion and debate. In short, we should ask why so many commentators are now confidently portraying these new digital technologies in terms of an imminent transformation of learning and teaching?

Here we should consider the changes that web 2.0 technologies are seen to bring to learning, learners and the settings within which they learn. In terms of learning, for example, strong links have been established between web 2.0 use and the highly influential socio-cultural view of learning. In short, socio-cultural theories of learning see 'active' and 'authentic' learning as best taking place within assemblages of people and objects where knowledge can be constructed actively by learners who are supported by communal social settings. As such, the widespread valorisation of the social dynamic of learning within the educational community now encompasses the personalised and socially situated forms of learning implicit within web 2.0 use. In this sense, as Charles Crook reasons, web 2.0 technologies are seen to offer learners:

> "a more *participatory* experience ... This is largely about making more opportunities for the user to publish and communicate. It is about uploading rather than downloading. About coordination, rather than delivery. So, for learners: it's about more audience, more collaboration, more resource" (Crook 2008, 30).

Much of the learning potential of web 2.0 is seen to derive from the co-construction of knowledge. Indeed, a constructivist ethos lies at the centre of practices such as folksonomies, mash-ups and wikis, as well as being a central tenet of popular web 2.0 philosophies such as '*Smart Mobs*' (Rheingold 2002), '*We Think*' (Leadbeater 2008a) and the '*Wisdom of Crowds*' (Surowiecki 2004). In an educational sense, the notions of constructivism and constructionism underpin recent celebration of the participative learning cultures of virtual societies such as *Second Life*[1] and multi-player online games such as *World of Warcraft* (Kemp and Livingston 2006). Similarly, the ability to collaboratively edit as well as individually read resources such as *Wikipedia*[2] is seen to lead young people to learn "what works and what does not in a way that was not possible with books. You wouldn't have even joined the debate" (Wales 2008, 23). The collaborative spirit of these web 2.0 activities and many others like them has therefore coalesced into a prevailing sense that "the internet has created greater opportunities for access, debate and transparency in the pursuit of knowledge than ever before" (Wales 2008, 23).

Aside from changing the nature of contemporary learning, web 2.0 technologies are also associated with significant shifts in the nature of contemporary learners. A popular characterisation of upcoming generations of learners is that they are 'digital natives' - i.e. individuals who have grown up in a world of computers, the internet and mobile telephony, and as a result lead lifestyles which are reliant upon the affordances of digital media. The lives of current generations of web 2.0 attuned learners are seen to be entwined with new digital cultures of creativity, collaboration and community. For these individuals at least, digitally-mediated everyday life is characterised by constant change, with commentators talking of a technologically-assisted fluidity and flexibility which lies at the heart of leading a mobile, reflexive, 'liquid' way of being (Bauman 2005, Lash 2002, Urry 2007). Crucially, these digital natives are seen to expect such characteristics to be woven into all aspects of their lives - not least the ways in which they learn and are educated. As Marc Prensky (2001, 1) warned nearly a decade ago, "our students have changed radically. Today's students are no longer the people our educational system was designed to teach".

These expected changes in digital learning and learners often lead to talk of the attendant need to change forms of digital schooling, in particular the reorganisation of education provision away from campus-based institutions and towards online envi-

1 http://www.secondlife.com/
2 http://www.wikipedia.org

ronments and spaces. One popular contention is that schools, colleges and universities are unable to deal with the challenges posed by web 2.0 technologies for a number of structural reasons. These include the many formal and informal systems of regulation and control which characterise the organisation of education institutions, as well as the continued reliance on broadcast pedagogies of various kinds and linear hierarchical relationships to facilitate learning and access to knowledge. As Bigum and Rowan (2008, 250) conclude,

> "whether or not the ramifications of a shift from a largely read-only Web to one that is read/write are as significant as some imagine, formal education is poorly placed to deal well with the social, cultural and economic changes that derive from the continuing use of these read/write web technologies".

In this sense, young people are felt to be turning to web 2.0 based forms of learning in spite of - rather than because of - their educational institutions. As Henry Jenkins (2004, n.p) reasons, it appears that "these teens are finding something online that schools are not providing them".

Indeed a spirit of using web 2.0 to bypass traditional education institutions is evident in online services such as the *School of Everything* – a popular web space designed to put teachers in contact with learners and therefore aiming to be "an eBay for stuff that does not get taught in school" (Leadbeater 2008b). Similarly, *NotSchool.Net* is a well established and officially endorsed online platform which aims to re-engage UK teenagers otherwise excluded from the formal education system with learning and the pursuit of qualifications. Yet rather than being cursory additions to traditional schooling, these examples and others like them are seen to mark the first steps in a radical rethinking and reorganisation of existing structures and organisation of education provision. As Leadbeater (2008b, 26) reasons, the imperative of web 2.0 based education provision ...

> "require[s] us to see learning as something more like a computer game, something that is done peer-to-peer, without a traditional teacher [...] We are just at the start of exploring how we can be organised without the hierarchy of top-down organisations. There will be many false turns and failures. But there is also huge potential to create new stores of knowledge to the benefit of all, innovate more effectively, strengthen democracy and give more people the opportunity to make the most of their creativity".

Recognising the Problems of Digital Education

Of course, these latter arguments are deliberately provocative and wilfully partial. The 'Education 2.0' thesis has a number of weaknesses, not least the significant shortfall between the rhetoric and realities of digital education. Yet such is the conviction with which these arguments are being made, and such is their influence in the minds of the education establishment, that time should be taken to highlight their inherent flaws and silences. This section of the chapter therefore considers some counter-arguments to the promises of education change outlined above.

One such area of contention is the mythologizing of the 'digital native' and the notion that educators are now faced with incoming cohorts of technologically-driven and technologically-dependent learners. To view 'children' and 'young people' as homogenous groups of like-minded individuals with similar technological resources, motivations and abilities has obvious limitations - in particular a denial of the possibility that young people may be as attuned differently to using digital media as they are engaged differently with any of the other activities in their lives, such as music, sport or learning. Instead, it could be argued that young people are not all technology-savvy individuals who make frequent and extensive use of a wide range of technologies. As Bennett et al. (2008, 9) argue:

> "The picture beginning to emerge from research on young people's relationships with technology is much more complex than the digital native characterisation suggests. While technology is embedded in their lives, young people's use and skills are not uniform. There is no evidence of widespread and universal disaffection, or of a distinctly different learning style the like of which has never been seen before. We may live in a highly technologised world, but it is conceivable that it has become so through evolution, rather than revolution. Young people may do things differently, but there are no grounds to consider them alien to us. Education may be under challenge to change, but it is not clear that it is being rejected".

Indeed, research studies suggest that young people's engagement with digital technologies remains differentiated along lines of socio-economic status and social class, as well as gender, geography and many other inequalities which continue to pattern early twenty-first century society. In short any discussion of a new digital education needs to acknowledge that the young learners of today continue to be as 'digitally-dependent' and as 'digitally-divided' as older generations - albeit in ways which are more subtle and perhaps less apparent to adult commentators than before (see Selwyn & Facer 2007). For example, the issue of age continues to be a fundamental but often overlooked influence on the technological needs, interests and practices of children and young people. The social, cultural and cognitive backgrounds of a seven year old child are very different to those of an eleven year old. In turn an eleven year old has very different social, cultural and cognitive backgrounds to a fifteen year old. It is perhaps unsurprising that these differences are reflected in the varying nature of technology engagement between *and* within these age groups.

Aside from inequalities in access and engagement, there is growing evidence that many young people's *actual* uses of digital technologies remain rather more limited in scope than the web 2.0 rhetoric would suggest, with internet use often blended with more passive forms of media consumption such as television viewing. Surveys of young people's technology use at home show a predominance of computer game playing, text messaging and retrieval of online content (as evidenced in the popularity of viewing content on *YouTube*[3] and *MySpace*[4]). Whilst some commentators may like to imagine collaborative communities of content-creating, globally-connected young 'power users' (Brumfield 2006), in reality many young people's engagement with technology is often far more sporadic and unspectacular (Livingstone 2009). Perhaps unsurprisingly, the mundane nature of home engagement with digital media is even more apparent in technology uses within educational settings. Belying the educational potential of digital media, in-school uses of new technologies remain dominated by the 'cut-and-pasting' of online material into word documents and PowerPoint presentations, and as young people pass through the education system the bounded use of 'virtual learning environments' (Selwyn et al. 2008, Nicholas et al. 2008). In short, for all but a minority of children and young people, technology use at home or at school remains rather less expansive and empowering than the rhetoric of Education 2.0 would lead us to believe.

If anything young people's use of web 2.0 technologies can be most accurately described as involving the passive consumption of knowledge rather than the active creation of content - in stark contrast to the descriptions of socially-situated authentic learning outlined earlier. This engagement leads, at best, to what Crook (2008) terms a 'low bandwidth exchange' of information and knowledge, with any illusion of collaborative learning described more accurately in terms of co-operation or co-ordination between individuals. At best then, web 2.0 applications appear to be used by young people to engage with learning content (and other learners) in a number of bounded and passive ways, rather than supporting unfettered active interaction with information and knowledge. Thus young people's current uses of these new technologies often show little evidence of the realisation of the 'learning gains' often attributed to digital media use.

---

3 http://www.youtube.com
4 http://www.myspace.com

Understanding the Practicalities of Digital Education: a Framework of Analysis

It is clear that many of the issues and controversies that surround the educational application of web 2.0 technologies follow familiar and longstanding lines of debate. Web 2.0 applications and other personalised technologies have undoubted potential when it comes to supporting learning and learners, yet it seems that this potential is only being realised on occasion. More often than not, educational use of these technologies in schools and homes remains far less transformatory than many commentators would have us believe. If the academic debate over web 2.0 can be moved forward then it is crucial that the education research community acknowledges this disjuncture. Most importantly, it is crucial that education researchers and commentators begin to develop sustained analyses of the seemingly problematic nature of the application of web 2.0 technologies in educational settings. We can now take some time to consider the forms that such analyses may take.

Firstly, there is a pressing need to move beyond the abstracted, context-free nature of the current discourse surrounding web 2.0 and education. At present many of the claims for an 'Education 2.0' are based upon a presumed "spontaneous appropriation of web 2.0 technologies by learners" (Crook 2008, 31), often independent of any commitments to learning through school or other formal modes of educational provision. More often than not the educational promise of web 2.0 technologies is imagined in terms of autonomous online activities taking place within neutral online environments. Yet as we have seen, a learner's engagement with web 2.0 is not abstracted or neutral, but instead rooted firmly within the realities of day-to-day life and the offline contaminations of school and home settings. Of course, a tendency to under-emphasise the human 'wetware' aspects of 'software' use can be found in most analyses of technology use (Kalnikaité and Whittaker 2007), yet it would seem foolhardy for education researchers to assume that the seemingly 'new' digital spaces of education are removed completely from pre-existing spaces of culture, society, economy and politics.

In particular it makes little sense to discount the school as the primary site of young people's education (at least in the short to medium-term). Similarly, it make little sense to assume schooling to no longer be the dominant form of learning in young people's lives. Instead, the focus of debate should be shifted towards gaining better understandings of the integral roles played by the spaces, institutions and practices of formal education in shaping the realities of young people's educational web 2.0 use. In short, there needs to be better recognition of the obduracy of school, college and university contexts - and the formal educational systems that such institutions represent - in framing learners' use of web 2.0 technologies.

This recognition of the socio-technical basis of web 2.0 use suggests a shift in thinking about technology, learning and learners. In particular it would seem appropriate that education researchers acknowledge that web 2.0 technologies can both shape - and themselves can be shaped by - the educational contexts in which they are situated. This reciprocal perspective places equal importance on both the technological and the social aspects of web 2.0 use, and allows researchers to account for the increasingly complex social settings within which technologies are produced and implemented. Seeking to understand the social shaping of new digital education suggests a number of levels of analysis for education research to pursue, all based around the aim of developing "a deep understanding of the social and interactional circumstances in which technologies exist, and through which they attain their meaning(s)" (Selwyn 2008, 25). Crucially this approach recognises that all aspects of the 'educational' use of technologies are shaped by a number of actors and agendas operating at macro, meso and micro levels. In this sense, educational use (and non-use) of web 2.0 technologies merit multi-layered analyses that move beyond consideration of the user/technology interface.

For instance, it could well be that where web 2.0 technologies do not 'fit' well with the micro-level concerns of being a student or learner (such as passing exams, gaining free time from studies, maintaining identity and status with peers) then young people are understandably unlikely make use of them. Where technologies do not fit well with the personal or professional concerns of teachers (such as maintaining disciplinary control, achieving expected levels of achievement) then use is similarly unlikely. From these micro-level perspectives, the apparently unsatisfactory use of web 2.0 technologies by learners and teachers could be seen less as a case of individual deficiency and more as a case of choice and sometimes 'tactic of resistance' within the constrained yet chaotic contexts of classroom and curriculum. Similarly, in terms of the shaping role of the school as organisation, the nature of educational web 2.0 use could also be seen in light of the meso-level operational concerns of schools along 'new managerial' lines of efficiency, modernisation, rationalisation and the reduction of spending costs. From this perspective, web 2.0 technologies may often be shaped by concerns of 'performativity' rather than pedagogy.

Aside from the immediate concerns of students, teachers and school administrators, attention could also be paid, for instance, to the macro-level influence of government policymaking - especially the continued positioning of education technology around the maintenance of political and economic control in the globalised, 'knowledge economy'. The involvement of IT firms in web 2.0 also merits scrutiny - from Google's ownership of YouTube through to Rupert Murdoch's News International ownership of MySpace web 2.0 applications are profoundly commercial spaces within which learning may (or may not) take place. Alongside government and commerce, an amalgam of 'other' stakeholders could also be considered - what has been termed by David Buckingham (2007) as the 'educational-technology complex'. These actors include journalists, educational technologists, advisory services, teacher groups and parental advocates, researchers, marketers, commercial interests and the local and central government bureaucracy which exists to oversee and steer policies and initiatives. From the micro-economies of the classroom and household to the political machinations of governments and industry, it should be clear that the shaping of digital education is a multifaceted and complex area of study.

Making Education Technology Research ‚Fit for Purpose'

We conclude by considering how education research could produce relevant and rigorous analyses of digital education which pay due attention to these issues. First and foremost is the need to focus on the present realities rather than future possibilities of technology-based education. As we have seen throughout this chapter, education technology is a forward-looking field with many educational technologists preferring to concentrate on 'state-of-the-art' issues. Whilst these abstracted concerns are laudable, there is clearly a need to redress the balance between what *could* happen and what *is* happening with digital technologies in education settings. In particular there is a need to enhance understanding of the subtle social, cultural, political and economic issues that underpin the messy realities of the *actual* use of digital technologies in educational settings.

From this perspective, more questions could be asked of who is (and who is *not*) using technologies in educational settings, how and why they are using them, and with what outcomes. Questions could be raised about the unintended and unexpected consequences of technology use *in situ* - especially the ways in which technologies may not appear to 'work' in the ways that their developers expected or hoped. Above all education researchers need to provide accounts of what can be really said to be 'new' about web 2.0 and new digital media - i.e. what are these technologies making possible that were not possible before? Does web 2.0 use really constitute a new educational era, or does it more accurately describe a set of continuities from the pre-digital age? In asking all these questions, researchers and writers need to consider questions of power, culture, inequality and identity. If education technology is as socially significant as many would have us believe, then it is essential that socially significant questions are asked of it.

Of course, developing this clarity of questioning necessitates a variety of appropriate yet imaginative methodological approaches. Researchers working in the area of education and technology could reconsider not only the ways in which they formulate research questions, but also the methods they choose to collect and analyse data that address these questions. In particular, there is a need to take a broad approach to the methodology of technology research. Whilst many research approaches are available, the field of education technology has tended towards a methodological conservativism (see McDougall et al. 2009). Indeed, it could be argued that education technology research is overpopulated by in-depth case studies of 'model' schools and classrooms with enthusiastic teachers and well-resourced students (Buckingham 2007). Unlike other areas of social science research, education technology is subject to far fewer studies that utilise ethnographic and visual methods, or large-scale cross sectional survey research and randomised-controlled-trials. There is clear scope for education researchers to adopt a more expansive and imaginative approach to investigating digital education - utilising the methods of data collection and analysis that best fit their research questions rather than personal convenience or habit.

Increased clarity of questioning and methodology would contribute greatly to the establishment of a body of education technology research which could be considered 'fit for purpose'. Yet in seeking to increase the quality of research and debate in the field it is perhaps necessary for researchers and writers to also reflect upon what the purposes of their endeavours actually are. In particular there is a need to challenge the underlying personal and political intentions of those researchers who have long been working in the field and have come to constitute the education technology 'community'. In raising these issues we recognise, of course, that all social researchers will assume that they are "doing good works or creating useful knowledge" (Scheurich 1997, 1). Yet few educational technologists would deny that identifying research topics, formulating questions and choosing methods of study are all ideological activities. In this sense personal interests and agendas shape every piece of work.

Against this background it could be argued that the study of education technology has been shaped by a particular set of intellectual and professional agendas which have left much research and writing imbued with a distinct techno-centric bias. Research studies are often, for example, rooted in the received wisdom that technology is inherently 'a good thing'. An implicit agenda of many researchers has been to demonstrate the 'effectiveness' of education technologies and to prove that technology 'works' - leading to a corresponding reluctance to address some of the more problematic and untidy issues highlighted throughout this chapter. For some researchers, this belief in the power of technology stems from a personal interest or even passion for their own new media use, leading to an air of technological fetishism pervading their accounts of education technology. For many other researchers this conviction is perhaps more pedagogically driven - having seen technology enhance their own practice they are keen to see these benefits extended to all.

In some cases, the pro-technology stance is accompanied by an underlying anti-schooling sentiment that has become increasingly evident as the web 2.0 debate continues. Indeed, much of the rhetoric to date surrounding web 2.0 and learning displays a distinct mistrust of the school and formal education, as well as an unsubstantiated over-valorising of the home and informal learning. This devaluing of school education in the face of web 2.0 development feeds into an anti-school discourse which has long been implicit in discussion of education and technology, and is often (although not always) based upon a range of utopian, anti-establishment ideals (see Robertson 2003). Whilst the intentions of most technologists may well be rooted in little more than benign counter-cultural sensibilities, the spirit of these arguments is now being used to support a insidious removal of the state from the provision of public education by a range of more neo-conservative and neo-liberal interests (see Kovacs 2007, Apple 2004).

Whilst one may have sympathy with some or all of these (over)enthusiams, such thinking imposes limitations on the ways in which technology use in education is discussed, leading in more extreme cases to undiluted forms of technological evangelising. Indeed, it seems that one of the most uncomfortable intellectual leaps for some researchers and writers to make is that of disconnecting any analysis of education and technology from their own personal biographies and points of view. Whilst usually fiercely critical in most other areas of their work it seems particularly difficult for academics to distance themselves from positions of technological privilege (either personally or professionally) and 'make the familiar strange'. In particular it appears a challenge for some education technologists to think critically about a topic that they are dependent upon and that many of them have become passionately absorbed by. Of course, social science research is a profoundly subjective activity, and it makes little sense to argue for analyses of education technology that are somehow *more* objective or *more* valid than those that have come before. Yet there would appear to be a need for education technology researchers to at least be accommodating of agendas other than those that currently dominate the field

With these issues in mind, the argument should be made in the strongest terms possible that it is not the place of education researchers (however well-meaning) to legitimise the removal of the state from education provision under the pretext of technological empowerment. It is also not the role of education researchers to 'sell' the latest technologies to the wider education community. There is a need to move research agendas away from overtly pro-technology or anti-school stances, and towards producing more disinterested analyses that seek to reconcile schooling and technology. Thus instead of advocating *de*-schooling perspectives on technology, the role of education research should be to explore opportunities for engineering a *re*-schooling for a digital age – i.e. re-imagining the structures of both the technological and the social elements of education. With this task in mind, the imperative for education research is to now reconcile the currently de-contextualised debate over new digital education with the messy realities of the use of these technologies in practice. We hope that this chapter has provided a starting point for such debates to take place.

References

Apple, Michael W. (2004): Are we wasting money on computers in schools?. In: Educational Policy, 18, 3, 513-522

Bauman, Zygmunt (2005): Liquid life. Cambridge: Polity.

Bennett, Sue/Maton, Karl/Kervin, Lisa (2008): The digital natives debate: a critical review of the evidence. In: British Journal of Education Technology, 39, 5, 775-786.

Bigum, Chris/Rowan, Leonie (2008): Landscaping on shifting ground: teacher education in a digitally transforming world. In: Asia-Pacific Journal of Teacher Education, 36, 3, 245-255.

Brabazon, Tara (2007): The University of Google. Education in a (post) information age. Aldershot: Ashgate.

Brumfield, Robert (2006): Power Users drive pedagogy. In: eSchool news, January 31. Online: http://www.eschoolnews.com/news/top-news/index.cfm?i=36780&CFID=16786431&CFTOKEN=32038049 [28.05.2009]

Buckingham, David (2007):Beyond technology: learning in the age of digital culture. Cambridge: Polity.

Crook, Charles (2008): Theories of formal and informal learning in the world of web 2.0. In: Livingstone 2008, 30-37.

Fumero, Antonio (2006): Eduweb 2.0: iCamp and n-gen educational web. In: Proceedings of WEBIST 2006 April, Setúbal, Portugal. Online: www.htk.tlu.ee/icamp/Members/antonio/webistdraft.doc [N/A]

Gabbard, David (ed) (2007): Knowledge and power in the global economy: the effects of school reform in a neoliberal/neoconservative age. 2nd Edition. London: Routledge.

Jenkins, Henry (2004): Why Heather can write. Technology Review [BizTech], February 6th. Online: http://www.technologyreview.com/business/13473/ [28.05.2009]

Kalnikaité, Vaiva/Whittaker, Steve (2007): Software or wetware? Discovering when and why people use digital prosthetic memory. In: Conference on Human Factors in Computing Systems: Proceedings of the SIGCHI conference on Human factors in computing systems, 71-80.

Kemp, Jeremy/Livingston, Daniel (2006): Putting a Second Life "Metaverse" Skin on Learning Management Systems. Livingston/Kemp 2006, 13-18.

Kovacs, Philip (2007): The anti-school movement. In Gabbard 2007, 239-250.

Lash, Scott M. (2002): Critique of Information. London: Sage.

Leadbeater, Charles (2008a): We-Think. London, Profile.

Leadbeater, Charles (2008b): People power transforms the web in next online revolution. In: The Observer, March 9th, 26.

Livingston, Daniel/Kemp Jeremy (Eds) (2006): Proceedings of the Second Life Education Workshop. SLCC conference, San Francisco, August. Online: www.simteach.com/SLCC06/slcc2006-proceedings.pdf [28.05.2009]

Livingstone, Sonia (ed) (2008): Theorising the benefits of new technology for youth: Controversies of learning and development. University of Oxford/London School of Economics. Online: http://www.education.ox.ac.uk/esrcseries/uploaded/08_0314%20ESRC%20report_web.pdf [28.05.2009]

Livingstone, Sonia (2009): Children and the Internet. Cambridge: Polity.

Lovink, Geert (2004): Uncanny networks. Cambridge MA: MIT Press.

McDougall, Anne/Murnane, John/Jones, Anthony/Reynolds, Nick (2009): Issues in research on IT in education. London: Routledge.

Nicholas, David/Rowlands, Ian/Huntington, Peter (2008): Information behaviour of the researcher of the future - Executive summary. Online: http://www.jisc.ac.uk/media/documents/programmes/reppres/gg_final_keynote_11012008.pdf [28.05.2009]

O'Reilly, Tim (2005): What Is web 2.0? Design patterns and business models for the next generation of software. Online: http://www.oreillynet.com/pub/a/oreilly/tim/news/2005/09/30/what-is-web-20.html [28.05.2009]

Prensky, Marc (2001): Digital natives, digital immigrants. In: On the Horizon, 9 ,5, October, 1-6.

Rheingold, Howard (2002): Smart mobs: the next social revolution. New York: Perseus.

Robertson, James (2003): Stepping out of the box: rethinking the failure of ICT to transform schools. In: Journal of Educational Change 4, 4,323-344.

Rosenfeld, Esther (2007): Beginning the conversation about education 2.0. In: Teacher Librarian 34, 4, 6.

Scheurich, James (1997): Research method in the postmodern. London: Routledge.

Selwyn, Neil (2008): Developing the technological imagination: theorising the social shaping and consequences of new technologies. in Livingstone 2008, 18-29.

Selwyn, Neil/Facer, Keri (2007): Beyond the digital divide: Rethinking digital inclusion for the twenty-first century. Bristol: Futurelab.

Shirky, Clay (2003): Social software and the politics of groups. Online: http://www.shirky.com/writings/group_politics.html [28.05.2009]

Surowiecki, James (2004): The wisdom of crowds: why the many are smarter than the few and how collective wisdom shapes business, economies, societies and nations. New York: Little Brown.

Urry, John (2007): Mobilities. London: Sage.

Wales, Jimmy (2008): It's the next billion online who will change the way we think. The Observer, June 15th, 23.

Wresch, William (2004): Review article: The information age. In: The Information Society, 20, 71-72.

Umbauten im und am Bildungsraum
Zum medieninduzierten Wandel der Kommunikationsstrukturen in der Hochschulbildung

von Christina Schwalbe und Torsten Meyer

Der Bildungsraum Universität befindet sich derzeit an verschiedenen Stellen in einem Umbauprozess. Neben dem Bologna-Prozess als zentralem Thema stellen auch der aktuelle medientechnologische Wandel und damit zusammenhängende kulturelle Veränderungen eine nicht zu unterschätzende Herausforderung für Hochschulen dar. Nahezu allgegenwärtig erhalten vernetzte Medien Einzug in den verschiedensten Bereichen unserer Gesellschaft. Damit einhergehende neue Kommunikations- und Kooperationsformen sowie veränderte Formen des Umgangs und der Übermittlung von Wissen und Information bringen den in der Tradition der Buchkultur gewachsenen Bildungsraum Universität zum Schwanken. Die Frage, die sich dabei stellt, ist: Wie könnte und müsste der Bildungsraum Universität in Zukunft gestaltet sein? Und welche Umbaumaßnahmen sind dazu derzeit erforderlich, in einer Phase, in der sich eine digitale Mediosphäre anzudeuten beginnt, die Folgen jedoch noch nicht vollständig absehbar sind? Im Zentrum steht dabei die Frage, welche Herausforderungen und Möglichkeiten sich aktuell und in Zukunft für Universitäten auf verschiedenen institutionellen Ebenen ergeben. Entscheidend ist hier die Frage nach dem grundsätzlichen Zusammenhang zwischen Bildungssystem und den jeweiligen technischen Medien der Übermittlung und Kommunikation. Nur wenn man versucht zu verstehen, welchen Einfluss Medien seit jeher auf das Konzept von Bildung, das Selbstverständnis von und die soziale Organisation in Bildungsinstitutionen hatten, kann man die Tragweite der aktuellen Entwicklungen erahnen und den Wandel entsprechend mitgestalten.

Die oben gestellte Frage nach den aktuell erforderlichen Umbau- und Umstrukturierungsmaßnahmen steht auch hinter dem Hochschulentwicklungsprojekt „ePUSH", das im Winter 2007 an der Fakultät für Erziehungswissenschaft, Psychologie und Bewegungswissenschaft (Fakultät EPB) der Universität Hamburg startete. In fünf parallel laufenden Teilprojekten werden in einem Zeitraum von zwei Jahren die ICT Entwicklungen im Bildungsbereich aktiv mitgestaltet und kritisch begleitet. Dabei geht es vornehmlich darum, die Einsatzmöglichkeiten digital-vernetzter Medien in Lehre und Studium in das Bewusstsein der Lehrenden und Studierenden zu rufen und dabei ausgehend von aktuell auftretenden Bedürfnissen und Problemen neue Handlungs- und Kommunikationsmöglichkeiten aufzuzeigen. In den einzelnen Teilprojekten werden unterschiedliche Themenfelder bearbeitet, die sich auf alle Ebenen der Fakultät EPB auswirken. Hierzu gehört z.B. der Ausbau digitaler und technischer Infrastrukturen, Community Building im universitären Kontext, die Qualifizierung von Lehrenden und Tutoren im Umgang mit dem neuen Medium, veränderte Prüfungsmöglichkeiten und -bedingungen und der Aufbau von Services und Dienstleistungen zur Unterstützung von Lehre und Forschung im digitalen Medium.

Vom Projekt ausgehend sollen einige grundsätzliche Fragen zur digitalen Zukunft der Universität erörtert werden. Dabei werden einige Vermutungen darüber angestellt, welche Auswirkungen die aktuellen und kommenden medientechnologischen Entwicklungen auf das Selbstverständnis von Universitäten und auf die soziale Organisation in Bildungsinstitutionen gehabt haben werden. Ausgehend von der Frage, was ein der Fragestellung angemessenes Verständnis von Medium ist, wird zunächst ein grundlegender Zusammenhang zwischen Medientechnologien und Bildungssystem hergestellt. Mit Bezug auf die französische Mediologie nach Régis Debray werden aus einer medien-kultur-historischen Perspektive Vermutungen über eine digitale Mediosphäre angestellt, die sich in erster Linie in Unterscheidungen zur Graphosphäre äußern. Über eine Verbindung der Mediologie nach Debray mit Vilém Flussers Kommunikologie folgen konkrete Überlegungen, wie sich Kommunikationsformen des Wissens und die soziale Organisation im Bildungsraum Universität in einer digitalen Mediosphäre verändern.

Medium, Kultur, Bildung

Wie bereits angedeutet, sind die aktuellen Herausforderungen an Bildungsinstitutionen und damit auch die derzeitigen Veränderungen auf das Engste verknüpft mit medientechnologischen und kulturellen Entwicklungen. Doch nicht erst seit die (immer noch so genannten) Neuen Medien, d.h. Computer und Internet, allmählich auch in Bildungsinstitutionen ankommen, sind Medien und Bildung auf vielfältige und grundsätzliche Weise miteinander verbunden. Nur, wenn man versucht zu verstehen, wie Medien und Bildung zusammen hängen, kann man auch verstehen, welche Herausforderungen sich derzeit tatsächlich für Bildungsinstitutionen ergeben.

Reaktion oder Transformation?

Den gegenwärtigen Auseinandersetzungen mit dem Thema Medien und Bildung liegt meist ein sehr verkürztes Verständnis von Medien zugrunde: ist von Medien die Rede, so sind vorwiegend die elektronischen, digital-vernetzten Medien gemeint, die auch heute, 15 Jahre nach der Einführung des WWW als vernetztem und vernetzendem Informations- und Kommunikationsmedium, immer noch häufig als ‚Neue Medien' bezeichnet werden. Medien werden in diesem Zusammenhang als elektronische Geräte verstanden, die als neue Medien zur Wissensvermittlung in pädagogischen Umgebungen Verwendung finden können und sollen. Aus unterschiedlichen Perspektiven wird dabei versucht, Antworten auf die Frage zu finden, wie diese (Neuen) Medien in der pädagogischen Praxis berücksichtigt werden müssen und welche Auswirkungen die Integration digitaler Medien auf Bildungsprozesse haben wird.

Aus Sicht der Medienpädagogik beispielsweise stellen eben diese elektronischen Medien eine neue Herausforderung an die erzieherischen und bildnerischen Aufgaben von Pädagogen[1]. Das Erlernen eines reflexiven Umgangs mit den (Neuen) Medien und die Ausbildung von Medienkompetenz stehen im Zentrum medienpädagogischer Überlegungen (vgl. Baacke 1997). Dieser Ansatz betrachtet zwar nicht nur die technische Seite der Geräte, sondern auch die Gestaltung und Kritik, ein tieferer Zusammenhang über kulturelle und strukturelle Zusammenhänge von Medien und Bildung wird jedoch nicht explizit hergestellt.

Ein eher mediendidaktischer Ansatz, der mit dem Begriff ‚eLearning' verbunden ist, zielt in erster Linie darauf ab, digitale Medien als neue Kanäle zur Wissensvermittlung zu nutzen, häufig mit der Idee, pädagogische Prozesse effizienter und effektiver zu gestalten. Der Begriff ‚eLearning' kam auf während der so genannten ‚dot.com-Euphorie' in den 1990ern, als auch Begriffe wie eCash, eGovernment und eBusiness entstanden. Mit der Bezeichnung der (potenziellen) neuen Kommunikationsmöglichkeiten und Handlungsfelder wurde unterstrichen, dass die traditionellen Kommunikations- und Handlungsmodelle durch elektronisch gestützte Modelle ergänzt und erweitert wurden. In Bezug auf eLearning suggeriert das dem ‚Learning' vorangestellte ‚e', dass, zusätzlich zu dem ‚normalen' Lernen ohne ‚e', Lernen nun auch mit elektronischen Medien möglich sei.

Mit der Entwicklung des Schlagwortes Web 2.0, das eine Art Versionierung des WWW impliziert, wurde analog dazu eine ‚zweite Version' des eLearnings vorgeschlagen, das ‚eLearning 2.0' (vgl. u.a. Kleimann 2007). War das WWW in seiner ‚ersten Version' vor allem als Distributionskanal verstanden worden – Informationen konnten neben der typographischen Speicherung und Distribution nun auch digital gespeichert und verbreitet werden – entwickelte es sich im Laufe der Jahre eher zu einer Ansammlung interaktiver, partizipativer Anwendungen und somit zu einem aktiven Informations- und Kommunikationsmedium, dem Web 2.0. Entsprechend findet unter dem Schlagwort eLearning 2.0 die zunehmende Nutzung interaktiver und partizipativer Anwendungen wie z.B. Wikis und Weblogs auch in mediendidaktischen Überlegungen Berücksichtigung; der Begriff eLearning bleibt gleichwohl weiterhin neben dem Begriff des Lernens bestehen, mediengestütztes Lernen wird ebenso vor allem als durch elektronische Medien, also durch elektronische Mittel und Mittler gestütztes Lernen verstanden.

Die Frage nach dem Zusammenhang von Medien und Bildung ist jedoch grundsätzlicherer Natur. Streng genommen waren Bildungsprozesse schon seit jeher auch

1 Wenn nicht ausdrücklich anders gekennzeichnet, sind auch bei monogeschlechtlicher Ausdrucksweise grundsätzlich alle Geschlechter gemeint

Prozesse der Entwicklung von Medienkompetenz. Vor der Erfindung der Schrift beispielweise, als Informationen und Wissen mündlich weitergegeben wurden und damit in den menschlichen Gedächtnissen gespeichert wurden, galt es, den Umgang mit dem gesprochenen Wort zu erlernen. So waren in der Antike die Kunst der Rhetorik und des Memorierens zentraler Bestandteil von Bildungsprozessen (vgl. Rotermund 1996). Medienkompetenz in der Buchkultur hingegen bezieht sich auf die Entwicklung von Lese- und Schreibkompetenz und einen kritischen Umgang mit Texten. In der aktuellen Mediosphäre geht es vor allem um einen operativen Umgang mit Komplexität (vgl. Baecker 2007).

Ebenso wie Bildungsprozesse nicht zu trennen sind von der Ausbildung von Medienkompetenz, so fungieren Übertragungsmedien schon seit jeher als Mittel, Mittler und Vermittler und sind als solche Grundlage von Lehr- und Lernprozessen. Allein die *Art* dieser Mittel und Mittler, die als pädagogische Medien galten und verwendet wurden, änderte sich im Laufe der Jahre und Jahrhunderte – ebenso wie auch die pädagogische Praxis und die Organisation von Lehr- und Lernsituationen einem andauernden Evolutionsprozess unterliegen.

Es geht also bei der Diskussion um Medien und Bildung nicht nur darum, auf die technische Entwicklung der jeweiligen Mittel und Mittler zu reagieren und die jeweils neuen Medien in die bestehende pädagogische Praxis zu integrieren, sondern es ist zu vermuten, dass ein grundlegender, wechselseitiger Zusammenhang besteht, der Auswirkungen auf das Konzept von Bildung sowie auf das Selbstverständnis und die Organisation von Bildungsinstitutionen hat.

Medium und Milieu[2]

Für die Beschäftigung mit den grundlegenden Zusammenhängen von Bildungssystem und Medientechnologie erscheint zunächst eine genaue Klärung des Begriffs ‚Medium' notwendig.

Die grundlegendste Definition des Mediums ist wohl die des ‚Dazwischen'. Der Begriff Medium als das ‚Dazwischen', z.B. als Kanal zwischen Sender und Empfänger, birgt in sich die Funktion als Träger und Übermittler von Informationen. Ein Medium als Mittler fungiert als passives technisches Werkzeug oder Instrument für die – zumeist intentional ausgerichtet gedachte – Übertragung und Verbreitung von Information. Das wäre (nach Tholen 2005, 151) ein „schwacher", weil harmloser, Medien-Begriff.

Wesentlich für einen weitsichtigen Zugriff auf die skizzierte Forschungsfrage wäre jedoch ein nach Tholen „starker" Medien-Begriff, der unterscheidet zwischen den jeweiligen Mitteln und Mittlern der Darstellung und Übertragung – und dem Medium

2 Zur weiteren Vertiefung der Überlegungen zum Medium als Milieu siehe Meyer (2008a), die folgenden Abschnitte zitieren einige Auszüge.

als einem System, das zusammen gedacht werden kann mit einem kulturellen Milieu. Medium kann, jenseits der Funktion als Mittel und Mittler, in Form einer konstitutiven Aktivität eines „informellen Dazwischen" (im Sinne Régis Debrays) gedacht werden. Von der „Prägekraft der Medien" ist in diesem Sinne (etwa bei Sybille Krämer 2003, 79) die Rede, und vom „Medium als Milieu". Medium würde hierbei nicht als etwas Äußeres verstanden werden, von dem man sich fernhalten könnte, das man einfach nicht anschaltet zum Beispiel, sondern als ein System, in dem wir uns befinden. Man könnte dieses ‚Medium' als ‚Milieu' denken in einer Weise, wie man sagt, Fische leben im Medium Wasser. Medium wäre dann – wie in physikalischen oder chemischen Kontexten – zu verstehen als eine Art Träger oder Stoff, in dem sich bestimmte Vorgänge abspielen (Luft als Träger von Schallwellen oder als Stoff, in dem bestimmte chemische Prozesse ablaufen). In unserem Kontext könnte man analog sagen: Medium als Träger und Stoff psychischer und sozialer Vorgänge.

Auf ähnliche Weise definiert auch Werner Sesink (2008, 14f) mit Bezug auf den systemtheoretischen Ansatz von Niklas Luhmann das „Medium der Medien" als „medialen Raum", als umfassende, einhüllende Instanz. Das Medium ist „nicht etwas, *zu* dem, sondern *in* dem Menschen sich verhalten" (Sesink 2008, 15).

(Medien-)historisches Apriori

Diese Art ‚Medium' ist zweigleisig zu verstehen. Zum einen ist ‚Medium' hier sehr abstrakt, systemtheoretisch zu interpretieren als Set von Bedingungen kognitiven, kommunikativen und sozialen Prozessierens, als ein System von Bezugspunkten der Reflexivität aufgrund kommunikativer Erfahrung gewonnener Handlungen – kurz: als *Kultur*. Jeder einzelne Mensch wird (u.a.) durch die technischen Medien sozialisiert.

Zum anderen – dem wird, wer sich mit Fragen der Darstellung und der Darstellbarkeit, also mit dem Ästhetischen auseinandersetzt, leicht zustimmen – sind diese kommunikativen Erfahrungen in Abhängigkeit von den jeweiligen Mitteln und Mittlern der Darstellung und Übermittlung – üblicherweise „Medien" genannt – zu denken. Das jeweils kulturell vorherrschende Medium hängt zusammen mit der Art und Weise, wie Wissen produziert, gespeichert und übermittelt wird und hat Auswirkungen auf den Status von Wissen bzw. auf die Definition dessen, was als Wissen angesehen wird, sowie auf die Strukturen der Kommunikation und Übermittlung. Der mediale Raum bzw. das Milieu, in dem wir leben, das uns umgebende Lebens-Mittel, ist in diesem Sinne zu verstehen als ein Möglichkeitsraum: wie einem Fisch das Wasser ermöglicht zu leben, so ermöglicht das Medium dem Menschen, sich auf je unterschiedliche Art und Weise zu verhalten und zu kommunizieren (vgl. Meyer 2002, 81ff). Ein typographisches Medium vermittelt uns gänzlich andere Kommunikationsmöglichkeiten und Möglichkeiten des Umgangs mit Wissen und Information als ein digital-vernetztes Medium. Dieses

Verständnis von Medium lehnt sich an den Begriff des „Archivs“ (als „historisches Apriori“) bei Michel Foucault an: „Das Archiv ist zunächst das Gesetz dessen, was gesagt werden kann. [...] es ist das, was an der Wurzel der Aussage selbst als Ereignis und in dem Körper, in dem sie sich gibt, von Anfang an das System ihrer Aussagbarkeit definiert. [...] es ist das, was den Aktualitätsmodus der Aussage als Sache definiert; es ist das System ihres Funktionierens“ (Foucault 1997, 187f). Dieses „historische Apriori“ kann man sich auch vorstellen als *medien-historisches* oder genauer noch *medien-kulturhistorisches* Apriori, als kulturtechnik-bedingte Episteme, als eine Art blinden Fleck des Denkens, Wissens, Erkennens. Blinder Fleck bedeutet: man sieht nicht, dass man dort nicht sehen kann.

Die Erkenntnis, dass es diese blinden Flecken gibt, und der Versuch, diese zu verstehen und sichtbar zu machen, ist wesentlich für das Verständnis der grundlegenden Zusammenhänge zwischen Medien und Bildungssystem. Es sind nicht nur die technischen Mittel und Mittler, die sich derzeit fundamental verändern. Die aktuelle Entwicklung des Internets eröffnet einen neuen Möglichkeitsraum, woraus sich gleichzeitig auch neue Herausforderungen ergeben – und eben diese Möglichkeiten und Herausforderungen müssen wahrnehmbar gemacht werden, um Gestaltungsspielraum für die Umbauten der Bildungsräume zu gewinnen.

Mediosphären

Eine Methode, mit der sich solche blinden Flecke untersuchen lassen, ist die der Mediologie. Dabei geht es um die Erforschung der höheren sozialen Funktionen vor dem Hintergrund der Ideologie, der Politik usw. und deren Beziehungen zu den zentralen technischen Trägern der Übermittlung. Mediologie ist, allgemein gesagt, eine Untersuchungsmethode der komplexen Korrelation zwischen einem symbolischen Körper (einer Doktrin, einer Religion, dem Selbstverständnis der Universität etc.), einer Form der kollektiven Organisation (einer Schule, einer Universität etc.) und einem technischen System der Kommunikation (technisches Medium, Archivierungssystem etc.; vgl. Weber/Mersmann 2007). Régis Debray, Begründer und Namensgeber der Mediologie, beschreibt das in einem einfachen, sehr anschaulichen Bild: „Wenn der Mediologe auf jemanden trifft, der mit dem Finger auf den Mond zeigt, dann betrachtet er nicht den Mond, sondern den Finger und die Geste des Zeigens“ (Debray 1999, 403).

Folgt man den mediologischen Betrachtungen Debrays, so lassen sich kulturelle Epochen nach den technischen Medien der Übermittlung unterscheiden. Debray benennt vier solcher Mediosphären: Logosphäre, Graphosphäre, Videosphäre und Hypersphäre.

> „Dominant ist das Hauptverfahren zur Speicherung und die Zirkulation der Spuren (Schrift, Typografie, Elektronik, das Digitale). Diesem hegemonischen Verfahren entspricht ein bestimmtes Milieu für die Übermittlung der Botschaften [...], ein Makromilieu, das wir ‚Mediensphäre[3]' nennen wollen. Diese legt eine bestimmte Art regulierender Überzeugungen fest, eine besondere Zeitlichkeit (oder eine typische Beziehung zur astronomischen Zeit) und eine bestimmte Art, wie Gemeinschaften eine Einheit, einen Körper bilden (mehr als nur einen Rahmen für ihren territorialen Zusammenschluss)" (Debray 2003, 57).

Der Begriff der „Sphäre" deutet das bereits angesprochene, räumlich zu denkende „Einhüllende" (Debray 2003, 63) an. Die Dreidimensionalität transportiert den eintauchenden, synergetischen Charakter der Mediosphäre. Die schematische Abgrenzung der Mediosphären, wie Debray sie vornimmt, ist jedoch als idealtypisch zu verstehen.

> „So wie ein neuer Träger den vorhergehenden nicht zum Verschwinden bringt (ihm aber zusätzlich zu neuen Möglichkeiten verhelfen kann) verdrängt eine neue [...] [Mediosphäre] nicht die vorhergehende. Sie restrukturiert sie nach ihren eigenen Bedingungen, nach langen Verhandlungen über Position und Funktion, so dass zum Schluss alle ineinander greifen, aber nicht beliebig" (Debray 2003, 60).

Derzeit erleben wir die Entwicklung eines neuen technischen Mediums der Übermittlung – des Internet und vor allem des WWW – dessen Folgen mit denen der Einführung des Buchdrucks verglichen werden. Ein Übergang in eine digitale Mediosphäre deutet sich an:

> „Vom 15. Jahrhundert bis gestern prägte der Buchdruck die Graphosphäre, heute umgibt uns die Videosphäre, in der auf Grund eines veränderten Zeitempfindens der Augenblick über die Dauer triumphiert, das Direkte über das Indirekte, das Reaktive über das Diskursive, und diese Videosphäre wiederum geht bereits über in eine Art Hypersphäre, die sich hauptsächlich aus digitalen Signalen zusammensetzt" (Debray 2001/2002, 6).

Debray ist mit seinen Vermutungen über das Entstehen einer auf die Graphosphäre folgenden neuen Mediosphäre in guter Gesellschaft: Schon in den Sechzigern sprach Marshall McLuhan vom Ende der Gutenberg-Galaxie. Sprachlich daran anschließend

3 In der Übersetzung der „Einführung in die Mediologie" wird der Begriff „Mediensphäre" verwendet. Im Folgenden verwenden wir jedoch „Mediosphären", da dies unserer Auffassung nach eine zutreffendere Wortwahl ist. Nach Debray bezieht sich die Mediologie auf die Schnittstellen zwischen einer symbolischen Form, einer Form der kollektiven Organisation und einem technischen System der Kommunikation – also auf das „informelle Dazwischen" – und nicht auf die technischen Medien, die technischen Mittel und Mittler, von Debray als „falscher Freund des Mediologen" bezeichnet (Debray 2004, 68).

befinden wir uns laut dem Soziologen Manuel Castells (2005) nun in den Anfängen der Internet-Galaxie. Der Soziologe Dirk Baecker (2007) analysiert mit Bezug auf Peter F. Druckers Bezeichnung der „next society“ aktuelle Veränderungen von der modernen Gesellschaft zur „nächsten Gesellschaft“. Ähnlich wie Debray, McLuhan und Castells schreibt auch er den technischen Medien der Übermittlung eine wichtige Funktion in Bezug auf die kulturelle Entwicklung zu:

> „Wir haben es mit nichts Geringerem zu tun als mit der Vermutung, dass die Einführung des Computers für die Gesellschaft ebenso dramatische Folgen hat wie zuvor nur die Einführung der Sprache, der Schrift und des Buchdrucks. Die Einführung der Sprache konstituierte die Stammesgesellschaft, die Einführung der Schrift die antike Hochkultur, die Einführung des Buchdrucks die moderne Gesellschaft und die Einführung des Computers die nächste Gesellschaft“ (Baecker 2007, 7).

Die digitale Mediosphäre und ihre nächste Gesellschaft wird man vermutlich dann am besten verstehen, wenn man sie von der nach Debray gestrigen Mediosphäre, der Graphosphäre, abgrenzt und so fundamentale Veränderungen und Entwicklungen aufzeigt. Die Graphosphäre beginnt nach Debray mit der Einführung des Buchdrucks als diejenige Epoche, in der das handschriftlich kopierte Buch als etabliertes technisches Medium der Übermittlung abgelöst wird durch gedruckte Bücher. Der Übergang von der oralen zur typographischen Kultur, von der Logosphäre zur Graphosphäre, rückte den Menschen selbst als lernendes Subjekt in den Mittelpunkt. War die Logosphäre geprägt von mündlicher Tradierung, der Mensch als eher passiver Empfänger von Informationen („Gott hat es mir gesagt“, Debray 2003, 64f), so förderte und erforderte die zunehmende Übermittlung von gedruckten Informationen eine Zuwendung zu einer aktiven Auseinandersetzung mit der Schrift („Ich habe es in einem Buch gelesen“, Debray 2003, 64f). „Lernen hieß nun ‚selbst Lesen lernen‘; hieß nun auch schreiben lernen, um diese Welt selbst in Text fassen zu können. Und Lehren hieß: den Menschen das Lesen und Schreiben beizubringen“ (Sesink 2008, 17). Mit der Alphabetisierung der breiten Masse änderte sich die Rolle der bisherigen Sinnverwalter, der gebildeten Geistlichen, die zuvor ihre Interpretationen der Schriften an das Volk weitergaben. Das subjektive Bild der Welt entstand nicht mehr in erster Linie aufgrund mündlich tradierter (fremder) Interpretationen von Schriften, sondern die Fähigkeit zu lesen und zu schreiben ermöglichte eine individuelle, eigenständige Auseinandersetzung mit den übermittelten Botschaften. Ein und derselbe Inhalt konnte in Folge der Entstehung von Druckereien und neuen Netzen der Distribution massenhaft kopiert und verteilt werden. Ohne diese technische, soziale und organisatorische Entwicklung hätte es wohl keine Notwendigkeit für die Alphabetisierung der Bevölkerung gegeben, weil das Medium Buch ohne maschinelle Vervielfältigung so knapp verfügbar geblieben wäre, dass es gar keinen Sinn gemacht hätte, wenn allzu viele Menschen über die Medienkompetenz des Lesens verfügten

Wissenschaftskommunikation

Michael Giesecke (2002) bringt die Entstehung der neuzeitlichen Wissenschaft in Zusammenhang mit der Entwicklung der Buchkultur. Die lineare Struktur von Produktion und Übermittlung von Wissen in typographischer Form ermöglicht es dem Leser eines Buches, den Gedankengang des Autors nachzuvollziehen, er folgt der Perspektive des Verfassers. Beim Lesen eines Buches kann man entweder den Standpunkt des Autors übernehmen, eine Gegenposition einnehmen oder den Gedankengang durch Referenzieren weiter fortführen. Giesecke bezeichnet diese Art der Kommunikation als soziale Informationsverarbeitung, jedoch ohne direkte Interaktion. Die neuzeitliche Wissenschaft und damit die traditionelle Struktur und das Selbstverständnis heutiger Universitäten beruht auf diesen Strukturen der interaktionsfreien, sozialen Informationsverarbeitung: Wissen wird akkumuliert und weiter entwickelt. Auf Basis vorhandenen Wissens wird neues Wissen erzeugt. Die Gründung der Universität als Ort der Einheit von Forschung und Lehre durch Wilhelm von Humboldt fällt in diese Epoche. Im Kern ging es nun nicht mehr hauptsächlich um Übermittlung, Verteilung und Speicherung von Wissen, sondern zunehmend auch um die Erzeugung von Wissen. Die Produktion und die Übermittlung von Wissen sind aneinander gekoppelt. Gleichzeitig ist durch die Möglichkeit der interaktionsfreien, sozialen Informationsverarbeitung die chronologische Reichweite und damit der Stellenwert der Übermittlung dieses Wissens sehr hoch.

Linie und Punkt, Individuum und Netz

Wie sich eine digitale Mediosphäre einmal formiert haben wird, kann man derzeit bestenfalls ahnen. Es ist zu beobachten, dass das Verhältnis zwischen den Medien der Verbreitung im Raum (also der Ubiquität der Kommunikation) und den Medien der Verbreitung von Wissen in der Zeit (also der Historizität der Transmission) zunehmend prekär wird. Die digitalen Infrastrukturen vergrößern die territoriale Reichweite, verkürzen aber die chronologische. Wurde nach Debray die Gestalt der Zeit in der Graphosphäre noch als Linie gedacht, strebt die Gestalt der Zeit in der digitalen Mediosphäre zum Punkt (vgl. Debray 2003, 65): Der Event, seine Aktualität und seine Performanz bestimmen die Gültigkeit von Wissen, nicht aber seine Tauglichkeit für die Ewigkeit. „Das fließende Wissen (oder das Know-How) ersetzt das bewahrte Wissen (oder die Weisheiten)“ (Debray 2003, 218; vgl. auch Lyotard 1979).

Wir erleben jedoch nicht nur eine Veränderung der zeitlichen und räumlichen Reichweite von Wissen, es entstehen ebenso andere Formen der Produktion von Wissen und der Kooperation. Die Möglichkeiten der Partizipation im WWW bringen verstärkt kollaborative Formen der Wissensproduktion hervor, die Weisheit der Massen steht dem Experten als gebildetem Individuum gegenüber. Wohl bekanntestes Beispiel dieses Phänomens ist die freie Online-Enzyklopädie Wikipedia. Statt linear organisierter Akkumulation von Wissen auf Basis interaktionsfreier, sozialer Informationsverarbeitung, wie voranstehend beschrieben, beruht die kollektive Wissensproduktion auf vernetzten Strukturen der Interaktion. Über solche, als Verteiler fungierenden Webanwendungen, z.B. auch Social Bookmarking-Diensten wie del.icio.us etc., finden wir Zugang zum kollektiven Wissen und zu einer Art Kollektivintelligenz.

Manfred Faßler (2007) beschreibt mit seinem Konzept der „Communities of Project" Veränderungen der sozialen Organisation, denen eben diese zunehmend vernetzten Strukturen zugrunde liegen und die nicht durch Linearität bestimmt sind. Anstelle von Zusammenarbeit in langfristig angelegten Arbeitszusammenhängen, die durch hierarchische Strukturen gekennzeichnet sind, vollzieht sich Kooperation zunehmend in Zusammenhängen, die auf ein gemeinsames Projektziel ausgerichtet sind und sich nach Erreichen dieses Ziels wieder auflösen. Das Individuum ist Teil sich immer neu organisierender, ergebnisorientierter „Communities of Project". Das Eingebundensein in Netzwerke wird hier zum grundlegenden Prinzip für Kooperation.

Gehört damit also Lacans *sujet supposé savoair*, das Subjekt, dem das Wissen unterstellt wird (Lacan 1996, 242ff), in die Logik der Graphosphäre? Ist das Subjekt nicht mehr ‚Ort' des Wissens? Wenn das Individuum als erkenntnistheoretisches Paradigma an Bedeutung verliert zugunsten des Wissen schaffenden Projekts und der sich darum bildenden Community, müsste dann für eine digital-vernetzte Mediosphäre eher vom *projet supposé savoir* die Rede sein? Und müsste gar über eine Grund legende „Theorie der Bildung der Communities" nachgedacht werden – mit der gleichen Tragweite, wie über die (auch anthropologischen) Grund legende „Theorie der Bildung des Menschen" (Humboldt) nachgedacht wurde?[4]

Universität zwischen Graphosphäre und Hypersphäre

Kommen wir zu unserer ursprünglichen Frage nach dem Zusammenhang zwischen Medientechnologie und Bildungssystem zurück. Traditionell ist die Universität ein durch eine typographische Kultur geprägter Bildungsraum. Dies spiegelt sich wider in ihrem Selbstverständnis, sowie auch in den Strukturen der Organisation und Kommu-

4 Diese Gedanken müssten näher ausgeführt werden. Anfänge gab es im Rahmen eines Beitrags von Torsten Meyer zur internationalen Forschungskonferenz „i hoch 4" (Forschungsnetzwerk Anthropologie des Medialen / FAME), Johann Wolfgang Goethe-Universität Frankfurt/M, 24.-26.10.2007. Weitere Gedanken folgten im Beitrag „projet supposè savoir" zum interdisziplinären Colloquium „Lehren bildet – Das Rätsel unserer Lehr-Anstalten" (Warburg-Haus Hamburg, 21.-23.11.2008). Entsprechende Publikationen folgen.

nikation und damit zu guter Letzt auch in der Praxis der Bildung. Durch die gegenwärtigen kulturellen Veränderungen, dem Übergang in eine andere Mediosphäre, werden Universitäten in ihrer gesamten organisatorischen Struktur und ihrem Selbstverständnis herausgefordert. Wichtig ist hierbei, nicht nur auf Veränderungen zu reagieren, sondern diesen Prozess kultureller Transformation aktiv gestaltend zu begleiten.

Begreift man die Universität als einen Raum, der aufgrund seiner strukturellen und auch architektonischen Beschaffenheit, seiner symbolischen Bedeutung und seiner organisatorischen Struktur Prozesse des Lehrens und Lernens und damit Bildungsprozesse ermöglicht, so kann man – in Analogie zum medialen Raum – von einem Bildungsraum ebenfalls in dem Verständnis eines Möglichkeitsraums sprechen. Technische Medien der Übermittlung von Wissen sind fundamentaler Bestandteil der strukturellen Beschaffenheit und bedingen ebenso soziale und organisatorische Prozesse wie auch die kulturelle Bedeutung. Es ist dieser mediale Bildungsraum, der die Formen und Möglichkeiten pädagogischer Praktiken einräumt und vermittelt, der aber im Gegenzug auch durch eben diese pädagogische Praxis mit gestaltet wird. Im Folgenden sollen aktuelle Transformationen des Bildungsraums Hochschule insbesondere hinsichtlich der pädagogischen Praxis genauer unter die Lupe genommen werden. Diese Überlegungen sind Ahnungen und Vermutungen über die Formierung und Ausgestaltung einer digitalen Mediosphäre.

Paideia: Übermittlung und Kommunikation

Einen gewinnbringenden Ansatz zum Verständnis der Evolution einer digitalen Mediosphäre und dem Zusammenhang zwischen Medien und Bildung liefert Vilém Flusser (2007) in seinen Vorlesungen zur „Kommunikologie"[5]. Die Begriffe *Übermittlung* und *Kommunikation* der Debrayschen Mediologie und Flussers Verständnis von *Kommunikation* sollen kurz dargelegt werden, um Überschneidungen, Unterschiede und Ergänzungen zu verdeutlichen.

Die Mediologie basiert auf der Unterscheidung zwischen Übermittlung und Kommunikation. Nach Debray besteht „Kommunizieren […] darin, eine Information im Raum innerhalb ein und derselben räumlich-zeitlichen Sphäre zu transportieren, und Übermitteln darin, eine Information in der Zeit zwischen unterschiedlichen räumlich-zeitlichen Sphären zu transportieren" (Debray 2003, 11). Der Kommunikation schreibt er also einen interindividuellen, soziologischen Horizont zu, während die Übermittlung durch die Nutzung eines Trägers der Informationen auch einen historischen Horizont

5 Vielen Dank an dieser Stelle an Michael Scheibel für den Hinweis auf Vilém Flussers „Kommunikologie", die auch bei der hier gedanklich im Hintergrund stehenden Masterarbeit zum Thema „Networking in universities – how universities can accept the challenge and take an active, formative role" von Christina Schwalbe eine wesentliche Rolle gespielt hat.

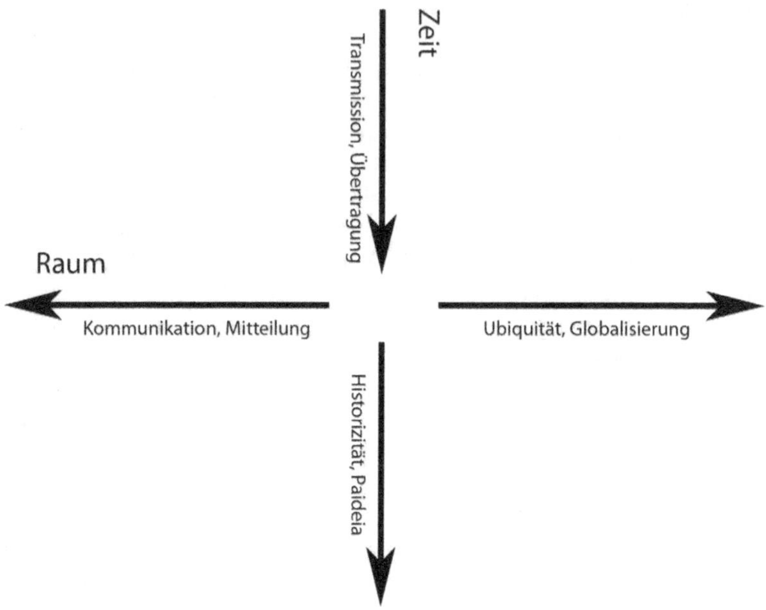

Abb. 1: Transmission und Kommunikation (T. Meyer nach Debray 2003)

haben kann. Kommunikation und Übermittlung sind nicht als gegenüberstehend zu betrachten, sondern greifen ineinander. „Kommunikation ist die notwendige, aber nicht hinreichende Bedingung der Übermittlung" (Debray 2003, 23). Oder anders gesagt: „Kommunizieren ist der Moment eines längeren Prozesses und das Fragment eines umfangreicheren Ganzen, das wir konventionsgemäß Übermittlung nennen werden" (Debray 2003, 11). Die Funktion der Übermittlung ist die Übertragung von Ideen, Glaubens- und Wissensinhalten über die Zeit, von einer Generation zur nächsten. Durch die Übermittlung werden kulturelle Inhalte langfristig in einem kollektiven Gedächtnis festgehalten und erzeugen damit kulturelle Kontinuität. Doch mit technischen Medien als Trägern der zu übermittelnden Information allein erreicht man keine Übermittlung. Zur Überwindung der Zeit braucht man einen Träger, ein Medium als äußeres Mittel, ebenso wie eine soziale Institution zur inneren Übermittlung. „Das äußere Gedächtnis der Bücher kommt nur durch das innere Gedächtnis einer Gruppe zu Kräften" (Debray 2003, 16). Bildungsinstitutionen erfüllen eben diese Funktion der Vermittlung zwischen den Medien der Übermittlung und der kulturellen und symbolischen Bedeutung.

Vilém Flusser betrachtet das, was Debray als Übermittlung bezeichnet, die „Paideia" als „Kernfrage der menschlichen Kommunikation überhaupt" (Flusser 2007, 309), da sie den Prozess beschreibt, der die Übertragung von im Gedächtnis einer Generation enthaltenen Informationen in das Gedächtnis der nächsten erlaubt. Bezieht sich die Mediologie eher auf die Schnittstellen zwischen dem Symbolischen, den technischen Medien zur Übermittlung und der sozialen Organisation, und beschäftigt sich damit eher mit der Funktion und Bedeutung von Kommunikation, so versucht Flusser in seiner Kommunikologie, Strukturen und Codes der Kommunikation in Zusammenhang mit den jeweils vorherrschenden Kommunikationsmedien zu untersuchen. Die von ihm hierzu entwickelten Modelle basieren auf einer stark formalisierten Beschreibung von Kommunikation, bestehend aus Sender, Information und Empfänger. Die Information wird dabei, je nach Situation, in der die Kommunikation stattfindet, unter Verwendung von spezifischen, nicht-natürlichen Codes und Kanälen ausgetauscht und weitergegeben. Nach Flusser umfasst menschliche Kommunikation formal das Speichern und Verarbeiten von Information durch deren Weitergabe, ebenso wie die Produktion derselben. Dabei unterscheidet er zwischen zwei Formen der Kommunikation, dem Diskurs und dem Dialog. Der Diskurs dient zur Weitergabe von Informationen. Durch dieses Verteilen von Information wird gleichzeitig auch das Bewahren derselben angestrebt. Dies wird von Debray als ein Teil der Übermittlung angesehen. Der Dialog ist eine Kommunikationsform, in der durch Austausch von Informationen neue Informationen synthetisiert und produziert werden. Diskurs und Dialog sind nicht unabhängig voneinander möglich und bedingen sich gegenseitig. Sowohl die Codes, in denen Informationen produziert, gespeichert und weitergegeben werden, als auch die dialogischen und diskursiven Strukturen der Kommunikation sind nur in Zusammenhang mit den Informations- und Kommunikationsmedien zu sehen.

Kommunikationsformen des Wissens

Die Beobachtung und Beschreibung von Wechselbeziehungen zwischen Medien und Kommunikation bzw. Übermittlung ist sowohl für die Mediologie als auch für die Kommunikologie von grundlegender Bedeutung. Die Übermittlung – die Paideia – als Kernaufgabe von Bildungsinstitutionen ist derzeit, angesichts der tiefgreifenden medientechnologischen Entwicklungen und der zunehmenden Ubiquität vernetzter, digitaler Medien ebenfalls einem Prozess der Veränderung unterworfen. Mit Hilfe des Kommunikationsmodels, das Vilém Flusser in seinen Vorlesungen zur Kommunikologie (2007) entwickelt hat, lassen sich aktuelle Veränderungen der Kommunikationsformen des Wissens und damit eventuelle Auswirkungen auch auf die pädagogische Praxis, beschreiben und analysieren. Flusser stellt Zusammenhänge her zwischen den Medien, die zur Speicherung und Weitergabe von Wissen und Information verwendet werden, sowie den Strukturen dieser Kommunikation. Flussers Kommunikationsmodelle sollen im Folgenden herangezogen werden, um die vermuteten neuen Kommunikationsformen in der pädagogischen Praxis zu beschreiben und Zusammenhänge zu einem möglichen Wandel der Mediosphären herzustellen.

Theaterdiskurs – Vorlesung

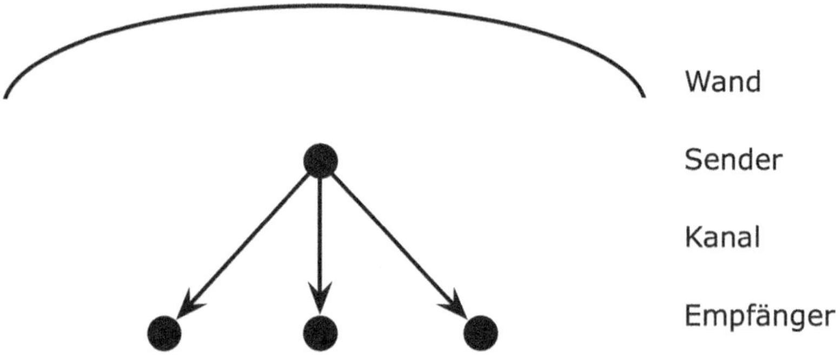

Abb. 2: Theaterdiskurs (Flusser 2007, 21)

Das charakterisierende Element des Theaterdiskurses (vgl. Flusser 2007, 21ff) ist die Wand, die den Sender nach hinten abschirmt und so gegen Einflüsse und Störungen von außen schützt. Der Sender gibt bei dieser Form des Diskurses die in seinem Gedächtnis gespeicherten Informationen, sein Wissen, an die Empfänger weiter, es ist eine eher interaktionsarme Kommunikationsstruktur. Durch die Abschirmung nach hinten und die räumliche Gegenüberstellung von Sender und Empfänger ist die gesamte Konzentration auf den Sender gerichtet. Die Hauptintention dieses Diskurses ist die Weitergabe von Information im Sinne der „Paideia" – die Übertragung von im Gedächtnis einer Generation enthaltenen Informationen in das Gedächtnis der nächsten; also das, was nach Debray Teil der Übermittlung ist. Dennoch besteht in eingeschränktem Maße die Möglichkeit, dass ein Dialog entsteht oder dass Empfänger und Sender die Positionen wechseln. Diesen Wechsel der Positionen nennt Flusser „Revolution" (Flusser 2007, 21).

Der Theaterdiskurs ist die traditionelle Kommunikationsstruktur des Frontalunterrichts oder der akademischen Vorlesung. Die in dieser Struktur enthaltene Rollenverteilung, bei der der Lehrende sein Wissen nach dem one-to-many-Prinzip an die Studierenden übermittelt, entspricht der linear-hierarchischen Struktur der Buchkultur. Der Umgang mit Wissen und Informationen in der Buchkultur geht von der Idee aus, dass ein Autor sein Wissen in einer linearen, schriftlichen Form weiter gibt und der Leser durch die lineare Form in die Lage versetzt wird, den Gedankengang des Autors nachzuvollziehen und weiterzuentwickeln (vgl. Giesecke 2002). Ebenso wie bei dieser auf typographischen Medien basierenden Kommunikation bzw. Übermittlung sind die Studierenden in den traditionellen Vorlesungen und in vielen Seminaren in erster Linie Empfänger von Informationen, die sie dann in ihre eigenen Wissensstrukturen einbauen. Auch die anfänglichen Ideen, digitale Medien in Form von ‚eLearning' in pädagogische Prozesse zu integrieren, sind noch typische Formen des Theaterdiskurses. Statt Vorlesungen in physischen Räumen abzuhalten, wurden virtuelle Klassenräume eingerichtet, in denen versucht wurde, die gängige pädagogische Praxis auf Online-Kurse zu übertragen. Der Schirm wird durch die Geschlossenheit von Lernplattformen simuliert. Die Möglichkeiten zur Kommunikation sind durch unterschiedliche Bearbeitungs- und Leserechte vorgegeben: Lehrende können Materialien erstellen, bearbeiten, zur Verfügung stellen, Studierende haben meist nur Leserechte und eingeschränkte Möglichkeiten, selber als Sender zu fungieren.

Kreisdialog – Seminar

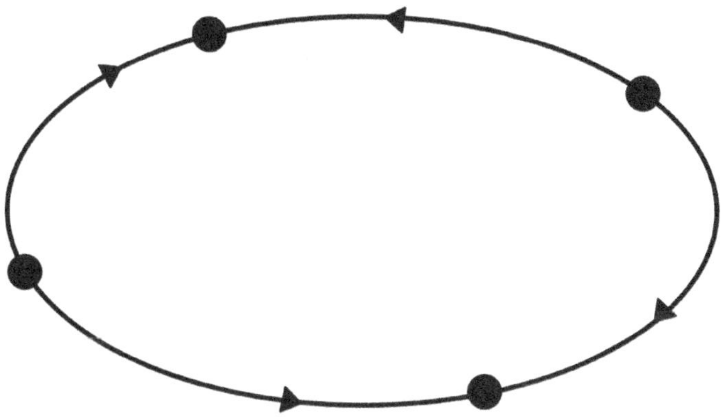

Abb. 3 : Kreisdialog (Flusser 2007, 29)

Der Kreisdialog (vgl. Flusser 2007, 29ff) ist nach Flusser eine in sich abgeschlossene Kommunikationsstruktur, in der verschiedene bestehende Informationen zu neuen Informationen synthetisiert werden. Die an einem Kreisdialog Beteiligten unterscheiden sich nicht nur in ihrem Bezug zu der Diskussion im Zentrum des Dialogs, sondern auch hinsichtlich der Kompetenzen, der verwendeten Codes und ihres eigenen Bewusstseins. Im Dialog wird nach einem gemeinsamen Nenner der in den verschiedenen Gedächtnissen gespeicherten Informationen gesucht. Durch diese Synthese unterschiedlicher Informationen entsteht neue, vorher so keinem der Beteiligten bekannte Information.

Flusser zufolge birgt die elitäre, abgeschlossene Form des Kreises Probleme, da fehlende Einflüsse von außen die Synthese wirklich neuer Information erschweren. Die Chance, neue Informationen zu generieren, ist in komplexen, intern stark differenzierten Strukturen zwar geringer, bei erfolgreicher Kommunikation ist jedoch ein qualitativ hochwertigeres Ergebnis zu erwarten.

Theaterdiskurs und Kreisdialog sind beides geschlossene, elitäre Formen der Kommunikation, die in ihrer Kombination charakteristisch sind für die traditionelle Organisation von Lehr- und Lernprozessen, wie sie aus der Buchkultur entstanden. Durch die Möglichkeit der Revolution kann sich aus einem Theaterdiskurs ein Kreisdialog entwickeln. Ebenso kann ein Kreisdialog als eine Abfolge vieler kleiner Theaterdiskurse gesehen werden, die darauf abzielen, die Informationsunterschiede innerhalb des Kreises zu verringern. Diese Art der Kommunikation ist Grundlage der meisten universitären Seminare.

Amphitheaterdiskurs – wissenschaftliche Recherche

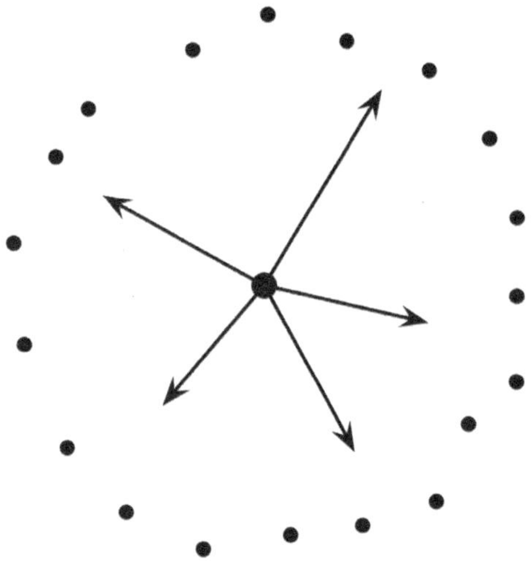

Abb. 4: Amphitheaterdiskurs (Flusser 2007, 27)

Im Gegensatz zum Theaterdiskurs ist der Amphitheaterdiskurs (vgl. Flusser 2007, 27ff) gekennzeichnet von Grenzenlosigkeit und einer „kosmischen Offenheit" (Flusser 2007, 27), da der Sender nicht, wie beim Theaterdiskurs, durch eine Wand abgeschirmt wird. Im Gegenteil, der Sender funkt von einem beliebigen Ort aus die in seinem Gedächtnis gespeicherten Informationen an ein ihm unbekanntes, beliebig großes Publikum. Der

Empfang geschieht zufällig, indem der Empfänger sich auf den Kanal einstellt. Charakteristisch für die Struktur des Amphitheaters ist, dass die Empfänger nur Kontakt zu den Kanälen, jedoch nicht zur Quelle der Information herstellen können. Die Unmöglichkeit der Interaktion von Sender und Empfänger verhindern das Entstehen eines Dialogs. Beispiele für einen Amphitheaterdiskurs sind u.a. Radio, Fernsehen und statische HTML-Webseiten, wie sie in den Anfängen des WWW typisch waren. Auch die Weitergabe von Informationen über Bücher kann als Amphitheaterdiskurs verstanden werden, als soziale Informationsverarbeitung ohne direkte Interaktion, wie Giesecke (2007) es nennt.

Der Amphitheaterdiskurs findet sich in der universitären Lehre eher versteckt wieder. Er funktioniert durch den fehlenden Kontakt von Sender und Empfänger nicht als ein Diskurs, der von Lehrenden direkt gesteuert wird, d.h. die Wissensinhalte werden nicht gezielt von Lehrenden an Studierende übermittelt, wie es – in der Tradition der Paideia – in theaterdiskursiven Vorlesungen geschieht. Allerdings kann die wissenschaftliche Recherche in Bibliotheken und im Internet mit dem Amphitheaterdiskurs verglichen werden. Jedoch gibt es hier Unterschiede hinsichtlich des Eingreifens der Bildungsinstitutionen in den Amphitheaterdiskurs. Durch Literaturhinweise in Seminaren und durch die Vorauswahl von Büchern durch Bibliotheken, werden die Informationen, die über Amphitheaterdiskurse verbreitet werden, eingegrenzt. Der Übertragungsprozess wird begleitet und damit gesteuert.

Das zunehmende Angebot an Informationen, die im Netz von jedermann bereit gestellt werden können und von jedermann jederzeit abrufbar sind fördert eine Übertragung, die nicht gesteuert wird. Dies verändert insbesondere auch die wissenschaftliche Recherche.

Die Paideia erfährt sozusagen eine teilweise Loslösung von der Person des Pädagogen. Die neuen Formen des Amphitheaterdiskurses im Netz in die universitäre Lehre zu integrieren würde bedeuten, dass die Lehrenden als Sinnverwalter sich auf die neuen Medien der Übermittlung einlassen und verstärkt die Prozesse der webbasierten Informationsrecherche einbinden und begleiten.

Netzdialog – informelle Kommunikation

Der Netzdialog (vgl. Flusser 2007, 32ff) als offene dialogische Form steht dem geschlossenen Kreis entgegen, die an einem Dialog Beteiligten bilden die Knotenpunkte in einem Netzwerk. Jeder einzelne dieser Knotenpunkte kann als Zentrum des Dialogs betrachtet werden. Der Dialog kann sich ohne Einschränkungen und Regeln in alle Richtungen ausbreiten. Durch Zerstreuung und äußere Einflüsse wird bestehende Information transformiert und damit (nicht notwendigerweise absichtlich) neue Information geschaffen. Der Netzdialog ist die archaischste Form der Kommunikation, die

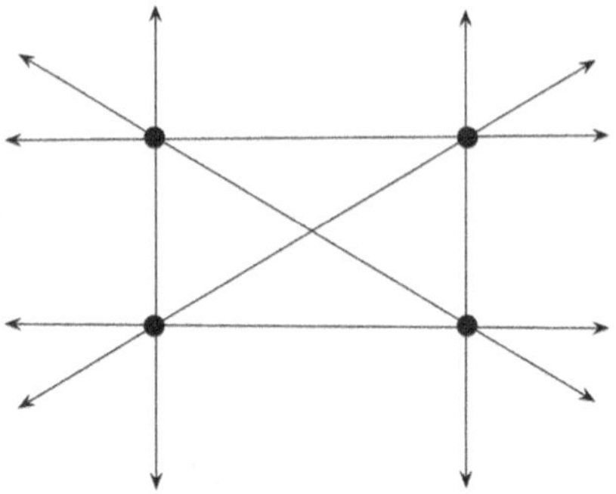

Abb. 5: Netzdialog (Flusser 2007, 32)

vermutlich in Form von *Klatsch* seit den ersten Gesellschaften der Menschen bis heute besteht. Als grundlegende Struktur stützt der Netzdialog alle anderen Formen der Kommunikation und saugt „letztlich alle von Menschen ausgearbeiteten Informationen in sich auf" (Flusser 2007, 32). Flusser bezeichnet die in einem Netz vorhandene Gesamtheit der Informationen, die durch permanentes Hintergrundrauschen verändert wird, als die öffentliche Meinung.

Amphitheater-Netz – Blogosphäre

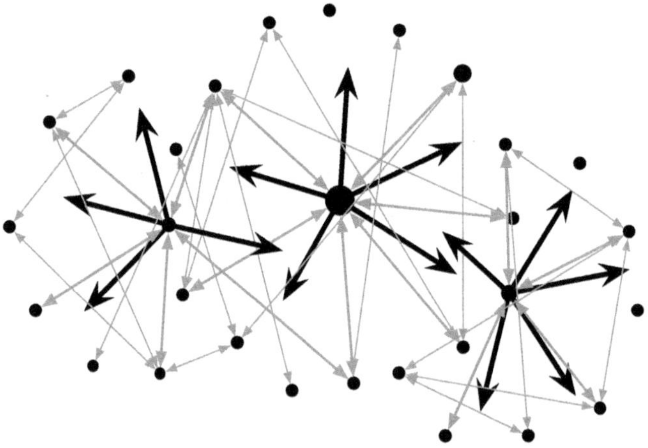

Abb. 6: Synchronisation von Amphitheaterdiskurs und Netzdialog. Adaption nach Flusser.

In Bezug auf eine Evolution der Mediosphären und der sich verändernden Kommunikations- und Übermittlungsstrukturen in einer möglichen digitalen Mediosphäre ist ein wesentliches Merkmal die Synchronisation von Amphitheaterdiskurs und Netzdialog. Diese Verbindung ist nicht neu, die alten römischen Amphitheater sowie die heutigen Massenmedien hatten seit jeher Einfluss auf die öffentliche Meinung. Doch Flussers Annahmen stammen aus einer Zeit vor der Entwicklung des Internets zu einem globalen Informations- und Kommunikationsmedium und demzufolge auch vor der Evolution des World Wide Web zu einer vernetzten technologischen Struktur, die soziale Interaktion und Partizipation an der Bereitstellung und Produktion von Inhalten ermöglicht. Insbesondere seitdem das WWW nicht mehr vorrangig als einseitig sendender, diskursiver Kanal, sondern als dialogisches Medium verstanden und genutzt wird, hat sich die Qualität der Synchronisation von Amphitheaterdiskurs und Netzdialog verändert.

Die Verbreitung von Informationen über das WWW ist zunächst einmal als Amphitheaterdiskurs anzusehen – es gibt keine bestimmten Empfänger, der Empfang geschieht nur durch das Einstellen des Empfängers auf den Kanal: Um die Information zu empfangen muss, man eine Webseite besuchen bzw. einen RSS-Feed abonnieren. In erster Instanz ist für den Empfänger nur der Kanal sichtbar, jedoch kann über die Möglichkeit zur Interaktion ein Kontakt zu dem Sender hergestellt werden – was diesen wiederum im Gegenzug dazu befähigt, mit dem Empfänger in einen Dialog zu treten. Ein weiteres Phänomen, das die Kommunikation über das WWW kennzeichnet, ist das, was Flusser als „Fortschritt" (Flusser 2007, 20) bezeichnet: Die Empfänger werden ihrerseits zum Sender und verbreiten die empfangene Information weiter, wieder in Form eines Amphitheaterdiskurses, der eingebunden ist in einen Netzdialog.

Was bedeutet es für Bildungsinstitutionen, wenn durch die sich zunehmend durchsetzende Synchronisation von Amphitheaterdiskurs und Netzdialog die Kommunikation, also die Verbreitung von Informationen in einem globalen Raum und die gleichzeitige permanente Transformation und Produktion immer neuer Informationen, sich schneller weiter entwickelt als die Übermittlungsinstitutionen? Wie können und müssen Bildungsinstitutionen sich bezüglich der Kommunikation verändern, ohne die Übermittlungsfunktion aufzugeben? Diese zentrale Frage ist handlungsleitend für das Teilprojekt Community Building des eingangs erwähnten Hochschulentwicklungsprojekts ePUSH.

Bildungsinstitutionen als Übermittlungsinstitutionen müssen sich auf die Ausweitung der Kommunikation in Form von Amphitheaterdiskursen gepaart mit Netzdialogen einstellen und dürfen nicht zu starr an Kommunikationsstrukturen festhalten, die der Graphosphäre entstammen. Übermittlung bzw. Paideia in einer kulturellen Epoche, in der die Weitergabe und Produktion von Informationen nicht mehr in erster Linie durch Universitäten getragen wird, sondern Informationen und Wissen jederzeit, überall verfügbar sind und jederzeit, überall und von jedem verfügbar gemacht werden können, bedeutet nicht mehr hauptsächlich, Ideen und Wissensinhalte zu übermitteln. Entscheidend wird zunehmend auch die Fähigkeit, mit Komplexität sinnvoll und reflexiv umzugehen (vgl. Baecker 2007, 143f).

Vernetzung statt Linearität

Mit dem Eindringen vernetzter, digitaler Medien in einen bis dato noch sehr geschlossenen, linear-hierarchisch organisierten Bildungsraum ist ein Trend hin zu offenen dialogischen Kommunikationsformen auch an Universitäten zu vermuten. Wenn, wie bereits angedeutet, die Übermittlung und damit die Paideia sich zunehmend von der Person des Pädagogen löst, und Lernen verstärkt in offenen, vernetzten Strukturen stattfindet, verändern sich dabei nicht nur die Kommunikationsformen, auch die sozialen Strukturen und Hierarchien sind hiervon betroffen. „Eine technische Veränderung der […] [Mediosphäre] bringt zugleich auch eine Veränderung des sozialen Status der Sinnverwalter mit sich" (Debray 2003, 61). Die Lehrenden als „Sinnverwalter" gelten bisher als Experten, die ihr Wissen in institutionell organisierten Lehr- und Lernsituationen an Studierende übermitteln bzw. als Vermittler zwischen den technischen Medien und Trägern zur Übermittlung und den symbolischen Bedeutungen fungieren. Dabei lassen sich anhand eines Modells von Vilém Flusser die traditionell aus der Graphosphäre gewachsenen sozialen Strukturen an Universitäten (schematisch vereinfacht) beschreiben. Verschiedene Kommunikationsebenen werden zueinander in Beziehung gesetzt: Die Lehrenden als Träger bzw. ‚Verwalter' des Wissens sind der Universalebene zuzuordnen, während die Studierenden die öffentliche Ebene bilden. Die Codes innerhalb der Universalebene sind jeweils abhängig von den wissenschaftlichen Disziplinen. Diese Codes gilt es für die Studierenden zu erlernen.

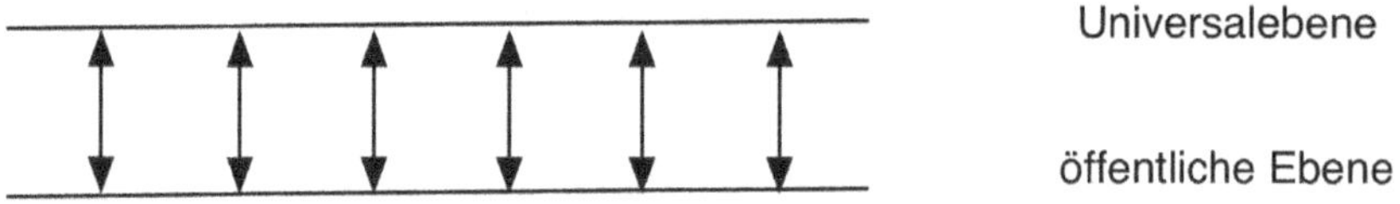

Abb. 7: Kommunikationsebenen an Universitäten

Die Kommunikation zwischen diesen beiden Ebenen ist immer noch deutlich geprägt von Theaterdiskursen, in denen Wissen und Informationen, zumeist gespeichert in äußeren Medien der Übermittlung, von der Universalebene an die öffentliche Ebene weitergegeben und in einen kulturellen bzw. wissenschaftlichen Kontext eingebettet werden. Feedback zwischen den Ebenen findet in Form von institutionell gelenkten Kreisdialogen statt. Innerhalb der Universalebene finden sowohl diskursive als auch dialogische Kommunikations- und Übermittlungsprozesse statt, die Studierenden hingegen befinden sich untereinander kaum in einem offenen Dialog. Diese bisher den Bildungsraum Universität prägenden sozialen und kommunikativen Strukturen sind aufgebaut auf linear organisierten, wissensbasierten Hierarchien zwischen Lehrenden und Studierenden.

Der sich andeutende Übergang zu einer digitalen Mediosphäre birgt jedoch, wie gesagt, Veränderungen der Kommunikationsstrukturen und damit Veränderungen in der Übermittlung, ebenso wie Veränderungen der sozialen Organisation. Universitäten können sich dem Trend zu einer offenen, vernetzten Kommunikation nicht verschließen, ohne sich nicht selber vom Diskurs abzuhängen und damit ihre Übermittlungsfunktion aufzugeben. Die Tendenz der Kommunikationsstrukturen und damit der Art und Weise der Übermittlung geht in Richtung offener und vermehrt dialogischer Strukturen, an denen Studierende und Lehrende gleichermaßen aktiv und passiv beteiligt sind. Mit der Zunahme offener, vernetzter, dialogischer Strukturen geht eine Verflachung der Hierarchien einher.

Auf Basis einer digital-vernetzten technischen Infrastruktur nimmt sowohl die Kommunikation innerhalb der bisherigen Universalebene, als auch die Kommunikation innerhalb der bisherigen Ebene der Studierenden zu. Ebenso ergeben sich neue Möglichkeiten, diskursive Strukturen – die Basis der Paideia – mit dialogischen Strukturen zu koppeln.[6] Die neuen technischen Medien bieten mehr Möglichkeiten zur Interaktion – Feedback und Dialog zwischen Lehrenden und Studierenden ist nicht mehr notwendigerweise an institutionell organisierte Kreisdialoge gekoppelt. Ebenso wird es Studierenden erleichtert, selber unabhängig von institutioneller Organisation als Sender zu fungieren und Dialoge anzuregen. Informelle Bildungsprozesse können mehr Platz auch innerhalb des Bildungsraums Universität erlangen. Um zu gewährleisten, dass die Übermittlung in einer sich andeutenden digitalen Mediosphäre nicht durch bloße Kommunikation, wie Debray sie betrachtet, verdrängt wird (also nur Zirkulation von Informationen in einem globalen Raum, ohne die Weitergabe von Wissensinhalten, Ideen und kulturellen Bedeutungen über die Zeit), muss die Rolle der Lehrenden neu definiert werden. Die Bedeutung der bisherigen eher geschlossenen Strukturen mit einem Sender aus der Universalebene und vielen, zumeist passiven Empfängern, den Studierenden, muss in diesem Zusammenhang überdacht werden. Anstelle der primären Übermittlung von typographischen Wissensinhalten tritt die Übermittlung von Kompetenzen, die zu einem reflexiven Umgang mit permanent verfügbaren und einem dynamischen Transformationsprozess unterworfenen Informationen in einer komplexen Informationsumgebung befähigen.

6 Im Rahmen des Projektes ePUSH werden die technischen Infrastrukturen der Fakultät erweitert, um zusätzlich zum Diskurs der Paideia auch verstärkt dialogische Strukturen in die universitären Kommunikationsstrukturen zu integrieren..

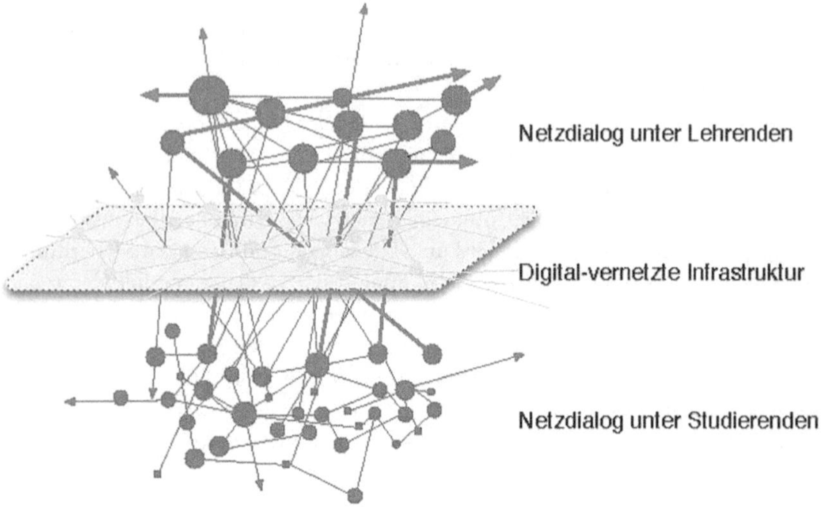

Abb. 8: Vernetzte Kommunikation an Universitäten (Schwalbe)

Offenes Ende

Es ist jedoch nicht allein die soziale Struktur und die Struktur der Kommunikation, die einem Veränderungsprozess unterworfen ist. Damit Bildungsinstitutionen auch in einer digitalen Mediosphäre ihre Funktion der Übermittlung wahrnehmen können, müssen auch die technischen Infrastrukturen, die gesamte soziale Organisation und das Selbstverständnis, die symbolische Bedeutung, neu gedacht und aktiv umgestaltet werden. Ein veränderter Status von Wissen, veränderte Kooperations-, Kommunikations- und Übermittlungsstrukturen wirken sich im Kern auf die Lehr- und Lernkultur an Universitäten aus. Der Rahmen des Bildungsraums Universität als Möglichkeitsraum muss neu gespannt werden. Daran arbeiten wir an der Universität Hamburg im Projekt ePUSH. Auf verschiedenen Ebenen wird der Umbau der Universität mit gestaltet und kritisch begleitet.

Zur kritischen Begleitung gehört es, die Verschiebung des bereits angesprochenen blinden Flecks des Denkens, Wissens, Erkennens zu realisieren und zu untersuchen, um so die Merkmale einer digitalen Mediosphäre erfassen zu können. Um die hier dargelegten theoretischen Annahmen zu stützen, werden während der Projektlaufzeit aktuelle Veränderungen des Mediennutzungsverhaltens Studierender evaluiert. Der Fo-

kus liegt dabei auf den Formen der Kommunikation, Kollaboration und dem Umgang mit Informationen.
Was sich in Hinblick auf eine digitale Mediosphäre schon jetzt deutlich abzuzeichnen beginnt, ist eine zunehmende Offenheit und permanente Vernetzung. Im Rahmen der ePUSH-Teilprojekte Community Building und eInfrastruktur wird daran gearbeitet, neben der auch weiterhin notwendigen geschlossenen Kommunikation und Übermittlung auch offene Kommunikation, Kooperation und Vernetzung zu fördern. Über die neue Fakultäts-Community „life" wird der Bildungsraum Universität als Übermittlungsinstitution eingebunden in den Netzdialog des neuen Mediums. Gleichzeitig werden vielfältige Schnittstellen zwischen digitaler und physischer Welt geschaffen, um die unkomplizierte und dauerhafte Anbindung an die digitalen Infrastrukturen der Fakultät und damit an den virtuellen Raum zu fördern.

ePUSH ist ein Hochschulentwicklungsprojekt mit experimentellem Charakter. Durch permanente Meta-Reflexion der angestoßenen Umbauten im und am Bildungsraum Universität wird der aktuellen Umbruchsituation Rechnung getragen. Der Ausgang der mediologischen Revolution ist bislang ungewiss ...

Literatur

Baacke, Dieter (1997): Medienpädagogik. Tübingen: Niemeyer.

Baecker, Dirk (2007): Studien zur nächsten Gesellschaft. Frankfurt am Main: Suhrkamp.

Debray, Régis (1994): Für eine Mediologie. In: Pias/Vogl/Engell 2004, 67-75.

Debray, Régis (2003): Einführung in die Mediologie: Facetten der Medienkultur. Berne: Haupt Verlag.

Fassler, Manfred (2007). Collaborative Intelligence/Communities of Project. In: Meyer/Scheibel/Münte-Goussar/Meisel/Schawe 2007: 136-150, 330-338.

Ferner, Christina (2007). Networking in Universities – How Universities Can Accept the Challenge and Take an Active, Formative Role. Masterthesis an der Universität Hamburg. Online: http://christinaferner.de/MA_ChristinaFerner.pdf [30.10.08]

Ferner, Christina/Meyer, Torsten (2008): ePush – Digitale Vernetzung und Integration in einer Fakultät. In: e-teaching.org, Themenspecial "Web 2.0 in der Lehre". Online: http://www.e-teaching.org/materialien/praxisberichte/ePush [30.10.08]

Flusser, Vilém (2007): Kommunikologie. 4. Ausgabe. Frankfurt am Main: Fischer.

Foucault, Michel (1981): Archäologie des Wissens. Frankfurt am Main: Suhrkamp.

Giesecke, Michael (2002): Von den Mythen der Buchkultur zu den Visionen der Informationsgesellschaft. Frankfurt am Main: Suhrkamp.

Kleimann, Bernd (2007): eLearning 2.0 an deutschen Universitäten. In: Merkt, Marianne/Mayrberger, Kerstin/Schulmeister, Rolf/Sommer, Angela/van den Berk, Ivo 2007, 149 – 158.

Krämer, Sibylle (2003). Erfüllen Medien eine Konstitutionsleistung? Thesen über die Rolle medientheoretischer Erwägungen beim Philosophieren. In: Münker/Roessler/Sandbothe 2003, 78-90.

Lacan, Jacques (1996). Die vier Grundbegriffe der Psychoanalyse. In: Das Seminar von Jacques Lacan, hg. von Haas, Norbert; Metzger, Hans-Joachim, Weinheim/Berlin: Quadriga, Bd. XI.

Lyotard, Jean-Francois (1979): Das Postmoderne Wissen. Ein Bericht. Wien: Passagen.

Merkt, Marianne/Mayrberger, Kerstin/Schulmeister, Rolf/Sommer, Angela/van den Berk, Ivo (Hrsg.) (2007): Studieren neu erfinden – Hochschule neu denken. Münster/New York/München/Berlin: Waxmann.

Meyer, Torsten (2002): Interfaces, Medien Bildung. Paradigmen einer pädagogischen Medientheorie. Bielefeld: transcript.

Meyer, Torsten/Scheibel, Michael/Münte-Goussar, Stephan/Meisel, Timo/Schawe, Julia (Hrsg.) (2007): Bildung im Neuen Medium. Wissensformation und digitale Infrastruktur/Education Within a New Medium. Knowledge Formation and Digital Infrastructure. Munster, New York, München, Berlin: Waxmann.

Meyer, Torsten (2008a): Zwischen Kanal und Lebens-Mittel: pädagogisches Medium und mediologisches Milieu. In: Sesink/Fromme 2008, 71-94.

Meyer, Torsten (2008b): Transmission, Kommunikation, Formation. Mediologische Betrachtungen der Bildung des Menschen. In: Weber/Mersmann 2008, 169-190

Meyer, Torsten/Scheibel, Michael/Münte-Goussar, Stephan/Meisel, Timo/Schawe, Julia (Hrsg.) (2007): Bildung im Neuen Medium. Wissensformation und digitale Infrastruktur/Education Within a New Medium. Knowledge Formation and Digital Infrastructure. Münster/New York/München/Berlin: Waxmann.

Münker, Stefan/Roessler, Alexander/Sandbothe, Mike (Hrsg.) (2003): Medienphilosophie. Beiträge zur Klärung eines Begriffs. Frankfurt am Main: Fischer.

Pias, Claus/Vogl, Joseph/Engell, Lorenz (Hrsg.) (2004): Kursbuch Medienkultur. Die maßgeblichen Theorien von Brecht bis Baudrillard. Stuttgart: DVA.

Roesler, Alexander/Stiegler, Bernd (Hrsg.) (2005): Grundbegriffe der Medientheorie. München: Fink.

Rotermund, Hermann (1996): Von der Keilschrift bis zum Internet. Verschwinden die Subjekte im Speicher? Online: http://www.weisses-rauschen.de/hero/96-03-keilschrift.html [09.10.08]

Scheibel, Michael (2001): Alma mater virtualis. Visionen einer neuen Hochschule. In: medien + erziehung 01/2001, 14-16.

Scheibel, Michael (2006): „Under construction". Ein Meinungsspiegel. In: medien+erziehung 02/2006, 71-74.

Sesink, Werner (2008): Bildungstheorie und Medienpädagogik. Versuch eines Brückenschlags. In: Sesink/Fromme 2008, 13-35.

Sesink, Werner/Fromme, Johannes (Hrsg.) (2008): Pädagogische Medientheorie. Wiesbaden: VS Verlag.

Sonvilla-Weiss, Stefan (Hrsg.) (2005). (e)Pedagogy – Visual Knowledge Building. Rethinking Art and New Media in Education. Bern/Berlin/Brüssel/Frankfurt am Main/New York/Oxford/Wien: Lang.

Tholen, Georg Christoph (2005): Medium/Medien. In: Roessler/Stiegler 2005, 150-172.

Weber, Thomas/Mersmann, Birgit (Hrsg.) (2008): Mediologie als Methode. Rodenbach: Avinus

Von der „kalifornischen Ideologie" zur „Folksonomy" - die Entwicklung der Internetkultur

von Udo Thiedeke

Internetkultur

Zunächst stellt sich die Frage, ob es Sinn macht das Internet als „Kulturraum" zu beschreiben und wenn ‚ja', was wir dann beobachten können? Anscheinend macht es Sinn, so hat es zumindest den Anschein, wenn man die Forschungslage beobachtet. Kaum verbreitete sich das Internet mit dem WWW in den 1990er Jahren, da entstanden u.a. in Deutschland erste sozialwissenschaftliche Forschungsprojekte zu einer Ethnographie des „Kulturraums Internet" (vgl. Helmers et al. 1997). Tatsächlich sind das Internet und der mit ihm entstehende Sinnhorizont der CMC (Computer mediated Communication) schon früh als kulturelle Phänomene identifiziert worden. Zu eigentümlich, zu neu erschienen die Technologie der dezentral vernetzten Computer und zu fantastisch die Möglichkeiten ihrer individuellen Fernsteuerung.

Bevor man hier weitermacht ist jedoch grundsätzlich zu klären, was unter „Kultur" verstanden werden soll? Kultur ist ein schwieriger, weil diffuser Begriff, obwohl er im alltäglichen, aber auch im wissenschaftlichen Sprachgebrauch Verwendung findet. Um nicht in die ausufernden Debatten von Kulturkämpfen zu geraten, wie sie nicht nur im 19. Jahrhundert um das Gegensatzpaar „Kultur" versus „Zivilisation" oder heute um den sog. Clash of Cultures (Huntington) geführt wurden und werden, möchte ich vorschlagen, den Kulturbegriff für unsere Zwecke ‚tiefer zu legen' und ihn damit seiner kulturellen Bewertung zu entziehen. Ich fasse Kultur dazu kommunikationstheoretisch von ihren Orientierungsleistungen her. So kann man die Definition vorschlagen:

Unter Kultur soll die Selbstbeschreibung von Individuen oder Kollektiven verstanden werden, die ein Orientierungswissen über Handlungs- und Bewertungsmodalitäten in umgrenzten Sinnbereichen vermittelt.

Bei Kultur geht es also um die Art und Weise, *wie* man die Welt in spezifischen Kontexten sieht und dementsprechende Gepflogenheiten des Umgangs mit dieser Welt erwartet. Kultur sagt uns wie wir etwas in einem bestimmten Umfeld machen oder bewerten sollen - Insofern ist Kultur immer auch ein Teil der Bildung.

Wenn wir uns so der Internetkultur annähern, so meint das, kommunizierte Selbstbeschreibungen zu beobachten, die von denjenigen hervorgebracht wurden und werden, die das Internet gestalten und nutzen. Da das Internet die Besonderheit aufweist, dass es dezentral durch alle vernetzbaren Computer steuerbar und veränderbar ist, heißt das, eine Kultur zu beobachten, die durch individuelle Impulse vieler Kommunikationsteilnehmerinnen und -teilnehmer in ständigem Fluss gehalten wird. Grob können wir dabei für die Kultur, die uns das ‚wie' im Umgang mit dem Internet beschreibt folgende Charakteristika festhalten:

Charakteristika der Internetkultur
- Dezentralität des Zugangs
- Individualität der Beteiligung
- Vernetzung der Kontakte
- Technizität des Umgangs
- Liberalität der Inhalte

Da es sich bei Kultur um *Beschreibungen*, also um tradierbare Erzählungen oder Texte der Kommunikation im und über das Netz handelt, treten diese Charakteristika in Symbolen, Geschichten, Mythen, Stilen oder Normen zu Tage. Träger der Internetkultur und ihrer Beschreibungsmuster sind aber nicht nur Individuen oder Gruppen, die das Netz reflektierend beobachten, wie Wissenschaftler oder Intellektuelle, sondern alle Nutzenden des Internets.

Hierzu fällt auf, dass sich mit dem Internet ein neues, kybernetisches, d.h., steuerbares *Interaktionsmedium* entwickelt hat, das eine universelle Anwendbarkeit und vollständige Durchdringung des Alltags verspricht. Entsprechend ist das Aufblühen der Internetkultur begleitet von großen Gefühlen der Zustimmung oder Ablehnung. Dieser Sachverhalt ‚kultureller Aufregung' lässt sich als Indikator dafür lesen, dass hier tatsächlich ein neues Medium gesellschaftlicher Kommunikation etabliert wurde.

Ich möchte mich dazu im Folgenden auf zwei kulturelle Selbstbeschreibungsmuster des Internets konzentrieren, die sich wiederum in differenzierte Selbstbeschreibungen untergliedern. Beide sind nicht vollständig voneinander zu trennen, zeigen aber an, wie sich die Entwicklungen des Netzes in seiner Kultur niederschlagen und das Internet damit zugleich ins allgemeine Orientierungswissen über unsere Welt einbetten.

Die „kalifornische Ideologie“ und der „Cyberspace“

Die Überraschung war groß, als die beiden Google-Gründer nach dem Börsengang ihres Unternehmens dieses Ereignis mit einem mehrtägigen ‚Abtauchen' im „burning man“ Happening feierten. Dieses Happening hat seine Wurzeln in der Hippiebewegung und wird als exstatisches Fest der Kreativität und Phantasie in alljährlich in der Wüste von Nevada gefeiert. Höhepunkt des Festes ist das Verbrennen einer überlebensgroßen Skulptur, des „burning man“.

Dass die Google-Gründer Sergey Brin und Larry Page den Börsengang nicht mit einer Campagner-Party für Finanzinvestoren, sondern im Rahmen eines Post-Hippie-Happenings feierten, wirkte als Signal, das Kreativität, Unkonventionalität und Spontaneität vermittelte und so die Bedeutung individueller Selbstverwirklichung für den wirtschaftlichen Erfolg andeutete.

Brin und Page lebten hier geradezu, was als kulturelles Selbstverständnis mit dem Internet möglich wurde. Das Internet wird demnach als raumsprengendes und Realitätsgrenzen überschreitendes Medium gesehen, weil jede und jeder Zugang zur vernetzten Wirklichkeitsmaschine Computer erhält, mit der sich Daten (das Gegebene) zu Fakten (dem Gemachten) manipulieren lassen. So werden die Tore geöffnet, um nach Gusto der Einzelnen die *letzte Grenze* physischer Eingebundenheit zu überschreiten.

Die Internetkultur basiert auf nichts weniger als auf dem Versprechen alle Realisierungschancen zu verwirklichen. Man möchte anders sein, in die Kindheit zurück oder zugleich Kind und Erwachsener sein, man möchte von ganz unten nach ganz oben, man möchte weiter hinaus, als irgendjemand vorher, man möchte sich selbst verwirklichen und dabei Teil einer idealen, weil schwerelosen Gemeinschaft sein - bitte sehr, just do it, click it!

Nicht von ungefähr scheint das Netz deshalb in einem Landstrich und auf der Grundlage einer Kultur zu entstehen, die wir *Kalifornien* und *kalifornisch* nennen. Kalifornien liegt nicht nur unter der ewigen Sonne, die das Leben erleichtert, an den Küsten des anbrandenden Pazifik, der zum Wellenreiten verführt, und auf einer tektonischen Erdbebenzone, die das Stabile in Frage stellt. Kalifornien stellt zugleich die Abrisskante des amerikanischen Traums von der „*final frontier*" dar. Hier geht der Treck nach Westen geographisch nicht mehr weiter. Er muss hinaus über das Meer, hinauf in den Weltraum und hinein in den kybernetischen Sinnraum des Internets, den Cyberspace. Eine Komponente der neuen Internetkultur scheint somit die kalifornische Version des amerikanischen Traums zu sein, das rastlose Vorwärtsdrängen. Aber warum ist diese Kultur eine „Kalifornische *Ideologie*"?

Die beiden Journalisten Richard Barbrook und Andy Cameron, die um 1997 die Bezeichnung prägten, suggerieren, ganz in der Tradition von Karl Marx, die Existenz einer „*virtuellen Klasse*". Diese stellt die Idee des kalifornischen Lebensstils in den Dienst der Verführung zum Marktliberalismus und zu reaktionärem Ordnungsdenken. Entsprechend stellt sich die Trägergruppe der Internetkultur dar:

> „Wer hätte vorausgesehen, daß [...] die Spießer und Hippies gemeinsam die kalifornische Ideologie ausbilden würden? Wer hätte gedacht, daß eine solch widersprüchliche Mischung aus technologischem Determinismus und liberalem Individualismus zur hybriden Orthodoxie des Informationszeitalters würde? Und wer hätte vermutet, daß es mit der zunehmenden Verehrung der Technologie immer weniger möglich würde, irgend etwas Sinnvolles über die Gesellschaft zu sagen, in der sie eingesetzt wird?" (Barbrook/Cameron 1997).

Die freie, basisdemokratische und friedlich utopische Haltung kalifornischen Lebens wird somit verraten. Die Kultur des Internets erscheint als indifferente Haltung, die Ungleichheiten ausblendet und nicht mehr dem Freiheitskampf verpflichtet ist, sondern der kommerziellen Expansion. Barbrook und Cameron weiter:

> „Wird die Ankunft der Hypermedien die Utopien der Neuen Linken oder der Neuen Rechten verwirklichen? Die *kalifornische Ideologie* als hybride Überzeugung reagiert glücklich auf diese Frage durch den Glauben an beide Visionen zur gleichen Zeit - und nicht durch Kritik an einer von beiden“ (Barbrook/Cameron 1997, Hervorh. im Orig.).

Nach dieser Sichtweise predigen die kalifornischen Ideologen nur: „das bizarre Mischmasch einer anarchistischen Hippieweltanschauung mit einem ökonomischen Liberalismus und mit einem großen Schuss an technologischem Determinismus“ (Barbrook/ Cameron 1997). Und sie wiederholen die Geschichte: „Die Technologien der Freiheit werden zu Maschinen der Herrschaft“ (Barbrook/Cameron 1997).

Tatsächlich können wir für den ‚Mainstream' der Internetkultur der 1980er und bis zum Ende der 1990er Jahre eine utopisch verklärte Bejahung der Computertechnik festhalten. Gebündelt wird dieser Technikdeterminismus einer neuen Gesellschaft in der Metapher des „Cyberspace“.

Es gilt, ganz in der Pioniertradition der USA, einen neuen Raum zu besiedeln und ein ‚neues Jerusalem' zu begründen. Das alles gipfelt in einer *Unabhängigkeitserklärung des Cyberspace*, wie sie vom Internetvisionär John Perry Barlow 1996 formuliert wird. Barlow zum Auftakt:

> „Regierungen der industrialisierten Welt, ihr erschöpften Giganten aus Fleisch und Stahl, ich komme aus dem Cyberspace der neuen Heimat des Geistes. Im Namen der Zukunft, fordere ich euch Gestrige auf, lasst uns allein. Ihr seid unter uns nicht willkommen. Wo wir uns versammeln da habt ihr keine Hoheitsrechte“ (Barlow 1996, Übersetzung UTh.).

Was wir hier registrieren, ist der Sachverhalt, dass uns die neue Kultur in den Formen der alten gegenüber tritt. Wir sehen uns einem Fortschrittsglauben konfrontiert, wonach individuelle und politische Freiheit durch Technik zu erlangen ist. Und wir registrieren das Misstrauen, dass eine technologische Klasse die Technik zur Verblendung und Ausbeutung manipulieren könnte. Will man die widersprüchlichen Charakteristika der „kalifornischen Ideologie“ und des „Cyberspace“ zusammenfassen, dann stellen sie sich wie folgt dar:

	Kalifornische Ideologie	Cyberspace
Trägergruppe	Virtuelle Klasse	Cybercitizens
Motto	Selbstverwirklichung	Selbstbefreiung
Ziel	marktliberale Ordnung	Freiheit durch Technik
Wirkung	Verblendungszusammenhang	Fortschrittsutopie

Tab. 1: Charakteristika der frühen Internetkultur. Quelle: eigene Darstellung

„Web 2.0" und „Folksonomy"

An dieser frühen Version der Internetkultur der 1980er und 90er Jahren fällt nicht nur die Widersprüchlichkeit auf. Zunächst deutet eine derart kontroverse kulturelle Debatte zum Umgang mit den vermeintlichen sowie tatsächlichen Hintergründen des neuen Mediums auf einen gesellschaftlichen Umbruch in den medialen Orientierungen hin. Eine solche Umbruchsituation lässt sich durch folgende Indikatoren kennzeichnen:

Indikatoren medialer Neuorientierung

- Gesellschaftliche Relevanz neuer Umgangsformen mit den Medien
- Kontrovers zugespitzte kulturelle Diagnosen
- Beschreibung des neuen Mediums in Termini der alten Medien
- Utopische und/oder dystopische Erwartungen eines Kulturwandels

Gerade die Dramatisierung der hier anschließenden kulturellen Utopien, etwa von idealen, egalitären „virtual Communities" (Rheingold 1993) oder kulturellen Dystopien, wie von „Pseudogemeinschaften" (Lockard 1997) sowie einer durch Cybereliten betrieben Segmentierung der Gesellschaft (Sassen 1997), zeigen Versuche an, Umgangsformen für das Internet zu finden.

Der Kulturumbruch wird deshalb auch im Auseinanderfallen der neuen Kommunikationsrealität und der neue Kommunikationskultur sichtbar. Die kulturellen Beschreibungen wirken wie ein Labor der Deutungen, in dem das ‚wie' im Umgang mit der neuen Wirklichkeit erst noch erprobt werden muss. So treten paradoxe Orientierungsmuster auf. Die einfache Formel „Freiheit durch Technik" (Brill 2003, 90) der „Cyberspace"-Orientierung erweist sich z.B. als nicht haltbar und wandelt sich in ein „Freiheit von der Technik durch Technik" und in virtuellen Gemeinschaften geht es bald darum „die freie Entfaltung, vor der Macht der freien Entfaltung, durch Macht und Sanktionen zu schützen“ etc..

Der tatsächliche Umgang mit dem Internet nahm auf diese Weise einen Weg, der sowohl den Einfluss der Netzutopisten, der ‚Unix-Priester‘ der ersten Internetstunden, der ‚Hacker‘, ‚Phreaks‘ und ‚Netiziens‘, als auch den Einfluss der ökonomischen und politischen Machtkartelle auf das Netz relativierte. Mit dem Platzen der sog. ‚Dotcom-Blase‘ im Jahr 2001 schien sich das Internet als wirtschaftliches Spielfeld sogar gänzlich selbst zerstört zu haben.

Unbeeindruckt davon haben die Millionen und Abermillionen Nutzerinnen und Nutzer das Netz und den virtualisierten Sinnhorizont des Cyberspace weiterentwickelt. In dieser „*Entwicklung durch Gebrauch*“ ist das Internet heute auf dem Weg ubiquitär zu werden. Es gehört zunehmend zur Erfahrung interaktionsmedialer Kommunikation, nicht mehr *ins* Netz zu gehen, sondern im Netz *zu sein*, wobei alle die kommunizierten Wirklichkeiten steuern und alleine durch ihre Zugriffe auf das Internet individuell verändern.

Das Netz, das beileibe noch nicht alle Kommunikationen der Weltgesellschaft erfasst hat, zeigt sich bereits jetzt als komplexer Raum selbstorganisierter Wissens- und Handlungsschwerpunkte, die je nach individueller Beteiligung aufblitzen und vergehen, wie Sternschnuppen am Nachthimmel.

Die darauf reflektierende neue kulturelle Beschreibung kommt wiederum als Dramatisierung daher. Zur Orientierung der Handelnden, wird jetzt der Aspekt des Mitmachens und Eingreifens der Kommunizierenden zur Kultur des „*Mitmach*“-Internet gesteigert. Hier soll ein *Update* des Netzes, ein „*Web 2.0*“ (O'Reilly 2005) entstanden sein. Man hat entdeckt, dass die Wege der Vernetzung viel weniger durch technische und ökonomische Eliten zentral vorherzubestimmen sind, wie etwa bei den Massenmedien.

So zeigt sich das Netz selbst als paradoxes Medium einer *massenhaften individuellen Beteiligung* und einer *mittelbaren Unmittelbarkeit* der sozialen Kontakte. Das Netz ist *soziotechnisch*, ohne, dass man genau bestimmen könnte, ob es die Technik oder die Nutzer sind, die seine Entwicklung vorantreiben. Es öffnet Wissenshorizonte und führt damit die Wissensfülle und unser aller Nichtwissen vor Augen, weil potenziell jede und jeder eine ganze Wirklichkeit der Kommunikation, ein ganzes globales soziales Netzwerk initiieren kann und so an die Grenzen der anderen individuellen Welten stößt. Und dabei geht es nicht darum, dass alle das auch *tun*, sondern dass es alle *könnten*.

Das Entstehen von Plattformen wie MySpace[1], Flickr[2], YouTube[3], StudiVZ[4] von Welten wie Second Life[5] oder vernetzter Computerspielwelten verweisen ebenso auf diese Eigendynamik des *Grossen aus dem Kleinen*, wie die vielen Blogs, Pod- oder Vidcasts, Chats und Foren. Immer wieder entstehen Gravitationszentren der Netzkommunikation, wie Google oder Second Life, World of Warcraft oder MySpace, die wirtschaftliche und politische Interessen fokussieren. Ob dieses Investment aber trägt, ob das Netz kontrolliert und ausgebeutet werden kann, ist ungewiss. Längst gehören sowohl die kalifornische Elite, wie die idealistischen Netzbürger zur Kulturgeschichte des Netzes. Die Regie seiner Eigendynamik scheinen *evolutionäre* Auswahl und Bestätigungsmechanismen übernommen zu haben.

Was ist darunter zu verstehen? Evolutionäre Strukturierungsmechanismen der Netzkommunikation treten auf, weil die Vielfalt von Millionen individueller Kommunikationsimpulse, die das Internet und seinen Sinnhorizont „Cyberspace" ständig verformen, nur sehr bedingt eine planbare Steuerung der Netzentwicklung zulassen. Die Wirklichkeit des Internets erscheint komplex, seine sozialen Beziehungs- und Beschreibungsstrukturen kontingent, d.h., in ihrem Entstehen und in ihrer Entwicklung unwägbar..

Als Grundbedingung der Netzkommunikation lässt sich daher *Variation* von Kommunikationen, Identitäten, Gruppen, Welten und Wirklichkeiten behaupten. Durch die große Zahl der individuellen Kommunikationsteilnehmer, deren Beteiligung typischerweise nicht massenmedial gebündelt oder individualmedial adressiert ist, findet Netzkommunikation auf der Grundlage zufällig ausgewählter Themen, Zeiten, Personen oder Orte statt. Wird eine solche *Selektion* für weitere Kommunikation genutzt, so hat die *Restabilisierung* einer unterscheidungsfähigen Struktur stattgefunden. Sie trägt dann z.B. als neues Thema, neues Netzwerk, neue Webidee wieder zur Variation der Netzkommunikation bei. Schematisch lässt sich dieser evolutionäre Strukturierungsprozess wie folgt skizzieren:

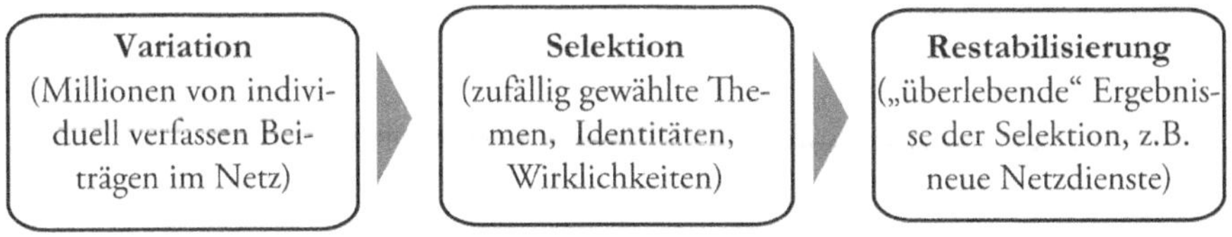

Abb. 1: Schematik der evolutionären Strukturentwicklung des Internets

1 http://www.myspace.com
2 http://Flickr.com
3 http://www.youtube.com
4 http://www.studivz.net
5 htttp://www.secondlife.com

Wie diese Strukturmechanismen arbeiten, zeigt z.B. die evolutionäre Kollaboration und ihr Abbild in der Internetkultur. Unterstützt durch sog. social software, die Verbindungen und Netzwerke der Kommunizierenden hervorhebt und beiläufig protokolliert, kann das Netz zufällige Zusammenarbeit und Wissenscluster als Meinungsballungen hervorbringen. Um Kommunikationsvorschläge und Interessenschwerpunkte herum, die attraktiv erscheinen, bilden sich Beziehungsnetzwerke und zeitlich relativ stabile virtuelle Gemeinschaften oder Gruppen aus (Thiedeke 2003, Thiedeke 2007). Die Attraktivität der Ballung wird dabei nach dem Prinzip der mitlaufenden Bewertung und Koppelung von den Aktionen der Kommunizierenden selbst erzeugt. Das erlaubt zeitweilige Bewertungsstrukturen, Schwerpunktbildungen und Orientierungsbewegungen.

Auf diese Weise ist die Kultur der „Folksonomy" entstanden, was nicht nur ein Bewertungsprinzip durch die Beteiligten meint (Folk = die Leute; -sonomy steht als Kürzel für Taxonomy = Bewertung), sondern eine Umgangsweise mit dem Netz, bei der die Einzelnen, unabhängig von Status, Alter und Geschlecht sich als Peers der Netzinhalte verstehen, die wie alle anderen, das betonen, was ihnen wichtig erscheint und das verwerfen, was ihnen persönlich unwichtig ist. Folksonomy ist eine Umgangsweise mit dem Web, die eine evolutionäre Form der Durchsetzung und Auflösung von Bedeutungsnetzen und sozialen Wirklichkeiten meint. Sie repräsentiert zugleich einen im Detail blinden Entstehungsprozess von Meinungsballungen, dem die Kommunizierenden in ihrem Handeln, wie ein Schwarm folgen und so das überkommenen Prinzip hierarchischer Meinungsbildung in Frage stellen. Und es überrascht daher nicht, dass man diesen Zusammenhang wiederum sowohl als „Weisheit der Massen" (Surowiecki 2004) feiert, als auch als „Maoismus der Massen" (Lanier 2006) verdammt.

	Web 2.0	**Folksonomy**
Trägergruppe	engagierte Netznutzer	Schwarm
Motto	Mitmachen	Bewerten
Ziel	Netzwerk	Überleben
Wirkung	soziale Vernetzung	Meinungsballungen

Tab. 2: Charakteristika der neuen Internetkultur. Quelle: eigene Darstellung

Zusammenfassung

Das Internet und der Computer haben sich zu einem, den Alltag durchdringenden neuen Medium entwickelt. Die Besonderheit dieser Entwicklung liegt darin, dass hier ein individuell verfügbares, steuerbares (kybernetisches) Interaktionsmedium entstanden ist, das bestehende physische, physikalische und soziale Beschränkungen entgrenzt. Mit dem Computer als Medium sowie mit durch dessen Vernetzung tritt Virtualisierung im Sinne einer ‚Machbarkeit von bisher nur Möglichem' ein. Man kann etwa die Identität kontrollieren, an mehreren Orten gleichzeitig sein, ‚Sterben' und ‚Wiederauferstehen', ohne Massenmedien weltweit bekannt werden, das Weltwissen individuell mitgestalten etc.

Mit dieser *Vermöglichung* der Wirklichkeit durch kybernetische Interaktionsmedien entsteht eine Eigendynamik der Selbstbeschreibung von Individuen und Kollektiven, die in der Internetkultur in Form orientierender Beschreibungen des Umgangs mit dem neuen Medium reflektiert wird. Dabei zeigen sich je nach Entwicklungsphase des Webs unterschiedliche kulturelle Erzählungen und Orientierungsmuster der Bewertung sowie der Handlungspraxis.

In der *Expansionsphase* des Netzes in den 1990er Jahren kann man diese Muster als „*kalifornische Ideologie*" und „*Cyberspace*" bezeichnen. Die Hoffnungen richten sich hier auf unbegrenzte Grenzüberschreitung, ideale Bedingungen der Beteiligung und Befreiung vom Diktat der Großtechnik. Die Befürchtungen gehen von einer Segmentierung der Öffentlichkeit, wachsenden ‚digitalen Ungleichheiten' und einer neoliberalen Manipulation aus.

In der *Konsolidierungsphase* des Netzes etwa ab dem Jahr 2000 treten Kulturmuster des „*Web 2.0*" und der „*Folksonomy*" in Erscheinung. Als Hoffnungen werden die Erwartungen individueller Kreativität der Nutzenden und eine evolutionäre Herausbildung der besten Lösungen und Netzwerke formuliert. Im Gegensatz dazu stehen hier Befürchtungen einer unkontrollierbaren Diktatur des schlechten Geschmacks, mittelmäßiger Ergebnisse und einer ‚digitalen Mitläuferhaltung'.

Diese utopischen und dystopischen Überzeichnungen zeigen uns einerseits an, dass Kulturmuster die soziale Wirklichkeit des Webs nur in Form einer ‚Übersetzung' in Bewertungen erfassen und andererseits, dass wir mit einem tatsächlichen Medienumbruch konfrontiert sind, der alte Kulturmuster relativiert.

Literatur

Barbrook, Richard/Cameron, Andy (1997): Die kalifornische Ideologie. In: Telepolis. Magazin der Netzkultur, hg. v. Christian Heise. Online: http://www.heise.de/tp/deutsch/inhalt/te/1007/1.html [22.04.2009]

Barlow, John Perry (1996): A Declaration of the Independence of Cyberspace. Online: http://eff.org/~barlow/Declaration-Final.html [22.04.2009]

Brill, Andreas (2003): Paradoxe Kommunikation im Netz: zwischen virtueller Gemeinschaft, Cyberspace und virtuellen Gruppen. In: Thiedeke 2003, 88-106.

Helmers, Sabine/Hoffmann, Ute/Hofmann, Jeanette (1998): Internet... The Final Frontier: Eine Ethnografie. Schlußbericht des Projekts ‚Interaktionsraum Internet' Netzkultur und Netzwerkorganisation. WZB Paper F SII 98-112. Berlin. Online:http://duplox.wzb.eu/endbericht/index.htm [22.04.2009]

Lanier. Jaron (2006): Digital Maoism. The hazards of the new online collectivism. In: Edge. The third culture. Online: http://edge.org/3rd_culture/lanier06/lanier06_index.html [22.04.2009]

Lockard, Joseph (1997): Progresive Politics. Electronic Individualism and the Myth of Virtual Community. In: Porter 1997, 219-232.

Münker, Stefan/Roesler, Alexander (Hrsg.) (1997): Mythos Internet. Frankfurt am Main: Suhrkamp.

Rheingold, Howard (1993): The Virtual Community: Homestanding on the Electronic Frontier. New York: Addison-Wesley.

O'Reilly, Tim (2005): What IS Web 2.0. Online: http://www.oreillynet.com/pub/a/oreilly/tim/news/2005/09/30/what-is-web-20.html [22.04.2009]

Porter, David (Hrsg.) (1997): Internet Culture. New York: Routledge.

Sassen, Saskia (1997): Cyber-Segmentierungen. Elektronischer Raum und Macht. In: Münker/Roesler 1997, 215-235.

Surowiecki, James (2004): The Wisdom Of Crowds: Why The Many Are Smarter Than The Few And How Collective Wisdom Shapes Business, Economies, Societies And Nations. London: Bantam Dell.

Thiedeke, Udo (Hrsg.) (2003): Virtuelle Gruppen. Charakteristika und Problemdimensionen. 2. Aufl. Wiesbaden: VS Verlag.

Thiedeke, Udo (2007): Trust, but test! Das Vertrauen in virtuellen Gemeinschaften. Konstanz: Uvk.

Digitale Medien und Transkulturalität

von Christina Schachtner

Weihnachten 2007: Durch die bundesdeutsche Presse ging eine Geschichte, die sich in einem Münchner U-Bahnhof zugetragen hatte. Ein pensionierter Lehrer war von einem türkischen und einem griechischen Jugendlichen zusammengeschlagen worden. ‚Scheiß Deutscher!' sollen die Jugendlichen gerufen haben, als sie den Mann attackierten. Wenige Tage später waren vor dem Münchner Rathaus auf dem Marienplatz junge Erwachsene zu sehen, die ein Transparent hochhielten, auf dem zu lesen war ‚Kriminelle Ausländer raus!'. Am selben Tag zitierte die Bild-Zeitung auf ihrer Titelseite einen der gewalttätig gewordenen Jugendlichen mit den Worten ‚Meine Heimat ist Deutschland!'. ‚Bild' interpretierte die Worte des Jugendlichen als geschickten Schachzug, der vor einer Abschiebung schützen sollte.

Soziologisch betrachtet, beschreiben die Worte des Jugendlichen eine neue soziokulturelle Situation, die nicht mehr nur eine Minderheit betrifft. Die Trennung zwischen Inländern und Ausländern, wie sie das erwähnte Transparent suggeriert, trifft für die Lebenssituation der hier geborenen oder seit langem hier lebenden Menschen mit Migrationshintergrund nicht mehr zu. Sie sind vielmehr beides, z.B. Türken und Deutsche oder Griechen und Deutsche, sie sind hier und dort; sie befinden sich in einer transkulturalen Situation. Sie reklamieren das Hier als Heimat wie der oben zitierte Jugendliche, aber vielleicht auch das Dort. Ja, sie unterscheiden vielleicht nicht einmal mehr zwischen dem Hier und dem Dort.

Wir wissen nicht, was genau die Aggression der Jugendlichen in der Münchner U-Bahn ausgelöst hat. Das Leben im Dazwischen ist schwierig genug und wenn es mit wenig Chancen ausgestattet ist, wie dies für Jugendliche mit Migrationshintergrund häufig der Fall ist, ist es umso schwieriger. Wenn sie in Elternhaus und Schule keine Handlungsstrategien gelernt haben, wie mit dieser Uneindeutigkeit, in der sie sich befinden, umzugehen ist, dann ist die Gefahr groß, dass sich Ohnmacht breit macht. Gewalt ist eine Möglichkeit, Ohnmacht aktiv zu wenden und sich zugleich Aufmerksamkeit zu sichern, die selbst als empörte öffentliche Aufmerksamkeit eine Form von Anerkennung darstellt.

Transkulturale Lebenssituationen werden immer selbstverständlicher in dieser Gesellschaft, aber kaum jemand ist auf die damit verbundene Verunsicherung vorbereitet. Insofern besteht die Gefahr, dass Aggression und Gewalt wachsen. Eine Alternative dazu wäre der ‚kosmopolitische Blick', den Ulrich Beck (2004) ins Gespräch gebracht hat.

In diesem Beitrag soll das Thema Transkulturalität primär nicht im Kontext der physikalischen Welt, sondern im Kontext der virtuellen Welt des Internets diskutiert und versucht werden, auf zwei Fragen eine Antwort zu geben:

1. Inwiefern entstehen auch in virtuellen Räumen transkulturale Situationen?
2. Inwieweit zeigen sich in den webbasierten Kommunikationsräumen Entwicklungen, die einen kosmopolitischen Blick offenbaren?

Für immer mehr Menschen verschiedenen Alters, verschiedener sozialer Herkunft und verschiedenen Geschlechts ist das Internet zu einem wichtigen Kommunikationsmedium geworden, das erlaubt, über geographische Grenzen hinweg kommunikative Verbindungen herzustellen. Der aktuellen ARD/ZDF-Onlinestudie 2008 zufolge, nutzen in Deutschland derzeit 42,7 Mio (=65,8%) Menschen ab 14 das Internet (vgl. Eimeren/Frees 2008, 333). Die intensivsten InternetuserInnen sind die 14- bis 19-Jährigen; 97,2% dieser Altersgruppe sind online. Die höchste Zuwachsrate ist in der Altersgruppe ab 60 Jahren zu verzeichnen; nutzten im Jahre 2005 erst 18.5% der ab 60-Jährigen das Internet, so sind es im Jahre 2008 bereits 26,4%. Frauen liegen bei der Internetnutzung wieder deutlicher hinter den Männern; 59,6% der Frauen, aber 72,4% der Männer nutzen das Internet gelegentlich. Innerhalb Europas liegt die Internetnutzung in den nordischen Ländern am höchsten mit den Niederlanden an der Spitze (90,1%), gefolgt von Norwegen (87,7%); am niedrigsten ist die Internetnutzung in Staaten wie Albanien (13%), Serbien (14,8%) oder im Vatikanstaat (16,9%) ausgeprägt (vgl. Miniwatts Marketing Group 2008). In den virtuellen Räumen des Internets finden sich global verteilte Akteure und Akteurinnen schneller und leichter zusammen als an geographischen Orten. Das Internet kann daher als Gegenstand einer auf Transkulturalität gerichteten Analyse nicht ausgespart bleiben.

Ich werde mich nun zunächst mit dem Konzept Transkulturalität und in diesem Zusammenhang mit dem hier verwendeten Begriff von Kultur sowie mit dem Konzept von Kosmopolitismus beschäftigen, um dann auf die Beziehung dieser beiden Konzepte zur digitalen Medienwelt einzugehen. Anschließend stelle ich webbasierte Projekte vor, die implizit oder explizit mit dem Anspruch auftreten, den kosmopolitischen Blick zu fördern. Abschließend werfe ich die Frage auf, welche Konsequenzen die Diskussion über Transkulturalität und Medien für die Pädagogik hat.

Transkulturalität und Kosmopolitismus

Transkulturale Situationen können auf verschiedene Weise initiiert werden: durch die geographische Mobilität von MigrantInnen, von Angehörigen globaler Unternehmen und Mitgliedern internationaler Gremien einerseits sowie durch die Bilder- und Textströme andererseits, die tagtäglich via Fernsehen, Printmedien, Digitale Medien in unsere Wohnzimmer, Büros und Kinderzimmer fließen. Mit den Menschen-, Text- und Bilderströmen werden Ideen, Werte, Lebensstile transportiert, die die national gedachten kulturellen Landkarten unterwandern (vgl. Hess/Lenz 2001, 19).

Mobilität ist nichts Neues; Wanderungsbewegungen sind im Verlauf der menschlichen Geschichte eher die Regel als die Ausnahme und wenn man sie lange genug zurückverfolgt, dann löst sich die Kategorie des Einheimischen auf (vgl. Beck 2004, 106). Neu jedoch ist – aufgrund eines beschleunigten Transfers medialer Inhalte und moderner Verkehrstechnologie -, dass ein globaler Erfahrungsraum entsteht, in dem Menschen aus verschiedenen Teilen der Welt gleichzeitig zu Augenzeugen politischer und medialer Ereignisse werden (vgl. Beck 2004, 14). Das Lokale ist nicht länger der Ort für Identitätsbildung; vielmehr setzt sich das Lokale, durchzogen von weltweiten Einflüssen und Mobilitätsströmen, neu zusammen (vgl. Hess/Lenz 2001, 16). Es bilden sich neue Kulturmixe heraus.

Was impliziert der Begriff Kultur? In Anlehnung an Alfred Schütz und Thomas Luckmann verstehe ich unter Kultur intersubjektiv hergestellte Sinnzusammenhänge, die sich in der Interaktion mit der Sozial- und Dingwelt herausgebildet haben (vgl. Schütz/Luckmann 1975, 26). Diese Sinnzusammenhänge beinhalten, was wir wissen müssen, um in einer von den Mitgliedern einer Gesellschaft akzeptierten Weise zu funktionieren (vgl. Goddenough, zit. n. Geertz 1983, 17): Werte, Normen, Deutungen und Bedeutungen, Lebensorientierungen, Handlungsmuster, die sich in Laut, Schrift, Bild oder in anderer Form objektivieren. Auch die Welt der Gegenstände zählt zur Kultur, denn Gegenstände sind ebenfalls Träger intersubjektiv hergestellten Sinns (vgl. Lorenzer 1981, 19). Dieser symbolistische Kulturbegriff, der auf Ernst Cassirer (1965) zurückgeht, schließt Digitale Medien und Technik als kulturelle Objektivationen ein, die kollektive Werte und Normen wie Rationalisierung, Beschleunigung, Vernetzung verkörpern. Thomas Hengartner und Johanna Rolshoven sprechen von einer „Kultürlichkeit der Technik", die sich darin ausdrückt, dass sich Technik tiefgreifend auf Alltagshandlungen auswirkt und im Zuge dessen zeitliche, räumliche und soziale Vorstellungs-, Machbarkeits- oder Kommunikationshorizonte verändern (Hengartner/Rolshoven 1998, 36).

Kultur ist öffentlich, weil Sinnzusammenhänge öffentlich sein müssen, sollen sie die Integration der Mitglieder einer Gesellschaft sichern. Kultur ist nicht starr, auch wenn es viele Versuche gab und gibt, kulturelle Muster von äußeren Einflüssen abzuschotten. Kultur verändert sich von innen, weil sie erworben und gestaltet und nicht bloß vorgefunden wird (vgl. Waldenfels 1985, 199) und sie verändert sich, weil es kaum möglich ist, jede Verbindung nach außen zu unterbinden, schon gar nicht mehr in einer globalisierten Welt, für die technische, politische, kommunikative Vernetzung konstitutiv ist. Wie erwähnt, mehren sich Erfahrungsräume, in denen die Verschiedenheiten von Kulturen fortbestehen und zugleich die Interdependenzen zwischen Kulturen zunehmen. Alltägliche Orte, egal, ob wir sie betreten oder ob sie medial vermittelt sind, werden zu Orten von Überlagerungen und Durchkreuzungen, die Begegnungen fördern, aber auch zu Abgrenzungen führen. Letzteres geschieht möglicherweise umso vehementer, als die Unterscheidung zwischen InländerIn und AusländerIn nicht mehr gelingt und die BewohnerInnen eines Ortes sowohl ein Wir bilden als auch die Anderen sind. Transkulturale Begegnung hieße im Unterschied zur Abgrenzung, sich auf das Sowohl-als-Auch der transkulturalen Situation einzulassen und das eigene Leben nach dem Prinzip einer „kulturellen Melange" zu gestalten (Beck 2004, 16f.). Das Melange-Prinzip beinhaltet nach Beck, dass sich lokale, nationale, ethische, religiöse Kulturen und Traditionen durchdringen, verbinden und mischen (vgl. Beck 2004, 16f.). Es verweist auf das Dritte, das in der Unterscheidung von Wir und den Anderen verborgen bleibt. Was transkultural ist, kann nicht der einen oder anderen Kultur zugerechnet werden (vgl. Beck 2004, 103). Transkulturalität ist eine Form der Verbindung des Fremden mit dem Eigenen.

Diese Verbindung erfolgreich für sich und andere zu leben, erfordert den „kosmopolitischen Blick"; es ist dies ein „historisch wacher, ein reflexiver Blick, ein dialogischer Blick für Ambivalenzen im Milieu verschwimmender Unterscheidungen und kultureller Widersprüche" (Beck 2004, 13). Der kosmopolitische Blick grenzt sich vom Universalismus insofern ab, als er ein für Differenzen sensibler Blick ist, während der Universalismus nicht die Andersheit des Anderen betont, sondern den Anderen als gleich respektiert. Die Stimme des Anderen interessiert im Universalismus als Stimme des Gleichen (vgl. Beck 2004, 76f.). Der kosmopolitische Blick dagegen macht die Differenz zum Ausgangspunkt, ohne sich strikt vom Universalismus abzugrenzen. Universalistisches Element einer kosmopolitischen Perspektive ist z.B. die Anerkennung global gültiger Menschenrechte. Ich schätze am Beck'schen Verständnis von Kosmopolitismus, dass es Aggression nicht tabuisiert. Der kosmopolitische Blick ist nicht nur ein von Mitgefühl, Empathie, Verstehen, Toleranz getragener Blick, sondern auch ein Blick, in den sich Zorn, Ärger, Ablehnung mischen dürfen, Gefühle, die die Verschiedenheit des Anderen hervorrufen kann. Gründe dafür können Verunsicherung, Angst vor Verlust sicher geglaubter Werte oder Empörung über verletzte Menschenrechte sein. Bloßes normengeleitetes Verstehen würde einen „wässrigen" Transkulturalismus befördern (Waldenfels 2006, 132). Das mögliche Dritte braucht die wechselseitigen Antworten, die sich nicht im Verstehen erschöpfen, sondern auch Widerspruch enthalten können, jedoch nicht ohne Reflexivität auskommen. Reflexivität schützt davor, von Aggressionen überwältigt zu werden. Den gewalttätigen Jugendlichen, von denen ich eingangs berichtet habe, hat es daran vermutlich gemangelt.

Transkulturale Begegnungen und Digitale Medien

Medien befördern die Möglichkeit von Transkulturalität, die ich am Beispiel Digitaler Medien begründen und exemplarisch veranschaulichen werde. Mit Waldenfels gehe ich davon aus, dass die mediale Struktur dem soziokulturellen Leben im Netz nicht äußerlich bleibt, genauso wie die Formen einer geographischen Landschaft in den Formen des Lebens und Zusammenlebens wiederkehren, „gelöst, zwanghaft oder wie auch immer“ (Waldenfels 1985, 198).

Eine Architektur des Übergangs

Ich betrachte den virtuellen Raum als eine Art Landschaft oder Architektur, durchzogen von Wegen, Bahnen, Knotenpunkten, die das ergeben, was wir ein Netzwerk nennen. Wege aber, die den Raum durchmessen, sind nach Waldenfels keine bloßen Strecken, die wir lediglich überwinden, um ans Ziel zu kommen. Es sind Bahnen, die bestimmte Bewegungsrichtungen und –abläufe vorschreiben, nahelegen oder ausschließen, die Durchlass gewähren oder Hindernisse enthalten (vgl. Waldenfels 1985, 189).

Welche Bewegungsrichtungen lässt ein Netzwerk zu? Netzwerke forcieren nicht die lineare Bewegung, sondern ein Zickzack der Bewegung durch den virtuellen Raum. Immer wieder tauchen Kreuzungen auf, an denen entschieden werden muss, wohin die Reise geht. Sie verlocken zum Vagabundieren, bei dem Richtungen und Räume gewechselt werden, die nicht nur mit unterschiedlichen Themen in Berührung bringen, sondern auch in verschiedene Länder und Kulturen reichen. Die Netzwerkarchitektur Digitaler Medien ist kein nachträgliches Zubehör zu einer autarken Aufführung; sie gehört zur Regie der Aufführung, indem sie Bewegungsformen und das Tempo der mentalen Bewegung sowie der Kommunikation mitbestimmt. Mit ihren Verschachtelungen, Verflechtungen, Verdünnungen und Verdichtungen repräsentiert die Netzwerkarchitektur eine Struktur, die die Konzentrik abgelöst hat zugunsten einer Architektur des Übergangs, die auf Endgültigkeit verzichtet (vgl. Zavarihin 1998, 2). In diesem Moment des Übergangs steckt die Möglichkeit von Transkulturalität, denn Übergang bedeutet eine Verflüssigung vom Hiersein zum Dortsein.

Transkulturalität impliziert eine Erschütterung tradierter kultureller Grenzen, was aber nicht heißen muss, dass die Menschen dadurch heimatlos werden, was der eingangs zitierte Jugendliche intuitiv erfasst hat. Wenn man dem Heimatbegriff von Bernhard Waldenfels folgt, dann deutet sich in einer Welt kultureller Übergänge aber ein neuer Typus von Heimat an. Ohne sagen zu können, wie diese Heimat aussieht, denn Heimat ist Produkt von Kommunikations- und Aushandlungsprozessen, kann man prognostizieren, dass sie auch in transkulturalen Settings möglich ist. Waldenfels distanziert sich von einem Heimatbegriff, demzufolge Heimat nur da ist, wo man herkommt und immer wieder zurückkehrt, wo alles vertraut ist (vgl. Waldenfels 1985, 207). Es ist dies ein Heimatbegriff, der sich ausschließlich an Sesshaftigkeit orientiert, aber Veränderung und Bewegung ignoriert, wenn nicht sogar diskriminiert. Heimat ist nach Waldenfels auch das, was vor uns liegt, wo noch niemand war; sie enthält Vertrautes und Unheimliches. Eine heimische Welt, die alle Fremdheit abstreifen würde, wäre nach Waldenfels keine Lebenswelt, sondern ein Mausoleum (vgl. Waldenfels 1985, 210). Mit diesem Heimatbegriff lässt sich eine transkulturale Heimat beschreiben, in die für die Einzelnen Vertrautes einfließt, das für die Anderen das Fremde ist und vielleicht bleibt; und gleichzeitig könnte in einem Klima des Sowohl-als-Auch aus der Mischung von Vertrautem und Fremdem, ein Drittes jenseits kultureller Grenzen entstehen, im Sinne der angesprochenen Melange verschiedener Kulturen und Traditionen.

Transkulturale virtuelle Räume

Anknüpfend an der These, dass virtuelle Netzwerke eine Architektur des Übergangs darstellen, möchte ich zwei Netzwerke vorstellen, die mit dem Anspruch auftreten, einen Raum für interkulturelle Kommunikation bereitzustellen, aus der Transkulturalität erwachsen kann. Es handelt sich um das von Gary Scudder, einem Professor am Champlain College im US-amerikanischen Bundesstaat Vermont initiierte studentische Kommunikationsnetz ‚Global Modules' und um das in Bahrain von Esra'a Al Shafei gegründete Netzwerk ‚Mideast Youth', das vorrangig von StudentInnen aus den arabischen Staaten, aber auch aus Europa und den USA besucht wird.

Global Modules

Das am Champlain College/Vermont angesiedelte Kommunikationsnetz ‚Global Modules' setzt sich aus einer Vielzahl von Diskussionssträngen zu Themen wie Frauenrechte, Globalisierung, Krieg im Irak, amerikanische Politik zusammen, an denen sich jeweils Studierende von zwei bis drei Universitäten aus unterschiedlichen Ländern beteiligen. Es handelt sich um einen ausschließlich textbasierten, zeitversetzt ablaufenden Dialog. Ziel des webbasierten Projekts ist es, unausgesprochene kulturelle Annahmen zu identifizieren, eigene nationale und regionale Vorurteile zu reflektieren und globale Sichtweisen auf dem Gebiet von Politik, Kultur, Bildung zu entwickeln (vgl. Scudder 2008).

In dem für die Analyse ausgewählten Diskussionsbeispiel treffen kulturelle Unterschiede aufeinander; von einer kulturellen Melange kann jedoch noch nicht die Rede sein. Lediglich Versuche, über Unterschiede hinweg Gemeinsamkeit herzustellen, werden sichtbar. Beteiligt an der Online-Diskussion sind US-amerikanische Studierende des erwähnten Champlain College und österreichische Studierende der Alpen-Adria Universität Klagenfurt, die im österreichischen Bundesland Kärnten angesiedelt ist.

Nachdem in dem Forum zunächst ausführlich über die Rolle der USA in aktuellen kriegerischen Konflikten (bezogen auf das Jahr 2006) diskutiert wurde, stellt der Moderator die Frage ‚How do Austrians see their place in the world?' Die Antwort von österreichischer Seite kommt knapp und deutlich. Sie lautet sinngemäß: ÖsterreicherInnen gehen nicht davon aus, dass Österreich außenpolitisch eine wichtige Rolle spielt, aber sie sind stolz auf ihre innenpolitischen Errungenschaften z.B. auf das Gesundheitssystem und die Neutralität Österreichs. Die Liste der als Erfolg definierten innenpolitischen Leistungen wird von den österreichischen Studierenden fortgesetzt mit Verweisen auf das österreichische Bildungssystem, auf berühmte Musiker, Dichter und Wissenschaftler. Die Beiträge zu den innenpolitischen Errungenschaften auf österreichischer Seite werden von amerikanischer Seite unterbrochen mit Fragen wie ‚Welche Ziele hat Österreich für die Welt?' oder ‚Was erwartet sich Österreich von anderen europäischen Ländern?', auf die aber nicht geantwortet wird. Während die amerikanischen Studierenden zunächst auf der außenpolitischen Perspektive in Bezug auf Österreich bestehen, verfolgen die österreichischen Studierenden konsequent eine innerpolitische Perspektive. Die Kernaussage der österreichischen Studierenden zur Charakterisierung ihres Landes lässt sich in den Worten zusammenfassen: Nach außen unbedeutend, aber nach innen fein. Die Kernfrage der amerikanischen Studierenden mit Blick auf Österreich dagegen lautet: Wie positioniert ihr euer Land im Verhältnis zu anderen Ländern?

Diese Kernaussagen/Kernfragen wurden gemeinsam mit den Studierenden bei der Analyse des Threads herausgearbeitet. In ihnen spiegeln sich kulturspezifische Perspektiven wider, die vermutlich in den politischen Ideologien der beiden Länder verankert sind. Für die amerikanischen Studierenden, die sich fragen, wie die USA ihrer Führungsrolle in der Welt gerecht werden kann, ist die außenpolitische Perspektive zentral, die sie auch von ihren österreichischen KommunikationspartnerInnen mit Blick auf Österreich einfordern. Für die österreichischen Studierenden dagegen scheint diese Perspektive irrelevant, was auf die im österreichischen Staatsvertrag festgeschriebene und kollektiv angeeignete Neutralität sowie auf traumatische Erfahrungen im 2. Weltkrieg (in Kärnten in zweifacher Hinsicht: Verluste an der Kriegsfront, Deportation und Ermordung der slowenischen Bevölkerung), auf die von den österreichischen Studierenden verwiesen wird, zurückzuführen sein dürfte.

Im weiteren Gesprächsverlauf zeichnet sich jedoch eine Wende ab, in der sich die Suche nach common ground widerspiegelt und die von amerikanischer Seite ausgeht. Als für die amerikanischen Studierenden klar zu sein scheint, dass ihre GesprächspartnerInnen dem Wunsch nach einer außenpolitischen Positionierung Österreichs nicht folgen, setzen sie einen neuen Gesprächsimpuls. Sie lassen sich auf die innenpolitische Perspektive ihrer GesprächspartnerInnen ein, übernehmen aber nicht deren erfolgsorientierte Sicht, sondern fragen nach den innenpolitischen Problemen in Österreich. Es fällt auf, dass sie dieses Angebot verbinden mit der Formulierung innenpolitischer Probleme in den USA wie Armut und ungleicher Bildungszugang. Dieser Hinweis soll es dem Gegenüber möglicherweise erleichtern, über eigene innenpolitische Probleme zu sprechen, wodurch eine Gemeinsamkeit hergestellt werden könnte. Ein weiterer Versuch common ground zu bilden, könnte in der Formulierung einer politischen Alternative zum Kapitalismus durch einen amerikanischen Studenten bestehen, in der er einen ökologischen Ansatz entwickelt und möglicherweise davon ausgeht, dass dieser konsensfähig ist.

Wie ist der webbasierte amerikanisch-österreichische Dialog aus transkulturaler Sicht zu bewerten? Er spielt sich weitgehend als interkultureller und noch nicht als transkulturaler Dialog ab, denn die Beteiligten bleiben weitgehend bei ihren jeweiligen kulturspezifischen Perspektiven. Eine Zäsur stellen der Wechsel der amerikanischen Studierenden von der außenpolitischen zur innenpolitischen Perspektive sowie die Suche nach gemeinsamen Erfahrungsfeldern in Form innenpolitischer Themen/Probleme dar. In der Diskussion über diese Themen könnte ein reflexiver, dialogischer, kurz, ein kosmopolitischer Blick entwickelt werden, weil sie nahelegen würde, über Werte und Prioritäten zu sprechen und sich dabei für beide Teile neue verbindende Orientierungen ergeben könnten. Ein amerikanischer Student macht zu dieser Option bereits einen Vorschlag, indem er sich als „grüner Sozialdemokrat" bezeichnet, eine politische Option, die er bei einem Besuch in Deutschland kennengelernt hat, also in einem Land, von dem er möglichweise annimmt, dass die dort entwickelten politischen Konzepte auch für Österreich von Interesse sind.

Die Reflexion der Diskussion durch die österreichischen Studierenden zeigte, dass, wie Beck ausführt, die Erarbeitung eines kosmopolitischen Blicks auch Emotionen evoziert. Der österreichisch-amerikanische Dialog ist einerseits von freudiger Neugier und Stolz getragen, andererseits lösten die auf Positionierung drängenden Fragen der amerikanischen Studierenden bei den österreichischen GesprächspartnerInnen Ärger und Zorn aus. Gefühle, die die Begegnung mit dem Fremden hervorruft, müssen genauso thematisiert werden wie kontrastierende Werte und Ideologien, sollen sie sich nicht als unüberwindbare Barriere für das Aufeinander-Zugehen erweisen.

Mideast Youth[1]

Ein weiteres Fallbeispiel eines interkulturellen Online-Netzwerkes, aus dem potenziell Transkulturalität erwachsen kann, ist das im Königreich Bahrain entstandene studentische Netzwerk ‚Mideast Youth'. Dieses Netz unterscheidet sich von den ‚Global Modu-

1 http://www.mideastyouth.com

les' insofern, als es nicht an einer etablierten Bildungsinstitution angesiedelt ist, sondern von einer politisch engagierten Studentin gegründet wurde, organisationsunabhängig existiert und die technischen Möglichkeiten Digitaler Medien ungleich stärker in Anspruch nimmt als ‚Global Modules'. Gemeinsam dagegen ist den beiden Netzwerken, dass sie beide im studentischen Milieu verankert sind und dass gesellschaftspolitische Diskussionsthemen im Vordergrund stehen. Die Analyse des arabischen Netzwerks setzt anders an als die Analyse des österreichisch-amerikanischen Dialogs im Rahmen der ‚Global Modules'. Ich werde mich auf die Analyse des auf der Homepage formulierten Selbstverständnisses beschränken. Mideast Youth ist ein multimediales Netzwerk, das neben Text auch Bilder und Filme z.B. über aktuelle politische Ereignisse enthält. Neben Diskussionsforen bietet das Netzwerk die Beteiligung an Projekten und Kampagnen; z.B. existiert eine Kampagne für die Freilassung des ägyptischen Bloggers Abdelkareem, der wegen regierungskritischer Äußerungen in seinem Weblog in einem ägyptischen Gefängnis inhaftiert ist.

Mideast Youth versteht sich als erste ‚Cyberdemokratie' des mittleren Ostens. Es wird in dem auf der Homepage formulierten Selbstverständnis ausdrücklich hervorgehoben, dass man keiner Organisation verpflichtet ist, sondern ein selbstorganisiertes unabhängiges Netzwerk darstellt, das von jungen AraberInnen aus dem mittleren Osten und Nordafrika organisiert wird. Bereits im dritten Satz des Selbstverständnisses wird mitgeteilt, dass es den InitiatorInnen ein wichtiges Anliegen sei, „to gather a diverse group of participants who represent various countries and religions within the region" im Bewusstsein darüber, dass „not all of us hold the same opinions regarding certain issues, most of which are sensitive, such as the status of women in Islam, modern Zionism or whether the current war in Iraq is justified or not" (Mideast Youth 2008). Nicht das Gemeinsame, die Differenz wird zum Ausgangspunkt des Netzwerks und des Demokratieverständnisses gemacht, das das Netzwerk repräsentieren soll.

Das Sowohl-als-Auch wird propagiert, wenn der ‚market place of ideas' als etwas vorgestellt wird, das es zu hegen und wertzuschätzen gilt, eine Haltung, die, dem Profil von Mideast Youth zufolge, eingebettet sein soll in wechselseitigem Respekt und Toleranz. Im Selbstverständnis von Mideast Youth wird für einen kosmopolitischen Blick plädiert, der auf Unterschiede achtet und gleichzeitig über Unterschiede hinweg im Dialog bleiben will. Positionen und Werte werden nicht als abgeschlossene starre Einheiten betrachtet, denn sonst könnte nicht das Anliegen formuliert werden „we want to promote bridge building".

Das Selbstverständnis des arabischen Netzwerks Mideast Youth repräsentiert Bedingungen von Transkulturalität, vielleicht aber auch schon den Anfang davon. Das über existierende Demokratieverständnisse Hinausweisende sehe ich zum einen darin, dass die Differenz als konstitutives Merkmal von Demokratie benannt wird und zum anderen, dass dieses Demokratieverständnis im virtuellen Raum mit dem eigenen

Netzwerk bereits in Szene gesetzt wird. Es ist ein Versuch, einen neuen Raum mit neuen Möglichkeiten zu besetzen, der aufgrund seiner Struktur als grenzüberschreitendes Netzwerk in besonderer Weise geeignet ist, Vielheit zu versammeln.

Zwischenbilanz

Digitale Netzwerke bieten eine Architektur, die die Entstehung transkulturaler Räume begünstigt, aber nicht zwangsläufig hervorbringt. Netzwerke können sich auch verknoten, was jene Communities belegen, in denen z.B. durch Sprache wie einem spezifischen Jargon, den nur Eingeweihte oder BewohnerInnen einer bestimmten geografischen Region verstehen, Zugangsbarrieren errichtet werden, die vor dem Fremden abschotten. Auch dies könnte eine Reaktion auf die transkulturalen Zumutungen der Gegenwartsgesellschaft sein; anstelle von Öffnung wird der Weg in die Abgeschlossenheit einer überschaubaren Welt der vermeintlich Gleichen gesucht. Aber selbst wenn – wie in den vorgestellten Beispielen – das Netz als Medium der Begegnung gewählt wird – die Struktur des Netzwerks allein reicht nicht aus als Stimulus für transkulturale Begegnungen. Es bedarf der Intention, die sich im Engagement eines Hochschullehrers bei Global Modules zeigt oder in einem politischen Konzept, wie es die InitiatorInnen von Mideast Youth formuliert haben. Mit dem Verweis auf das erforderliche intentionale Engagement ist die Pädagogik herausgefordert.

Transkulturalität und Bildung

Abschließend wird der Frage nachgegangen, was es Menschen ermöglicht, sich auf transkulturale Situationen einzulassen und was sie befähigt, in diesen Situationen einen kosmopolitischen Blick zu entwickeln. Die Antwort auf diese Frage skizziert ein pädagogisches Programm. Menschen stehen – wie ich versucht habe, ausgehend von dem Gewaltakt in einer Münchner U-Bahn aufzuzeigen – heutzutage vor der Aufgabe, heimisch zu werden in einer Welt, die sich zunehmend als Konglomerat von Differenzen, Widersprüchen und einer Pluralität an Zugehörigkeiten und Seinsweisen darstellt (vgl. Wulf 2006, 42). Die Situation des vielfältigen Neben- und Ineinanders nicht nur zu ertragen, sondern als Chance für die Entwicklung einer transkulturalen Lebensperspektive zu nutzen, diese Chance ist im menschlichen Sein angelegt, und zwar:

1. in der menschlichen Fähigkeit zur Weltoffenheit,
2. in der Angewiesenheit des menschlichen Subjekts auf Andere,
3. in dem Bedürfnis und in der Fähigkeit des Menschen, in ein Interaktionsspiel mit der Welt einzutreten, in dem sich der einzelne Mensch und die Welt verändern.

ad 1

Transkulturalität setzt Öffnung voraus, andernfalls würde man des Fremden nicht gewahr werden. Christoph Wulf beschreibt Weltoffenheit unter Bezug auf Jakob von Üxküll als die Besonderheit des Menschen, die ihn vom Tier unterscheidet (vgl. Wulf 2006, 135f.). Tiere sind in die ihnen entsprechende Umwelt eingebunden und können ihr nicht entkommen. Für Menschen dagegen existiert diese Abhängigkeit von Umwelt so nicht. Soziale und kulturelle Umwelten sind zwar prägende Faktoren, aber Menschen sind nicht in ihr gefangen. Kommunikation und Sprache öffnen den Weg in die Welt. Weltoffenheit ist nach Wulf Menschliches per se, die Formen, die das Offen-Sein annimmt aber, entwickeln sich je nach Kultur, Umwelt, historischer Zeit unterschiedlich (vgl. Wulf 2006, 137). Weltoffenheit kann durch Erziehung gefördert und gestaltet werden.

ad 2

Weltoffenheit beschreibt nicht nur eine Fähigkeit, sondern auch eine Notwendigkeit (vgl. Schachtner i.E.). Sie gründet in der Angewiesenheit des menschlichen Subjekts auf Andere. Käthe Meyer-Drawe veranschaulicht diese Angewiesenheit mit dem Mythos von Narziss und Echo. Diese beiden mythologischen Figuren verkörpern Extreme unserer Existenz, das bloße Sein zu sich selbst und das pure Sein durch den Anderen. Beide gehen an dieser Ausschließlichkeit zugrunde (vgl. Meyer-Drawe 1990, 116). Demnach haben Menschen nicht die Möglichkeit, auf andere zu verzichten. Vielmehr beglaubigt der Widerhall, den sie im anderen finden - sei es in Form von Blicken, Berührungen, verbalen Reaktionen – ihre Existenz (vgl. Wulf 2006, 38). Der Andere dient, wie Wulf ausführt, als Spiegel, sich selbst zu sehen und zu erforschen. Mithilfe dieses Spiegels lernen wir, Repräsentationen von uns selbst aufzubauen und Selbstbewusstsein zu entwickeln.

Die Komplexität des Widerhalls signalisiert das Risiko von Verunsicherung und Verwirrung und zugleich die Möglichkeit von Transkulturalität. Beispielsweise haben sich die österreichischen Studierenden in der hier vorgestellten Diskussion gefragt, wer sind wir, dass uns die amerikanischen DiskussionspartnerInnen so sehen und wie sehr deckt sich das Fremdbild mit dem Selbstbild. Die entdeckte Diskrepanz hat auch, wie erwähnt, Verunsicherung ausgelöst. In einer Welt des Neben- und Ineinanders kultureller Strömungen blicken Menschen in einen Spiegel mit vielen Gesichtern, vergleichbar einem Kaleidoskop, das in verschiedenen Farben schillert und das natürlich verstören kann.

ad 3

Ging es mir bisher darum zu begründen, warum Menschen gar nicht anders können, als sich zu öffnen, was ich als Voraussetzung für Transkulturalität betrachte, so wende ich mich nun dem möglichen Wie dieser Öffnung zu. Nach Alfred Lorenzer sind es Interaktionsspiele, mit denen sich die Subjekte zur Welt ins Verhältnis setzen. Diese entfalten sich nach Lorenzer im Hinblick auf die kulturellen Symbole wie Worte, Laute, Bilder, Dinge, mit denen das Subjekt konfrontiert ist.

Lorenzer beschäftigt sich vorrangig mit der Symbolik der dinglichen Welt, weshalb sein Ansatz für die hier geführte Diskussion über die transkulturalen Möglichkeiten Digitaler Medien besonders geeignet ist. Die von den Dingen repräsentierte Symbolik stellt nach Lorenzer eine Manifestation sozialer Konsense dar. Lorenzer unterscheidet in Anlehnung an Susanne Langer zwischen einer diskursiven und einer präsentativen Symbolik (vgl. Lorenzer 1981, 31). Eine diskursive Symbolik verkörpert z.B. die Sprache, weil sich die Bedeutungen hintereinander erschließen. Bilder, Kunstwerke und mediale Artefakte dagegen stellen präsentative Symbole dar, weil sich deren Bedeutung nicht nacheinander vermittelt, sondern als ein Ganzes. Auch das menschliche Subjekt repräsentiert, so möchte ich dem Ansatz von Lorenzer hinzufügen, eine diskursive und eine präsentative Symbolik. In seinen sprachlichen Fähigkeiten zeigt sich eine diskursive Symbolik, in seiner Körperlichkeit eine präsentative Symbolik.

Menschen entwickeln im Hinblick auf die diskursive Symbolik laut Lorenzer sprachsymbolische Interaktionsformen, die vorrangig den kognitiven Fähigkeiten verhaftet sind und im Hinblick auf präsentierte Symbole sinnlich-symbolische Interaktionsformen (vgl. Lorenzer 1981, 161f.), die den Emotionen und dem Leiblichen verhaftet sind. Mit dem Begriff Interaktionsspiel verweist Lorenzer darauf, dass die Subjekte die Bedeutungen, mit denen sie in der Ding- und Sozialwelt konfrontiert sind, nicht einfach nur übernehmen, sondern sie drehen und wenden und dabei verändern. Dieses Spiel ist der Ansatzpunkt für die Annahme, dass kulturelle Bedeutungen und Unterschiede, die in transkulturalen Begegnungen auftauchen, miteinander kombiniert und vermischt werden können im Sinne einer kulturellen Melange.

Transkulturale Kompetenzen

Die beschriebenen Chancen zur Entwicklung eines kosmopolitischen Blicks eröffnen sich in der Auseinandersetzung mit dem Anderen. Es bedarf jedoch spezifischer Fähigkeiten, um die Chancen Wirklichkeit werden zu lassen, die konstitutiv sind für Bildung in der Gegenwartsgesellschaft. Unter Bezug auf Christoph Wulf, Nira Yuval-Davis und Annelie Knapp-Potthoff werde ich einige dieser mir zentral erscheinenden Fähigkeiten diskutieren.

Weltoffenheit verlangt nach einem Denken, das Wulf als heterologisches Denken bezeichnet. Im Mittelpunkt heterologischen Denkens steht das Verhältnis von Vertrautem und Fremden, von Wissen und Nichtwissen, von Gewissheit und Ungewissheit (vgl. Wulf 2006, 45). Es kommt darauf an zu lernen, vom Anderen her wahrzunehmen und zu denken. Dieses Lernen kann gleichwohl in der eigenen Kultur beginnen, denn auch diese ist nicht homogen, sondern ein Konglomerat von Differenzen (vgl. Wulf 2006, 42), ja, das Subjekt selbst bildet keine homogene Einheit. Je besser es gelingt, die Paradoxien und Widersprüche im Eigenen zu sehen und sich mit ihnen auseinander zu setzen, so die Annahme, desto eher kann ich externe Differenzen annehmen.

Setzt das heterologische Denken beim Anderen an, so hat das von Yuval-Davis in die Diskussion eingeführte transversale Denken seinen Ausgangspunkt in der Formulierung des eigenen Standpunkts, ohne essentialisierte Vorstellungen von Identität zu entwickeln (vgl. Yuval-Davis 2001, 210 ff.). Als Beispiel für eine transversale Strategie nennt Yuval-Davis Versuche italienischer Frauenzentren, Frauen aus miteinander in Konflikt geratenen Gruppen z.B. Serbinnen und Kroatinnen in einen Dialog einzubinden, bei dem jede Teilnehmerin vom eigenen Standpunkt her spricht im Bewusstsein, dass der individuelle Standpunkt ein unabgeschlossenes Wissen repräsentiert (vgl. Yuval-Davis 2001, 206). Dieses Bewusstsein ermöglicht Empathie und Respekt den anderen gegenüber, ohne dass die eigene Perspektive aufgegeben werden muss. Für Yuval-Davis spielt sich das transversale Denken als ein gleichzeitiges rooting und shifting ab. Ein digitales Übungsfeld für die Entwicklung transversalen Denkens könnten multimediale Projekte sein, bei denen z.B. Kinder und Jugendliche aus verschiedenen Ländern Filme über ihren Alltag drehen, die sie sich via Internet wechselseitig zur Verfügung stellen. Die Rezeption dieser Filme eignet sich dazu, die Identität anderer Kulturen kennenzulernen und Vergleiche mit der eigenen Lebenswelt anzustellen, Differenzen und Gemeinsamkeiten wahrzunehmen und zu benennen.

So sehr sowohl das heterologische als auch das transversale Denken die Nichthintergehbarkeit der Differenz betont, so wenig kann auf universalistische Elemente verzichtet werden. Bereits das Bestehen auf Differenz bringt eine universalistische Position zum Ausdruck. Oftmals braucht es eine gemeinsame Basis oder common ground, wie Annelie Knapp-Potthoff sagt, um Differenzen überhaupt zum Thema machen zu können (vgl. Knapp-Potthoff 1997). Wenn in dem digitalen Netzwerk Mideast Youth eine Diskussion mit dem Titel ‚Which countries operate the best democracies?' geführt wird, dann erfolgt dies auf der gemeinsamen Annahme, dass es verschiedene Formen von Demokratie gibt, dass es schlechtere und bessere Demokratien gibt und dass Demokratien Produkte politischen Handelns sind. Als ein zweiter Schritt der Entwicklung von common ground in diesem thread kann der Versuch der DiskussionsteilnehmerInnen gewertet werden, Qualitätsmerkmale für gute Demokratien zu definieren, wie z.B. Religionsfreiheit, gleiche Rechte für MigrantInnen, Partizipation, Freiheit, Sicherheit. In Bezug auf einige Qualitätsmerkmale konnte unter den DiskussionsteilnehmerInnen Einigkeit erzielt werden, andere blieben umstritten. Die Herstellung von common ground wird nach Knapp-Potthoff auch durch Mehrfachzugehörigkeit der am Diskurs beteiligten Personen gefördert (vgl. Knapp-Potthoff 1997, 191). Die nationale Zugehörigkeit der TeilnehmerInnen an dem angesprochenen Demokratiediskurs im Netzwerk ‚Mideast Youth'war zwar unterschiedlich, aber gemeinsam war ihnen die Zugehörigkeit zur jüngeren Generation, der Status als StudentInnen, das Interesse am transkulturalen Dialog.

Die beschriebenen Kompetenzen, die die Bereitschaft fördern, sich auf transkulturale Situationen einzulassen und einen kosmopolitischen Blick zu generieren, können zwar auch in Lernsettings jenseits digitaler Medien eingeübt werden, doch bietet die Technik des Cyberspace erweiterte Gelegenheitsstrukturen für transkulturales Lernen aufgrund der grenzüberschreitenden Qualität Digitaler Medien (vgl. Schachtner 2008, 14) sowie aufgrund der Möglichkeit, Dialoge nicht nur textbasiert zu führen, sondern sie durch Bilder, Klang und Stimme anzureichern, was die kulturellen Besonderheiten noch stärker hervortreten lässt.

Das hier vorgetragene Plädoyer, digitale Räume transkultural zu gestalten und sie als Experimentierfeld für die Generierung kosmopolitischer Perspektiven zu nutzen, wirft gleichwohl Fragen auf wie ‚Wie viel Weltoffenheit verträgt der Mensch? Wie viel Veränderung ist möglich?'

Solche Fragen zu stellen, führt zur Wahrnehmung von Grenzen und schützt vor einer Idealisierung des Netz-Mediums. Wenn wir Bourdieu folgen, so ist Weltoffenheit möglich und zugleich begrenzt. Sie ereignet sich stets auf der Basis unseres Habitus, den wir beginnen zu entwickeln, sobald wir in diese Welt hineingeboren werden und der zur Grundlage der Wahrnehmung und Beurteilung aller späteren Erfahrung wird. Der Habitus lässt sich als System von Dispositionen beschreiben, die als strukturierende Strukturen fungieren, d.h. als Erzeugungsbasis von Kommunikations- und Interaktionsformen (vgl. Bourdieu 1987, 97). Das schließt neue Erfahrungen und Experimente, wie sie für die Entwicklung von Transkulturalität unverzichtbar sind, nicht aus, im Gegenteil. Für Bourdieu ist der Habitus die unbegrenzte Fähigkeit, in völliger Freiheit Gedanken, Wahrnehmungen, Handlungen zu erzeugen, die aber stets in den historischen und sozialen Grenzen seiner Erzeugung liegen (vgl. Bourdieu 1987, 103). Die Chancen transkulturalen Lernens liegen in der wechselseitigen Stimulierung der auf die Erschließung neuer Erfahrungen gerichteten Tätigkeit und in der Nutzung der entstehenden Schnittflächen für eine kulturelle Melange.

Literatur

Beck, Ulrich (2004): Der kosmopolitische Blick oder: Krieg ist Frieden. Frankfurt am Main: Suhrkamp.

Bourdieu, Pierre (1987): Sozialer Sinn. Fankfurt am Main: Suhrkamp.

Eimeren, Birgit van/Frees, Beate (2008): Internetverbreitung: Größter Zuwachs bei Silver-Surfern. Ergebnisse der ARD/ZDF-Onlinestudie 200. In: Media Perspektiven H. 7, 330 - 344.

Funiok, Rüdiger/Pietraß, Manuela (Hrsg) (i.E.): Mensch und Medien, Beiträge zu einer Anthropologie des „homo medialis". Wiesbaden: VS Verlag.

Geertz, Clifford (1983): Dichte Beschreibung, Beiträge zum Verstehen kultureller Systeme. Frankfurt am Main: Suhrkamp.

Hengartner, Thomas/Rolshoven, Johanna (1998): Technik - Kultur Alltag. In: Hengartner/Rolshoven 1998, 17 - 49.

Hengartner, Thomas/Rolshoven, Johanna (Hrsg.) (1998): Technik-Kultur, Formen der Veralltäglichung von Technik – Technisches als Alltag. Zürich: Chronos.

Hess, Sabine/Lenz, Ramona (2001): Kulturelle Globalisierung und Geschlecht – ein Buchprojekt. In: Hess/ Lenz 2001, 10-33.

Hess, Sabine/Lenz, Ramona (Hrsg.) (2001): Geschlecht und Globalisierung. Ein kulturwissenschaftlicher Streifzug durch transnationale Räume., Königstein: Helmer.

Knapp-Potthoff, Annelie (1997): Interkulturelle Kommunikationsfähigkeit als Lernziel. In: Knapp-Potthoff/ Liedke 1997, 181-206.

Knapp-Potthoff, Annelie/Liedke, Martina (Hrsg.) (1997): Aspekte interkultureller Kommunikationsfähigkeit, München: Iudicium.

Lorenzer, Alfred (1981): Das Konzil der Buchhalter. Frankfurt am Main: Suhrkamp.

Meyer-Drawe, Käte (1990): Illusionen von Autonomie, München: Kirchheim.

Mideast Youth (2008): About us. Online: http://www.mideastyouth.com/about-us [15.12.2008]

Miniwatts Marketing Group (2008): Internet World Stats. Usage and Population Statistics. Online: http:// www.internetworldstats.com [15.12.2008]

Schachtner, Christina (2008): Virtualität, Identität, Gemeinschaft, Reisende im Netz. In: Herbert 2008, 103-118.

Schachtner, Christina/Höber, Angelika (Hrsg.) (2008): Learning Communities. Das Internet als neuer Lern- und Wissensraum. Frankfurt am Main: Campus.

Schachtner, Christina (i.E.): Kommunikation und Subjektivierung, Verbundenheit als anthropologische Größe und die Absage an das ‚starke Subjekt'. In: Funiok, Rüdiger/Manuela Pietraß (i.E.).

Schütz, Alfred /Luckmann, Thomas (1975): Strukturen der Lebenswelt. Darmstadt: Luchterhand.

Scudder, Gary Evans (2008): Global Modules – Nutzung des Internets zum Aufbau interkultureller Communities. In: Schachtner/Höber 2008, 109-120.

Waldenfels, Bernhard (1985): In den Netzen der Lebenswelt. Frankfurt am Main: Suhrkamp.

Waldenfels, Bernhard (2006): Grundmotive einer Phänomenologie des Fremden. Frankfurt am Main: Suhrkamp.

Willems, Herbert (Hrsg.) (2008): Weltweite Weiten. Internet-Figurationen aus wissenssoziologischer Perspektive, Wiesbaden: VS Verlag.

Wulf, Christoph (2006): Anthropologie kultureller Vielfalt. Interkulturelle Bildung in Zeiten der Globalisierung. Bielefeld: Transcript.

Yuval-Davis, Nira (2001): Geschlecht und Nation. Emmendingen: Die Brotsuppe.

Anerkennung und Zugehörigkeit im Social Web
Tendenzen der Identitätsbildung am Beispiel junger Migranten

von Kai-Uwe Hugger

Im Folgenden werde ich die Frage thematisieren, welche Bedeutung die Vergewisserung von sozialer Zugehörigkeit sowie die Suche nach Anerkennung für Jugendliche im Internet hat. Dies verdeutliche ich am Beispiel von Jugendlichen mit Migrationshintergrund, die sich aktiv in speziellen Community-Angeboten des Social Web[1] bewegen. Zu diesem Zweck werde ich in zunächst grundlegender Weise den Stellenwert von Zugehörigkeit und Anerkennung im Identitätsbildungsprozess von Migranten der zweiten und dritten Generation diskutieren; auf der Basis einer eigenen empirischen Studie frage ich dann im zweiten Teil dieses Beitrags fokussiert, welche Möglichkeiten der Identitätsentwicklung Online-Communities eröffnen, die sich vorwiegend an Jugendliche mit Migrationshintergrund in Deutschland richten.

Als Ergebnis der jüngeren Identitätsforschung kann festgehalten werden: Identitätsbildung lässt sich gegenwärtig kaum noch angemessen mit den Begriffen Einheit, Kontinuität und Vorhersagbarkeit beschreiben. Identität im Kontext der zurzeit zu beobachtenden gesellschaftlichen Wandlungsprozesse, zu denen verstärkt Medialisierung und Globalisierung gehören, wird nicht mehr von einem zentralen Ich bestimmt. Der Identitätsbildungsprozess ist als kontinuierliches und offenes Aushandlungsprojekt zu begreifen, in dem verstärkt Gegensätzliches zur Wirkung kommt und ausgehalten werden muss. Für das Identitätsprojekt bleibt zwar die Vergewisserung von *sozialer Zugehörigkeit* sowie die Suche nach *Anerkennung* zentral. Allerdings: Angestammte soziale Zugehörigkeiten und Traditionen werden von den Individuen als weniger verbindlich erlebt, sie schwächen sich in ihrer identitätsbildenden Kraft ab. Dagegen erhält der einzelne Mensch zunehmend die Verantwortung über seinen Identitätsbildungsprozess. Soziale Zugehörigkeiten verlieren für das Individuum nicht grundsätzlich an Bedeutung, jedoch können sie von ihm auf neue Art und Weise verstanden und erfahren werden. Zudem gilt: Mit der *Individualisierung der Anerkennung* muss der Einzelne seine Leistung zwar nicht mehr „einem ganzen Kollektiv" (Honneth 2003, 209) zurechnen, vielmehr kann er sie positiv der eigenen Person gutschreiben. Da aber die Normen

1 Die technikzentrierte Unterscheidung Web 1.0/Web 2.0 hat meines Erachtens den Nachteil, von der Lebenswelt der Menschen abgehoben zu sein. Die (jugendlichen) Mediennutzer sind interessiert an den neuen Möglichkeiten, Chancen und Risiken der neuen Medien bzw. Medienangebote und nur im Ausnahmefall an der Technologie. Im Falle der Internetangebote, die in diesem Beitrag relevant sind, geht es vor allem um Fragen, die sich auf Kommunikation, Interaktion wie die Pflege und Erweiterung des sozialen Netzwerkes betreffen. Da es in empirischen Studien entscheidend ist, am Alltagsverständnis der Befragten anzusetzen, gebe ich im Folgenden dem Begriff *Social Web* den Vorzug – verwende ihn jedoch gleichbedeutend mit dem Begriff Web 2.0.

gesellschaftlicher Instanzen gegenwärtig weniger wirksam sind, bedeutet dies zugleich, dass das Subjekt selbst erhöhte Anstrengungen unternehmen muss, um Anerkennung zu erhalten und sich seiner Zugehörigkeit zu vergewissern. Die Vermittlungsformen für Anerkennung verändern sich. Diese waren in früheren Zeiten an die *Traditionen* von Kollektiven, Gruppen oder Gemeinschaften gebunden: Kulte, Rituale und Bräuche, die in einer „posttraditionalen Gesellschaft" (Giddens 1996) nicht mehr auf traditionelle Art und Weise bewahrt werden können. Mit dem Verlust angestammter, unbezweifelter Vermittlungsformen von Anerkennung werden *offene, dialogische* Vermittlungsrahmen entscheidend. Was bedeutet dies für das dezentrierte Subjekt? Es ist nun viel mehr auf sein soziales Netzwerk „mit jeweils unterschiedlichen Anerkennungsklaviaturen angewiesen. Das Spiel auf einer dermaßen individualisierten Anerkennungsklaviatur ist anspruchsvoller bzw. erfordert weit mehr beziehungsorientierte Aushandlungskompetenzen als in modernen Zeiten" (Keupp et al. 1999, 260). Das Internet mit seinen Sozialräumen scheint einen neuen Rahmen für die Vergewisserung von Zugehörigkeit und die Suche nach Anerkennung in der posttraditionalen Gesellschaftsformation anzubieten.

Dezentrierung, Hybridität, Migration

Die Entstehung solcher zunehmend offenen und gegensätzlichen Identitätsformationen lässt sich am Beispiel von Migrationsphänomenen aufzeigen. So hat vor allem die sozialwissenschaftliche Postkolonialismusdebatte (vgl. etwa Bhabha 1994; Hall 1994; literarisch: Rushdie 1997) darauf aufmerksam gemacht, dass die Subjektkonstitution derjenigen Menschen, deren Biografie durch Entwurzelungserfahrungen im Rahmen von Migrationsprozessen geprägt ist, nicht mehr in „moderner" Form beschrieben werden kann. Bhabha (1994) verdeutlicht dies anhand der vielschichtigen Beziehungen zwischen Kolonisierten und Kolonisatoren: Eine klassische, binäre Gegenüberstellung zwischen machtvollen Kolonisatoren und machtlosen Kolonisierten mache blind für Räume des Widerstandes und der Verhandlung – „third spaces" oder „Räume des Dazwischen" –, die über die koloniale Grenze hinweg funktionieren. Menschen jedoch, die sich in solchen dritten Handlungsräumen bewegten, überbrücken Dualitäten und erhalten dadurch eine subversive Kraft, indem sie dominante koloniale Symbole und Bilder verfremden. Dies meint der Begriff Hybridisierung, der allerdings nicht als harmonische und ästhetische Form „kultureller Vermischung" zu denken ist, so Ha (2005, 87f.), sondern eine Möglichkeit bezeichnet, „das kulturelle Feld gegen hegemoniale Kräfte für Marginalisierte zu instrumentalisieren, wodurch der koloniale Rahmen überschritten und neue Assoziationen und Bedeutungen geschaffen werden, die Eindeutigkeit in Zwiespalt verwandelt". In Bhabhas Verständnis kann die Hybridität von Migranten also nicht angemessen analysiert werden, ohne zugleich auch die gesellschaftlichen Machtverhältnisse zu berücksichtigen, durch die sie mit Diskriminierung und Ausgrenzung konfrontiert werden. Auch Hall (1994) argumentiert in die Richtung neuer mehrdeutiger Identiätsformationen, wenn er die Menschen, die „Kulturen der Hybridität" angehören, als „Übersetzer" bezeichnet. Er meint diejenigen Migranten, die einerseits starke Bindungen zu den Orten und Traditionen ihrer Herkunftskultur aufweisen, andererseits jedoch nicht unbedingt in ihr Heimatland zurückkehren wollen. Einerseits sind sie dazu gezwungen, sich in der Ankunftskultur einzuleben, andererseits assimilieren sie sich nicht vollständig. Auf diese Weise haben sie gelernt, sich mindestens zwei Identitäten anzueignen und diese miteinander auszuhandeln, ohne dass sie noch historisch fest verankerten Identitätsmustern folgen könnten. Hybride sind nicht etwa diejenigen, die sich *noch* nicht für die eine oder andere Identität entschieden haben. Sie sind das, was Zygmunt Bauman (2005, 100f.) die „im Prinzip Unentscheidbaren" nennt.

Hybrididentität versucht, diese Gemengelage von Ambivalenzen, Brüchen und Komplexitäten für die Subjektkonstitution von Migranten unter kulturellen Globalisierungsbedingungen auf den Begriff zu bringen. Sie bricht mit den Entweder-Oder-Zuordnungen des modernen Subjekts und tauscht diese für ein Sowohl-als-auch ein. Freilich sollte Zurückhaltung gegenüber einem vorschnellen *Feiern von Hybridität* geübt werden. Die kritische sozialwissenschaftliche Auseinandersetzung mit dem Hybriditätskonzept (z.B. Rätzel 1999; Ha 2005) macht deutlich, dass bei der Untersuchung der Identitätsbildung von hybriden Migranten die Schwierigkeiten, die sie mit ihrem Identitätsstatus haben, nicht außer Acht gelassen werden dürfen. Die Kritik des Hybridmodells an essenzialisitischen Ansätzen der Identität muss berücksichtigen, wie es Mecheril (2003, 334) formuliert, „dass die relationalen Identifizierungen der Anderen materialisieren, zu ‚Substanzen' im Sinne von habitualisierten (Un-)Vermögen werden". Hybridität ist also nicht mit einem postmodernen Gesamtkunstwerk zu verwechseln, mit dessen Hilfe der Alltag per se kreativ und souverän gemeistert werden kann; vielmehr muss auch bedacht werden, dass Mehrwertigkeit dort zum Problem wird, wo sie von anderen nicht anerkannt wird. Und von dieser fehlenden Anerkennung ihres Identitätsstatus sind hybride Migranten nicht nur in der Offline-, sondern auch in der Online-Welt betroffen, wie ich auf den folgenden Seiten Hinblick auf Jugendliche noch deutlicher machen will.

Transmigration, soziale Zugehörigkeit und Anerkennung

Beispiele für Hybridisierungsprozesse sind in der Identitätsbildung von Migrantenjugendlichen zu finden, die (nicht nur) in der deutschsprachigen erziehungswissenschaftlichen Debatte freilich sehr unterschiedlich wahrgenommen wird. Noch bis zum Ende der 1980er Jahre wurde der in Deutschland lebenden zweiten Migrantengeneration gemeinhin „Identitätsdiffusion" aufgrund eines „Kulturkonflikts" diagnostiziert.

In dieser defizitzuschreibenden Perspektive ging man davon aus, dass die jungen Migranten mit (mindestens) zwei widersprechenden Kulturen konfrontiert sind: zum einen die, die durch die Eltern oder durch die im Herkunftsland verbrachte Kindheitsphase, zum anderen jene, die sich in „fremdethnischen Verhaltens- und Handlungsstandards“ (Hill 1990) zeigt, und die durch Ausbildung, Peers und Medien des Ankunftslandes vermittelt wird. Die Folge dieser Konfliktsituation seien, so die vorherrschende Auffassung, „Persönlichkeitsstörungen“ oder krisenhafte Zustände des „Hin- und Hergerissenseins“ zwischen unterschiedlichen kulturellen Orientierungen. Erst ab den 1990er Jahren zeichnet sich ein Paradigmenwechsel ab.

> „Migranten werden nun „als deutende und handelnde Subjekte entdeckt, die in der Lage sind, sich in Handlungsräumen, die auch durch ihren rechtlichen und/oder sichtbaren Migrantenstatus konstituiert sind, sinn-voll auf Andere und sich selbst zu beziehen. Anstelle des behaupteten Kulturkonflikts (…) rücken (…) soziale und identitäre Aspekte des praktischen und symbolischen Hantierens mit ethnischen, nationalen und kulturellen Kategorien in den Vordergrund, welches als ein kreatives Grenzgängertum bezeichnet und verstanden wird“ (Mecheril 2003, 18).

In den letzten Jahren liefert insbesondere das Konzept der *Transmigration* eine geeignete Erklärungsfolie für die über zwei oder mehrere ethnisch-kulturelle Kontexte aufgespannten Erfahrungen und Identitätskonstellationen, die vor allem bei der zweiten dritten Generation von Migranten in Deutschland beobachtet werden können. Transmigranten *pendeln* zwischen zwei oder mehreren national-ethnisch-kulturellen Kontexten hin und her, wie etwa Glick Schiller, Basch und Blanc-Szanton (1992, 1f.) zum Ausdruck bringen: „Transmigrants take actions, make decisions, and feel concerns, and develop identities within social networks that connect them to two or more societies simultaneously.“ Für die Untersuchung der Lebenspraxis von jugendlichen Transmigranten – sowohl online wie offline – erachte ich zwei Foki als zentral, die ich im Folgenden vorstellen und erläutern werde: Soziale Zugehörigkeit und soziale Anerkennung.

Soziale Zugehörigkeit

Paul Mecheril (2003) zeigt die Wichtigkeit von „Zugehörigkeitsverhältnissen“ bei der Untersuchung der hybriden Identitätsbildungsprozesse von jungen Migranten in Deutschland auf: Er thematisiert in zugehörigkeitstheoretischer Perspektive, dass für die Mitglieder von Migrationsfolgegenerationen ihr Verhältnis zu mehreren natio-ethno-kulturellen Kontexten problematisch geworden ist. Für die Untersuchung solcher neuer Zugehörigkeitskonstellationen sind alltägliche Bezeichnungen und geläufige Unterscheidungspraxen wie „türkisch“, „deutsch“ oder „italienisch“ wenig praktikabel, weil sie diffus und wenig trennscharf sind. Die Bezeichnung „natio-ethno-kulturell“

soll dies zum Ausdruck bringen. Sie rufe in Erinnerung, „dass die sozialen Zugehörigkeitsordnungen, für die Phänomene der Migration bedeutsam sind, von einer unbestimmten ‚Wir'-Einheit strukturiert sind" (Mecheril/Hoffarth 2006, 230). Da die Begriffe „Nation", „Ethnizität" und „Kultur" miteinander verschwimmen, Nationalstaaten im Hinblick auf das ethnische Selbstverständnis ihrer Bevölkerung sowie deren kulturelle Praktiken und Traditionen nicht einheitlich sind, Nationalstaaten aber dennoch durch Dominanzverhältnisse gekennzeichnet sind, stellten *natio-ethno-kulturelle Zugehörigkeitskontexte* aus der Perspektive des Subjekts „faktische und imaginäre Räume" zugleich dar (Mecheril 2003, 25). Diese Kontexte seien dem Einzelnen nicht einfach gegenübergestellt. Vielmehr seien sie so verstehen, dass die Menschen in ihnen „ein handlungsrelevantes Verständnis ihrer selbst erlernen und praktizieren" (Mecheril 2003, 25). Auf der Basis der Zugehörigkeitserfahrungen einer Person konstituieren sich „Zugehörigkeitsverständnisse" aus, d.h. „übergeordnete Strukturen der Kenntnis, des Handelns und Befindens [...], in denen der und die Einzelne ihren kontextspezifischen Zugehörigkeitsstatus versteht" (Mecheril 2003, 132). Zugehörigkeitsverständnisse sind somit Bestandteil des Selbstverständnisses einer Person. Da im Jugendalter die Suche nach und Aushandlung von sozialer Zugehörigkeit eine zentrale Rolle spielt, bilden sich gerade bei Jugendlichen aus Erfahrungen von Zugehörigkeit bzw. Nicht-Zugehörigkeit Zugehörigkeitsverständnisse aus (vgl. Riegel/Geisen 2007), die freilich jenseits von angestammten Herkünften verortet sein können. Mecheril fragt nun in seiner Untersuchung, unter welchen idealtypischen Bedingungen, sich Menschen einem natio-ethno-kulturellen Kontext als „fraglos zugehörig" beschreiben. Sie tun dies,

> „wenn sie sich selbst als symbolisches Mitglied des Kontextes erkennen und von bedeutsamen Anderen als Mitglied erkannt werden, wenn sie in dem Kontext in einer ihnen gemäßen Weise habituell wirksam sein können und schließlich an den Kontext lebensgeschichtlich gebunden sind" (Mecheril 2003, 28).

Junge Migranten verfügen über eine „prekäre natio-ethno-kulturelle Zugehörigkeit", die von dem Idealtyp fragloser Zugehörigkeit abweicht. Mecheril (2003) verdeutlicht dies am Beispiel von Rava Mahabi, dessen Eltern aus Indien stammen, und der in Deutschland aufgewachsen ist. In Deutschland bezeichnet Rava sich als Inder, weil dies den Erwartungen vieler Deutscher, die er neu kennen lernt, entspreche. Auf diese Weise ist es für ihn weniger wahrscheinlich, dass er in identitätsrelevante Herkunfts- und Legitimationsdialoge verwickelt wird und sich darin erklären muss. Im Prinzip – so äußert sich Rava – kann er aber auch sagen, er ist Deutscher, wenngleich dies für viele schwieriger zu verstehen ist. Die Prekarität der Zugehörigkeit von Migrantenjugendlichen ist deshalb als prekär zu kennzeichnen, weil sie erst aufgrund von gesellschaftlich vorherrschenden Zugehörigkeitskonzepten entstehen kann, die die Einwertigkeit von Zugehörigkeitsverhältnissen zum Maßstab haben. Fraglos zugehörig zu sein, bleibt eine

Art Referenzpunkt derjenigen, die hybrid sind, ob nun konkret ausgesprochen, implizit in der Vorstellungswelt des Einzelnen oder unbewusst. Dies bedeutet jedoch nicht, dass für diejenigen, die sich zwei oder mehr Zugehörigkeitskontexten verbunden fühlen, die fraglose Zugehörigkeit eine sinnvolle Ziel- oder Entwicklungsperspektive darstellte, und zwar deshalb nicht, weil diese von ihnen verlangt, „sich der Exklusivitätslogik des Entweder-Oder zu beugen, die ihre Mehrfachzugehörigkeit bestenfalls als irrelevantes (‚symbolisches') Relikt einer identitätsdiffusen Phase" (Mecheril 2003, 303) akzeptiert.

Soziale Anerkennung

Charles Taylor (1997) weist darauf hin, dass in unserer „modernen" Gesellschaftsformation die Frage der sozialen Anerkennung zum Problem geworden ist. In vormoderner Zeit sei von Identität und Anerkennung nicht etwa deshalb keine Rede gewesen, weil die Menschen keine Identität besessen hätten oder auf Anerkennung nicht angewiesen wären, sondern weil Anerkennung als Teil gesellschaftlich abgeleiteter Identität auf gesellschaftlichen Kategorien beruhte (z.B. Klasse, Milieu), die niemand anzweifelte. Für Taylor ist es vor allem die monologische Perspektive der modernen Philosophie, die Identität als alleine individuellen Prozess verstanden und den *dialogischen* Charakter menschlichen Daseins (vgl. Mead 1934) übersehen hat. Das Bedürfnis nach Anerkennung habe es schon immer gegeben. „Neu", sagt Taylor (1997, 24) vor allem mit Bezug auf die Bestrebungen kultureller Minderheiten, sei vielmehr, „dass wir in Verhältnissen leben, in denen das Streben nach Anerkennung scheitern kann". Zwar haben die Individuen heute mehr Möglichkeiten, eigene Identitätsvorhaben autonom umzusetzen, zugleich stehen sie aber – nach wie vor – Schwierigkeiten beim konkreten Versuch gegenüber, Anerkennung von anderen bekundet zu bekommen. Wenn Keupp et al. (1999, 260f) in ihrem Anerkennungskonzept davon sprechen, dass Anerkennung ein „prekäres Gut" sei, dann meinen sie genau diesen Aspekt. Denn *erstens* haben oftmals diejenigen, denen Zustimmung von anderen schmerzlich versagt bleibt, die notwendigen sozialen Kompetenzen verloren, um die Vielfalt der Anerkennungskulturen gemäß ihren prinzipiellen Möglichkeiten für sich zu nutzen. Hinzu kommt eine *zweite* Schwierigkeit, die darin besteht, so Keupp et al. (1999, 260f), „dass mit Veränderungen in sozialen Netzwerken nur diejenigen gut zurechtkommen, die bereits frühzeitig die gestalterischen Fähigkeiten eines Baumeisters des eigenen Netzwerks erworben haben" .

Die natio-ethno-kulturelle Mehrfachzugehörigkeit von jungen Migranten steht mit der Frage der Anerkennung in einem konzeptionellen wie empirischen Zusammenhang: Denn mit der Mehrfachzugehörigkeit sind für Migrantenjugendliche Schwierigkeiten der Art verbunden, dass sie sich wegen ihres mehrwertigen Zugehörigkeitsverständnisses nicht in die Einwertigkeit der vorherrschenden Zugehörigkeitsordnung einpassen lassen. Weder im Hinblick auf den einen Zugehörigkeitskontext (z.B. Türkei) noch auf den anderen (z.B. Deutschland) machen sie Erfahrungen, „eindeutig" zugehörig zu sein. Den einwertigen Anderen im jeweiligen Zugehörigkeitskontext erscheinen sie als fragwürdig und nicht vollwertig. Dieser Zusammenhang wird auch in Mecherils Konzept „prekärer Zugehörigkeit" deutlich. Der Anerkennungsaspekt ist dort insofern mitgedacht, als infolge des für prekäre Andere charakteristischen „Zwischenstatus" bei ihnen ein Mangel an persönlicher Anerkennung entstehen kann: „Staatsbürgerliche Exklusion, ethnozentristisch-rassistische und kulturelle Exklusion durch eine dominante Ein- und Ausschlusswirklichkeit" (Mecheril 2003, 304) bilden das Missachtungspotenzial für die jungen Migranten, mit dem sie in dem natio-ethno-kulturell einwertigen Umfeld konfrontiert sind, in dem sie aufwachsen.

Nun ist zu fragen, ob es „Orte" gibt, an denen sich der „prekäre" Identitätsstatus von Migrantenjugendlichen als solcher Geltung verschaffen kann. Typisch ist für sie, wie bereits deutlich werden sollte, dass sie sich keinem der für sie wichtigen Zugehörigkeitskontexte eindeutig und fraglos zugehörig wissen. Sie sind *natio-ethno-kulturell ortlos*. Sie finden, so Mecheril (2003, 314), „zunächst keine öffentlichen Orte der Darstellung ihres natio-ethno-kulturellen Status und ihrer natio-ethno-kulturellen Ortlosigkeit vor". Wenn Stuart Hall (1995, 181) in diesem Zusammenhang darauf hinweist, dass wir unseren (kulturellen) Identitäten eine geografische Rahmung geben: „We give it a background, we put it in a frame, in order to make sense of it", lässt sich allerdings vermuten, dass es dennoch sozial-räumliche Konstellationen gibt, in denen sich diejenigen verorten können, „die sich im Raum des Natio-ethno-Kulturellen nicht eindeutig positionieren [lassen] können" (Mecheril 2003, 315). Wenn dies so ist, welche sozial-räumliche Rahmung geben sich Migrantenjugendliche, die es ihnen ermöglicht, ihre „prekäre" Zugehörigkeit und die damit verbundenen Anerkennungsprobleme zu verarbeiten bzw. diese in die eine oder andere Richtung auszuhandeln?

Meines Erachtens findet dies zunehmend in der kommunikativen Welt des Internets statt, im *Social Web* der zweiten und dritten türkischen Migrantengeneration in Deutschland.

Anerkennung, Zugehörigkeit, Internet

Offline-Lebenswelten sind nicht mehr von Online-Lebenswelten zu trennen. Das Netz bietet den Jugendlichen heute einen immer gewichtiger werdenden Teil derjenigen Ressourcen, die sie für ihr soziales Miteinander und das Aushandeln eines authentischen Bildes von sich selbst benötigen. Das gilt selbstverständlich auch für Migrantenjugendliche. Die Online-Erfahrungen (nicht nur) junger Migranten sind somit – analog zum Thema der Mehrfachzugehörigkeit von jungen Migranten – ebenfalls durch *Hybridität*[2]

2 Winfried Marotzki (2003a, 136) bezeichnet dies als „Virtualitätslagerung", d.h. ein sich immer weiter ausprägendes *Komplementärverhältnis* zwischen Offline- und Online-Lebenswelt, woraus seiner Meinung nach ein

gekennzeichnet. Sie offenbaren zwar ein *Durchdringungsverhältnis* von Virtuellem und Realem (vgl. Welsch 2000). Dennoch macht es einen Unterschied aus, wenn sich Zugehörigkeits- und Anerkennungsverhältnisse in der Online-Welt statt in der Offline-Welt entwickeln. Damit sind die unterschiedlichen *Bedingungen* des Handelns in nicht-medialen Umgebungen und in der Online-Kommunikation angesprochen, unter denen sich die Identitätskonstruktion einer Person gestaltet. So verändert sich unter den kommunikativen Bedingungen des Internets die Struktur der Anerkennungsverhältnisse, und zwar deshalb, weil sich das Bild, welches sich andere von einer ‚Person' machen, alleine auf die Konstruktion der Persona[3] beziehen kann, d.h. „*was* also Anerkennung finden kann, ist immer nur dieses symbolische Konstrukt, dieses durch die eigene Selbstwahrnehmung gefilterte Bild" (Zirfas/Jörissen 2007, 183). Nun ist es aber so, dass auch diejenigen, die Anerkennung bekunden, ausschließlich als Personae handeln. Da die Personen in diesem Anerkennungsverhältnis keine direkten Rückschlüsse auf die Person hinter der Persona ziehen können, also die, die im eigentlichen Sinne erst in der Lage wäre, sich gegenseitig Anerkennung zuteil werden zu lassen, sind die Personen auf die Imaginationen angewiesen, die sie im Hinblick auf den Wert des jeweils anderen entwickeln.

Während diese Form des Anerkennungsverhältnisses in kulturkritischer Perspektive beklagt oder im „theoretizistischen" Fokus (Sandbothe 2001, 12) vor allem als „Verlustphänomen" (Krämer 2000) gekennzeichnet wird, scheint es mir angesichts der Feststellung eines sich zunehmend *ergänzenden* Verhältnisses zwischen Offline- und Online-Lebenswelten naheliegender zu sein, danach zu fragen, *wie* es das Individuum eigentlich schafft, die in der Online-Welt gesammelten Anerkennungserfahrungen in sein hybrides Selbst zu integrieren – oder eben auch nicht. Voraussetzung dafür ist das „Medialitätsbewusstsein" (Groeben 2002) eines Menschen. Diese Basis-Fähigkeit zur Entwicklung von Medienkompetenz besteht darin, über ein Bewusstsein für die Unterscheidung zwischen Realität und Medialität bzw. Virtualität zu verfügen. Für den Gegenstand der veränderten Anerkennungsstruktur im Netz bedeutet dies in zunächst normativer Hinsicht, davon auszugehen, dass der Agierende als prinzipiell dazu in der Lage anzusehen ist, sich über das *Risiko* einer Anerkennungsbekundung in der Online-Welt bewusst zu sein. Dieses Risiko besteht darin, nicht genau wissen zu können, wer sich hinter dem Anerkennenden verbirgt. Da grundsätzlich nur Annahmen darüber getroffen werden können, ob es die Person hinter der Persona mit ihrer bestätigenden (oder auch missachtenden) Geste ernst meint, besteht im Vergleich zur Offline-Welt ein erhöhtes Enttäuschungspotenzial für den Handelnden.

Möglichkeitsraum entstehen kann, „wie Menschen online Erfahrungen machen, ihre Identität entwerfen und damit ihr Offline-Leben erweitern"..

3 In der Online-Kommunikation wird aus einer Person zwangläufig das, was in der Begrifflichkeit der Internetforschung üblicherweise als „Persona" bzw. „Personae" verstanden wird, eine Maskierung also, mit anderen Worten: die *Konstruktion* einer dahinterstehenden Person.

Solche unterschiedlichen Bedingungen von Anerkennungssuche und ihrer sozialräumlichen Verortung online wie offline müssen berücksichtigt werden, sollen die Identitätsbildungsprozesse junger Migranten im Internet untersucht werden.

Jugendliche mit türkischem Migrationshintergrund im Internet

Nutzungsaspekte

Für junge Türken in Deutschland ist das Internet in den letzten Jahren zunehmend zu einem selbstverständlichen Bestandteil ihrer Medienwelten geworden, womit sich zunächst einmal zeigt, dass sie ebenso wie Nicht-Migranten in die durch die Einführung des Internets mit beeinflussten sozialen Wandlungsprozesse in unserer Mediengesellschaft eingebunden sind. In empirisch-quantitativer Hinsicht wird die wachsende Bedeutung der Online-Welt für türkische Heranwachsende in Deutschland besonders durch die Ergebnisse von zwei zentralen Nutzungsstudien belegt (vgl. bereits Fritzsche 2000):

1. Die Nutzung „heimat- und deutschsprachiger Medien" bei sechs Migrantengruppen hat die Repräsentativstudie der ARD/ZDF-Medienkommission „Migranten und Medien 2007" untersucht (vgl. Simon 2007). Neben klassischen Medien Fernsehen, Radio und Tageszeitung wurde auch das Internet in den Blick genommen. Dabei haben die Forscher aus den Daten die Anzahl der sog. „Stammnutzer" berechnet, der Personen also, die an mindestens vier Tagen pro Woche ein bestimmtes Medien- oder Programmangebot nutzten. In den Ergebnissen wird deutlich, dass sich unter den Jugendlichen mit türkischem Migrationshintergrund (14-29 Jahre) 62 % Stammnutzer des Internets befinden. Nimmt man als Maßstab die *gelegentliche* Nutzung des Internets hinzu – diese wird in der Studie nicht eigens ausgewiesen –, ist also anzunehmen, dass der Anteil der Internetnutzer unter den jungen Türken sogar weitaus höher ist und sich vermutlich dem Anteil der Gesamtnutzerschaft der Jugendlichen in Deutschland annähert. Dieser liegt nach Angaben der ARD/ZDF-Online-Studie 2007 (vgl. Eimeren/Frees 2007) bei etwa 95 % (14-19 Jahre: 95,8 %; 20-29 Jahre: 94,3 %), was nahezu einer Vollversorgung entspricht[4]. Während also die

4 Dies wird durch die Ergebnisse einer Sonderauswertung zum „(N)Onliner Atlas 2008" bestätigt, die sich mit dem Zusammenhang von Internetnutzung und Migrationshintergrund beschäftigt. Die Studie der Initiative D21, durchgeführt von TNS Infratest, kommt zum Resultat, dass bei den 14 bis 29-jährigen Personen mit und ohne Migrationshintergrund der Unterschied bei der Internetnutzung gering ist: Während der Anteil der Internetnutzer bei den jungen Menschen „ohne Migrationshintergrund" 92,7 % beträgt, liegt dieser Anteil bei den Personen dieser Altersgruppe, deren Eltern über eine Migrationserfahrung verfügen, bei 90,4 %. Der Migrationshintergrund alleine, so die Autoren der Untersuchung, sei deshalb kein Merkmal digitaler

Studie „Migranten und Medien 2007" zur gelegentlichen Nutzung des Internets nur implizit Angaben darstellt, liefert sie interessante Ergebnisse zur sprachspezifischen Nutzung von Internetseiten. Demnach besuchen die jugendlichen Stammnutzer mit türkischem Migrationshintergrund vor allem „nur deutschsprachige" Internetseiten (42 %), an zweiter Stelle sowohl „deutschsprachige" als auch „türkischsprachige" Internetseiten (16 %) und an dritter Stelle „nur heimatsprachige" Websites (4 %).

2. Die zweite relevante Untersuchung – freilich älteren Datums – ist in der Markt- und Meinungsforschung angesiedelt, was sich aus dem zunehmenden Interesse von Unternehmen am „Ethno-Marketing" erklären lässt. So stellt Joachim Schulte (2003) in einer Studie des Markt- und Meinungsforschungsinstituts „Data 4U" zur Internetnutzung von Türken in Deutschland fest – befragt wurden insgesamt 1.027 Personen ab 14 Jahren, mittels Telefoninterviews –, dass von 2001 bis 2003 der Anteil der 14-29-jährigen (mindestens gelegentlichen) türkischen User von 40 % auf etwa 53 % gestiegen ist. Aus den Data 4U-Ergebnissen geht darüber hinaus hervor, dass es 2003 vor allem jüngere, männliche Personen aus Haushalten mit einem gehobenen Einkommen sind, die den Kern der türkischen Online-User darstellen. Bei den genutzten Onlineanwendungen dominieren die kommunikativen Funktionen E-Mail und Chat/Newsgroups. Nachgeordnet rangiert die Suche nach Informationen und Nachrichten.

Obwohl beide Studien zwar die grundsätzlich immer größer werdende Relevanz der Online-Welt bei den türkischen Jugendlichen in Deutschland belegen können, ist die Aussagekraft ihrer Ergebnisse für die Fragestellung dieses Beitrages doch eher beschränkt: Erstens, weil die quantitativen Daten kaum eine Antwort auf das Warum der Mediennutzung liefern. Dazu ist (zusätzlich) die Verwendung qualitativer Verfahren notwendig. Ein Beispiel dafür werde ich im folgenden Abschnitt darstellen. Zweitens liefert vor allem die Untersuchung der ARD/ZDF-Medienkommission keinerlei Ergebnisse zu denjenigen Online-Angeboten, die bei den Jugendlichen zwischen 14 und 29 Jahren besonders große Aufmerksamkeit hervorrufen, d.h. das Social Web (vgl. allgemein zu deren Nutzung durch Jugendliche: Eimeren/Frees 2007; Schmidt/Paus-Hasebrink/Hasebrink 2009; Wagner/Brüggen/Gebel 2009). Teil des Social Web sind Online-Communities, die sich speziell an junge türkische Migranten in Deutschland richten, von einigen Autoren auch Ethnoportale oder „Multikulti-Portale" (Azrak 2002) genannt. Sie stehen in diesem Beitrag im Mittelpunkt (vgl. differenziert zur Internetlandschaft von Jugendlichen mit türkischem Migrationshintergrund in Deutschland: Hugger/Özcelik 2009).

Spaltung. Alter – und darüber hinaus Bildungsabschluss sowie Einkommen – würde in ähnlicher Weise auf die Nutzung des Internets wirken wie bei der Bevölkerung ohne Migrationshintergrund (Initiative D21 2008).

Solche Online-Communities können sich als *dialektische* Räume abbilden – jenseits homogener, begrenzter nationaler, kultureller und ethnischer Einheiten liegend –, die sich für die Jugendlichen als *natio-ethno-kulturelle Hybrid-Umgebung* der identitären Vergewisserung konkretisieren, d.h. in der sie ihre „prekäre“ Zugehörigkeit zum Ausdruck bringen und die damit verbundenen Anerkennungsprobleme verarbeiten können. Im Zentrum solcher dialektischer Räume im Internet steht also in analytischer Hinsicht nicht der kommunikative Aspekt, sondern der Identitätsstatus der Migranten. Davon zu unterscheiden sind solche Räume der Identitätsbildung im Internet, die sich für die jungen Migranten als *natio-ethno-kulturell fixierte Umgebungen* konkretisieren. Dabei handelt es sich um Internetseiten bzw. Online-Communities, die den Jugendlichen eine vor allem natio-ethno-kulturell einwertige Vergewisserung von Zugehörigkeit und Anerkennung ermöglichen bzw. die von den Jugendlichen als solche Seiten wahrgenommen werden. Dies muss sich gar nicht unbedingt auf Websites beziehen, deren sozial-räumliches Gefüge eine Dominanz der Mehrheitsgesellschaft im Ankunftsland widerspiegelt; genauso gut kann es Internetseiten betreffen, die auf die natio-ethno-kulturelle Einwertigkeit des Herkunftslandes bezogen sind, z.B. Seiten, die ausschließlich auf die Alltagswelt von Menschen abgestellt sind, die in der Türkei leben. Dies bedeutet: Der Begriff der *natio-ethno-kulturellen Umgebung identitärer Vergewisserung im Internet* transzendiert die Rede von einer dualistischen Zuordnung von Internetprodukten zum Herkunfts- oder Ankunftsland. Bei der Frage der Einordnung von Websites, die für die Identitätsbildung von jungen Migranten relevant sind, geht es dann darum, welcher *natio-ethno-kulturellen Umgebung* diese Sites zugeordnet werden können.

Wie im Folgenden deutlich werden soll, konkretisieren sich die Online-Communities, die sich speziell an junge türkische Migranten in Deutschland richten, für viele Jugendliche als ‚natio-ethno-kulturelle Hybridumgebungen'. Nach den Marktforschungsdaten der Data 4U-Erhebung werden sie von fast 60 % aller deutsch-türkischen Onliner genutzt, insbesondere den Jugendlichen. Allerdings unterlaufen diese Angebote die Klassifizierung der ARD/ZDF-Studie, die ausschließlich nach einem deutsch- und heimatsprachigen Internet unterteilt. Wie sich auf den folgenden Seiten noch detaillierter zeigen soll, ist diese Trennung sowohl aus der Perspektive der Angebots- wie der Nutzerseite problematisch: Auf der Angebotsseite zeigt sich etwa bei Vaybee.de[5], dass die redaktionellen Inhalte teils in deutscher, teils in türkischer Sprache präsentiert werden. Der User hat hier sogar die Möglichkeit, seine favorisierte Sprache auszuwählen. Aber auch im Hinblick auf einen weiteren Aspekt scheint mir die Trennung von deutsch- und heimatsprachigem Internet wenig zielführend zu sein, um auf dieser Basis geeignete Schlüsse für das „Integrationspotenzial“ des Internets zu ziehen, so wie es die Studie versucht. Denn schaut man auf die Kommunikation der jungen Türken untereinan-

5 http://www.vaybee.de

der, also die Inhalte, die die Mitglieder der Online-Community eigenständig veröffentlichen, zeigt sich, dass diese oft durch Sprachwechsel, also dem Wechsel zwischen dem Türkischen und dem Deutschen gekennzeichnet ist (vgl. Androutsopoulos 2006). Eine Unterteilung zwischen deutsch- und heimatsprachigen Websites bleibt auch hier unangemessen, weil sie das Angebot nicht treffsicher zu erfassen vermag.

Dieser eindimensional verengte Blick auf Internetangebote bzw. Sozialräume im Internet für Jugendliche mit (nicht nur) *türkischem* Migrationshintergrund, zeigt beispielhaft, dass in der (empirischen) Medienforschung in Deutschland der Zusammenhang von Transmigration, hybrider Identität und Internet bisher noch zu wenig fruchtbar gemacht wird. Dies gilt freilich nicht nur für die Medien- sondern in anderer Weise auch für die Migrationsforschung, die, wenn sie die Mediennutzung (junger) Türken untersucht, vor allem die Massenmedien Fernsehen, Radio und Print berücksichtigt, die zunehmende Bedeutung des Internets jedoch noch weitgehend unberücksichtigt lässt (vgl. Hafez 2003, 2005; Geißler/Pöttker 2006; Sauer/Goldberg 2006; Halm 2007).

Vergewisserung von Zugehörigkeit und Suche nach Anerkennung im Internet

Um tiefergehende empirische Hinweise darüber zu erhalten, ob bzw. in welcher Art und Weise die Verarbeitung hybrider Identitäten von jungen Migranten in der Online-Welt erfolgt, habe ich im Jahr 2005 eine face-to-face-Befragung von 20 jungen Türken der zweiten Migrantengeneration in Deutschland durchgeführt. Bei diesen Jugendlichen bzw. jungen Erwachsenen handelt es sich um Mitglieder der Online-Communities Vaybee, Bizimalem[6] und Aleviler[7], die sich dort aktiv am kommunikativen Austausch in den asynchronen Diskussionsforen beteiligt haben (vgl. zur Beschreibung dieser Communities Hugger 2009).

Vergewisserung von „prekärer" Zugehörigkeit

Online-Communities wie Vaybee.de, Aleviler.de oder Bizimalem.de stellen für die türkischen Migrantenjugendlichen Orte dar – dies wird in den Ergebnissen meiner Untersuchung deutlich –, in denen sie ihre „prekäre" Zugehörigkeit insofern ‚verarbeiten' können, als sie sich dort ihrer gemeinschaftlichen wie biografischen Wurzeln vor dem Hintergrund national-ethnisch-kultureller Hybridität vergewissern können. Obwohl junge Migranten, wie Mecheril (2003, 314) feststellt, „zunächst keine öffentlichen Orte der Darstellung ihres natio-ethno-kulturellen Status und ihrer natio-ethno-kulturellen Ortlosigkeit" vorfinden, kann ihr Agieren in den national-ethnisch-kulturellen Hybridumgebungen des Internets als *sozial-räumlicher Rahmungsversuch* interpretiert werden,

6 http://www. bizimalem.de

7 Aleviler.de ist seit Juli 2007 offline. Die Betreiber stellen auf ihrer Website einen Relaunch in Aussicht, der jedoch bis Juni 2009 noch nicht erfolgt ist.

der es ihnen ermöglicht, ihre „prekäre" Zugehörigkeit zu ‚verorten'. Insgesamt werden bei den Befragten unterschiedliche *Muster der Vergewisserung* national-ethnisch-kultureller Zugehörigkeit in den Online-Communities sichtbar, m.a.W. zeigt sich eine Vielfalt unterschiedlicher Verarbeitungsweisen „prekärer" Zugehörigkeit:

1. Der Versuch, erst mithilfe des Agierens in der Online-Community biografische wie gemeinschaftliche türkische Wurzeln zu *entdecken.* Dieses Muster wird bei Hasan deutlich, für den Bizimalem.de die Funktion eines Türöffners zum türkischen Zugehörigkeitskontext hat, wodurch es ihm gelingt „Berührungsängste" gegenüber dem Türkischen und den Türken abzubauen, somit die seines Erachtens vernachlässigte Seite seines mehrwertigen Zugehörigkeitsverständnisses fruchtbar zu machen. Dies unternimmt er freilich nicht mit dem Ziel, Mehrwertigkeit durch Einwertigkeit zu ersetzen, sondern Mehrwertigkeit *auszubalancieren.*
2. Der Versuch, „prekäre" Zugehörigkeit mithilfe der Vergewisserung biografischer wie gemeinschaftlicher Wurzeln im Rahmen der Online-Community zu *vereindeutigen.* Dieses Muster zeigt sich bei Haluk, dem es Probleme bereitet, Mehrfachzugehörigkeit in seinem Selbstverständnis aufrechtzuerhalten. Für eine sinntragende Zukunftsperspektive sieht er sich dazu gezwungen, sich für den einen oder anderen national-ethnisch-kulturellen Kontext zu entscheiden und damit die Frage nach seiner Zugehörigkeit idealtypisch zu einer Entweder-oder-Entscheidung zu machen.
3. Der Versuch, mithilfe des Agierens in der Online-Community biografische wie gemeinschaftliche türkische Wurzeln zu *bewahren.* Dieses Muster wird bei Ildiz sichtbar, der sich seiner Mehrfachzugehörigkeit bewusst ist, der aber zugleich aufgrund des von ihm beobachteten gesellschaftlichen Enttraditionalisierungsprozesses das Überleben seiner türkischen, genauer ausgedrückt: alevitisch-kurdischen Wurzeln gefährdet sieht. Mithilfe seines Agierens in der Online-Community will er deshalb vor allem die alevitischen Traditionen späteren Generationen zur Aufbewahrung weitergeben.
4. Der Versuch, mithilfe der Vergewisserung biografischer wie gemeinschaftlicher Wurzeln in der Online-Community „prekäre" Zugehörigkeit zu *festigen und anderen zu vermitteln.* Dieses Muster zeigt sich vor allem bei Ünay. Sie erkennt sich im spezifischen biografischen So-geworden-sein ihres hybriden national-ethnisch-kulturellen Zugehörigkeitsverständnisses an und will die positiven wie negativen Zugehörigkeitserfahrungen, die sie gesammelt hat, anderen vermitteln, weil sie davon überzeugt ist, anderen türkischen Jugendlichen, die unter einer „prekären" Zugehörigkeit zu leiden haben, helfen zu können.
5. Der Versuch, mithilfe der Vergewisserung biografischer wie gemeinschaftlicher türkischer Wurzeln im Rahmen der Online-Community *biografische Kontinuität herzustellen.* Dieses Muster zeigt sich verstärkt bei Duru, für die das Agieren in der

Online-Community den sozial-räumlichen Rahmen zur biografischen Reflexion zur Verfügung stellt, und zwar indem sie immer wieder einen Zusammenhang herstellt zwischen den „Mischkultur"-Themen in den Diskussionsforen der Vaybee.de-Community und ihren eigenen Kindheitserfahrungen. Dadurch erinnert sie sich aber nicht nur ihrer Wurzeln, sondern kann auf dieser Basis überprüfen, inwieweit diese mit ihrem heutigen hybriden Selbstverständnis in Passung zu bringen sind.

Jenseits aller Unterschiede, die sich in den verschiedenen Verarbeitungsweisen „prekärer" Zugehörigkeit widerspiegeln, können – zu den Ergebnissen der Einzelfallanalysen Hugger (2009) – zwei *übergreifende* Aspekte entdeckt werden, die die Vergewisserung von Zugehörigkeit in den Communities des Internets zu strukturieren scheinen:

1. Die Frage, ob die Vergewisserung, oder anders ausgedrückt: *Reflexionsarbeit* der jungen Türken gelingt, nur episodisch gelingt oder gar scheitert, ist offen. Dass die sozial-räumlichen Rahmungsversuche für das Individuum nicht zufriedenstellend verlaufen *müssen*, mithin die national-ethnisch-kulturellen Hybridumgebungen des Internets kein Erfolgsgarant zur Selbst-Findung junger Türken in Deutschland sind, kann als wichtiges Ergebnis festgehalten werden. Dieser Aspekt relativiert aber nicht nur ein vorschnelles Feiern des türkischen Social Web und seiner Bedeutung für das Ausleben von Hybriditität. Zugleich ist dieses Ergebnis ein Hinweis darauf, dass die Kritik an einem naiven Verständnis von national-ethnisch-kultureller Hybridität durchaus Berechtigung hat, wenn darunter verstanden wird, dass junge Migranten grundsätzlich und immer souverän mit ihrem mehrwertigen Selbstverständnis umzugehen in der Lage sind.
2. Im Rahmen der Vergewisserung von Zugehörigkeit in den national-ethnisch-kulturellen Hybridumgebungen des Internets lassen sich sowohl *synchrone* als auch *diachrone* Orientierungsformate wiederfinden (vgl. Marotzki 2007). Neben die Betrachtung der Identitätsbildung von jungen Migranten im Hier und Jetzt (synchrone Perspektive) tritt die des *historischen* Sinnbildungsprozesses (diachrone Perspektive), in dessen Rahmen sich der Einzelne zum einen seiner individuellen, biografischen und zum anderen seiner gruppenorientierten Wurzeln vergewissert. Im Hinblick auf die diachrone Seite vermischt sich die Suche nach biografischen und gemeinschaftsorientierten Wurzeln des Einzelnen. In den individuellen Verarbeitungsweisen „prekärer" Zugehörigkeit werden in der Regel beide Elemente sichtbar und können nur analytisch voneinander getrennt werden. Dies bedeutet: Wenn die Personen über die Frage kollektiver Eigenschaften in historischer und gegenwärtiger Perspektive zusammen mit anderen reflektieren, dann kann dies nicht unabhängig von ihren ganz persönlichen Zugehörigkeitserfahrungen und Verarbeitungsweisen derselben betrachtet werden. Um auf die Frage der Vergewisserung „prekärer" Zugehörigkeit

im Internet eine Antwort zu finden, müssen also – dies offenbart sich in den Selbsterzählungen der jungen Türken – sowohl kulturelle wie persönliche Aspekte von Identität berücksichtigt werden.

Suche nach Anerkennung

Der anfangs aufgezeigte Zusammenhang zwischen der national-ethnisch-kulturellen Mehrfachzugehörigkeit der jungen (türkischen) Migranten und der Frage der Anerkennung (vgl. auch Stojanov 2006) kann im Hinblick auf das Agieren in Online-Communities auch empirisch fruchtbar entfaltet werden. Ich hatte darauf hingewiesen, dass durch die mit dem „prekären" Zugehörigkeitsstatus verbundenen Schwierigkeiten sich nicht bruchlos in die Einwertigkeit des vorherrschenden gesellschaftlichen Zugehörigkeitsverständnisses einpassen zu lassen, die Migrantenjugendlichen einen *Mangel an persönlicher Anerkennung* erleben können, d.h., dass ihnen zumindest im Kontext der (deutschen) Mehrheitsgesellschaft die Möglichkeit vorenthalten zu werden scheint, ihren eigenen durch national-ethnisch-kulturelle Hybridität gekennzeichneten Orientierungen und biografischen Leistungen einen sozialen Wert beizumessen und diesen intersubjektiv zum Ausdruck zu bringen. Vor diesem Hintergrund machen die Einzelfallanalysen darauf aufmerksam: Die national-ethnisch-kulturellen Hybridumgebungen des Internets bieten den jungen Türken einen sozial-räumlichen Rahmen, in dem sie jenseits des einwertigen deutschen, aber auch des einwertigen türkischen Zugehörigkeitskontextes Bestätigung durch andere Personen erfahren können, die ebenfalls über einen „prekären" Zugehörigkeitsstatus verfügen und damit über ähnliche Alltagserfahrungen (z.B. mit verwehrter Anerkennung im deutschen oder türkischen Kontext) wie biografische Hintergründe verfügen. Dies muss freilich nicht notwendigerweise bedeuten, dass dieser Rahmen für die Suche nach Anerkennung in jedem Fall auch ‚erfolgreich' genutzt werden muss. Über die unterschiedlichen Muster der Anerkennungssuche in den Online-Communities hinaus, die die jungen Türken auf der Basis ihrer Selbsterzählungen zum Ausdruck bringen, werden zwei übergreifende Aspekte sichtbar:

1. Verwehrte Anerkennung in Form von *Rassismuserfahrungen* in Deutschland ist ein zentraler Antriebsfaktor für den Versuch der jungen Türken, ihre „prekäre" Zugehörigkeit im Rahmen national-ethnisch-kultureller Hybridumgebungen im Internet zusammen mit anderen zu verarbeiten. Missachtungserfahrungen aufgrund von Rassismus sind ein bestimmendes Strukturmuster der Anerkennungssuche von Migrantenjugendlichen, also nicht nur in der Offline-Welt, sondern auch im Netz. Dies wird beispielhaft bei Hasan deutlich, der von persönlichen und institutionellen Rassismuserfahrungen – offline wie online – erzählt. Hasan versucht, diese zu vermeiden, indem er sich verstärkt seinem türkischen Kontext zuwendet, der ihm durch das soziale Miteinander bei Bizimalem.de eröffnet wird: „Bei Bizimalem habe ich mich viel wohler gefühlt, einfach, weil niemand sagen konnte 'Scheiß-

türke'. Das war für mich sehr wichtig" (Hasan, 233-234). Da die Mitglieder von Bizimalem.de ebenfalls einen türkischen Migrationshintergund haben, kann sich Hasan sicher sein, dort nicht mit der Beschimpfung „Scheißtürke" konfrontiert und erniedrigt zu werden. Insofern ist seine Mitgliedschaft in der türkischen Online-Community eine *Reaktion* auf im deutschen Kontext verwehrte Anerkennung. Die durch alltäglichen Rassismus erzwungene permanente Vergegenwärtigung, nicht fraglos dem deutschen Kontext zugehörig zu sein, scheint hier zu entfallen. Dieses Muster lässt sich in der einen oder anderen Weise in allen Einzelfallanalysen entdecken, wenngleich die Rassismuserfahrungen nicht unbedingt so unmittelbar als wichtiges Motiv für das Agieren in den ‚türkischen' Online-Communities formuliert sein müssen, wie dies bei Hasan der Fall ist. Rassismuserfahrungen können auch *imaginären* Charakter haben, dennoch wirksam für das Subjekt sein und somit als wichtiger Antriebsfaktor für eine Mitgliedschaft in Frage kommen. Dies wird an Durus Beispiel sichtbar, wenn sie die Rezeption eines „türkischen Macho-Typen" im Fernsehen und die daraus von ihr abgeleiteten negativen Folgen im deutschen Alltag thematisiert: Duru befürchtet nicht einfach nur, dass die deutsche Mehrheitsgesellschaft das Verhalten des türkischen Machos mit dem der türkischen Hybriden gleichsetzen könnte, zu denen sie sich zählt. Sie befürchtet vor allem, von *den Deutschen* mit Missachtung bestraft zu werden („jetzt werden alle normal denkenden Deutschen in Deutschland sich das angucken und sich denken ‚oh Gott, nein, Hilfe, was ist das für eine Einstellung'" [Duru, 94-96]). Die mögliche Missachtung, die die Rezeption des türkischen „Macho-Typen" im Fernsehen für sie zur Folge haben könnte, würde für sie einen Entzug von Anerkennung bedeuten, zu der sie im biografischen Prozess erst schwer hat finden müssen. Insgesamt wird bei den jungen Türken im Netz ein Muster der Erwartung von Anerkennung durch Andere aus dem deutschen Zugehörigkeitskontext deutlich, das durch *Fragilität* gekennzeichnet ist. Dies bedeutet am Beispiel von Duru: Sie kann sich nicht in selbstverständlicher Weise sicher sein, dass ihr von den „normal denkenden Deutschen in Deutschland" Wohlwollen entgegengebracht wird. In solchen Situationen wird Duru die Unsicherheit bewusst, bei der Suche nach sozialer Anerkennung kaum dem deutschen Zugehörigkeitskontext vertrauen zu können – im Gegensatz zu der erwarteten Bestätigung durch Andere, von der sie prinzipiell im Rahmen der türkischen Online-Community ausgeht.

2. Die Anerkennungssuche der türkischen Migrantenjugendlichen im Rahmen der national-ethnisch-kulturellen Hybridumgebungen des Internets kann als Prozess rekonstruiert werden, der idealtypisch vier Phasen umfasst: Entdeckung, Bestätigung/Missachtung, Prüfung, Konsolidierung. Dieser Prozess und die mit ihm verbundenen Phasen haben einen dynamischen und variablen Charakter, d.h. obwohl

sie zwar als Ablaufmuster in – mehr oder weniger – allen analysierten Fällen zu finden sind, können die einzelnen Phasen

a) für das Subjekt unterschiedlich stark ausgeprägt sein (Intensität, Zeitdauer etc.),
b) in veränderter oder erweiterter Reihenfolge zum Ausdruck kommen oder
c) sich miteinander vermischen.

So kann nach der Konsolidierungsphase eine erneute Prüfung vorgenommen werden, die Phasen Bestätigung/Missachtung und Prüfung fallen zusammen usf. Solange aber die Person in der Online-Community aktiv ist, kann auch die dortige Anerkennungssuche fortdauern. Zudem ist darauf hinzuweisen, dass die rekonstruierten Phasen nicht als ‚Erfolgsmodell' misszuverstehen sind. Am Ende des Prozesses, sofern er in den Selbsterzählungen der Jugendlichen als ‚abgeschlossen' erkennbar wird, muss für den Einzelnen nicht Anerkennung stehen, vielmehr kann ihm diese auch von anderen vorenthalten werden.

Entdeckungsphase

Diese Phase steht am Beginn des Anerkennungsprozesses in den natio-ethno-kulturellen Hybridumgebungen des Internets. Sie ist in der Regel dadurch geprägt, dass der Jugendliche zwar von der Annahme ausgeht, dass er in der Online-Community diejenige Bestätigung als Individuum mit „prekärer" Zugehörigkeit erhält, die ihm im einwertigen deutschen bzw. einwertigen türkischen Zugehörigkeitskontext außerhalb der Community verwehrt wird. Allerdings ist sein Verhalten noch durch Unsicherheit darüber gekennzeichnet, ob sich seine Annahme im sozialen Miteinander bewahrheitet. Als Neu-Mitglied verfügt er zu diesem Zeitpunkt noch nicht über Erfahrungen, wie die anderen Mitglieder der Community auf eigene kommunikative Äußerungen in Postings reagieren werden, ob positiv oder negativ oder gleichgültig.

Bestätigungs-/Missachtungsphase

Kennzeichnend für diese Phase ist die Reflexion der Migrantenjugendlichen, wie die Reaktionen der Anderen nicht nur, aber insbesondere auf das erste Posting zu bewerten sind. Dies ist insofern für die Verarbeitung „prekärer" Zugehörigkeit relevant, als der erste Beitrag von den Jugendlichen auch immer – ob implizit oder explizit – als persönliche Positionierung oder gar Offenbarung im Hinblick auf das Thema der national-ethnisch-kulturellen Hybridität verstanden wird. Und aus diesem Grund werden die Reaktionen der Anderen als eine Art Gradmesser hinsichtlich der Frage interpretiert, ob man als Hybrid willkommen ist, ob die Annahme, hier tatsächlich soziale Anerkennung erfahren zu können, berechtigt war oder nicht. Fallen die Rückmeldungen der Anderen positiv aus, kann dies bei der Person ein Gefühl der sozialen Wertschätzung hinterlassen. Fallen die Rückmeldungen negativ aus, kann dies bei der Person ein Gefühl fehlender sozialer Wertschätzung bzw. Missachtung hinterlassen.

Prüfungsphase
Diese Phase im Anerkennungsprozess ist dadurch charakterisiert, dass die Migrantenjugendlichen den Sinn und Zweck ihres Agierens in der jeweiligen national-ethnisch-kulturellen Hybridumgebung des Internets für sich und ihr Selbst kritisch in Frage stellen. Zugleich überprüfen sie damit, ob es ihnen hier gelungen ist, sich mit ihrem „prekären" Zugehörigkeitsstatus Geltung verschafft haben zu können. Somit hat diese Phase den Charakter einer Bestandsaufnahme, in der die bisherigen Online-Erfahrungen zur Reflexion kommen. Verläuft die Prüfungsphase für die Jugendlichen positiv, d.h. können sie für sich insgesamt festhalten, sich in der jeweiligen national-ethnisch -kulturellen Hybridumgebung des Internets mit ihrem „prekären" Zugehörigkeitsstatus Geltung verschafft zu haben, leitet dies über in die *Konsolidierungsphase*. Verläuft die Prüfungsphase dagegen negativ, stellt die Person also fest, dass sie sich alles in allem keine Geltung verschaffen konnte, kann dies einerseits zur Beendigung der Mitgliedschaft in der Online-Community führen bzw. zum vorzeitigen Abschluss des dort mit der Entdeckungsphase begonnenen Anerkennungsprozesses oder es kann andererseits zum Versuch eines *Neubeginns* dieses Prozesses mithilfe eines veränderten Identitätsprofils führen.

Konsolidierungsphase
Für diese Phase des Anerkennungsprozesses ist Voraussetzung – dies ist bereits angeklungen –, dass für den einzelnen die Prüfungsphase positiv verläuft und er für sich festhalten kann, sich insgesamt in der jeweiligen national-ethnisch-kulturellen Hybridumgebung des Internets mit seinem „prekären" Zugehörigkeitsstatus Geltung verschafft zu haben. Kennzeichnend für diese Phase ist die *Festigung* des persönlichen Agierens in der Online-Community, indem die Person beschließt, Mitglied zu bleiben und das eigene Engagement vielleicht sogar zu verstärken, obwohl im Anerkennungsprozess durchaus Missachtungserfahrungen aufgetreten sein können.

Schlussbetrachtung

Die Ergebnisse dieser Untersuchung können zweifelsohne *bildungstheoretisch* gelesen bzw. fruchtbar gemacht werden. Bildung – in der Perspektive einer strukturalen Bildungstheorie (Marotzki 1990, 2007) verstanden, die Bildungsprozesse als „orientierende Reflexion" begreift – ist für die Identitätssuche des Menschen von zentraler Wichtigkeit. Sie lässt sich in zwei Dimensionen entfalten: „Synchrone" und „diachrone" Orientierungsformate:

> „Diachrone sind solche, die den Einzelnen aus seiner individuellen, gemeinschaftlichen, gesellschaftlichen und nationalen Traditionslinie heraus verstehen. Synchrone

Orientierungsformate sind solche, die den Einzelnen aus den zum gegenwärtigen Zeitpunkt bestehenden Zugehörigkeits- und Anerkennungsverhältnissen verstehen" (Marotzki 2007, 93).

Beide Formate gehören zusammen, bedingen sich gegenseitig, können aber analytisch voneinander getrennt werden. Ich habe die Inbesitznahme der sog. Ethnoportale im Internet durch türkische Migrantenjugendliche auf der Basis meiner Untersuchungsergebnisse als *Verortung ihrer natio-ethno-kulturellen Ortlosigkeit* gekennzeichnet. Die untersuchten Online-Communities konkretisieren sich für die jungen Türken – wie gezeigt – als *natio-ethno-kulturelle Hybrid-Umgebungen der identitären Vergewisserung*, in der sie ihre „prekäre" Zugehörigkeit und die damit verbundenen Anerkennungsprobleme *verarbeiten* können. Was dort stattfindet ist – bildungstheoretisch ausgedrückt – „orientierende Reflexion". Wenn es richtig ist, dass gesellschaftliche und soziale Enttraditionalisierungsprozesse das Bedürfnis nach Selbstvergewisserung und einem Experimentieren mit dem Selbst erzeugen, dann scheinen also die untersuchten Hybridumgebungen im Netz für die jungen Türken den Rahmen für eine solche ‚Reflexionsarbeit' liefern zu können. Insofern stellen sie sich als *Bildungsräume* dar.

Literatur

Androutsopoulos, Janis. (2006): Mehrsprachigkeit im deutschen Internet: Sprachwahl und Sprachwechsel in Ethnoportalen. In: Schoblinski 2006, 172-19.

Azrak, Atilla (2002): Links zum Leben und Überleben. In: medien concret 1/2002, 10-11.

Bauman, Zygmunt (2005): Moderne und Ambivalenz. Hamburg: Hamburger Edition.

Becker, Jörg/Behnisch, Reinhard (Hrsg.) (2003): Zwischen kultureller Zersplitterung und virtueller Identität. Türkische Medienkultur in Deutschland III. Rehburg-Loccum: Ev. Akademie Loccom.

Bhabha, Homi (1994): The Location of Culture. London: New York: Routledge.

Eimeren, Birgit. van/Frees, Beate. (2007): Internetnutzung zwischen Pragmatismus und YouTube-Euphorie. ARD/ZDF-Online-Studie 2007. In: Media Perspektiven, 8/2007, 362-378.

Fischer, Arthur/Fritzsche, Yvonne/Fuchs-Heinritz, Werner/Münchmeier, Richard (Hrsg.) (2000): Jugend 2000. 13. Shell Jugendstudie. Opladen: Leske + Budrich.

Fritzsche, Yvonne (2000): Modernes Leben. Gewandelt, vernetzt, verkabelt. In Fischer/Fritzsche/Fuchs-Heinritz/Münchmeier 2000, 181-219.

Geißler, Rainer/Pöttker, Horst (2006) (Hrsg.): Integration durch Massenmedien. Medien und Migration im internationalen Vergleich. Bielefeld: transcript.

Glick Schiller, Nina/Basch, Linda/Blanc-Szanton, Christina (1992): Transnationalism: A new analytic framework for understanding migration. In: Glick Schiller/Basch/Blanc-Szanton 1992, 1-24.

Glick Schiller, Nina/Basch, Linda/Blanc-Szanton, Christina (Hrsg.) (1992): Towards a transnational perspective on migration. Race, class, ethnicity and nationalism reconsidered. New York: The New York Academy of Sciences.

Groeben, Norbert (2002): Dimensionen der Medienkompetenz. Deskriptive und normative Aspekte. In: Groeben/Hurrelmann 2002, 160-197.

Groeben, Norbert/Hurrelmann, Bettina (Hrsg.) (2002): Medienkompetenz. Voraussetzungen, Dimensionen, Funktionen. Weinheim und München: Juventa.

Ha, Kien Nghi (2005): Hype um Hybridität. Kultureller Differenzkonsum und postmoderne Verwertungstechniken im Spätkapitalismus. Bielefeld: transcript.

Hafez, Kai (2003): Türkische Mediennutzung in Deutschland: Hemmnis oder Chance der gesellschaftlichen Integration? Eine qualitative Studie im Auftrag des Presse- und Informationsamtes der Bundesregierung. Hamburg/Berlin: Presse- und Informationsamt der Bundesregierung.

Hafez, Kai (2005): Mythos Globalisierung. Warum die Medien nicht grenzenlos sind. Wiesbaden: VS Verlag.

Hall, Stuart (1990): Cultural Identity and Diaspora. In: Rutherford 1990, 222 - 237.

Hall, Stuart (1992):The Question of Cultural Identity. In: Hall/Held/McGrew 1992, 273 - 316.

Hall, Stuart/Held, David/McGrew, Tony (Hrsg.) (1992): Modernity and its Futures. Milton Keynes: Polity Press/The Open University.

Hall, Stuart (1994): Rassismus und kulturelle Identität. Hamburg: Argument.

Hall, Stuart (1995): New Cultures for Old. In: Massey/Jess 1995, 175-213.

Halm, Dirk (2007): Freizeit, Medien und kulturelle Orientierungen junger Türkeistämmiger in Deutschland. In: Wensierski/Lübcke 2007, 101 - 113.

Esser, Harmut./Friedrichs, Jürgen (Hrsg.) (1990): Generation und Identität. Theoretische und empirische Beiträge zur Migrationssoziologie. Opladen: Westdeutscher Verlag.

Hill, Paul B. (1990): Kulturelle Inkonsistenz und Stress bei der zweiten Generation. In: Esser/Friedrichs 1990, 100-126.

Hugger, Kai-Uwe (2009): Junge Migranten online. Suche nach sozialer Anerkennung und Vergewisserung sozialer Zugehörigkeit. Wiesbaden: VS Verlag.

Hugger, Kai-Uwe (Hrsg.) (2009): Digitale Jugendkulturen. Wiesbaden: VS Verlag (im Druck).

Hugger, Kai-Uwe/Özcelik, Ferdal (2009): Intraethnische jugendkulturelle Gesellungen im Internet als Ressource. In: Hugger 2009 (im Druck).

Honneth, Axel (2003): Kampf um Anerkennung. Zur moralischen Grammatik sozialer Konflikte. Mit einem neuen Nachwort. Frankfurt am Main: Suhrkamp.

Keupp, Heiner et. al. (1999): Identitätskonstruktionen. Das Patchwork der Identitäten in der Spätmoderne. Reinbek: Rowohlt.

King, Vera/Koller, Hans-Christoph (Hrsg.) (2006): Adoleszenz – Migration – Bildung. Bildungsprozesse Jugendlicher und junger Erwachsener mit Migrationshintergrund. Wiesbaden: VS Verlag.

Kompetenzzentrum Informelle Bildung (Hrsg.) (2007): Grenzenlose Cyberwelt? Zum Verhältnis von digitaler Ungleichheit und neuen Bildungszugängen für Jugendliche. Wiesbaden: VS Verlag.

Kossek, Brigitte (Hrsg.) (1999): Gegen-Rassismen. Konstruktionen, Interaktionen, Interventionen. Hamburg/Berlin: Argument.

Krämer, Sybille (2000): Subjektivität und Neue Medien. Ein Kommentar zur ‚Interaktivität'. In: Sandbothe/Marotzki 2000, 102-116.

Marotzki, Winfried (1990): Entwurf einer strukturalen Bildungstheorie: Biographietheoretische Auslegung von Bildungsprozessen in hochkomplexen Gesellschaften. Weinheim: Deutscher Studienverlag

Marotzki, Winfried (2007): Erinnerungskulturen im Internet. In: Kompetenzzentrum Informelle Bildung 2007, 93-103.

Massey, Doreen/Jess, Pat (Hrsg.) (1995): A Place in the World? New York: Oxford University Press/The Open University.

Mead, George Herbert (1934): Mind, self and society from the standpoint of the social behaviorist. Chicago: The University of Chicago Press.

Mecheril, Paul (2003): Prekäre Verhältnisse. Über natio-ethno-kulturelle (Mehrfach-)-Zugehörigkeit. Münster: Waxmann.

Mecheril, Paul/Hoffarth, Britta (2006): Adoleszenz und Migration. Zur Bedeutung von Zugehörigkeitsordnungen. In: King/Koller 2006, 221-240.

Räthzel, Nora (1999): Hybridität ist die Antwort, aber was war noch mal die Frage? In: Kossek 1999, 204 - 219.

Riegel, Christine/Geisen, Thomas (2007) (Hrsg.): Jugend, Zugehörigkeit und Migration. Subjektpositionierungen im Kontext von Jugendkultur, Ethnizitäts- und Geschlechterkonstruktionen. Wiesbaden: VS Verlag.

Rutherford, Jonathan (Hrsg.) (1990): Identity: Community, Culture, Difference. London: Lawrence & Wishart.

Sandbothe, Mike/Marotzki, Winfried (2000): Subjektivität und Öffentlichkeit. Köln: Herbert von Halem.

Sandbothe, Mike (2001): Pragmatische Medienphilosophie. Grundlegung einer neuen Disziplin im Zeitalter des Internet. Weilerswist: Velbrück Wissenschaft.

Sauer, Martina/Goldberg, Andreas (2006): Türkeistämmige Migranten in Nordrhein-Westfalen. Ergebnisse der siebten Mehrthemenbefragung. Essen: Stiftung Zentrum für Türkeistudien.

Schmidt, Jan-Hinrik/Paus-Hasebrink, Ingrid/Hasebrink, Uwe (2009) (Hrsg.): Heranwachsen mit dem Social Web. Zur Rolle von Web 2.0-Angeboten im Alltag von Jugendlichen und jungen Erwachsenen. Kurzfassung des Endberichts für die LfM. Online: http://www.hans bredow-institut.de/webfm_send/367 [20.06.2009]

Schlobinski, Peter. (Hrsg.): Von *hdl* bis *cul8r*. Sprache und Kommunikation in den Neuen Medien. Mannheim: Dudenverlag.

Schulte, Joachim (2003): Die Internet-Nutzung von Deutsch-Türken. In: Becker/Behnisch 2003, 115-123.

Simon, Erik (2007): Migranten und Medien 2007. Zielsetzung, Konzeption und Basisdaten einer repräsentativen Studie der ARD/ZDF-Medienkommission. In: Media Perspektiven, 9/2007, 426-435.

Stojanov, Krassimir (2006): Bildung und Anerkennung. Soziale Voraussetzungen von Selbst-Entwicklung und Welt-Erschließung. Wiesbaden: VS Verlag.

Taylor, Charles (1997): Multikulturalismus und die Politik der Anerkennung. Frankfurt am Main: Fischer.

Wagner, Ulrike/Brüggen, Niels/Gebel, Christa (2009): Web 2.0 als Rahmen für Selbstdarstellung und Vernetzung Jugendlicher. Analyse jugendnaher Plattformen und ausgewählter Selbstdarstellungenvon 14- bis 20-Jährigen. Erster Teil der Studie „Das Internet als Rezeptions- und Präsentationsplattform für Jugendliche" im Auftrage der BLM. Online: http://www.jff.de/dateien/Bericht_Web_2.0_Selbstdarstellungen_JFF_2009.pdf [29.06.2009]

Welsch, Wolfgang (2000): Virtual to Begin With? In: Sandbothe/Marotzki 2000, 25-60.

Wensierski, Hans-Jürgen von/Lübcke, Claudia (Hrsg.) (2007): Junge Muslime in Deutschland. Lebenslagen, Aufwachsprozesse und Jugendkulturen. Opladen & Farmington Hills: Verlag Barbara Budrich.

Zirfas, Jörg/Jörissen, Benjamin (2007): Phänomenologien der Identität. Human-, sozial- und kulturwissenschaftliche Analysen. Wiesbaden: VS Verlag.

Virtuelle Räume und die Hybridisierung der Alltagswelt

von Alexander Unger

Einleitung

In der sozialwissenschaftlichen Diskussion wird zunehmend die Frage behandelt, wie sich die Verbreitung digitaler Medientechnologien auf die soziale Lebenswelt sowie die individuelle Existenzbewältigung und Persönlichkeitsentwicklung auswirkt. Blickt man zurück, so wurde die Frage nach dem Für und Wieder von Technisierung und Medialisierung zumeist mit einer euphorischen Bejahung oder einer extremen Ablehnung beantwortet. In der öffentlichen Diskussion finden sich dementsprechend auch eine Vielzahl von Stimmen, die in der Verbreitung neuer Medien und Medientechnologien einen Verfalls- und Degenerationsprozess sehen (Nolda 2002, 40f.; Unger 2009, 109f.). Nach dem Kino, Comics und dem Fernsehen stehen heute besonders die so genannten neuen Medien im Verdacht, das soziale und kulturelle Leben zu deformieren und die individuelle Bewusstseinsbildung durch die Ausbildung einer medialen Scheinwelt zu unterlaufen.[1] Weitgehend unstrittig ist in der wissenschaftlichen Diskussion hingegen, dass Neue Medien und softwarebasierte Umgebungen, sowohl in der Arbeitswelt als auch im Bereich der Freizeit, zu einem integralen Bestandteil unseres alltäglichen Handelns werden. Vor diesem Hintergrund wird es immer schwerer sie bei der Untersuchung gesellschaftlicher Strukturen und des Sozialraums auszublenden.

Ein entscheidender Unterschied der Neuen Medien im Vergleich zu den klassischen Massenmedien ist dabei, dass Neue Medien zunehmend Anwendungen anbieten, die eine neue, virtuelle Handlungssphäre eröffnen, die in vielfältiger und sehr enger Weise mit realen Handlungen und Sozialität verknüpft sind. Viele Aktivitäten und Handlungsformen, die als nicht-medialisiert und in materiellen Räumen verankert geläufig sind, verlagern sich in oder verbinden sich mit dieser Sphäre, die auf Digitalität, Interaktivität und Vernetzung basiert (vgl. Issing/Klimsa 2002; Schulmeister 2002). Dies reicht vom Austausch von Dokumenten über die Organisation von Arbeitsprozessen, das kooperative Erstellen von Inhalten, die private Peer-Group Kommunikation und die eigene Selbstdarstellung, bis hin zu neuen Formen des gemeinschaftlichen Spielens und der Partnersuche. Trotzdem ist man auch in der sozialwissenschaftlichen Diskussion eher zurückhaltend geblieben, was die Integration der virtuellen Sphäre bzw. von Virtualität in tragende Theoriekontexte anging.

1 Da die Bezeichnung „Neu“ eine relative ist, wechseln im Laufe der Zeit die Medien, welche als neu bezeichnet werden. So wurden u.a. Kabelfernsehen, BTX oder Multimedia-Computer als Neue Medien bezeichnet. Die Argumente zu ihrer Kritik, aber auch zu ihrer Befürwortung, bleiben dabei weitestgehend gleich.

Dabei liegt es auf der Hand, dass in einer Gesellschaft, die grundlegend durch neue Medientechnologien geprägt ist, auch mediale Formate, Architekturen und Interaktionsformen einen integralen Bestandteil von Sozialität darstellen und sich in Sozialisationsprozesse einschalten, was nicht zu letzt die Diskussion um Mediensozialisation verdeutlicht (vgl. Hoffmann/Mikos 2007; Süss 2004). Damit stellt sich allerdings auch die Frage, in welchem Verhältnis diese medialen Formate und die durch sie eröffneten Räume zum „realen" Sozialraum stehen bzw. wie sie in diesem zu verorten sind. Haben wir es mit getrennten Bereichen und Formen von Sozialität zu tun? Findet eine Überschreibung bzw. Virtualisierung des lebensweltlichen Raums und seiner Sozialität statt, was möglicherweise zu deren Verschwinden führt (vgl. Baudrillard 1996)? Oder verbinden sich diese beiden Sphären vielmehr zu einem hybriden Konglomerat, das zunehmend als Hintergrund von Sozialität und Sozialisation zu sehen ist?

Der vorliegende Artikel geht von der These aus, dass mit der Verbreitung digitaler, softwarebasierter Medientechnologie eine neue Stufe der Vermischung von real-materiellen und virtuell-softwarebasierten Räumen eingesetzt hat, die zu einer Entgrenzung und Hybridisierung innerhalb der sozialen Lebenswelt führt und Anlass bietet gängige Konzepte von Sozialität, Raum und Räumlichkeit zu überdenken. Die sich so ergebende Perspektive sieht die Medialisierung bzw. Hybridisierung der Lebenswelt weniger als einen Verfallsprozess, sondern vielmehr als Kernphänomen nachmoderner Gesellschaftskonstellationen, die zu grundlegenden Transformationen führen, welche auch für die Sozialwissenschaften von zunehmender Bedeutung sind. Diese Transformationsprozesse wurden und werden in vielfältigen Theoriekontexten diskutiert. Dabei scheint es, obwohl die Bezeichnungen ‚virtuelle Räume' oder ‚mediale Architekturen' mittlerweile geläufig sind, gerade in Hinblick auf die Kategorie Raum noch Nachhohlbedarf in der (sozial-) wissenschaftlichen Auseinandersetzung zu geben.[2] Vor dem Hintergrund einer voranschreitenden Medialisierung der Lebenswelt bzw. des Sozialraums scheint es daher angemessen zu sein, diesen (medien-) technologischen Vermischungsprozess und seine Konsequenzen auch aus einer raumtheoretischen Perspektive stärker in den Blick zu nehmen.

Der Artikel gliedert sich dabei in fünf Abschnitte. Im ersten Teil wird kurz auf die Konstitution der Wissensgesellschaft und die basale Bedeutung digitaler Medientechnologie für diese gesellschaftliche Figuration eingegangen. Hieran schließt sich eine Auseinandersetzung mit Donna Harraways Manifest für Cyborgs an, dessen zentrale These der Hybridisierung nachgezeichnet und dann auf die Vermischung real-materieller und virtuell-softwarebasierter Räume bezogen werden soll. Im folgenden Abschnitt werden

2 Es scheint demnach für die Gesellschaftskonstellation der so genannten Informations- und Wissensgesellschaft typisch zu sein, dass sie sich durch eine neue Stufe der Durchdringung der sozialen Lebenswelt mit Technik und Medien auszeichnet (vgl. Unger 2008). Diese These ist u.a. unter der Bezeichnung „mediatic turn" diskutiert worden (vgl. Hug 2007).

Beispiele für verschiedene Formen der Hybridisierung des lebensweltlichen Raums angeführt. Diese sollen veranschaulichen, dass Hybridisierung einerseits technologisch induziert wird, auf der anderen Seite aber auch eine individuelle Integrations- und Sinnstiftungsleistung darstellt. Wie gezeigt werden soll sind diese beiden Formen der Hybridisierung weniger getrennt, als vielmehr als zwei Seiten desselben Phänomens zu behandeln. Im vierten Teil des Artikels findet eine vertiefte Auseinandersetzung mit der Erschließung und Aneignung des Sozialraums und der Verortung virtueller Räume in diesem Prozess aus einer phänomenologischen Perspektive statt. Abschließend werden die Ergebnisse dieser Auseinandersetzung mit dem Phänomen der Hybridsierung abgeglichen und einige Schlussfolgerungen aus medienpädagogischer Perspektive gezogen.

Zur Konstitution der Wissensgesellschaft

In der Diskussion um die Wissensgesellschaft herrscht weitgehend Einigkeit über die immense Bedeutung der Wissen bei der gesellschaftlichen Reproduktion und Weiterentwicklung einerseits, sowie bei der gesellschaftlichen Partizipation und damit auch der individuellen Persönlichkeitsentwicklung andererseits, zukommt (Höhne 2003, 27 ff.). Zu den vielen bejahenden Stimmen dieser Entwicklung mischen sich allerdings auch durchaus kritische Töne dieser neuen, wissensbasierten gesellschaftlichen Formation, die u.a, von Richard Sennett (2006 und 2007) und Allan Ehrenberg (2004) vorgetragen werden. Betrachtet man diese Kritik genauer, so ist festzustellen, dass der Wandel zu einer Wissensgesellschaft den Begriff des Wissens nicht unberührt lässt und zudem über den Bereich des Wissens hinausweist. Wissen scheint in diesem Kontext vielmehr als Chiffre für die Fähigkeit zu stehen, auf die sich mit erhöhter Geschwindigkeit wandelnden gesellschaftlichen Bedingungen zu reagieren; ein Prozess, der nicht zu letzt durch die Verbreitung neuer Medien forciert wird. Diese gesteigerte Anpassungsforderung gilt sowohl für Wirtschaftsunternehmen als auch für die Individuen, die zunehmend vor der Herausforderung stehen sich wandelnden Gegebenheiten flexibel anzupassen und dabei auch zunehmend für Risiken die Verantwortung zu tragen, die jenseits ihres Einflussbereichs liegen (vgl. Sennett 2006, 35).

Diese Entwicklungstendenz, die immer weitere Bereiche und Bevölkerungsgruppen betrifft, wird durch zwei grundlegende Entwicklungen in extremer Weise beschleunigt und potenziert: die Globalisierung einerseits und eine umfassende Medialisierung durch den Einsatz von Informations- und Kommunikationstechnologien (IuK-T) andererseits. Diese beiden Entwicklungen werden oft getrennt voneinander behandelt, dabei lässt sich durchaus zeigen, dass beide Prozesse eng miteinander verknüpft sind und die Verbreitung neuer Medientechnik die technologische Voraussetzung für den Prozess der Globalisierung bereitstellt. Der Prozess der Globalisierung wird dabei in der sozialwissenschaftlichen Diskussion als einer verstanden, der mit massiven Tendenzen zur

Entgrenzung, Enttraditionalisierung und zur Steigerung von Komplexität bzw. Kontingenz einhergeht. In diesem Sinne sind die Subjekte zunehmend mit einer Situation konfrontiert, in der bekannte und tradierte Strukturen in einen Auflösungsprozess übergehen. Die oben beschriebene Bereitschaft zum permanenten Wandel und Transformation scheint die einzige Form von Sicherheit in einer Konstellation darzustellen, die kaum mehr Planungssicherheit ermöglicht.

Diese veränderten Bedingungen beschränken sich dabei allerdings nicht nur auf den Bereich Erwerbstätigkeit, sondern zunehmend auch auf den Bereich der Freizeit und Regeneration. Stellt man die Bedeutung neuer Medientechnologie für die Entstehung der Wissensgesellschaft in Rechnung, so deutet sich schon an, von welcher zentralen Bedeutung eine entsprechende Kompetenz im Umgang mit Medien auch für eine befriedigende Gestaltung der Freizeit ist (vgl. Süss 2004, 56 ff.). Auch im privaten Bereich sind Kommunikation, Konsum, regenerative und kreative Aktivitäten zunehmend an digitale Technologien, softwarebasierte Anwendungen und Datennetzwerke geknüpft. In der sozialwissenschaftlichen Diskussion setzt sich daher zunehmend die Einsicht durch, dass besonders die Lebensphase der Jugend heute stark medialisiert ist und es insofern gerechtfertigt ist, von einer „Jugend der Medien" bzw. einer „Medienjugend" zu sprechen (vgl. Treumann et. al. 2007, 27 ff.). Die Anforderungen im Bereich der Handlungskompetenzen, die mit dieser Entwicklung einhergehen, werden dabei zunehmend zu einer Selbstverständlichkeit. Im Folgenden soll nun dieser Prozess der Medialisierung und die mit diesem einhergehenden Entgrenzungsprozesse - als Kernphänomene der gegenwärtigen gesellschaftlichen Verfassung - stärker in den Blick genommen werden.

Hybridisierung als Signum der postindustriellen Gesellschaft

Ende der 1990er Jahre veröffentlichte Donna Harraway ihr provokantes Manifest für Cyborgs, indem sie den Versuch unternahm, den feministischen Diskurs auf eine Basis zu stellen, die sich auf Augenhöhe mit der aktuellen Entwicklungen in Wissenschaft und Technik und deren Konsequenzen und Herausforderungen für die Konstitution von Subjektivität, bewegte. Harraway (1995, 33) entwickelt in ihrem Manifest einen „ironischen, politischen Mythos", mit dem sie ein kritisches Schlaglicht auf die dualistische Konzeption des westlichen Denkens wirft. Eine der zentralen Thesen, die im Manifest für Cyborgs entwickelt wird, ist, dass die wissenschaftlich-technische Entwicklung die Dualismen, die das westliche Denken bestimmten, in einen Entgrenzungs- und Auflösungsprozess überführt hat. Klassische dualistische Unterscheidungen wie die von Mensch/Tier, künstlich/natürlich, Mensch/Technik und damit letztlich auch Mann/Frau seien vieldeutig und schillernd geworden und hätten ihre klare, distinktive

Kraft verloren.[3] Viele der Merkmale, mit denen der Mensch von Technik oder dem Tier abgegrenzt wurde, werden zunehmend im Verhalten von Tieren nachgewiesen (Werkzeugeinsatz, Sozialverhalten usw.) oder von Technik, besonders von der Computertechnologie, simuliert:

> „Die Maschinen des späten 20. Jahrhunderts haben die Differenz von natürlich und künstlich, Körper und Geist, selbstgelenkter und außengesteuerter Entwicklung, sowie viele andere Unterscheidungen, die Organismen und Maschinen zu trennen vermochten, höchst zweideutig werden lassen" (Harraway 1995, 37).

Auch durch Fortschritte im medizinischen Bereich wird die Abgrenzung Mensch/Technik unterlaufen, da zunehmend technische Artefakte zum Bestandteil des Körpers werden. Diese reichen von der Brille über Prothesen bis hin zu Herzschrittmachern. Harraway stellt hier die provokante Frage, wo die Grenze zu ziehen sei, bei der der natürliche Mensch durch technische Implantate zum Cyborg wird. Entgegen der konservativen Argumentation, die diese Entwicklung als Entfremdung beklagt oder mit ihr sogar das Ende des Subjekts eingeläutet sieht (vgl. Anders 1994, 45 ff.), hebt Harraway vor allem die Potenziale dieser durch Technologie provozierten Auflösung hervor.[4] Die natürliche Einheit, die als grundlegend für das westliche Subjekt angesehen wird und deren Verletzung durch Technik die zentrale Angst der kulturpessimistischen Technik- und Medientheorie darstellte, wird hier ironisch unterlaufen und als eine überholte Setzung bzw. als repressive Erzählung enttarnt. Mit dem „Zusammenbruch aller Bezeichnungen des Menschen" sieht Harrawy an die Stelle der klassischen Identität „eine von Andersheit und Differenz ausgehende Form postmoderner Identität" (Harraway 1995, 41) treten, die hochpolitisch sei.

Harraway plädiert daher dafür, den Status des westlichen Subjekts zu überdenken und mit dieser neuen technisierten Subjektkonstitution zu experimentieren, die ohne die Momente der Ursprünglichkeit, Einheit und Natürlichkeit auskommt. In diesem Sinne proklamiert sie: „Cyborgs sind unsere Ontologie" (Harraway 1995, 34). Diese neue Subjektkonstitution kann als „hybrid" verstanden werden, als ein Zustand, der durch

3 Die von Harraway beschriebene „Hybridisierung" , die sie u.a. an der Vermischung von Biotechnologie und dem menschlichen Körper beschreibt und die zu einer Auflösung des westlichen Selbst führt, lässt sich meiner Meinung nach auch auf das Verhältnis von Realität und Virtualität übertragen. Harraway selbst führt im Kontext der Auseinandersetzung mit der „Informatik der Herrschaft" die Dichotomie „Repräsentation/Simulation" (Harraway 1995, 48) als Erste an.

4 Anders bezeichnet den Wunsch nach der Verschmelzung mit der (Industrie-) Maschinerie bzw. die Anpassung an deren Maßstab als „angemaßte Selbsterniedrigung und hybride Demut" (Anders 1994, 47), als Selbstmord und „Vernichtung des Menschen qua Menschen" (Anders 1994, 48). Indem der Mensch diese Verbindung mit den Maschinen eingeht erfindet er sich selbst neu, ähnlich wie dies Harraway sieht. Allerdings bedeutet für Anders diese Neuerfindung die Aufgabe des Subjektstatus und damit der menschlichen Freiheit, was letztlich seinen Untergang bedeutet. Hier zeigen sich die Bewertungen der voranschreitenden Technologisierung von Harraway und Anders als diametral entgegengesetzt.

die zunehmende Verschmelzung des menschlichen Leibs mit neuen Technologien sukzessive hergestellt wird und die den „Cyborg“ als eine positive Verbindung von Mensch und Technik hervorbringt. Diese Entwicklung erfordert allerdings auch eine neue Form des politischen Denkens, das sich ebenfalls nicht mehr über vermeintlich natürliche Konzepte definieren kann: „Daneben entwickelt sich aber auch eine andere mögliche Strategie der Koalitionsbildung: Affinität statt Identität“ (Harraway 1995, 41). Die These einer anti-essentialistischen „Ontologie“, als Ausgangsbasis für politisches Handeln, die vor allem das Moment affirmativer oder zufälliger Verbindungen von Menschen als Grundlage der sozialen Organisation betont, ist sicher streitbar. Allerdings zeigt sich gerade im virtuellen Raum des WWW die Form der affirmativen Bindung als prägend. Harraway selbst sieht „das Weben von Netzen“ (Harraway 1995, 60) als eine mögliche neue, soziale und politische Praxis an, die man durchaus mit den interaktiven Räumen der virtuellen Sphäre in Verbindung bringen kann. Die Figur des Cyborgs bringt demnach eine Perspektive ins Spiel, die auf die Verbindung von Mensch, Sozialität, Politik und neuen Technologien verweist und die Potenziale dieser vermeintlich unnatürlichen Kopplung auslotet. Vor dem Hintergrund einer solchen Theorie muss dann auch „die Beziehung von Organismus und Maschine“ nicht mehr als „Grenzkrieg“ (Harraway 1995, 35) dargestellt werden. Vielmehr können Übergänge und Vermischungen, die zur Entgrenzung tragender Dualismen führen, auch hinsichtlich neuer Gestaltungsoptionen und Möglichkeiten untersucht werden. Harraway plädiert vor diesem Hintergrund dafür, „die Vermischung dieser Grenzen zu *genießen* und *Verantwortung* bei ihrer Konstruktion zu übernehmen“ (Harraway 1995, 35, Hervorh. im Orig.).

Ob die hier angesprochene biologische Technisierung in Form der Implementierung technischer Geräte in den menschlichen Leib es rechtfertigt, nicht mehr vom Menschen, sondern vom Cyborg zu sprechen, kann kontrovers diskutiert werden. Weniger strittig scheint zu sein, dass die ‚Hybridisierung‘ zunehmend prägend für die Konstitution der gegenwärtigen gesellschaftlichen Verhältnisse ist, in der sich die Individuen bewegen und ihre Existenz bestreiten. In diesem Sinne betrifft Hybridisierung nicht nur unseren Leib durch Formen der technischen Implementierung, sondern neben dieser biopolitischen Perspektive zeigt sich auch die Arbeits-, Alltags- und Sozialwelt von Hybridisierung betroffen, was sich auch auf die Räumlichkeit des Sozialraums auswirkt. Der Fokus liegt dann allerdings weniger auf dem Dualismus natürlich und künstlich, sondern auf dem Dualismus von Virtualität und Realität, wobei diese durchaus auch gewisse Überschneidungen aufweisen.

Eine ähnliche anti-essentialistische Argumentation findet sich auch in Wolfgangs Welsch bekannten Aufsatz zum Thema „Wirklichkeit“, in dem er geläufige Realitätsmodelle vergleicht und diskutiert (vgl. Welsch 2000). Er unterscheidet hierbei ontologische und formale Realitätskonzepte, die jeweils den Blick auf Welt, Gesellschaft und letztlich auch auf die Bedeutung von Medien prägen. Im Rahmen von ontologischen

Realitätskonzepten wird Virtualität als Gefahr für Realität und Wahrheit angesehen. Dieses Konzept basiert auf einer Zwei-Welten-Lehre, in der die alltägliche oder medial erzeugte Wirklichkeit sich als Scheinwirklichkeit zeigt, durch die hindurch zu einer wahrhaften, objektiven Wirklichkeit vorzustoßen ist. Besonders den neuen Medien und so genannten virtuellen Realitäten (VR), wird zugerechnet eine Scheinrealität zu produzieren und so die eigentliche Realität zu verdecken, zu verdrängen oder gar unwiederbringlich zu überschreiben. Vor dem Hintergrund formaler Realitätskonzepte zeigt sich die vermeintliche Bedrohung durch Virtualität allerdings nicht als sonderlich dramatisch, weil hier Wirklichkeit und gesellschaftliche Realität schon immer als Ergebnisse eines sozialen Aushandlungs- und Konstruktionsprozesses angesehen werden: Alle Hervorbringungen des Menschen, seine ganze Kultur und der Sinnhorizont seines Handelns sind in diesem Sinne „künstlich" (vgl. Berger/Luckmann 2007). Aus dieser Perspektive zeigt sich die virtuelle Sinnsphäre weniger als eine Bedrohung, sondern vielmehr als eine basale und unersetzbare Sinndimension der sozialen Lebenswelt. Trotz der positiven Grundeinstellung gegenüber Medien und medial erzeugter „Realitäten", die aus einem formalen Ansatz resultiert, bleibt hier die konkrete Rolle, die Medien in den angesprochenen Prozessen der Sinnkonstitution und der Anreicherung der Lebenswelt spielen, unklar.

Eine Auslegung der Hybridisierungsthese, die weniger Medizin- und Biotechnologien in den Blick nimmt, sondern die Neuen Medien und den Bereich des Bewusstseins sowie der Wahrnehmung, muss dabei nicht im Widerspruch zu Harraways Intention stehen. Vielmehr wird hier nur der Fokus etwas anders justiert. Die Frage, die sich nun stellt, ist, mit welchen Formen der Vermischung wir konfrontiert sind, wie diese „genossen" und nicht mehr als „Grenzkrieg" behandelt werden könnten und was in diesem Kontext unter einer bewussten Gestaltung zu verstehen ist. Die kurze Auseinandersetzung mit den von Welsch behandelten Realitätskonzepten hat dabei verdeutlicht, dass durch eine ontologische Argumentation ausgeblendet wird, dass das Handeln des Menschen schon immer virtuelle Anteile bzw. eine virtuell-sinnhafte Dimension aufweist. Wenn nun die Individuen ihre Aktivitäten zunehmend an eine technologisch erzeugte virtuelle Sphäre koppeln, dort Erfahrungen machen und Gemeinschaften ausbilden, ist es wenig hilfreich, diese Erfahrungen und Handlungen als per se defizitär zu behandeln. Vielmehr ist zu klären, welche Bedeutung diese Erweiterung der Lebenswelt für den Menschen und für sein Welt- und Selbstverhältnis aufweist und welche Rolle neue Medientechnologien hierbei spielen.

Hybride Räume in der Alltagswelt

Die Beispiele für virtuelle Räume, die durch die Neuen Medien eröffnet werden und deren Tendenz zur Verschmelzung mit dem real-materiellen Raum, sind mittlerweile zahllos. Es sollen daher hier nur einige wenige Beispiele angeführt werden, die zwei unterschiedliche Formen der räumlichen Hybridisierung erkennen lassen. Dies ist zum einen eine technologisch induzierte Form der Hybridisierung, die Schnittstellen zwischen dem virtuellen und dem lebensweltlichen Erfahrungsraum schafft. Zum anderen soll ein näherer Blick auf hybride Verknüpfungen und Übergänge gelegt werden, die quasi vom Individuum selbst geschaffen werden und die etwas umfassender diskutiert werden soll. Auch für diese zweite Form der Hybridisierung sind die Neuen Medien als technologische Basis grundlegend. Diese werden hier aber weniger als determinierend für die Art und Weise der Aneignung oder der geschaffenen Verbindungen gesehen, sondern sie eröffnen vielmehr einen komplexen Möglichkeitsraum, der, wenn auch nicht frei von kommerziellen und machtvollen Strukturen, zur Selektion und Integration auffordert (vgl. Sesink 2004, 96f.). Beide hier vorgestellte Formen der Hybridisierung sind daher nicht als getrennt zu verstehen, sondern vielmehr als zwei Seiten desselben Prozesses zusehen, der, wie gezeigt werden soll, sowohl einer spezifischen technologischen Grundlage als auch der Handlungs-, Selektions- und Sinnstiftungsfähigkeit des Menschen bedarf.

Wirft man einen kurzen Blick auf die technologische Seite, so zeigt sich, dass im WWW zunehmend Anwendungen und Angebote zu finden sind, die keinen eigenständigen geschlossenen Sinnbereich etablieren wollen, sondern die stark an den real-materiellen Raum an- bzw. rückgebunden sind und auf dessen Anreicherung abzielen. Diese ‚Funktion' der medialen Anreicherung bzw. Erweiterung wird oft unter dem Stichwort ‚augmented Reality' diskutiert. Eine solche Anreicherung kann durch den Einsatz von Cybergoggles oder das Einblenden von Head-up-Displays auf der Windschutzscheibe eines Autos realisiert werden. Über diese Technologie können kontextspezifische Zusatzinformationen visualisiert und mit dem „realen"' Raum verbunden werden, die dieser so nicht bietet, die aber das individuelle Handeln nachhaltig beeinflussen können. Bekannt ist das Beispiel aus der Automobilherstellung, bei der dem Mechaniker über Cybergoggles virtuell veranschaulicht wird, wie und wo ein bestimmtes Teil (z.B. das Türschloss) einzubauen ist. Es handelt sich bei solchen Formen der augmented Reality also um eine direkt-visuelle Vermischung von real-materiellen und virtuellem Raum, die einen hybriden Erfahrungs- und Handlungsraum erzeugen. Die Anwendungen, auf die nun eingegangen werden soll, sind in technischer Hinsicht sehr viel einfacher aufgebaut und die Hybridisierung findet hier auch nicht in so unmittelbarer Weise über die visuelle Ebene statt. Trotzdem kann an ihnen verdeutlichen werden, wie der lebensweltliche

Raum und dessen Sinnstrukturen durch neue softwarebasierte Anwendungen erweitert und angereichert werden kann.

Ein populäres Beispiel für eine solche „anreichernde" Anwendung ist ‚Google-Maps'[5]. Google-Maps kann wie eine ganz normale Karte benutzt werden, d.h. man kann einen bestimmten Ort, Geschäfte oder Einrichtungen suchen und diese aus der Vogelperspektive betrachten. Gegenwärtig kann bei der Darstellung zwischen der Anzeigeform einer normalen Karte, eines Satellitenbildes oder einer kombinierten Geländedarstellung gewählt werden. Ebenso kann diese Anwendung als Routenplaner verwendet werden. Neben diesen klassischen Funktionen, die auch schon „virtuelles" Wissen über bestimmte Orte und Gegenden vermitteln, können Nutzer in Google-Maps (in der Kombination mit Webangeboten wie Qype[6] und Wikipedia[7]) auch Zusatzinformationen wie Bilder, Hinweise, Bewertungen, Abhandlungen und Erfahrungsberichte einstellen. Auf diese Weise werden nicht nur Adressendatenbanken mit Karten und Satellitenbildern kombiniert, sondern auch Alltagserfahrung oder biografische Erlebnisse in visueller und textueller Form eingebunden.

Als Nutzer kann man so auf die „objektivierten" Erfahrungen, Bedeutungen und Sinnstrukturen anderer Personen zugreifen, ohne zu diesen in einen persönlichen Kontakt zu treten. Zudem können bei mehreren Berichten zu einem Ort oder einer Einrichtung die verschiedenen Beurteilungen und Darstellungen verglichen und die relevanten Informationen herausgefiltert werden, wobei durchaus Widersprüche in den Darstellungen auftreten können. Oft enthalten diese Bewertungen auch biografische Notizen oder Berichte über „singuläre" Erfahrungen und Ereignisse. Sucht man z.B. in den Bewertungen zu Discotheken, so finden sich oft auch Anmerkungen zu der Rolle, die dieser Ort in der Jugend der bewertenden Person gespielt hat oder unter welchen Umständen der Ort besucht wurde und was sich dort ereignete. Die Anwendung integriert in diesem Sinne auch eine lebensweltliche Sinndimension und ermöglicht es, Bedeutungen und Sinnstrukturen in das eher formal-objektive Format ‚Karte' einzuschreiben. Auf diese Weise können Erwartungen, Bedeutungen und Einschätzungen, mit denen eine Person bestimmte Orte aufsucht, virtuell vorgeprägt werden, wodurch die Trennung des real-materiellen und des virtuellen Erfahrungsraums zunehmend schwieriger wird.[8]

Als weiteres Beispiel für diese technische Hybridisierung des lebensweltlichen Erfahrungsraums kann ‚Plazes'[9] angeführt werden. Auch dieses Angebot ist interessant

5 http://maps.google.com

6 http://www.qype.com

7 http://www.wikipedia.org

8 Ein entscheidender Unterschied zu gängigen Reise- oder Stadtführen, die eine ähnliche Funktion der virtuellen „Vorprägung" haben können, ist dabei die hohe Dynamik und Flexibilität dieses Formats, die große Masse an Beitragenden und die Ausrichtung auf „User-generated Content", die sehr viel stärker biografisch geprägtes Wissen und singuläre Ereignisse ins Spiel bringt.

9 http://www.plazes.com

in Hinblick auf die gegenseitige Durchdringung von virtuellem und real-materiellem Raum, sowie auf die „Objektivierung“ lebensweltlicher Bedeutungs- und Handlungsstrukturen. Während bei Google-Maps eher eine individuelle Beschreibung und Bewertung aller möglichen Orte im Vordergrund steht, erlaubt Plazes eine individuelle Geodatenbank anzulegen, in der die jeweiligen Lieblings- und Alltags- und Arbeitsorte mit den aktuellen Aktivitäten eingespeichert werden können. Als Nutzer von Plazes kann man diese Informationen für Freunde, Bekannte und Kollegen freigeben. So erfährt man dann z.B. dass ein Kollege gerade einen Vortrag auf einer Computermesse hält oder ein Bekannter in einem schwedischen Möbelhaus zu Mittag isst. Ohne detaillierter auf die weiteren Funktionen von Plazes einzugehen oder Anwendungen mit einem ähnlichen Charakter wie z.B. ‚Twitter'[10] zu diskutieren, zeigt sich hier eine deutliche Verzahnung von real-materiellem und virtuellem Raum, die die Objektivierung von und den Zugriff auf den Alltagsraum bestimmter Personen sowie dessen Handlungsstrukturen und sinnhafte Gliederung erlaubt. Anwendungen wie Plazes oder Google-Maps eröffnen in diesem Sinne neue Formen und Möglichkeiten der „Ent-fernung“ (vgl. Heidegger 1993, 105), d.h. der Auflösung von Ferne und Distanz zu Orten und Personen, aber auch zu lebensweltlichen Erfahrungs- und Bedeutungsstrukturen, durch softwarebasierte Anwendung.[11] In diesem Sinne regt Hybridisierung zum Nachdenken über die Konstitution von Raum und Räumlichkeit, von Nähe und Distanz, sowie der Auswirkung von Hybridisierung auf die soziale Alltagswelt als Erfahrungs- und Existenzraum an.

Um diese räumliche Hybridisierungstendenz durch Medialisierung noch etwas näher zu beleuchten, soll nun der Fokus von den technologischen Angeboten auf die Aneignungs- und Integrationsformen aus der Perspektive der Nutzer gelegt werden, also auf die subjektive Seite der Hybridisierung. Die Vermischung und Entgrenzung des Sozialraums findet aus dieser Perspektive über die subjektive Erfahrungswelt statt, dem u.a. in der sozialwissenschaftlichen Tradition des symbolischen Interaktionismus (SI), aber auch des Konstruktivismus, eine eigenständige Bedeutung gegenüber einer (vermeintlich) objektiven Wirklichkeit zukommt. Bei der Ausbildung dieser Erfahrungswelt kommt der Etablierung von Bedeutungsstrukturen und der intersubjektiven „Anreicherung“ von Objekten mit Bedeutung eine zentrale Rolle zu (vgl. Charon 2001).

Welche Rolle in diesem Bedeutungsgefüge mediale Angebote spielen und inwiefern sie in den Prozess der Hybridisierung des lebensweltlichen Raums eingebunden sind, kann ein stückweit an der Studie „Neue Wege durch die konvergente Medienwelt“ (Wagner/Theunert 2006) verdeutlicht werden. Diese Studie untersucht, wie sich Ju-

10 http://www.twitter.com

11 Auch wenn diese diskutierten Beispiele auf der technologischen Seite verortet wurden, zeigt sich deutlich, dass solche Anwendungen nur dann existieren, wenn sie genutzt und entsprechende Informationen eingestellt und abgerufen werden.

gendliche durch das ständig wachsende crossmediale Medienuniversum bewegen und welche Wege sie hierbei einschlagen. Ein solches ‚crossmediales Universum' entsteht einerseits durch technische Konvergenz, d.h. mit dem Zusammenwachsen unterschiedlicher Medien und Medienformate, durch Digitalisierung, Vernetzung und Multimedialität, zum anderen durch Vermarktungsstrategien, die einen Inhalt über unterschiedliche Medien hinweg anbieten und so crossmediale Verweise, Verknüpfungen und Übergänge schaffen (vgl. Wagner/Theunert 2006, 15ff.). So werden zu einem bestimmten Inhalt ein Buch, zu diesem Buch ein Film und zum Film ein Computerspiel auf den Markt gebracht. Ergänzt werden diese Angebote durch Webseiten, virtuelle Kommunikationsplattformen bis hin zu kooperativen Online-Spielewelten und Webcommunities.

Eine der Ausgangsüberlegungen der Studie ist dabei, dass vor dem Hintergrund einer zunehmenden Medienkonvergenz die Einzelmedienforschung zunehmend an ihre Grenzen stößt und daher die verschiedenen Verknüpfungen zwischen den medialen Angeboten und ihre Qualität zu erforschen sei (vgl. Wagner/Theunert 2006, 14). Auf diese Weise kann untersucht werden, wie sich Jugendliche das crossmediale Universum aneignen und ob sie hierbei vor allem marktförmigen Verweisen folgen oder eigene Wege einschlagen, was als Anzeichen für einen mündigen Umgang gewertet werden kann. Im Hintergrund steht also die Vermutung, dass das vernetzte Medienuniversum neue und differenzierte Handlungs- und Aneignungsformen hervorbringt, die stärker selbstbestimmt oder (ökonomisch) determiniert sein können und die mit der individuellen Aneignung und Verknüpfung bestimmter medialer Angebote und Orte einhergeht.

Zu den interessanten Ergebnissen der Studie gehört auch eine Nutzertypologie, die fünf unterschiedliche Muster konvergenter Medienaneignung umfasst (vgl. Wagner/Theunert 2006, 83ff.). Diesen lassen u.a. eine andere Dimension des „Digital Divides" jenseits der Zugangs erkennen: Es sind vor allem Jugendliche mit hohem Bildungshintergrund, die sich ihre eigenen Wege durch das Medienuniversum suchen, die partizipative und eigenproduktive Formen nutzen und virtuelle Angebote und Gemeinschaften ganz selbstverständlich in ihren Alltag integrieren. Jugendliche mit niedrigerem Bildungshintergrund folgen hingegen eher marktförmigen Verknüpfungen und nutzen nur einen kleinen Teil des crossmedialen Angebots (vgl. Wagner/Theunert 2006, 130ff.).[12] Neben dieser grundsätzlichen Tendenz unterscheiden sich die verschiedenen Muster hinsichtlich der Nutzungsintensität, dem Grad der Integration bzw. Immersion in mediale Angebote, sowie den gesuchten „Gratifikationen" und verfolgten Interessen. Diese reichen von der Suche nach Zusatzinformationen, über den planvollen Ausbau des eigenen Erlebens und der Zugehörigkeit zu einer Kultwelt, bis zur Nutzung des

12 Allerdings finden sich auch in vermeintlich bildungsfernen Milieus eine überraschend hohes Mass an aktiver, produktiver und partizipativer Mediennutzung, wie die an die Konvergenzforschung anschließende Folgestudie „Medienhandeln in Hauptschulmilieus" zeigt (vgl. Wagner 2008).

medialen Raums als Präsentations- und Gestaltungsraum (vgl. Wagner/Theunert 2006, S. 83 ff.).

Die Studie zeigt zudem, dass in der medialen Sphäre nicht nur neue Angebote und „Orte" erschlossen, Interessen verfolgt oder Bindungen ausgebildet werden, sondern dass auch bereits bestehende Aktivitäten und Interessen fortgeführt und erweitert werden. Dies wird besonders deutlich an einem ergänzenden Untersuchungsinstrument, welches in der Studie eingesetzt wurde, das so genannte Präferenzbild. Mit diesem Instrument konnten die Befragten zeigen, welche medialen Interessen sie in welchem Ausmaß, mit welcher Funktion und in welchem sozialen Kontext verfolgen (vgl. Wagner/Theunert 2006, 49ff.). Die Auswertung der Präferenzbilder zeigte dabei, dass viele der medialen Interessen der Befragten stark sozial eingebunden sind und so vielfache Bezüge zum real-materiellen Raum und seiner Sozialität zeigen. Letztlich kann dies als Indiz für die zunehmende Integration der medialen oder virtuellen Sphäre in die jugendliche Lebenswelt interpretiert werden: Es zeigt sich, dass Jugendliche ihre Aktivitäten zunehmend mit virtuellen Elementen anreichern oder in die virtuelle Sphäre verlagern und dabei nicht nur passiv, sondern auch produktiv und sozial agieren.

Interpretiert man diese Ergebnisse etwas weiter als dies in der Studie intendiert wurde, so drängt sich der Eindruck auf, dass die Übergänge zwischen dem real-materiellen und dem medialen Raum von den Befragten kaum als deutliche Brüche wahrgenommen werden. In der subjektiven Wahrnehmung scheinen sich die Übergänge vielmehr fließend in einem einheitlichen Handlungsraum zu vollziehen, indem real-materielle und virtuelle Elemente stark miteinander verwoben sind und indem versucht wird Interessen zu folgen, Bedürfnisse zu befriedigen, Prestige zu erlangen oder soziale Kontakte herzustellen. Die vermeintlich harten Grenzen zwischen realen und virtuellen Räumen oder realer und virtueller Sozialität scheinen sich im alltäglichen Umgang zu verflüssigen und so eine hybride Erfahrungs- und Alltagswelt zu entstehen, in der sowohl den Eltern, Freunden, Institutionen und Gruppen, aber auch Chatpartnern und den medialen Unterhaltungs- wie Informationsangeboten ein Platz im individuellen „Präferenzraum" zugewiesen wird. Virtuelle Angebote und Orte werden so als bedeutungshaft integriert und mit Bedürfnissen und Interessen verknüpft. Die Rede von „neuen Wegen" legt dabei nahe, dass die Angebote der digitalen Medien durchaus als räumliche Umwelt(en) verstanden werden können, durch die man sich bewegen, in denen man agieren, produzieren sowie verschiedene Orte aufsuchen und diese mit Sinn anreichern kann - in denen man sich aber auch orientieren und die Gefahren vorgepflasterter Wege und Verweisungen erkennen können muss. Die Rede vom „Raum" und von „Wegen" geht in diesem Sinne über eine rein metaphorische Bedeutung hinaus, da diese aus der subjektiven Sicht eine sehr reale Bedeutung für das Alltagshandeln erhalten. Sie sind bedeutsamer Bestandteil der individuell angeeigneten Umwelt und zeigen sich zunehmend mit anderen Orten, Personen und Ressourcen materieller wie medialer Art verwoben und in ein individuelles Verweisungsnetz integriert. Gerade die Erforschung und Analyse solcher individuell eingerichteter Umwelten mit ihren Verweisungsstrukturen könnte Einblick in den tatsächlichen Grad der lebensweltlichen Hybridisierung geben.

Zur Räumlichkeit der Lebenswelt

Die oben angeführten Beispiele legen nahe, dass neben der Medientechnologie und entsprechender Softwareformate die Individuen und ihre Sinnstiftungsfähigkeit selbst einen entscheidenden integrierenden „Faktor" bei der Hybridisierung des lebensweltlichen Raums darstellen. Die Frage nach der Bedeutung oder Bedeutungslosigkeit virtueller Räume erfordert aus dieser Perspektive daher weniger eine pauschale Beantwortung als vielmehr ein fallspezifisches Wissen über die individuell erschlossene Umwelt und die Einbindung virtueller Elemente und Räume in diese. Dass es Sinn macht dieser Frage verstärkt über die Kategorie Raum nachzugehen, wurde bereits an einigen Beispielen verdeutlicht und soll nun durch das Aufzeigen von Bezügen zu der Daseinanalyse von Martin Heidegger und dem dort entwickelten Verständnis von Raum und Räumlichkeit weiter vertieft werden.

Der zentrale Ansatzpunkt der Heideggerschen Daseinsanalyse, wie sie in „Sein und Zeit" (Heidegger 1993) entfaltet wird, ist das *In-der-Welt-Sein.* Versteht man den für die Analyse zentralen Begriff des „Daseins" als Chiffre für die allgemeine Konstitution von Subjektivität, so klingt die Aussage, dass ein Subjekt in der Welt ist, zunächst banal. Heidegger impliziert mit dem In-der-Welt-sein allerdings einen bestimmten Modus, der eine grundsätzliche Zugangsweise zur sozialen Lebenswelt markiert. So wie der symbolische Interaktionismus davon ausgeht, dass Sinn und Bedeutung nicht objektiv gegeben sind, sondern in einem intersubjektiven Aushandlungsprozess hergestellt werden (vgl. Charon 2001, 26ff.), geht auch die Daseinsanalyse davon aus, dass der Mensch nicht in einem distanzierten Verhältnis zu einer Objektwelt steht, die quasi unabhängig von ihm existiert, sondern mit der er in sinnhafter und existenzieller Weise verbunden ist. Dieser existenzielle Bezug stellt den eigentlichen und primären Zugang zur Welt dar, der der Daseinsanalyse zu Folge vor aller objektiven Erkenntnis gegeben ist. Das Dasein kann zwar auch in einen objektiv-distanzierten Modus gegenüber der Welt gelangen, der als „Vorhandenheit" bezeichnet wird (vgl. Heidegger 1993, 54). Der primäre Modus des „Da-seins" ist allerdings die „Zuhandenheit", die als Modus des routinierten alltäglichen Umgangs beschrieben werden kann und zu dem der Modus „Vorhandenheit" nachläufig ist (vgl. Heidegger 1993, 102).

Dieser Modus der Zuhandenheit hat der Heideggerschen Philosophie massiv Kritik eingebracht, dass es sich hierbei um einen Zustand des mehr oder weniger unbewussten Aufgehens in der Lebenswelt und des unmittelbaren und vertrauten Umgangs mit dieser und ihrer „Objekte" handelt.[13] Da dieser Modus das entfremdete, aber reflexivere Vorhandensein massiv überwiegt und eher durch singuläre Ereignisse oder die Widerständigkeit der Welt als durch eine auf das Subjekt zurückgehenden Willensakt aufgebrochen wird, steht dies dem Entwurf eines mündigen, permanent reflektierenden Subjekts tendenziell entgegen. Dessen ungeachtet kann dem Modus der Zuhandenheit eine gewisse empirische Evidenz nicht abgesprochen werden. Diese zeigt sich z.B., wenn wir nach einem langen Arbeitstag nach Hause kommen, ganz selbstverständlich die Haustür aufschliessen wollen und in diesem Moment bemerken, dass der Schlüssel noch im Büro liegt. In diesem Moment wird „Welt" bzw. das Verweisungssystem unserer Handlungen, dass auf der Handlung des Türöffnens aufbaut – die Wohnung zu betreten, einen Kaffee zu kochen, den Fernseher einzuschalten, noch schnell eine dringende E-Mail beantworten etc. – thematisch. Erst dieser negative Modus reißt das Subjekt aus der „unauffälligen Vertrautheit" (Heidegger 1993, 104) und lässt die Umwelt und ihre Objekte als etwas „vorhandenes" und distanziertes erscheinen. Ohne diese Störung ist das Individuum allerdings nicht bei der vorhandenen Welt, sondern es ist vielmehr bei dem Projekt, dass es gerade „besorgt" bzw. verfolgt (vgl. Heidegger 1993, 86f.).

Folgt man der These, dass das Subjekt zunächst im alltäglichen Umgang in der Lebenswelt aufgeht, so können aus dieser Vorstellung von Raum und Räumlichkeit sowohl erkenntnistheoretische wie forschungsmethodische Implikationen abgeleitet werden: Der lebensweltliche Raum ist nicht als objektiver gegeben, sondern er entsteht vielmehr über das individuelle Handeln und die Projekte, die in ihm verfolgt werden. Entscheidend ist hierbei, dass Heidegger diese Um-wendung des geläufigen Verständnis von Raum als objektiv-gegeben in radikaler Weise ausbuchstabiert: Nicht der Mensch ist in einem gegeben Raum, sondern er konstituiert in der Entfaltung seiner Existenz Raum. So wie ein „Ding" erst ist bzw. ins Sein kommt, wenn es von einem Menschen erschlossen bzw. mit Sinn belegt wird, so existiert auch der lebensweltliche Raum nicht ohne ein Dasein: „Nicht gibt es einen Raum, in dem dann ein Dasein agiert, […] sondern es gibt keinen Raum ohne das Dasein" (Luckner 1997, 39). Der Mensch ist somit ein räumliches, ein raumschaffendes und raumaufspannendes Wesen. Wie basal und konstitutiv diese Idee für die Daseinsanalyse ist, zeigt sich, wenn in Betracht gezogen wird, dass das Dasein einen sehr dynamischen Charakter aufweist. Es gibt hier keinen festen und überdauernden Identitätskern, sondern das Dasein ist sein „Entwurf". Anders, aber auch missverständlicher formuliert: Der Mensch ist das, was er sein will. Der Selbstentwurf einer Person konstituiert sich demnach weniger essentialistisch über objektive Eigenschaften oder Fähigkeiten, sondern vielmehr über das, was sie sein will und von dem her sie sich entwirft und Welt begegnen lässt (vgl. Heidegger 1993, 42f.).

13 Im Gegenzug kritisiert allerdings Heidegger einen rein rational-objektivierenden Zugang zur Lebenswelt als verkürzt: „Der nur ‚theoretische', hinsehende Blick auf Dinge entbehrt des Verstehens von Zuhandenheit." (Heidegger 1993, 73)

Letztlich „ist" der Mensch die vielen kleinen Projekte, über die er sich entwirft und seine Existenz entfaltet. Das Selbst wird so zu einem dynamischen, unabgeschlossenen Projekt, das auf einen zukünftigen „Zustand" ausgerichtet und in das Jetzt zurückgeworfen wird.

Der entscheidende Aspekt an diesem Konzept ist dabei, dass die Realisierung dieser identitätskonstituiven Projekte räumlich erfolgt: Das Individuum spannt seine Umwelt auf und richtet sich diese für seine Projekte ein. Dieses Einrichten kann wörtlich im Sinne der materiellen Manipulation verstanden werden, das heißt „Objekte" werden so angeordnet, dass sie in der richtigen Entfernung für die Handlungen und Handgriffe liegen. Heidegger wählt für die Verdeutlichung des Einräumens primär das Beispiel der Werkstatt, in der die Dinge bzw. die (Werk-) Zeuge so angeordnet werden, dass alles in greifbarer Nähe ist, was zur Verwirklichung des Werks gebraucht wird (vgl. Heigegger 1993, 70f.). Das Einrichten zeigt zugleich aber auch eine sinnhaft Dimension, indem eine Person einen Gegenstand, einen Ort, eine Gegend, eine andere Person usw. sinnhaft mit ihrem Projekt verbindet und diese Dinge über Verweisungsstrukturen in eine räumliche Relation zu anderen bringt.[14] Anders formuliert: Ein Individuum spannt in der Realisierung seiner Existenz ein Bedeutungs- und Verweisungsgefüge als seine Umwelt auf, in der all die Orte, Objekte, Personen usw. integriert sind, die im Rahmen des Selbstentwurfs eine Rolle spielen und die über dieses ihre Bedeutung und Relationen erhalten (vgl. Heidegger 1993, 102). Das Projekt bzw. der Entwurf gibt somit auch vor, wie dem Individuum Welt und die Dinge in der Welt begegnen lässt (vgl. Heidegger 1993, 86).

Bei aller Relevanz dieser Form von Räumlichkeit gerade für einen qualitativen Zugang zur Lebenswelt muss der radikale Subjektivismus dieses Konzepts relativiert werden, um auch für soziale bzw. intersubjektive Umwelten fruchtbar gemacht zu werden (vgl. Unger 2006). Neben der Kritik am Fokus auf die vorindustriellen Arbeitsprozesse der Werkstatt (vgl. Heidegger 1993, 70 f.) kritisieren Autoren wie Romano Pocai (2001) das übermächtige und solipsistische Subjekt der Daseinsanalyse, durch das die Vermittlung der individuellen Um-welt mit einer materiellen und sozial-historischen Welt quasi übersprungen wird.[15] Wird allerdings dieses in der Daseinsanalyse angelegte

14 Die Entfernung der Objekte zueinander und zur Person ist dann nicht mathematisch bzw. metrisch zu verstehen, sondern sie ergibt sich aus der Bedeutung für das zu realisierende Projekt. So kann die Antarktis für einen Antarktisforscher sehr viel näher sein, als z.B. die Autowerkstatt, die nur wenige Meter von seiner Wohnung entfernt liegt, weil in seinem Identitätsentwurf die Antarktis eine große Rolle spielt und mit vielen Projekten verbunden ist, er aber kein Auto fährt und er so keinen Grund eine Autowerkstatt in irgendeiner Weise in seine Umwelt integrieren.

15 Es muss hier allerdings angemerkt werden, dass Heidegger dies soziale Dimension über das Mit-sein und den Modus der Fürsorge einzuholen versucht (vgl. Heidegger 1993, 117 ff.). Diese Erweiterung bleibt aber ein stückweit additiv zum Modus des In-Seins und überbrückt den Bruch zwischen der subjektiven Um-welt und der sozialen Welt nicht vollständig.

Vermittlungsmoment stärker in den Blick genommen und die „Faktizität der Welt“ berücksichtigt, dann zeigt sich, dass auch der individuelle Entwurf und seine räumliche Ausprägung keine freie Konstruktion jenseits der sozialen Realität ist, sondern dieser durch die jeweilige gesellschaftlichen und materiellen Verhältnisse gerahmt und beeinflusst wird, wozu nicht zu letzt die Auswirkungen der Transformation von Lebenswelt durch Medientechnologien zu zählen sind.

Erweitert man das Heideggersche Verständnis in diesem Sinne, so ist das Subjekt nicht nur räumlich im Sinne der Konstitution seiner Umwelt, sondern auch in dem Sinne, dass es sich bei seiner Selbstverwirklichung Welt aneignen und für seine „Projekte“ erschließen muss. Welt in diesem Sinne kann sich aber auch widerständig oder dem Projekt entgegenstehend erweisen, so dass eine Anpassung stattfinden oder im Extremfall das Projekt verworfen werden muss. Bei einer gelungen Aneignung und „Vereinnahmung“ für ein Projekt entsteht so eine räumlich-virtuelle Verweisungsstruktur, die eine Person um sich herum aufspannt und durch die die intersubjektive Lebenswelt mit einer individuellen Bedeutungsstruktur belegt und angereichert wird. Diese existiert quasi parallel zu einer materiellen und intersubjektiven Realität, mit der die individuelle Umwelt und damit auch der individuelle Selbstentwurf „vermittelt“ ist. Diese vermittelte, aber dennoch individuelle Umwelt kann dabei entscheidende Hinweise für das Verständnis der Auswirkung neuer Medientechnologien und der virtuell-softwarebasierten Sphäre auf die Transformation der individuellen Umwelt, deren Niederschlag in den individuellen Selbstentwürfen und der Art und Weise wie dieser realisiert werden kann, haben. Virtuelle Räume scheinen dabei zu einer weiteren räumlichen Entgrenzung oder Ent-fernung beizutragen, die sich ja schon als Grundtendenz des Daseins gezeigt hatte. Die Bedingungen zur Ausbildung von Sinnstrukturen und zur Integration in die individuellen Projekte sind dabei in Relation zu der datentechnischen Umgebung virtueller Räume zu sehen. Neben dieser Entgrenzung zeigt sich allerdings auch, dass bestimmte virtuelle Anwendungen die Möglichkeit eröffnen, die individuellen Strukturen des vertrauten Umgangs zu objektivieren und einem breiten Publikum zugänglich zu machen.

Ausblick

Folgt man der hier entwickelten Argumentation, so sind virtuell-softwarebasierte Orte und Räume, deren Ausbreitung vor allem durch die rasante Verbreitung softwarebasierter und vernetzter Anwendungen forciert wird, nicht als abgegrenzt von realer Sozialität zu verstehen. Sie stellen vielmehr eine Erweiterung bzw. Anreicherung des lebensweltlichen Raums dar, die mit einer grundlegenden Transformation in Verbindung steht: Materielle und virtuelle Anteile verbinden und vermischen sich zunehmend und führen zu einer hybriden Alltagswelt. Virtuelle Räume betreffen in diesem Sinne die Erfahrungswelt der Individuen, d.h. die Welt die sich diese erschließen, aneignen, in der diese soziale Bindungen ausbilden, sowie produktiv agieren und über die sie sich nicht zuletzt reflektieren und entwerfen. Virtuelle Räume schalten sich in diesem Sinne in Entwicklungs- und Bildungsprozesse ein und schaffen neue Möglichkeiten der Ausbildung individueller Umwelten und Entwürfe, die zunehmend einen hybriden Charakter aufweisen.

Die individuelle Umwelt kann aus dieser Perspektive als ein Produkt des biografischen Entwicklungs- oder Bildungsprozesses verstanden werden, die zunehmend durch die medientechnologische Entwicklung beeinflusst wird. Für die jeweilige Person ist es dabei zunächst irrelevant, ob es sich bei den Räumen und Objekten, die es erschließt, um virtuelle oder real-materielle handelt, ob die Kontakte im Modus leiblicher Anwesenheit oder technologisch vermittelt stattfinden. Entscheidend ist vielmehr, ob diese den „Raum" anbieten um individuelle Sinnstrukturen auszubilden bzw. um diese in die individuelle Umwelt und die verfolgten Projekte zu integrieren. Wie die Sozialforschung im Bereich der Neuen Medien gezeigt hat, bieten virtuelle Räume durchaus eine Form von Räumlichkeit an, die es erlaubt, diese sinnhaft zu belegen und entsprechend zu integrieren. Die Bedingungen dieser Integration und sinnhaften Erschließung unterscheiden sich dabei von der real-materieller Räume und sind u.a. durch das Interface, den Programmcode (vgl. Fromme/Jörrissen/Unger 2008; Unger 2007) und spezifische soziale Praktiken (vgl. Marotzki/Nohl 2004) geprägt, die sich durchaus auch als widerständig gegen eine individuelle Funktionalisierung und Vereinnahmung zeigen können oder bestimmte Aneignungsweisen, ähnliche wie dominante Lesarten, nahelegen.

Dieser Blick auf unterschiedliche Bedingungen, Rahmungen und Strukturen, spricht aber nicht dagegen, bei der empirischen Erforschung der Sozialwelt virtuelle wie realmaterielle Räume als integrale Bestandteile einer (individuellen) Umwelt zu behandeln und Übergänge, Vermischungen und Schnittstellen in den Blick zu nehmen. Ein solcher Zugang könnte u.U. mit dem sozial- oder medienökologischen Ansatz verbunden werden, der ebenfalls bei der Lebenswelt ansetzt und nach der Bedeutung unterschiedlicher Zonen und Orte im Prozess der Sozialisation fragt (vgl. Zimmermann 2006, 45f.). Schon Baacke u.a. hatten im Rahmen des Projekts „Lebenswelten sind Medienwelten" gezeigt, dass zu den relevanten Orten auch „Medienorte" zu zählen sind (vgl. Baacke/Sander/Vollbrecht 1990). Auch wenn das Verständnis von Medienorten vor dem Hintergrund der Ausbreitung digtial-vernetzter Medientechnologie und der durch diese eröffneten Räume zu aktualisieren wäre, wurde hier die Perspektive auf hybride Konstellationen und die Einbindung medialer Orte in den Alltag quasi schon angedeutet.

Aus medienpädagogischer Perspektive kann dieser Zugang auch noch in einer anderen Hinsicht fruchtbar gemacht werden. Nimmt man Harraways Aufforderung „Verantwortung für die sozialen Beziehungen, die durch die gesellschaftlichen Wissenschafts- und Technologieverhältnisse strukturiert werden, zu übernehmen" (Harraway 1995, 72), ernst, dann kann dies sowohl auf die Gestaltung medialer Architekturen und Formate als auch auf deren Integration in den pädagogischen Raum übertragen werden. In Hinblick auf die Etablierung einer medialisierten Gesellschaftsformation und der Relativierung eines einheitlichen Wissenskanons kommt Pädagogen zunehmend die Aufgabe zu als Raum- und Settinggestalter tätig zu werden (Anfang 2001, 13). Hierzu gehört auch das Arrangieren hybrider Seetings, eine Aufgabe, die Wissen über die Gestaltung real-materieller sowie virtueller Räume und deren Einrichtung für die Förderung von Lern- und Bildungsprozessen erfordert (vgl. Unger 2007). Die Gestaltung hybrider Settings bietet auch die Chance Erfahrungsräume zu eröffnen, die es einerseits ermöglichen an die medientechnologische Transformation der Lebenswelt und somit an die Alltagserfahrung der Jugendlichen und ihre individuellen Umwelten anzuschließen. Andererseits können solche Räume gegenüber dem Alltagshandeln verstärkt Reflexionsmöglichkeiten für die scheinbar fließenden Übergänge zwischen der medialen und real-materiellen Sphäre anbieten und in diesem Kontext zur Vermittlung eines „transformierten“ Orientierungswissen genutzt werden (vgl. Unger 2009, 238 ff.). Diese Optionen eröffnen sich durch eine „hybride“ Perspektive und können weder durch das Beharren auf technikfreier Um- oder Lernwelten noch durch das radikale Umschalten auf rein virtuelle Umwelten, wie sie teilweise in der Hochphase des E-learnings angestrebt wurden, aktualisiert werden.

Literatur

Anders, Günther (1994): Die Antiquiertheit des Menschen. Band I. München: Beck.

Anfang, Güther: Computer in der Kinder-und Jugendarbeit. In: Anfang/Demmler/Lutz 2001, 9-18.

Anfang, Günther/Demmler, Kathrin/Lutz, Klaus (Hrsg.) (2001): Erlebniswelt Multimedia. München: kopead.

Baacke, Dieter/Sander, Uwe/Vollbrecht, Ralf (2000): Medienwelten Jugendlicher. Opladen: Leske + Budrich.

Berger, Peter/Luckmann, Thomas: Die gesellschaftliche Konstruktion der Wirklichkeit. Frankfurt am Main: S. Fischer.

Baudrillard, Jean (1996): Das perfekte Verbrechen. München: Matthes & Seitz.

Charon, Joel (2001): Symbolic Interactionism. New Jersey: Prentice Hall.

Ehrenberg, Alain (2004): Das erschöpfte Selbst. Frankfurt am Main: Campus.

Ferdig, Richard E. (Hrsg.) (2008): Handbook of Research on Effective Electronic Gaming. Volume II. Hershey/New York: Information Science Reference.

Fromme, Johannes/Jörissen, Benjamin/Unger, Alexander (2008): (Self-) Educational Effects of Computer Gaming Cultures. In: Ferdig 2008, 757-775.

Haraway, Donna (1995): Die Neuerfindung der Natur. Frankfurt am Main: Campus.

Heidegger, Martin (1993): Sein und Zeit. Tübingen: Niemeyer.

Heil, Reinhard/Kaminski, Andreas/Stippak, Marcus/Unger, Alexander/Ziegler, Marc (Hrsg.) (2007): Tensions - Technological and Aesthetic (Trans)Formations of Society. Bielefeld: Transcript.

Hoffmann, Dagmar/Mikos, Lothar (Hrsg.) (2007): Mediensozialisationstheorien. Heidelberg: VS Verlag.

Issing, Ludwig J./Klimsa, Paul (Hrsg.) (2002): Information und Lernen mit Multimedia und Internet. Weinheim: Beltz.

Krämer, Sybille (Hrsg.) (2000): Medien Computer Realität. Frankfurt am Main: Suhrkamp.

Luckner, Andreas (1997): Martin Heidegger: Sein und Zeit. Paderborn: UTB.

Marotzki, Winfried/Nohl, Arnd-Michael (2004): Bildungstheoretische Dimension des Cyberspace. In: Thiedeke 2004, 335-354.

Nolda, Sigrid (2002): Pädagogik und Medien. Stuttgart: Kohlhammer.

Pocai, Romano (2001): Die Wirklichkeit der Welt und ihre abgedrängte Faktizität (§ 14-18). In: Rentsch 2001, 51-68.

Rentsch, Thomas (Hrsg.) (2001): Martin Heidegger. Sein und Zeit. Berlin: Akademie Verlag.

Schulmeister, Rolf (2002): Grundlagen hypermedialer Lernsystem. München: Oldenburg.

Sennett, Richard (2006): Der flexible Mensch. Berlin: BVT.

Sennett, Richard (2007): Die Kultur des neuen Kapitalismus. Berlin: BVT.

Sesink, Werner (2004): In-formatio. Die Einbildung des Computers. Berlin: LIT-Verlag.

Sesink, Werner (Hrsg.) (2006): Subjekt - Raum - Technik. Beiträge zur Theorie und Gestaltung neuer Medien in der Bildung. Münster: LIT-Verlag.

Süss, Daniel (2004): Mediensozialisation von Heranwachsenden. Wiesbaden: VS Verlag.

Thiedecke, Udo (Hrsg.) (2004): Soziologie des Cyberspace. Wiesbaden: VS Verlag

Treumann, Klaus P./Meister, Dorothee M./Sander, Uwe/Burkatzki, Eckhard/Hagedorn, Jörg/Kämmerer, Manuela/Strotmann, Mareike/Wegener, Claudia (2007): Medienhandeln Jugendlicher. Wiesbaden: VS Verlag.

Unger, Alexander (2006): Umgebungsanalyse - Nachhaltige Gestaltung von virtuellen Lernumgebungen. In: Sesink 2006, 91-117.

Unger, Alexander (2007): Technological Transformation of Education. In: Heil et. al. 2007: Tensions - Technological and Aesthetic (Trans)Formations of Society. Bielefeld: Transcript.

Unger, Alexander (2009): Zur Hybridisierung der Lernkultur in der Wissensgesellschaft. Berlin: LIT-Verlag.

Wagner, Ulrike/Theunert, Helga (2006): Neue Wege durch die konvergente Medienwelt. München: Reinhard Fischer.

Wagner, Ulrike (Hrsg.) (2008): Medienhandeln in Hauptschulmilieus. München: kopaed.

Welsch, Wolfgang (2000): >Wirklich<. Bedeutungsvarianten – Modelle – Wirklichkeit und Virtualität. In: Krämer 2000, 169-212.

Zimmermann, Peter (2006): Grundwissen Sozialisation. Wiesbaden: VS Verlag.

Strukturale Ethnografie Virtueller Welten

von Benjamin Jörissen

Die Existenz so genannter „Virtueller Welten" ist seit dem Medienhype um „Second Life" weithin bekannt. Auch wenn virtuelle Rollenspieluniversen wie *World of Warcraft* – von den reinen Nutzerzahlen her betrachtet – das weitaus auffälligere Phänomen darstellen, existiert doch eine Vielzahl nicht primär ludisch organisierter Angebote, mit steigender Tendenz vor allem für jüngere Zielgruppen, insbesondere Schulkinder.[1] Das Marktforschungsinstitut KZERO registrierte Anfang 2009 über dreiundvierzig Virtuelle Welten für ca. 8- bis 13-Jährige, eine etwas geringere Anzahl für 15- bis 25-Jährige sowie vereinzelte Angebote für Ältere, darunter das besagte Second Life, dessen Nutzer durchschnittlich um die 35 Jahre alt sind (für diese und die folgenden Angaben: KZERO 2009). Auffällig ist dabei, dass ungefähr die Hälfte dieser Welten in der Erprobungsphase sind, was auf eine rege Entwicklungstätigkeit in diesem Bereich verweist. Der Medienkonzern Nickelodeon allein brachte im Jahr 2007 ein Investitionsvolumen von 100 Millionen US-Dollar zur Entwicklung einer (an Altersphasen orientierten) Kette Virtueller Welten auf (Barnes 2007). Hierzulande bekannte Angebote Virtueller Welten sind, um eine Auswahl zu nennen, „Barbie Girls" (17 Millionen Accounts, davon 5 Millionen neu seit Anfang 2008), „Poptropica" (40 Millionen Accounts, davon 20 Millionen neu seit Herbst 2008); „Habbo Hotel" (124 Millionen Accounts, davon ca. 35 Millionen neu seit Anfang 2008), die virtuelle Chat-Welt „IMVU" (30 Millionen Accounts, davon 10 Millionen neu seit Herbst 2008) sowie Second Life (17 Millionen Accounts, davon 4 Millionen neu seit 2008). Für den deutschsprachigen Raum ist zusätzlich die virtuelle Kinderwelt „Panfu" mit über 4 Millionen Accounts (Eigenauskunft Panfu) zu nennen.[2]

Angesichts dieser Entwicklungen stellt sich die Frage nach dem Bildungswert Virtueller Welten – erneut, wie man sagen muss, denn tatsächlich handelt es sich dabei an sich nicht gerade um ein neues Phänomen. Grafische Virtuelle Welten existierten in einfachen Formen bereits in den 1990er Jahren und wurden kontinuierlich, in den Grenzen der jeweils verfügbaren Rechnerleistung und Datenübertragungskapazitäten, weiterent-

1 Der Unterschied zwischen Virtuellen Welten und genuinen Virtuellen Spielwelten kann an formalen Merkmalen des Spiels, wie etwa der Existenz expliziter oder impliziter Spielziele und -regeln, festgestellt werden. Virtuelle Welten haben keinen vorgegebenen Handlungszweck, keinen narrativen Ablauf, keine ludische Topologie im Sinne von Orten, die für bestimmte Aspekte des Spiels funktional sind, etc. Sie haben auch keine Spielregeln, wohl aber – wie jede Onlinecommunity auch – soziale Verhaltensregeln. Virtuelle Welten können dabei durchaus eine Vielzahl von eingebetteten Spielen enthalten. Das macht aus ihnen jedoch ebensowenig ein Spiel wie Flashgames im Webbrowser aus dem World Wide Web oder dem Sozialen Netzwerk, in welches sie eingebunden sind, ein Spiel machen wrüden.

2 Einige Beispielvideos sind unter http://www.youtube.com/user/joeriben versammelt; eine (selektive) Linkliste Virtueller Welten ist unter http://www.diigo.com/list/benjamin/virtualworlds zu finden.

wickelt.[3] Entsprechend ist die Forschungslage so, dass Virtuelle Welten oder Aspekte derselben – insbesondere die Körperrepräsentationen Virtueller Welten, so genannte „Avatare“ – schon seit einiger Zeit im Fokus der Aufmerksamkeit stehen: selbstredend ist dies in der Informatik der Fall (Bormann 1994), aber auch im Kontext der Cultural Studies (Featherstone/Burrows 1995), der Kommunikationswissenschaften (Steurer 1996; Hillis 1999), der experimentellen Sozialpsychologie (vgl. Bente/Krämer/Petersen 2002) und schließlich in disziplinenübergreifenden Sammelbänden (Schröder 2002a; Schröder/Axelsson 2006).

Der hier vorgeschlagene Zugang ist im Kontext der Strukturalen Medienbildung verortet (Jörissen/Marotzki 2009). Dieser Ansatz verbindet den Gedanken der strukturalen Bildungstheorie (Marotzki 1990) mit medialen Strukturanalysen, so dass die Bildungspotenziale medialer Architekturen empirisch thematisierbar werden. Bildung wird dabei in einem engeren, genuin bildungstheoretisch verankerten Sinn als Transformation der *Strukturmuster* von Selbst- und Weltverhältnissen aufgefasst. Es geht mithin im Folgenden um die Frage, ob und inwiefern die Strukturelemente Virtueller Welten Potenziale für Prozesse der Identitätsfindung und -transformation, für den Aufbau von Orientierungswissen, mithin für das Reflexivwerden des eigenen Welt- und Selbstbildes bieten. Ich möchte dabei so vorgehen, dass innerhalb der drei sogleich zu benennenden Analyseebenen jeweils die relevanten Binnenstrukturen aufgezeigt und anschließend in bildungstheoretischer Perspektive diskutiert werden.[4]

Virtuelle Welten sind, zumindest potenziell, hochkomplexe Gebilde. In ihnen treffen eine Vielzahl unterschiedlicher Teilnehmer aus unterschiedlichen sozialen und kulturellen Kontexten, aufeinander, geben sich eine oder mehrere Identitäten (in Form von Avataren), schließen Bekanntschaften, bilden Gruppen, kommunizieren, spielen, kooperieren miteinander, und machen dabei oft eine Vielzahl neuer *Formen* von persönlichen und sozialen Erfahrungen. Die anthropologische Studie von Tom Boellstorf, der *Second Life* über mehrere Jahre in Teilnehmender Beboachtung beforscht hat, zeigt in eindrucksvoller Weise auf, in welch hohem Ausmaß eine virtuelle Welt zur Lebenswelt und zum Ort biografischer Erfahrungen werden kann.[5]

3 So besteht z.B. die heute noch verbreitete „Active Worlds“-Plattform bereits seit 1995. Vor allem in Form grafischer Chat-Anwendungen wie „The Palace“ oder grafischen MUDs wie der „Worlds Chat Space Station“ fanden einfache Virtuelle Welten seit Mitte der 1990er Jahre zunehmende Verbreitung. Gegen Ende dieser Dekade kamen zunehmend dreidimensionale Welten im Stil von Active Worlds auf. Moove Rose 3D (1999) und die Pseudo-3D-Welten Habbo-Hotel (2000) und Playdo (2000) zählen zu den verbreiteten frühen Angeboten.

4 Insofern dieser Ansatz zunächst anhand von Avatar-Technologien entwickelt wurde, sind einige Passagen des nachfolgenden Textes bereits an anderer Stelle veröffentlicht worden (vgl. insbes. Jörissen/Marotzki 2009, 224 ff.).

5 Boellstorf (2008); vgl. auch die journalistisch-populärwissenschaftlichen, nichtsdestotrotz interessanten Erfahrungsberichte von Guest (2007) sowie Stöcker (2007).

Virtuelle Welten entfalten gemäß ihrer technologischen und technosozialen Grundstrukturen jeweils eigene, komplexe Gesetzmäßigkeiten und eröffnen somit jeweils sehr spezifische Erfahrungsoptionen, die sich von denen anderer Virtueller Welten zumeist deutlich unterscheiden. Ein Weg, diese komplexen Gefüge empirisch aufzuschlüsseln, wäre die Teilnehmende Beobachtung im Feld, wie sie Boellstorf oder zuvor T. L. Taylor (2002) durchgeführt haben. Ein anderer, angesichts der Vielzahl und Entwicklungsdynamik unter forschungspragmatischen Aspekten gangbarerer, weil erheblich weniger zeitaufwändiger Weg liegt in der Strukturanalyse, wie sie Winfried Marotzki (2003) zur Analyse von Onlinecommunities eingeführt hat. Strukturkategorien machen es möglich, Komplexität zu reduzieren und dabei zugleich auch Möglichkeiten des Quervergleichs zu schaffen. Vor allem erlauben sie, wie erwähnt, bildungstheoretische Anschlüsse im Kontext einzelner Strukturbereiche differenziert zu diskutieren.

Virtuelle Welten können in soziografischer Hinsicht als eine besondere Form von Onlinecommunities betrachtet werden, denn sie lassen sich als Gefüge öffentlicher und privater Arenen zum Zweck der Kommunikation und Interaktion beschreiben. Allerdings lässt sich die Virtuelle *Umgebung* ihrerseits nicht auf Onlinecommunity-Merkmale reduzieren. Insofern Virtuelle Umgebungen für eine Vielzahl anderer Anwendungsbereiche offen sind – von der wissenschaftlich-technischen Simulation über Computerkunst bis zum erwähnten Online-Rollenspiel – liegt es nahe, diese als eigenen Strukturbereich zu analysieren. Die Verbindung beider Bereiche liegt dann beispielsweise in der simulierten Räumlichkeit der Arenen, die mithin zu „begehbaren" virtuellen Orten und sozialen Interaktionsräumen werden. Von dieser Virtuellen Umgebung ist wiederum der *Avatar* analytisch zu trennen. Dies ist nicht selbstevident, denn Avatare setzen in aller Regel auf der gleichen technologischen und grafischen Basis auf wie die virtuelle Welt, in der sie auftreten. Dies ist jedoch nicht nicht *notwendig* der Fall. Zum einen wird immer wieder daran gearbeitet, Avatare mittels Standardisierungen so zu beschreiben, dass sie in verschiedenen Virtuellen Umgebungen verwendet werden können, so dass eine Avatar-Identität in verschiedenen Kontexten und diesen gegenüber relativ autonom bestehen würde.[6] Zum anderen finden Avatare auch außerhalb virtueller Welten Anwendung (so z.B. die im Webbrowser beheimateten „Weblin"-Avatare)[7]. Wichtiger jedoch als diese technischen Aspekte ist das besondere Verhältnis des Avatars zu seinem Besitzer oder Benutzer. Nicht zufällig existiert eine Avatarforschung, die den Aspekt der Virtuellen Umgebung nur sehr marginal berücksichtigt (Petersen/Bente/Krämer 2002; Schroeder 2002a; Bailenson/Beall 2005; Yee 2007). Die komplexen – und aus-

6 In einfacher Form, nämlich mit statischen „Avataren" (keine interaktiven Avatare wie hier behandelt, sondern kleine quadratische Bilder), ist dies bereits gegeben. Gravatar.com ist ein verbreiteter Service, der es erlaubt, den eigenen „Avatar" dynamisch an verschiedenen Stellen im WWW einzubinden (z.B. neben eigenen Kommentaren in fremden Weblogs etc.).

7 http://tinyurl.com/Weblin-Demo

gesprochen bildungsrelevanten – Effekte der Beziehung von Avatar und Nutzer lassen sich weder auf die Gestaltung der Virtuellen Umgebung noch auf Community-Funktionalitäten zurückführen. Sie stellen, wie nachfolgend auch im Detail aufgezeigt wird, einen eigenständigen und sehr zentralen Aspekt von Virtuellen Welten dar.

Somit lassen sich folgende drei Strukturbereiche Virtueller Welten voneinander unterscheiden:

1. Die Virtuelle Umgebung,
2. die Avatar-Technologie sowie
3. die Community-Umgebung und -Funktionalität.

Als ein vierter Strukturbereich, der hier allerdings nicht einbezogen werden soll, können soziale Arenen des „real life", also von Bereichen außerhalb der Virtuellen Welt, die diese dennoch durchziehen, gelten. Ein klassisches Beispiel dafür wäre eine reale Ökonomie, die zugleich *innerhalb* der Welt als Währung auftritt und *außerhalb* dieser in andere Währungen umgetauscht werden kann. Die *Second Life*-Währung „Linden Dollar" etwa ist so eine Währung. Durch sie wird es möglich, dass Personen „in" – was auch immer diese Präposition in diesem Fall bedeuten mag – Virtuellen Welten arbeiten. Im Fall von *Second Life* kommen durch die hybride virtuell-realweltliche Währung zugleich viele andere soziale Arenen ins Spiel, die ohne ökonomische Anbindung dort kaum, oder in erheblich geringerem Maße, von Bedeutung wären. Insofern dieser Bereich im Nachfolgenden nicht systematisch verfolgt wird (weil er erstens den Rahmen dieses Aufsatzes sprengen würde und zweitens einen Spezialfall einiger weniger virtueller Welten darstellt), sei anhand der Karte sozialer Welten und Arenen in Second Life ein Eindruck der potenziellen Vielfalt und Komplexität dieses vierten Strukturbereichs vermittelt (Abb. 1; vgl. zum methodologischen Hintergrund der hier angewandten „Situational Analysis": Clarke 2005). Damit nun zur ausführlichen Diskussion der drei genannten Strukturbereiche.

Strukturebene I: Die Virtuelle Umgebung

Dieser Strukturbereich fasst alles zusammen, was mit dem Charakter der Situierung des Users in einer Virtuellen Welt (vermittels einer Avatar-Technologie und anderen Aspekten wie dem Interface etc.) zusammenhängt, also die Räume, Objekte, Objekt-Aktionen, Gestaltung usw. Die virtuelle Umgebung ist für den Grad der sensorischen und sozialen Lebendigkeit digitaler Umgebungen, die nach Johannes Fromme (2008, 191) ein wesentliches Moment und Merkmal Virtueller Welten darstellt, maßgeblich: Je mehr eine digitale Umgebung in diesem Sinne ein lebendiges Geschehen darstellt, desto größer sind beispielsweise Möglichkeiten des Involvements, der sozialen Perspekti-

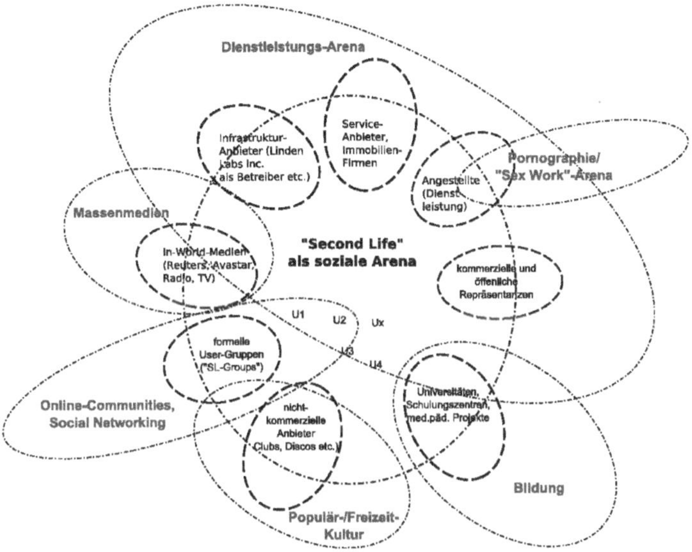

Abb. 1: Karte: Second Life: Soziale Arenen/Welten

venübernahme und des partizipatorischen sozialen Lernens. Zur Virtuellen Umgebung zählen folgende Aspekte:

1. Als erster Aspekt im Sinne einer rahmenden Grundstruktur kann im Anschluss an Ralph Schroeder (2002b, 10ff.) die *Fokussierung* der digitalen Umgebung genannt werden. Die jeweilige Art der sozialen Bühne, auf der das Geschehen stattfindet – ob es sich also etwa um eine pädagogische Lern- und Spielwelt, eine Discowelt, eine Produkwelt (Barbie, Disney) etc. oder um eine offene, nicht festgelegte Virtuelle Welt handelt – geht mit situativen Rahmungen aus der Perspektive ihrer Nutzer einher, die den Gesamtcharakter der Umgebung wesentlich mitbestimmt und so das Spektrum möglicher (erlaubter, gebotener) Handlungen rahmt. Im Anschluss an Erving Goffmans Theorie der Rahmenanalyse (Goffman 1996), auf die Schroeder Bezug nimmt, geht es also bei der Fokussierung um Ensembles von nicht expliziten Regeln und Normen, die sowohl das Handeln als auch die Wahrnehmung der (und in der) digitalen Umgebung beeinflussen.
2. Die technische und grafische Umsetzung, insbesondere die Dimensionalität des virtuellen Raumes, die Perspektivität und der grundlegende Darstellungscharakter der digitalen Umgebung markieren die augenfälligsten Unterschiede zwischen den verschiedenen digitalen Umgebungen. Zweidimensionale Umgebungen sind

Abb. 2: Playdo, isometrische oder 2,5D-Welt

in den Avatarchatumgebungen der 1990er Jahre die Regel (zumeist in Form von Pseudo-3D-Visualisierungen). Isometrische Räume (sog. „2,5D-Welten") sind vorwiegend bei Virtuellen Welten für Kinder und Jugendliche verbreitet (z.B. Playdo, Habbo Hotel), dreidimensionale Welten schließlich bilden die räumlich und technisch anspruchsvollste Kategorie. Der Aspekt der Perspektivität ist bei 2D- und 2,5D-Welten festgelegt: Die Benutzer schauen jeweils aus der Außenperspektive auf eine Fläche bzw. einen isometrischen Raum; sie sind von ihren Avataren insofern dissoziiert, als sie sich nicht mit ihnen bewegen (in ludologischer Hinsicht erinnert diese Perspektive sehr an Puppenstuben; vgl. Abb. 2). Im Gegensatz dazu sind die Benutzer von 3D-Avataren in aller Regel mit diesen assoziiert, wobei die Egoperspektive eher in Spielen (wie z.B. den *first person shootern*) anzutreffen ist, während in Virtuellen 3D-Welten der Betrachterstandpunkt typischer Weise den eigenen Avatar aus leicht erhöhter Perspektive von hinten sehen lässt, so dass dieser bei jeder Aktion im Blick des Benutzers ist (*third person-Perspektive*). Letzterer Modus erzeugt eine *Distanz* zum Avatar (er ist visuell als „Anderer" markiert), erlaubt aber zugleich eine stärkere Identifikation mit seinen Aktionen, die ja vom User mitinitiiert und -kontrolliert werden. Der *Darstellungscharakter* von digitalen Umgebungen schließlich ist überwiegend in zwei Kategorien einzuteilen: entweder liegt eine comic-ähnliche, weniger naturalistische Ästhetik vor, oder aber die Welt bildet Farb-, Licht- und Schattengebung natürlicher Umwelten in naturalistischer Weise (im Rahmen der technischen Möglichkeiten) nach. Dimensionalität, Perspektivität und Darstellungscharakter sind für die Art und Weise, wie eine Virtuelle Welt vermittels ihrer Avatare sich erfahren lässt, von grundlegender Bedeutung (s.u., Präsenzstruktur).

3. Zur Virtuellen Umgebung zählen weiterhin die Interface-Elemente (sowohl das Hardwareinterface – die Steuerungsmodi des Avatars – als auch das Softwareinterface, etwa grafische Bedienungselemente und Steuerungsmenüs). Auch die Interfacegestaltung ist für die Erfahrungsmöglichkeiten in einer virtuellen Umgebung von großer Bedeutung. Zum einen ist dies die Schnittstelle mit den körperlichen Aktionen des Benutzers – also der unmittelbare Anschluss von leiblicher und digitaler Sphäre –, zum anderen bestimmt die Gestaltung des visuellen Interfaces die Sichtbarkeit des Mediums und disponiert damit eine eher immersive oder auch eine eher reflexiv-distanzierte Haltung zum Geschehen in der digitalen Umgebung (vgl. Fromme 2006).

Bildungstheoretische Diskussion

Die bildungstheoretische Bedeutung der Virtuellen Umgebung ergibt sich wie erwähnt aus der jeweiligen Art und Weise der *techno-sozialen Situierung* des Users. Das Thema der „Situierung“ ist selbst relativ komplex, da soziale Situationen immer gleichsam doppelt codiert sind: einerseits entstehen sie aus den einzelnen Perspektiven (oder Situationsdefinitionen) der Individuen, liegen also in einer Erfahrungsdimension; andererseits stellen sie das Interaktionsgefüge dar, das sich durch diese Einzelperspektiven insgesamt ergibt. Hierbei spielen konstruktive Anteile eine bedeutende Rolle: Situationen sind nicht „objektiv“ gegeben, sondern sie sind vielperspektivische Geschehnisse. Sie sind kulturell und historisch geprägte Deutungen dessen, was als Welt (oder Umwelt) wahrgenommen wird, dar. Genau darin liegt ein Potenzial der *Neu-* und *Umdeutung* von Situationen, das unter bildungstheoretischen Aspekten als relevant im Sinne eines Wandels der Welt- und Selbstreferenz betrachtet werden kann.

Inwiefern eine solche Umdeutung möglich ist, hängt nicht nur von der situationsdeutenden Kreativität oder Flexibilität der Beteiligten ab, sondern auch von den situationsimpliziten Regeln und Rahmungen. Denn ob medial vermittelt oder nicht: Situationen beinhalten in sozialen Settings immer auch die Perspektiven der anderen Situationsteilnehmer, die in der Regel niederschwellig und aufgrund nonverbaler Kommunikationen bekannt gegeben werden (zum Beispiel durch entsprechende Gesten, Bewegungen, Mimiken, Sprechweisen etc., die als Hinweise fungieren) – im Zweifelsfall muss daher ausgehandelt werden, unter welcher Rahmung sich eine Situation gemeinsam verstehen lässt. Hierbei spielen Macht- und Anerkennungsgefüge eine Rolle, die schon im Alltagsleben eine Umdeutung von Situationen nur in gewissen Grenzen erlauben. In interaktiven medialen Umgebungen treten zudem mediale Strukturbedingungen hinzu, welche das Spektrum möglicher Situationsdefinitionen soziotechnisch kanalisieren. D.h., dass einerseits *situationsermöglichende* Strukturelemente bestehen, die andererseits mehr oder weniger *beschränkend* wirken. Hierbei sind, was die rahmende Kraft Virtueller Umgebungen betrifft, (mindestens) zwei Dimensionen zu unterscheiden: 1) Je unspezifischer die „Fokussierung", also vorgegebene situative Rahmung einer digitalen Umgebung ist, desto größer ist das Potenzial – aber auch die Notwendigkeit – sozialer Aushandlungen von Situationsdefinitionen. 2) Je präsenter, also je weniger „immersiv" die Gestaltung des Interface einer digitalen Umgebung ist, desto größer ist das Potenzial einer impliziten Situationsdistanz und folglich des reflexiven Potenzials des jeweiligen medialen Settings (vgl. Fromme 2008; Fromme/Jörissen/Unger 2008).

Strukturebene II: Avatare

Um die Komplexität von Avatartechnologien zu handhaben – und auch, um voneinander funktional oder in ihren Auswirkungen unterscheidbare Bereiche voneinander abzugrenzen, werden drei Strukturbereiche unterschieden: a) die Präsentationsstruktur (visueller Aspekt); b) die Interaktionsstruktur (Handlungsaspekt); c) die Präsenzstruktur (Erfahrungsaspekt).

a) Präsentationsstruktur

Die Präsentationsstruktur bezeichnet das visuelle Erscheinungsbild von Avataren unabhängig von ihren interaktiven Optionen (wie Bewegungen und Handlungen) angesprochen. In aller Regel existiert für die visuelle Gestaltung ein eigenes Menü, das den Avatar in einer neutralen Umgebung mit wenigen oder keinen Körperbewegungen darstellt. Hierbei sind zu unterscheiden:

1. Die wählbaren Grundformen: Das Spektrum reicht von der Beschränkung auf menschliche Avatare über Humanoide (z.B. Fantasy-Charaktere, Science-Fiction-Charaktere) und Tiere bis hin zu völlig unbeschränkter Wahl der Grundform.
2. Gestaltungsparameter: Die meisten Avatartechnologien bieten eine Reihe von Gestaltungsparametern an, deren Anzahl allerdings erheblich variiert. Typische Gestaltungsparameter sind beispielsweise: Geschlechtszugehörigkeit, Körperform, Gesichtsform, Augenfarbe, Frisur, Haarfarbe, Kleidung, sowie (selten anzutreffen) Altersmerkmale. Vereinzelt sind Angebote zu finden, die lediglich eine Grundauswahl vorgefertiger Avatare ohne weitere Gestaltungsoption zur Verfügung stellen.
3. Freiheitsgrade der Gestaltung: Die Beeinflussung der Gestaltungsparameter kann in einem sehr einfachen Interface als diskrete Wahl zwischen wenigen Alternativen realisiert sein (z.B. die Wahl aus 6-8 vorgegebenen Haarfarben); sie kann aber auch

(quasi-) kontinuierlich über Schieberegler implementiert sein. Die meisten Freiheitsgrade bieten solche Technologien, welche die Erstellung eigener Hautoberflächen, Frisuren, Körperformen, Kleidungsstücke etc. ermöglichen.

Bildungstheoretische Bedeutung der Präsentationsstruktur
Auf der Ebene der Präsentationsstruktur erscheinen Avatare als visuelle Artefakte, die einen hohen Artikulationswert aufweisen können. Die Präsentationsstruktur ist eng mit Fragen der Identität und Alterität, der „Veranderung“, dem Rollenspiel und der Maskerade, aber auch mit „mikropolitischen“ Artikulationen von Lebensstilen und Selbstverhältnissen verbunden: Avatare in sozialen digitalen Umgebungen, so formuliert es Michel White (2006, 123),

> „produce a kind of ‚speaking‘. They stand in for ideas about what bodies are, describe the physiognomy of the spectator, represent what spectators are seeking, and present a form of art that can only be read by some spectators“ .

Wie bereits angeführt, weisen die verschiedenen Avatartechnologien sehr verschiedene Freiheitsgrade der Gestaltung, Grundformen und Gestaltungsparameter auf. Manche (wenige) Angebote erlauben lediglich die Auswahl eines vorgefertigten Avatars ohne weitere Veränderungsmöglichkeiten; was unter der Perspektive des ermöglichten visuellen Selbstausdrucks eher unergiebig erscheinen muss. In eine ähnliche Kategorie fallen solche Angebote, die ihre zur Auswahl stehenden Gestaltungselemente strukturell beschränken (die MTV Virtual Worlds beispielsweise erlauben es nicht, gegengeschlechtliche Frisuren, Accessoires etc. zu verwenden). In der Regel aber besteht ein größerer Freiraum. Insbesondere solche Anwendungen, die nur eine beschränkte Auswahl zulassen, können logischerweise nur recht selektive Vorgaben anbieten. Typisch für die zumeist kinder- und jugendorientierten isometrischen Welten (bekannteste Vertreter sind Habbo Hotel und Playdo) ist ein mehr oder weniger differenziertes Auswahlmenü an vorgefertigten Körperformen, Haarformen und -farben, Kleidungsstücken und Accessoires (Sonnenbrillen etc.).[8] Weitere Elemente können zumeist im Rahmen einer bezahlten Mitgliedschaft erworben werden. Es folgt aus der technologischen Struktur, dass solche Angebote eine Festlegung auf bestimmte Körper- und Darstellungsstile mit sich bringen, die allerdings durch ungewöhnliche Kombinationen unterlaufen werden können, etwa im Sinne einer „Ästhetik des Hässlichen“. Auch ein Durchkreuzen der zumeist technologisch implementierten binären Geschlechtermatrix (männlich/weiblich) ist durch entsprechende Kombination gegenläufig „gendermarkierter“ Elemente dann möglich – das performative Unterlaufen der „heterosexuellen Matrix“ (Butler) ist auch in solchen Avataranwendungen realisierbar. In der Regel jedoch werden diese Ava-

8 http://tinyurl.com/Playdo-Avatar-Creation-Demo

tare eher konventionell verwendet, indem bestimmte jugend- und subkulturelle Zugehörigkeiten durch entsprechende Auswahl typisierender Haar- und Kleidungsformen angezeigt werden. Die Option des monetären Erwerbs von Avatar-Grundformen und Zubehör bringt zudem einen Distinktionsaspekt mit sich. Insgesamt ergibt sich der Eindruck, dass die artikulative Grundlogik solcher Avatartechnologien eher in der Inszenierung von Identitätszugehörigkeiten und jugendkulturellen Stilen liegt; sich also eher im Rahmen einer Identitätslogik und weniger dem einer Logik des reflexiven Wandels von Selbstverhältnissen bewegt, was der psychosozialen Entwicklungsphase der Zielgruppe solcher 2.5D-Welten, in der es primär um die Ausprägung außerfamiliärer Peergroup-Zugehörigkeiten geht, ja auch entspricht.

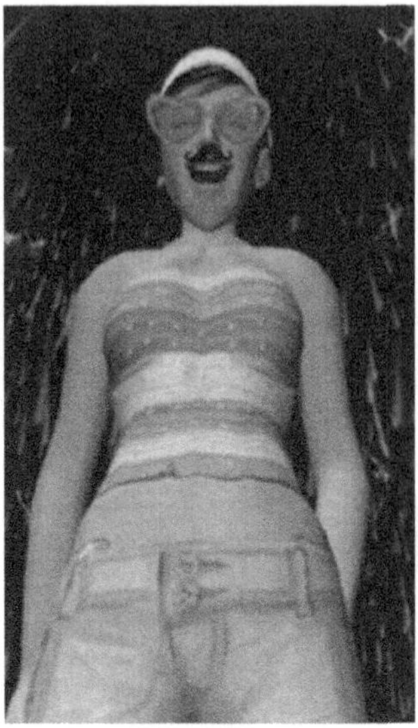

Abb. 3: Gender-Play in Second Life (Quelle: Svarog 2007)

Eine dritte Kategorie bilden solche Technologien, die eine weitestgehend freie Gestaltung von Avataren ermöglichen. Interessanter Weise bieten die Avatar-Chatanwendungen der 1990er Jahre (wie z.B. der Virtual Places Chat) zwar kaum Interaktionsmöglichkeiten, dafür aber eine fast völlige visuelle Gestaltungsfreiheit der Avatare – denn diese bestanden lediglich aus austauschbaren zweidimensionalen Grafiken, die von den Usern in das System hochgeladen werden konnten. Eine der komplexesten Avatar-Technologien stellt *Second Life* zur Verfügung: Dort stehen Hunderte von Parametern bereit, anhand derer Körperformen, Augen, Hauttypen (inklusive Alterungserscheinungen), Farben etc. durch Schieberegler, also praktisch stufenlos, festgelegt werden können.[9] Zudem können beliebige Körperformen in externen Programmen erstellt und in das System hochgeladen werden. Kleidungsstükke und Accessoires können „inworld" kopiert oder gekauft, aber auch selbst angefertigt oder modifiziert werden. Der Verkauf von Körperformen, Hautoberflächen und Kleidungsstücken macht einen bedeutenden Anteil der Ökonomie in Second Life aus. Die grundlegende Technologie, aber auch die konkrete Implementation z. B. von vorgefertigten Teilen zur Auswahl hat einen großen Einfluss auf die Möglichkeiten der visuellen Artikulation im Sinne eines Ausdrucks kultureller, ethnischer, politischer, subkultureller, generationaler etc. Zugehörigkeiten. Während ethnische Zugehörigkeiten in allen gesichteten Angeboten zumindest andeutungsweise dargestellt werden können

9 http://tinyurl.com/Second-Life-Avatar-Generierung

(anhand unterschiedlicher Hautfarben), bieten die wenigsten Technologien die Möglichkeit, Alterskennzeichen wie z. B. Falten zu applizieren oder den Avatar bewusst unattraktiv zu gestalten.

Bereits an dieser Stelle treffen kulturelle oder subkulturelle auf mediale Formangebote. Man kann in Second Life leicht feststellen, dass sehr unterschiedliche Artikulationsniveaus bzw. Avatarkulturen existieren. Während eine nicht geringe Anzahl von Mitgliedern ihren Avatar (bzw. mehrere Avatare) „in-world" in einem der vielen Läden vorkonfektioniert kauft – Avatare „von der Stange" sozusagen – und diesen allenfalls mit einigen Accessoires (Schmuck etc.) ausstatten, betreiben andere Mitglieder einen wesentlich höheren Aufwand, um aus vorhandenen Elementen und Eigenkreationen individuelle, oft auch sehr außergewöhnliche Avatare zu erstellen. Der Avatar stellt in diesen Fällen nicht selten eine dezidiert diskursive visuelle Form des Selbstausdrucks (aber nicht notwendig der visuellen Selbstrepräsentation) dar, in der Körpernormen und -ideale, Genderaspekte, subkulturelle Inklusionen und Exklusionen performativ verhandelt werden (Svarog 2007).

b) Interaktionsstruktur

Die Interaktionsstruktur stellt den wohl komplexesten Strukturaspekt von Avataren dar. Während die Präsentationsstruktur sich grundsätzlich auch auf andere Gestaltungsobjekte übertragen ließe (z.B. auf die Gestaltung von Puppen oder Marionetten), kommt bei der Interaktionsstruktur die außerordentliche „Mächtigkeit" digitaler Objekte zur Geltung. Es handelt sich hierbei um Objekteigenschaften, die ausschließlich in digitalen Umgebungen existieren können – mithin hat man es also mit einer interaktiven visuellen Objektsorte zu tun, die kulturgeschichtlich neu und ohne Vorbild ist (vgl. Bausch/Jörissen 2005). Der grundlegende, in seinen Auswirkungen aber variierende Effekt dessen liegt darin, dass die Aktionen eines Benutzers („User") mit den interaktiven Algorithmen programmierter digitaler Objekte (z.B. Körperteile des Avatars) interagieren. Je nach Komplexität und Mächtigkeit des Avatar-Systems kann der Avatar eigenständige Anteile zu Interaktionen beitragen – er wird damit zu einem Aktanten, also einer eigenständigen, nicht-menschlichen Handlungsinstanz (vgl. Akrich/Latour 1992, 259). Das Ergebnis ist eine im Wortsinn „emergente" Interaktion, die sowohl den, technisch gesprochen, „User-Input" als auch die (an sich berechenbaren) algorithmischen Anteile in der konkreten Ausführung zu einem Amalgam verschmilzt. Körperhaltungen und -bewegungen in komplexen Virtuellen Welten wie Second Life bestehen überwiegend aus beiden Anteilen. Dazu kommt, je nach Technologie, die weitere Komplikation, dass eine automatische Interaktion mit anderen digitalen Objekten der Umwelt (seien es andere Avatare oder auch sonstige Dinge) implementiert sein kann. Der Punkt hierbei ist also, dass die resultierenden Aktionen von Avataren häufig weder von den Usern noch von den Algorithmen vollständig kontrolliert werden, so dass man von einem *hybriden Akteur* sprechen kann. Zu unterscheiden sind auf dieser Strukturebene mithin folgende Aspekte:

1. Handlungsinitiation und -kontrolle: Hierbei sind die existierenden Interaktionsoptionen im Einzelnen danach zu unterscheiden, ob sie vom User kontrolliert (also „manuell", etwa durch Tastaturbefehl ausgelöst werden), hybrid gesteuert (halbautomatisch oder indirekt induziert) oder aber algorithmeninduziert (vollautomatisch) umgesetzt werden.
2. Verbale Interaktionensoptionen: Überlicherweise (aber nicht in jedem einzelnen Fall: vgl. etwa die kleine Virtuelle Welt *The Endless Forest*)[10] stellt die verbale Kommunikation einen zentralen Aspekt von Digitalen Multiuser-Umgebungen dar. Diese ist entweder in Textform oder per Stimme („Voicechat") implementiert; im letzteren Fall häufig auch mit zusätzlicher Textchat-Option. Beim Textchat wie beim Voicechat ist zu unterscheiden, ob die Kommunikation „am" Avatar stattfindet (z.B. durch Comic-Sprechblasen über dem Kopf des Avatars bzw. durch akustische Lokalisierung der User-Stimme am Avatar in Form eines entfernungsabhängigen „Proximity-Voicechats"), oder ob sie von diesem getrennt und damit nicht „in-world", sondern auf der Ebene des Programminterfaces stattfindet (z.B. angebundene Chatfenster; externe Voicechat-Lösung wie z.B. *Skype*[11] oder *Teamspeak*[12]). Dieser verbale Interaktionsaspekt ist insbesondere für die Präsenzstruktur (s.u.) von Bedeutung.
3. Nonverbale Interaktionsoptionen: Hierzu zählen implizite und explizite Gesten (Körperhaltungen, Posen, Augenbewegungen/Blicke, Mimik; Winken, Klatschen, Handgesten etc.), Bewegungsgesten (wie Gehen, Tanzen, Rennen, Schwimmen, Fliegen) sowie räumliche Bewegungsoptionen (durch Veränderung der Position des Avatars im Bildraum beispielsweise ermöglichte Annäherung an bzw. Entfernung von anderen Avataren, Teilnahme an informellen oder formellen „szenischen Arrangements" wie räumliche Gruppenbildung; gemeinsame „sportliche" Bewegungsweisen wie Autorennen, etc.). Ein zubeachtender Punkt hierbei ist, ob Avatare mit anderen Objekten und Avataren kollidieren können, oder ob von der Programmierung her keine Kollisionen vorgesehen sind.

Bildungstheoretische Bedeutung der Interaktionsstruktur

Die Interaktionsstruktur hängt, wie die Bezeichnung bereits andeutet, primär mit den symbolischen Handlungsoptionen in virtuellen Umgebungen zusammen. Thematisierbar werden auf dieser Ebene einerseits tentative Handlungsentwür-

10 http://tale-of-tales.com/TheEndlessForest

11 http://www.skype.com

12 http://www.teamspeak.com

fe (Als-ob-Handeln), aber auch Reflexionsleistungen, die sich aus dem Transfer alltäglicher Handlungsmuster und -normen in einen neuen Kontext (den der virtuellen Welten) ergeben. Zum anderen geht es um eine potenzielle Rekonstitution des Handlungssubjekts auf der Basis hybrider technosozialer Handlungsstrukturen. Die Ebene der „Interaktionsstruktur" fokussiert damit auf eine besondere Eigenschaft vieler Avatar-Technologien, nämlich ihren sozial *eigendynamischen, teilweise autarken Charakter*. Es geht hierbei um die Frage, *wer* in einer avatar-basierten digitalen Umgebung Handlungen vollzieht, und auf welcher Ebene diese vollzogen werden, d. h. welche soziale Welt symbolisch durch die mit dem Avatar vollzogenen Handlungen referenziert wird. Für einige Arten von Handlungsvollzügen oder kommunikativen Akten lässt sich relativ klar zeigen, dass sie Handlungen des Benutzers (Users) des Avatars sind: Wenn z. B. in Second Life durch den Klick auf einen Gegenstand ein (real-ökonomischer) Kaufvorgang eingeleitet wird, ist der Avatar daran zwar gestisch beteiligt, aber man wird kaum behaupten können, der Avatar selbst „kaufe" etwas. Desgleichen würde man etwa bei beleidigenden Gesten, die ein Avatar gegenüber anderen vollzieht, kaum sagen können, dass ein Avatar einen anderen beleidige (wobei bereits unklar ist, ob in einem solchen Fall der handelnde Benutzer einen anderen Benutzer oder einen anderen Avatar mit seiner beleidigenden Geste adressiert). In vielen anderen Fällen ist die Sachlage jedoch unklarer. Aktiviert man per Tastendruck eine Tanzbewegung, würde man schlecht sagen können, dass der User tanze. Der Druck auf die Taste des Computerkeyboards ist analytisch, d. h. technisch, aber auch von den vollzogenen virtuellen Bewegungen des Avatars her klar zu trennen. Tanzt also der Avatar? (Oder genauer: vollzieht er im virtuellen Raum virtuelle Bewegungen, die strukturell vergleichbar mit Tanzbewegungen sind?) Und wenn der User per Knopfdruck die Tanzschritte passend zum Musikwechsel in der virtuellen Disco und passend zu den Bewegungen der anderen Avatare wechselt – wer tanzt dann? Das Beispiel zeigt eindrücklich: es lässt sich letztlich nicht mehr unterscheiden, welcher Part im Ensemble von User und Avatar die eigentiche Handlungsinstanz ausmacht. Die Interaktionsoptionen am Avatar – Blicke, Gesten, Mimik, Posen, Bewegungsgesten (Gehbewegung, Rennen, Schwimmbewegung etc.) und die damit verbundenen räumlichen (Fort-) Bewegungsmöglichkeiten verweisen auf die anthropologisch hochkomplexe Frage des Körpers, seiner Grenzen und seines Status als Objekt sozialer und kultureller Konstruktion. Dass den Gesten und Bewegungsformen potenziell eine artikulative Bedeutung zukommt, zeigt sich bereits daran, dass die Gesten von Avataren kulturabhängig unterschiedlich gestaltet und interpretiert werden (Koda 2007; generell zur Konstruktion von „race" mit Avataren: Nakamura 2007, 131 ff.). Da die nonverbale Kommunikation in allen Kulturen eine große Rolle spielt, kann diese Information zunächst nur bedingt verwundern. Avatar-Gesten stellen kulturelle Aufführungen dar, die gerade durch ihre „Verdopplung", also ihren Bezug auf kulturelle Herkunftsgesten, einen stark performativen Charakter annehmen. Dies gilt zumal für subkulturelle Gesten und Posen, mit denen Zugehörigkeiten und Abgrenzungen angezeigt werden. Hier liegt zudem ein besonderes mimetisches Potenzial, indem die jugendkulturell-„coolen" Posen und die oft sehr „gekonnten" Bewegungen der Avatare durchaus als nachahmenswert erscheinen können, so z. B. die erwähnten Tanzbewegungen in darauf spezialisierten virtuellen „Disco-Welten".[13]

Wenn Avatartechnologien die Möglichkeit bieten, Gesten und Bewegungen selbst zu programmieren oder zu modifizieren – was allerdings eher die Ausnahme darstellt – können sie zu einem besonders elaborierten und differenzierten (sub-) kulturellen Artikulationsmedium werden. Auch in diesem Bereich stellt derzeit Second Life die technologisch avancierteste Plattform dar. Skripte für Gesten können programmiert und in beliebigen Formen – in der Regel als kleine Bälle – in der virtuellen Welt platziert werden (werden sie dort angeklickt, vollführt der eigene Avatar die entsprechende Geste). Die vorhandenen Standardgesten unterscheiden überwiegend zwischen weiblichen und männlichen Gesten (und zwar indem die Gestenbällchen rosa bzw. blau gefärbt sind);[14] dieses technosoziale „Doing Gender" auf Basis der heterosexuellen Matrix wird adaptiert, aber auch modifiziert und subvertiert, wenn etwa schwule Communities in Second Life sich eigene (hell- und dunkelblaue) Gestenbällchen programmieren.

Gesten und Bewegungen von Avataren spielen also wie gesehen eine Schlüsselrolle für die Art der in digitalen Umgebungen kultivierten Sozialität. Avatare sind aufgrund ihrer soziotechnologischen Struktureigenschaften ein besonders komplexes Beispiel dessen, was in der Actor-Network-Theorie (ANT) „Aktant" genannt wird. Akrich/ Latour verstehen darunter nichthumane Elemente sozialer Handlungsvollzüge und Handlungsketten. Ein Aktant ist „whatever acts or shifts actions; action itself being defined by a list of performances through trials; from these performances are deduced a set of competencies with which the actant is endowed [.]"; während ein Akteur („actor") ein „actant endowed with a character (usually anthropomorphic)" ist (Akrich/ Latour 1992, 259).

In dieser allgemeinen Definition werden auch „nicht-intelligente" Aktakten als Handlungsträger thematisierbar.[15] Die Avatare fungieren also nicht als passive Objek-

13 http://www.vside.com

14 http://tinyurl.com/Second-Life-Gendergesten

15 Aus der Perspektive der ANT steht der Avatar in einer „flachen" Verkettung von menschlichen und nichtmenschlichen Aktanten – Usern, Bildschirmen, Computermäusen, virtuellen Objekten, Grafikkarten, Internetverbindungen, Tastaturen, Programmen (Software) usw. –, die jeweils die Art der entstehenden Verbindungen formen. Auch im Sinne solcher flacher Akteur-Netzwerke würde der Avatar u.E. ein besonders komplexes soziales Objekt darstellen, insofern er am Kreuzungspunkt mehrerer Transmissionslinien liegt: einer technischen (etwa: Interfaceeingaben – Serverkommunikation – Digitale Umgebung/Virtuelle Welt), einer visuellen (Blick – Bildschirm – Bild), einer sozialen (User – Avatar – Avatar – User) und einer taktilen (Hand – Computermaus – Avatarbewegunen g/Gesten). Der Avatar ist also ein Objekt, an dem diese

te; vielmehr spielen die Interaktionen der Avatare in digitalen Umgebungen aufgrund ihrer sozialen Eigendynamik eine zentrale Rolle für die sozialen Abläufe, mithin für die in einer digitalen Umgebung entstehende Sozialität überhaupt. Sie sind in dieser Eigenschaft gleichsam teilautonom: Bereits die User der technologisch eher schlichten Avatarchat-Community *Virtual Places Chat*[16] berichteten von ihrer Erfahrung, dass sie nicht wirklich das zukünftige Verhalten ihres (relativ statischen) Avatars vorhersagen oder kontrollieren könnten: „You are kidding yourself if you think you will be able to control or predict what will happen to your avatar. It is the ultimate learning experience", so ein VP-Chat- User (Taylor 2002, 56).

Im Extremfall können Avatare so kontextsensitiv programmiert sein, dass sie den Charakter sozial eigenständig sensibler „Agenten" erhalten. Ein Beispiel dafür ist „Virtual Eve", eine für Lehrzwecke (Distance Learning) eingesetzte Avatar-Technologie, bei welcher der Lehrer-Avatar automatisch mimisch auf die von Kameras erfassten und in Echtzeit analysierten Gesichtsausdrücke der Schüler reagiert.[17] Im Kontext einer digitalen Umgebung ist es zudem zumindest prinzipiell denkbar – wenn auch derzeit u.W. nicht implementiert –, dass Avatare aufeinander gestisch und mimisch reagieren, dass sie also eine Ebene selbstständiger Gestenkommunikation vollziehen und somit eine eigenständige soziale Dynamik erzeugen.

c) Präsenz und Kopräsenz

In der Avatar-Forschung ist der Aspekt der mit Avatartechnologien einhergehenden Präsenz- und Kopräsenzeffekte, also etwa der Eindruck, an einem Ort zu sein, und dort ggf. mit anderen Personen gemeinsam zu sein, von großer Bedeutung (vgl. Jensen 2001; Becker/Mark 2002; Petersen/Bente/Krämer 2002). Präsenz- und Kopräsenzeffekte ergeben sich weniger aus isolierten einzelnen soziotechnischen Eigenschaften; sie stellen vielmehr einen „emergenten" Gesamteffekt aller anderen Strukturebenen dar (also teilweise auch der oben erwähnten Aspekte der Virtuellen Umgebung): Die Erfahrungen, die Benutzer in digitalen Umgebungen machen, berühren alle vorgenannten Strukturbereiche zugleich; sie lassen sich dabei nicht unbedingt auf einzelne Aspekte zurückführen. In der Beurteilung von Avatartechnologien muss dies entsprechend berücksichtigt werden. Bei der Präsenzstruktur von Avataren handelt es sich entsprechend um eine synthetische Strukturebene, die keine eigenen soziotechnischen Merkmale besitzt, sondern deren Merkmale sich aus Elementen der vorhergehenden Ebenen zusammensetzen. Es lassen sich dabei zwei Aspekte unterscheiden:

Handlungsketten im Sinne der ANT sich überschneiden und transformieren, indem sie aufeinander Einfluss ausüben.

16 http://www.vpchat.com/

17 http://tinyurl.com/virtual-eve

1. *Präsenz:* Hierbei geht es darum, in welchem Maße eine Virtuelle Welt den Eindruck der „Präsenz“, des „an-einem-Ort-Seins“ mit sich bringt. Relevant sind dabei u.a. die visuelle Umsetzung (v.a. die Perspektivität), die Art des Interfaces, die Qualität und Dichte der Handlungsoptionen insgesamt sowie die Bandbreite und Art möglicher visueller Gestaltungsweisen der Avatare.
2. *Kopräsenz:* Das Maß, in dem sich in digitalen Umgebungen die Erfahrung einstellt, dass man sich mit anderen Personen gemeinsam an einem „Ort“ befindet, hängt u.a. von der Qualität der nonverbalen Kommunikation, der Sichtbarkeit oder Verdecktheit der medialen Rahmung, aber auch dem ermöglichten persönlichen Eingebundenheitsgefühl (Involvement) und Engagement ab.

Bildungstheoretische Bedeutung der Präsenzstruktur

Die Präsenzstruktur zielt primär auf eine Erfahrungsperspektive ab. Thematisierbar werden hier zum Beispiel andere, „appräsente“ Körpererfahrungen, Entgrenzungserfahrungen (Hybridität), Erfahrungen transformierter Präsenz (Raum und Zeit), sowie Erfahrungen transformierter sozialer Präsenz im Umgang mit anderen „User/Avatar-Einheiten“. Mit dem an Edmund Husserl angelehnten Ausdruck der „Appräsenz“ bezeichnet der Medienphilosoph Mike Sandbothe (2001, 200)

> „die für die Kommunikation im Internet charakteristische Form der Telepräsenz, das heißt eine Weise der virtuellen Anwesenheit, welche auf der Abwesenheit der realen körperlichen Präsenz beruht. Die appräsente Präsenz ist dadurch ausgezeichnet, daß die körperliche Präsenz aufgeschoben bleibt, das heißt im Modus der Appräsenz mitgegenwärtig, aber nicht im Sinne einer reinen Präsenz gegenwärtig ist“.

Aufgrund des Aktantencharakters von Avataren lässt sich das Verhältnis User – Avatar nicht nach einem Subjekt-Objekt-Schematismus, etwa nach dem Modell des Marionettenspielers, verstehen. Die durch Avatar-Interaktionen entstehende soziale Dynamik wirkt auf den Benutzer zurück. Dieses rückwirkende Verhältnis ist von Nick Yee in einem sozialpsychologischen Setting untersucht und als „Proteus-Effekt“ bezeichnet worden (Yee 2007). In einer Reihe von Experimenten bekamen Probanden einen Avatar zugewiesen, der unterschiedlichen Attraktivitätswerten (z. B. hinsichtlich der Körpergröße und der Gesichtsform) entsprach. In einem virtuellen Raum sahen die Probanden ihren eigenen Avatar kurz in einem (virtuellen) Wandspiegel. Eine weitere im virtuellen Raum anwesende TeilnehmerIn interagierte anschließend mit diesem Avatar bzw. Probanden, sah aber nicht denselben Avatar wie der Proband, sondern immer dieselbe (neutral-attraktive) virtuelle Person. Yee konnte im Ergebnis hochgradig signifikante Verhaltensänderungen der Probanden nachweisen: mit attraktiven Avataren ausgestattet, hielten sie eine erheblich geringere interpersonelle Distanz zu anderen Avataren, gaben erheblich mehr Informationen über sich preis und tendierten in Spielsettings dazu, ihre Gegener zu übervorteilen. Yee (2007, passin) schlussfolgert:

> „The appearances of our avatars shape how we interact with others. As we choose our self-representations in virtual environments, our selfrepresentations shape our behaviors in turn. These changes happen not over hours or weeks, but within minutes".

Was Yee auf eine visuelle Selbstbeziehung zurückführt (also in unserer Strukturdifferenzierung eher der Präsentationsstruktur zugerechnet werden muss), weist für den Medienphilosophen Mark Hansen (2006) ein wesentlich tiefer gehendes körperliches Moment auf, das die Interaktionsstruktur betrifft. Hansen sieht virtuelle Körperlichkeit grundsätzlich dadurch gekennzeichnet, dass sich in das Verhältnis von Körperschema und Körperbild, also zwischen die taktil-motorische Erfahrungsdimension des Körpers und die visuell-propriozeptive Selbstwahrnehmung, ein technogenes drittes Element einschreibt. Virtuelle Körperlichkeit sei insofern nicht als informationelle oder digitale Abstraktion eines alltäglichen Körpers zu verstehen. Vielmehr sei von einem „body submitted to and constituted by an unavoidable and empowering technical deterritorialization" zu sprechen – einen solchen Körper, der nur durch die Verbindung mit Technik realisiert werden kann, nennt Hansen „body-in-code" (Hansen 2006, 20).
Dieser Konstellation schreibt Hansen das Potenzial zu, das Körperschema, also die taktile Erfahrungsdimension vom Körperbild zu entkoppeln mit dem Ziel „to increase his agency as an embodied being" (Hansen 2006, 20). Die Vermittlung über einen visuellen Techno-Körper hätte nach Hansen unter bestimmten Bedingungen – Hansen entwickelt seine Argumentation anhand der interaktiven Kunstwerke von Monika Fleischmann und Wolfgang Strauss, also an einem hochgradig avancierten und reflcktierten künstlerisch-experimentellen Setting – also nachgerade das Potenzial einer Neuentdeckung des Körpers. Hansens phänomenologische Theoretisierung virtueller Körperlichkeit korrespondiert mit den Befunden der Avatar-Forschung insofern, als, wie Ralph Schroeder (2002b) aufzeigt, das Gefühl der körperlichen Präsenz am virtuellen Ort, der „sense of being there", nicht von einer naturalistischen Grafik abhängig ist. Vielmehr seien es die Interaktivität und Reaktivität der Avatare, sowie deren Fähigkeiten zur nonverbalen Kommunikation, die solches bewirkten. In diesem Sinne berichtet Tom Boellstorf, der während einer über drei Jahre dauernden Teilnehmenden Beobachtung in Second Life zahlreiche Interviews geführt hat, von der Bedeutung der mit den Second Life-Avataren einhergehenden *agency*:

> „One resident noted how ‚experimenting with appearance or behavior in Second Life potentially opens up new ways to think of things in real life.' Another emphasized how ‚despite everything, who I am still seems to come out, so perhaps I

discover my essential nature [through my avatar]'; a third observed that ,my offline self is becoming more like my avatar, personality-wise. It's like SL [Second Life, B.J.] has grown on me and looped back'" (Boellstorf 2008, 148).

„This theme of Second Life permitting access to an interior self that in the actual world is masked by an unchosen embodiment and social obligations was common", stellt Boellstorf fest (Boellstorf 2008, 148), und schlussfolgert aus seinen Beobachtungen: „Avatars were not just placeholders for selfhood, but sites of self-making in their own right " (Boellstorf 2008., 149).

Die hier erwähnten Untersuchungen aus unterschiedlichen disziplinären Blickwinkeln machen Folgendes deutlich: Je höher die Präsenz einer (wie auch immer realisierten) Avatar-Technologie im Sinne einer solchen *agency* ist, desto größer ist die Wahrscheinlichkeit, dass sie neue Selbsterfahrungsräume eröffnet. Der Präsenz korrespondiert – das sei hier nur am Rande erwähnt – in digitalen Multiuser-Umgebungen eine soziale Kopräsenz, also die Möglichkeit der Erfahrung eines „artikulierten Anderen". Erst dadurch werden letztlich die visuellen und gestischen Artikulationen in einem deliberativen digitalen Raum sozial wirksam.

Zusammenfassung: Zur Bildungsrelevanz von Avataren

Jede einzelne Avatar-Technologie weist Eigenschaften auf, die von anderen verschieden sind. Die hier hervorgehobenen Strukturebenen zeigen Potenziale virtueller Körperlichkeit auf, die in medienanthropologischer und auch in bildungstheoretischer Perspektive relevant sind, und die angesichts der gegenwärtigen Trends zukünftig womöglich immer mehr im Blickpunkt des (besorgten oder engagierten) Interesses stehen könnten. Auf der Basis der genannten Beobachtungen erscheint es angemessen zu sagen, dass die „Handlungsinstanz" in virtuellen Welten ein Nutzer/Avatar-Hybrid, also ein hybrider Akteur ist. Die Kopplung von User und Avatar zeigt sich letztlich auf allen Strukturebenen der Analyse: Erstens kommt es auf der Ebene der Virtuellen Umgebung (Strukturebene I) zu einer *hybriden Situierung* in der digitalen techno-sozialen Umgebung (also beispielsweise einer Virtuellen Welt). Zweitens kommt es auf der Ebene der Präsentationsstruktur zu einer Überlagerung eigener und medial vorstrukturierter Artikulationsoptionen. Drittens kann man auf der Ebene der Interaktionsstruktur eine Hybridisierung von (intendierten) User-Aktionen und teilautonomen Avatar-Aktionen feststellen. Viertens schließlich war auf der Ebene der Präsenzstruktur eine Hybridisierung der Erfahrung im dem Sinne zu beobachten, dass der User mit seinem Avatar eine enge identifikatorische Beziehung eingeht („Proteus-Effekt"), und dass darüber hinaus die Grenzen der eigenen Körperlichkeit in der visuo-motorischen Erfahrungsdimension aufgelöst werden.

Strukturebene III: Communityfunktionen

Als dritte Strukturebene sind die Community-Aspekte Virtueller Welten zu betrachten, die sich weitgehend mit den in der Online-Ethnographie Winfried Marotzkis decken (Marotzki 2003). Dabei kommt es zu typischen Überschneidungen mit den anderen Strukturebenen; etwa was die Kommunikationsfunktionen von Avataren und den Öffentlichkeits- oder Privatheitscharakter von Räumen in virtuellen Umgebungen betrifft. Marotzki (2003) unterscheidet sieben online-ethnographische Strukturmerkmale:

1. *Leitmetapher*: In der Frühphase des World Wide Web (WWW) folgte die Aufmachung WWW-basierter Onlinecommunities in der Regel bestimmten *Leitmetaphern*, welche zugleich die Navigationsstruktur wie auch die Interaktions- und Kommunikationsmöglichkeiten versinnbildlicht darstellten (z.B. „Cybercafe" für einen Online-Chatraum).Während moderne Onlinecommunities und Soziale Online-Netzwerke Leitmetaphern kaum mehr verwenden, wirkt die in Strukturebene I beschriebene Rahmungsfunktion durchaus in diesem Sinn. Dieser Aspekt der Community-Ethnographie kann in Virtuellen Welten mithin unter dem Titel der Virtuellen Umgebung angemessen abgehandelt werden.
2. Jede Onlinecommunity besitzt eine spezifische *soziographische Struktur*. Diese umfasst die Zugangsbedingungen und -prozeduren (Anmeldung), das Regelwerk, das Status-System (nicht-zahlende, einfache und Premium-Mitgliedschaften sind in fast allen kommerziell betriebenen Communities zu finden), das Gratifikations- und Sanktionssystem, das Buddy- und Ignore-System (Freunde/Feinde-Kennzeichnung) sowie die oft sehr wichtigen (i.d.R. Frei einrichtbaren) Gruppen. Diese Merkmale können ausschlaggebend für die Form der etablierten sozialen Beziehungen in Onlinecommunities bzw. Virtuellen Welten sein. Die Art des Zugangs etwa (anonyme Anmeldung vs. Anmeldung mit vollem Namen und Überprüfung der E-Mailadresse, evtl. sogar Identitätsfeststellung) legt fest, ob der Community-Charakter eher unverbindlich ist oder aber die Form eines „ernsten Spiels" annimmt, in das die Beteiligten sich letztlich mit ihren realen Identitäten einbringen. Das Gratifikations- und Sanktionssystem fördert bestimmte (gewollte) regelmäßige Aktionsformen in Communities – etwa die Teilnahme an Forendiskussionen –, die häufig ritualisierten und gemeinschaftlichen Charakter aufweisen. Das Buddy-System schließlich etabliert Anerkennungsstrukturen und kann somit innerhalb der Community (je nach Implementation und Nutzung) stabile Gemeinschaften wie auch Statustransformationen – bspw. die Aufnahme in eine bestehende Peergroup – bewirken. Die Gruppen schließlich bieten die Option der Organisation von Gemeinschaft, in der Regel an Interessen orientiert. Als Beispiel sei *Second Life* angeführt: hier ist die Gruppenfunktion primär in einem eigenen Optionsinterface untergebracht, das nicht zur

Welt selbst gehört. Gruppenzugehörigkeiten können wahweise „in-world“ in Form entsprechender Kennzeichnungen der Avatare erscheinen (Name und Gruppenname werden dann oberhalb des Kopfes eingeblendet), so dass die Zugehörigkeit zu einer Gruppe ein dominantes Merkmal sein kann.

3. Onlinecommunities sind von der Mitwirkung ihrer Mitglieder abhängig. Der Grad an Mitbestimmung wird durch die *Partizipationsstruktur* geregelt, welche die Mitbestimmungsoptionen der Mitglieder differenziert festlegt. Sie varriiert sehr stark zwischen verschiedenen Communities und ist häufig auch vom Status der Mitglieder abhängig (Neulinge haben weniger Rechte als seit langem aktive Mitglieder, zahlende mehr als nicht-zahlende etc.). Unterscheiden lassen sich hierbei die *inhaltliche Partizipation* (z.B. in der Welt agieren), die *strukturelle Partizipation* (z.B. die Welt verändern, z.B. bauen) und die *organisatorische Partizipation* (z.B. Entscheidungen über Grundcharakter und grundlegende Veränderungen der Virtuellen Welt mitbestimmen). Mit diesen Partizipationstypen gehen potenziell unterschiedliche Grade von Einbindung und Verpflichtung einher.
4. Jede Onlinecommunity verfügt über mindestens eine Möglichkeit der gegenseitigen Kommunikation ihrer Mitglieder. In aller Regel handelt es sich um ein ganzes Bündel verschiedener Optionen, das die spezifische *Kommunikationsstruktur* einer Community ausmacht. Dies umfasst bei Web-basierten Communities sowohl „one-to-one“- als auch „many-to-many“-Kommunikationdienste (Chat, Privatchat, Foren, Email, Instant-Messaging, SMS-Interface, Mailinglisten, etc.). Auf Virtuelle Welten bezogen, wird die Kommunikationsstruktur zum großen Teil über die Interaktionsstruktur der Avatartechnologie realisiert, jedoch existieren auch hier regelmäßig zusätzliche Kommunikationswege, die zwar innerhalb des Interfaces der Virtuellen Welt voerortet sein kann, jedoch nicht dem Geschehen in der Welt angehört (dementsprechend zählen hierzu auch Kommunikationsmöglichkeiten auf etwa zusätzlich angeschlossenen Profilseiten im Web).
5. Communities sind an mehr oder weniger stark abgegrenzten gemeinsamen Themen oder Interessen orientiert. Unter der *Informationsstruktur* sind alle Dienste zu verstehen, durch welche die Mitglieder mit für sie relevanten Informationen versorgt werden. Dies können Themen- oder auch Community-bezogene Informationen sein, also etwa Newsletter, thematische Linksammlungen und Datenbanken, Kalender zur Organisation gemeinsamer Aktivitäten sowie auf der Website integrierte Glossare und Wikis. Für Virtuelle Welten ist dieser Aspekt sehr wichtig, insofern sie in aller Regel nicht ohne weiteres bedienbar sind. Sehr häufig werden Neulinge deshalb zunächst mit Tutorial-Videos oder sogar angeleiteten ersten Schritten in der Virtuellen Umgebung selbst mit der Bedienung bekannt gemacht (in *Second Life* beispielsweise landen Neulinge automatisch auf „Orientation Islands“).

6. Die *Präsentationsstruktur* einer Community umfasst das in allen Onlinecommunities vorhandene Identitätsmanagement, also die zur Verfügung stehenden Möglichkeiten der Selbstpräsentation der einzelnen Mitglieder. Darüber hinaus ist in einigen Communities die Möglichkeit einer Präsentation auf Gruppenebene oder sogar der Visualisierung von Freundes-Netzwerken vorhanden. Die Präsentation kann in Web-basierten Communities in privaten oder halböffentlichen Arenen erfolgen (eigene Homepage oder Weblog innerhalb der Community-Seiten; Identitätskarte mit aufgelisteten Persönlichkeitseigenschaften und Vorlieben). Im Fall von Virtuellen Welten stellt selbstredend der Avatar eine zentrale Instanz der Präsentationsstruktur dar (s.o.), aber wie erwähnt bestehen nicht selten zusätzliche öffentliche und private Arenen (Profilseiten) außerhalb der Virtuellen Umgebung.
7. Schließlich spielt das *Verhältnis Online-Offline* häufig eine große Rolle: Bei vielen Communities bestehen strukturelle Vorkehrungen, die ein offline-Treffen der Mitglieder ermöglichen oder gezielt befördern, indem per Email bspw. Termine von Treffen oder sonstigen Aktivitäten an Interessierte weitergeleitet werden. Dies können User-Treffen von Themencommunities sein oder auch Treffen zwischen einzelnen Mitgliedern oder Gruppen. Zum Verhältnis Online-Offline gehören außerdem etwa in Communities integrierte Shop-Angebote, die also zu realweltlichen Warenlieferungen führen. Während Offline-Treffen für Virtuellen Welten er eine untergeordnete Rolle spielen – man ist ja bereits in „appräsenter" Form mit anderen zusammen – , beinhalten die allermeisten Virtuellen Welten kostenpflichtige Shop-Angebote, indem Accessoires und Kleidung für den Avatar oder Möbel und Gegenstände zur Einrichtung der eigenen Virtuelle Wohnung angeboten werden. Ein Sonderfall, der bereits erwähnt wurde, sind Welten wie *Second Life* mit ihrer hybriden Ökonomie und entsprechend vielfältigen Offline-Online-Verbindungen.

Fazit

Die vorangegangenen Ausführungen sollten die strukturelle Komplexität Virtueller Welten aufzeigen, dazu mögliche Analysekategorien vorstellen und bildungstheoretische Anschlussmöglichkeiten skizzieren. Die hier hervorgehobenen Strukturebenen zeigen *Potenziale* Virtueller Welten und Avatartechnologien auf, die in medienpädagogischer und auch in bildungstheoretischer Perspektive relevant sind, und die angesichts der gegenwärtigen Trends zukünftig womöglich immer mehr im Blickpunkt des öffentlichen Interesses stehen könnten. Jede einzelne Virtuelle Welt weist Eigenschaften auf, die von anderen, oft in wesentlichen Aspekten, verschieden sind. Im Anschluss an Norbert Meder lässt sich die Bildungsrelevanz digitaler Umgebungen dadurch charakterisieren, dass diese einer „Logik der Reduktion auf das Wesentliche" entsprechen: „Einerseits werden die Räume für Bildungsprozesse eng gemacht, andererseits wird ein unbestimmter Raum eröffnet, in dem ‚alles' möglich ist. Das heißt, der Kreativität und Phantasie wird freier Raum gelassen" (Meder 2008, 231). Ihre Potenziale liegen in der gestaltenden Artikulation sowie in der handelnden Partizipation – dies aber *erstens* in unterschiedlichem Ausmaß und in *zweitens* unterschiedlicher Ausrichtung:

1. Wie anhand der verschiedenen Strukturaspekte zu sehen war, ist das Verhältnis von Engführung und Freiheit in den verschiedenen Virtuellen Welten sehr unterschiedlich gelagert. Durchaus finden sich auch solche Beispiele, die kaum Raum für eigenen Ausdruck lassen und statt dessen lediglich stereotype Identitäts- und Interaktionsangebote bieten. Andere Welten suchen in gelungener Weise ein Gleichgewicht von „didaktischer Reduktion" und Gestaltungs- und Handlungsfreiheit. Wieder andere bieten beinahe unbeschränkte Optionen, setzen dafür jedoch eine erhebliche Lernbereitschaft voraus.
2. Weiterhin bieten Virtuelle Welten sehr unterschiedliche Rahmungen an, die ebenfalls in Betracht gezogen müssen. Der Grundcharakter der Welt kann eher pädagogisch-wissensorientiert oder spielerisch-tentativ gestaltet sein; er kann auf Identitätsangebote fokussieren, indem die Identifikation mit jugendkulturellen Subkulturen und Szenen forciert wird, oder aber das Spiel mit der Identität, das Ausprobieren anderer, bis hin zu Grenzen unterlaufenden Formen (Cyborgs, mehr- oder ungeschlechtliche Wesen, Chimären etc.) ermöglichen. Er kann schließlich auf Handlungspotenziale fokussieren (etwa dort, wo gemeinsame Handlungsformen und/oder das Mitarbeiten am Aufbau der Welt im Vordergrund stehen oder sogar realweltliche soziale Arenen in die Virtuelle Welt hineinwirken).

Deutlich wird in der Gesamtbetrachtung, dass Virtuelle Welten ein mediales Feld mit vielfältigen Lern- und Bildungspotenzialen darstellen. Sie bieten die Möglichkeit, Selbst- und Weltbezüge in einem alternativen Raum tentativ zu erfahren und zu erweitern. Angesichts der aufgezeigten Komplexitäten kann dieses Potenzial jedoch keinesfalls pauschal beurteilt werden. Vielmehr bedarf es jeweils am konkreten Fall der Einzel- oder Vergleichsanalyse der bildungsrelevanten Strukturaspekte und ihres Zusammenspiels.

Literatur

Akrich, Madeline/Latour, Bruno (1992): A Summary of a Convenient Vocabulary for the Semiotics of Human and Nonhuman Assemblies. In: Bijker/Law 1992, 259- 264.

Bachmair, Ben/Diepold, Peter/de Witt, Claudia (Hrsg.) (2003): Jahrbuch Medienpädagogik 3. Opladen: VS Verlag.

Bailenson, Jemery N./Beall, Andrew C. (2005): Transformed Social Interaction: Exploring the Digital Plasticity of Avatars. Online: http://vhil.stanford.edu/pubs/2006/bailenson-digital-plasticity.pdf [7.6.2009].

Barnes, Brooks (2007): Web Playgrounds of the Very Young. In: New York Times vom 31.12.2007. Online: http://www.nytimes.com/2007/12/31/business/31virtual.html [7.6.2009]

Bausch, Constanze/Jörissen, Benjamin (2005): Das Spiel mit dem Bild. Zur Ikonologie von Action-Computerspielen. In: Wulf/Zirfas 2005, 345-364.

Becker, Barbara/Mark, Gloria (2002): Social Conventions in Computer-mediated Communication: A Comparison of Three Online Shared Virtual Environments. In: Schroder 2002a, 19-39.

Bente, Gary/Krämer, Nicole C./Petersen, Anita (Hrsg.) (2002): Virtuelle Realitäten. Göttingen: Hogrefe.

Bijker, Wiebe E./Law, John (Hrsg.) (1992): Shaping Technology / Building Society: Studies in Sociotechnical Change. Cambridge, Mass.: MIT Press.

Boellstorf, Tom (2008): Coming of Age in Second Life: An Anthropologist Explores the Virtually Human. Princeton: Princeton University Press.

Bormann, Sven (1994): Virtuelle Realität: Genese und Evaluation. München: Addison Wesley.

Butler, Judith (1991): Das Unbehagen der Geschlechter. Frankfurt am Main: Suhrkamp.

Clarke, Adele (2005): Situational Analysis. Grounded Theory after the Postmodern Turn. Thousand Oakes: Sage.

Svarog, Forseti (Hrsg.) (2007): Avatar Expression. (Selbstverlag)

Dery, Mark (1996): Escape velocity. Cyberculture at the end of the century. London: Grove Press.

Featherstone, Mike/Burrows, Roger (Hrsg.) (1995): Cyberspace, Cyberbodies, Cyberpunk. London: Sage.

Ferdig, Rick (Hrsg.) (2008): Handbook of Research on Effective Electronic Gaming in Education. Hershey: Information Science Reference.

Freyermuth, Gundolf S. (1996): Cyberland. Eine Führung durch den High-Tech-Underground. Berlin: Rowohlt.

Fromme, Johannes (2006): Socialisation in the Age of New Media. In: MedienPädagogik 11/2006. Online: http://www.medienpaed.com/05-1/fromme05-1.pdf [16.7.2007].

Fromme, Johannes (2008): Virtuelle Welten und Cyberspace. In: Gross/Marotzki/Sander (2008), 169-201.

Fromme, Johannes/Jörissen, Benjamin/Unger, Alexander (2008): (Self-) Educational effects of computer gaming cultures. In Ferdig 2008, 757-775.

Goffman, Erving (1996): Rahmen-Analyse. Ein Versuch über die Organisation von Alltagserfahrungen. (4. Aufl). Frankfurt am Main: Suhrkamp.

Gross, Friederike von/Marotzki, Winfried/Sander, Uwe (Hrsg.) (2008): Internet – Bildung – Gemeinschaft. Wiesbaden: VS Verlag.

Hansen, Mark B. N. (2006): Bodies in code. Interfaces with digital media. New York: Routledge .

Hillis, Ken (1999): Digital sensations: space, identity, and embodiment in virtual reality. Minnesota: University of Minnesota Press.

Ishida, Toru/Fussell, Susanne R./Vossen, Piek T. J. M. (Hrsg.))(2007): Intercultural Collaboration (IWIC 2007). Wien/New York: Springer.

Jensen, Jens F. (2001): Virtual Inhabited 3D Worlds: Interactivity and Interaction Between Avatars, Autonomous Agents and Users. In: Qvortrup 2001, 23-47.

Jörissen, Benjamin (2008): The Body is the Message. Avatare als visuelle Artikulationen, soziale Aktanten und hybride Akteure. In: Paragrana 17/2008, 277-295.

Jörissen, Benjamin/Marotzki, Winfried (2009): Medienbildung – eine Einführung. Theorie – Methoden – Analysen. Bad Heilbrunn: Klinkhardt/UTB.

Koda, Tomoko (2007): Cross-Cultural Study of Avatars' Facial Expressions and Design Considerations Within Asian Countries. In: Ishida/Fussell/Vossen 2007, 207-220.

KZERO (2009): Virtual Worlds Registered Accounts Q1 2009. Online: http://www.kzero.co.uk/blog/?page_id=2537 [7.6.2009].

Latour, Bruno (2007): Reassembling the social. an introduction to Actor-Network-Theory. Oxford: Oxford University Press.

Marotzki, Winfried (1990): Entwurf einer strukturalen Bildungstheorie. Biographietheoretische Auslegung von Bildungsprozessen in hochkomplexen Gesellschaften. Weinheim: Deutscher Studienverlag.

Marotzki, Winfried (2003): Online-Ethnographie – Wege und Ergebnisse zur Forschung im Kulturraum Internet. In: Bachmair/Diepold/de Witt 2003, 149-165. Online: http://www.uni-magdeburg.de/iew/web/Marotzki/03/virt_Communities/Marotzki_2003.pdf [20.06.2009]

Marotzki, Winfried (2008): Weisen der Artikulation in bildungstheoretischer Perspektive am Beispiel von Web 2.0 Phänomenen. In: Schachtner/Höber 2008, 57-70.

Meder, Norbert (2008): Bildung und virtuelle Welten - Cyberbildung. In: Gross/Marotzki/Sander 2008, 227-239.

Nakamura, Lisa (2007): Digitizing Race: Visual Cultures of the Internet. Minnesota: University Of Minnesota Press.

Petersen, Anita/Bente, Gary/Krämer, Nicole C. (2002): Virtuelle Stellvertreter: Analyse avatar-vermittelter Kommunikationsprozesse. In: Bente/Krämer/Petersen 2002, 227 - 253.

Qvortrup, Lars (Hrsg.) (2001): Virtual Interaction: Interaction in Virtual Inhabited 3D Worlds. London: Springer.

Rheingold, Howard (1992): Virtuelle Welten. Reisen im Cyberspace. Reinbek: Rowohlt.

Sandbothe, Mike (2001): Pragmatische Medienphilosophie: Grundlegung einer neuen Disziplin im Zeitalter des Internet. Weilerswist: Velbrück Wissenschaft.

Schachtner, Christina/Höber, Angelika (Hrsg.) (2008): Learning Communities. Das Internet als neuer Lern- und Wissensraum. Frankfurt am Main: Campus.

Schlette, Magnus/Jung, Matthias (Hrsg.) (2005): Anthropologie der Artikulation. Begriffliche Grundlagen und transdisziplinäre Perspektiven. Würzburg: Königshausen & Neumann.

Schroeder, Ralph (Hrsg.) (2002a): The social life of Avatars. presence and interaction in shared virtual environments. London: Springer.

Schroeder, Ralph (2002b): Social Interaction in Virtual Environments: Key Issues, Common Themes, and a Framework for Research. In: Schroeder 2002a, 1-18.

Schroeder, Ralph/Axelsson, Ann-Sofie (Hrsg.) (2006): Avatars at Work and Play. Collaboration and Interaction in Shared Virtual Environments. Dordrecht: Springer.

Stephenson, Neal (1993): Snow crash. London: Bantam.

Steurer, Siegfried (1996): Schöne neue Wirklichkeiten? Die Herausforderung der virtuellen Realität. Wien: Wuv Universitaets Verlag.

Taylor, T. L. (2002): Living Digitally: Embodiment in Virtual Worlds. In: Schroeder 2002a, 40-62.

White, Michele (2006): The body and the screen. theories of internet spectatorship. Cambridge, Mass: MIT Press.

Wulf, Christoph/Zirfas, Jörg (Hrsg.) (2005): Ikonologie des Performativen. München: Wilhelm Fink.

Yee, Nick (2007): The Proteus Effect: The Effect of Transformed Self-Representation on Behavior. Online:: http://vhil.stanford.edu/pubs/2007/yee-proteus-effect.pdf [19.10.2007].

Digitale Konsumwelten als politische Bildungsräume?
Zur Typologisierung der Online-Praktiken von Verbrauchern

von Jörn Lamla

Einleitung

Wie sehen Bildungsprozesse der Bürgerschaft in einer Verbraucherdemokratie aus, in der klassische Konflikte um private, politische und soziale Bürgerrechte allmählich in den Hintergrund treten und Auseinandersetzungen um die Angebote und Angebotsstrukturen in Marktkontexten an Bedeutung gewinnen? Was mit Ralf Dahrendorf (1994) als Verschiebung im modernen sozialen Konflikt um Anrechte und Angebote, Optionen und Ligaturen der Lebensführung bezeichnet werden kann, hat Anthony Giddens (1991) durch die Gegenüberstellung von emanzipatorischer Politik und Politik der Lebensführung in eine griffige Formel gefasst. „Life politics" bezeichnet den in der fortgeschrittenen Moderne immer zentraleren Bereich solcher kollektiver und individueller Entscheidungsprobleme, den die Demokratie lange ins Reich des Privaten verbannen konnte, der nicht zuletzt wegen seiner existenziellen Aspekte und seines Folgenreichtums (Gesundheit, Umwelt, globale Interdependenzen, Armut usw.), dort aber nicht verbleibt, sondern auf unterschiedlichen Wegen eine Re-Politisierung erfährt. Am Handeln von Regierungen ebenso wie zivilgesellschaftlichen Bewegungen, in profanen Alltagskontexten ebenso wie an strukturellen Marktdynamiken lassen sich Prozesse einer bürgerschaftlichen Mobilisierung der Verbraucherinnen und Verbraucher ebenso wie diskursiven Auseinandersetzung über ihre Konsumpraktiken beobachten. Eine spannende und offene Frage ist dabei, ob und in welcher Richtung sich Haltungen oder Habitusformationen von Konsumsubjekten überhaupt verändern. Eine solche Frage wird hier unter bildungstheoretischen und soziologischen Gesichtspunkten aufgegriffen und auf den Gegenstandsbereich der in den digitalen Konsumwelten des Internets sich abspielenden Online-Praktiken von Verbrauchern bezogen. Dies macht deshalb Sinn, weil das Internet oft als die technologische, soziale, ökonomische und kulturelle Infrastruktur schlechthin für Bildungs- oder Formierungsprozesse zu sogenannten „Consumer Citizen" angesehen wird (vgl. dazu Scammell 2000; Baringhorst 2007; Lamla 2008a).

Auf Basis empirischer Fallanalysen, die im Rahmen des von der Deutschen Forschungsgemeinschaft geförderten Projekts „CyberCash – Konsumpraktiken in der virtuellen Alltagsökonomie" durchgeführt worden sind, soll dieser Fragenkomplex im Folgenden aufgehellt werden. Dabei bediene ich mich einer typologisierenden Darstellung der Online-Praktiken von Verbraucherinnen und Verbrauchern, die im Rahmen einer mehrstündigen Erhebung mittels (medien)biografisch-narrativem Interview und teilnehmender Beobachtung ihrer Computer- und Internetnutzung im privaten Haushalt erfasst worden sind – auch wenn die Individualität dieser Fälle durch diese Darstellung etwas leidet. Es ist das Ziel dieses Beitrags, die Fälle durch minimale und maximale Kontrastierung von als typisch für einzelne Fälle anzusehenden Online-Praktiken in einen theoretischen Zusammenhang zu bringen (3). Zuvor werden die Ausgangsfragen, die Zielsetzungen und das Forschungsdesign des Projektes kurz vorgestellt (2). Einige knappe Schlussfolgerungen zur Verbraucherdemokratie und den Perspektiven bürgerschaftlicher Autonomie im Internetzeitalter schließen den Text ab (4).

Ausgangsfragen, Zielsetzungen und Forschungsdesign des Projekts

Das Forschungsprojekt zielte zunächst ganz allgemein und offen darauf ab, Zusammenhänge und Wechselwirkungen zwischen den dynamischen Strukturentwicklungen digitaler Marktplätze im Internet und Konsumpraktiken der privaten Haushalte, einschließlich der Gebrauchsweisen internetspezifischer Geldformen und Zahlungssysteme, empirisch zu rekonstruieren und typologisch zu erschließen. In Übereinstimmung mit einer Reihe neuerer Ansätze in der sozialwissenschaftlichen Kultur-, Medien-, Wirtschafts- und Technikforschung war davon auszugehen, dass sich die Nutzungsweisen des ökonomischen Angebots im Internet nur angemessen erfassen lassen, wenn die Konsumpraktiken als in den Alltagskontexten der kulturellen Praxis privater Haushalte situiert und eingebettet begriffen werden. Dem wurde mit einem primär ethnographischen Zugang Rechnung getragen, der auf die jeweilige alltagskulturelle und insbesondere (familien-)biografische Rückbettung der Internetnutzung, der Medienkompetenz, des Geldgebrauchs und der kommerziellen Orientierungen abhob. Zugleich war für die Untersuchung die Einsicht entscheidend, dass die Konsumpraktiken im Rahmen der virtuellen Alltagsökonomie auf einen sozial dezentrierten Handlungsraum treffen, der sich dynamisch entwickelt und durch komplexe ökonomische, technische und kulturelle Prozesse strukturiert wird. Weder war davon auszugehen, dass sich die alltäglichen Konsumgewohnheiten einfach bruchlos in die digitale Alltagsökonomie verlängern, noch war anzunehmen, dass sich die Marktstrukturen der Internet-Ökonomie der Alltagskultur privater Haushalte einfach bemächtigen und den Eigensinn eingelebter Konsummuster schlicht übergehen.

Die Kulturen des Alltags und der Lebensführung wurden nicht als Randbedingung, sondern als Fundament ökonomischen Handelns betrachtet, dessen Parameter deshalb zunächst unbestimmt bleiben konnten. Die neuere wirtschaftssoziologische Forschung fasst Märkte und Marktbeziehungen im Vergleich zur neoklassischen Modellbildung in höherem Maße als kulturabhängig auf. Aus diesem Grund wurde in der Erhebung kein Bild vom Internet und seinen Märkten vorab fixiert, um den privaten Umgang damit anschließend zu untersuchen. Vielmehr bilden die kulturellen Dispositionen einen maßgeblichen (aber nicht ausschließlichen) Hintergrund, von dem aus nicht nur die Märkte, sondern auch das Internet insgesamt sozial konstruiert werden. [Das] Internet – diese Sprechweise ist schon reifizierend und sollte sozialwissenschaftlich nicht unhinterfragt verdoppelt werden – eröffnet einen relativ neuen, alles andere als scharf konturierten Kommunikationsraum, in dem [das] ökonomische Handeln - und wiederum gilt es, den bestimmten Artikel einzuklammern - seinen Platz und seine Bestimmung erst noch finden muss. Diese alltags- und kultursoziologische Perspektive auf die Praktiken des Konsums und Geldgebrauchs (vgl. auch Zelizer 1994) schlägt sich damit auch auf die Typenbildung nieder, insofern die Typisierungen und Klassifizierungen, die im ökonomischen Feld nicht selten entlang kommerziell definierter Lebensstilkategorien erfolgen, hier nicht unhinterfragt übernommen werden sollen. Vielmehr sind es eher die im kulturellen Feld verankerten, impliziten lebensweltlichen Ansprüche, die hier als Bezugspunkt typologisierender Kontrastierungen gewählt werden. Genau das begründet die Affinität des Projekts zu bildungs- und demokratietheoretischen Fragestellungen und Forschungsansätzen. Konsumpraktiken sind in dieser Perspektive nicht auf kommerzielle Sinnkontexte festgelegt, sondern entfalten – wie etwa Michel de Certeau (1988) an der Konsumpraktik des Lesens verdeutlicht – ihre eigene „Ökonomie", die mit der institutionalisierten ökonomischen Rechts- und Eigentumsordnung in Konflikt geraten kann, wie im Bereich des Internets insbesondere die Praktiken des „File-Sharing" zeigen.

Nun setzt ein „theoretisches Sampling" (vgl. Strauss/Corbin 1996) der Fälle nach kontrastierenden Konsumpraktiken neben haushalts- oder akteursbezogenen Unterscheidungslinien der Alltagskultur aber auch Kenntnisse über den sich dynamisch wandelnden *Möglichkeitsraum* internetbezogener Konsumpraktiken voraus. Aus diesem Grund wurden aus dem Repertoire an qualitativen Methoden verschiedene Ansätze aufgegriffen und zu einem mehrstufigen Forschungsdesign zusammengefügt: Zum einen betrifft dies die Ebene ethnographischer Erhebung und fallrekonstruktiver sowie kontrastierender Analyse internetbezogener Konsumpraktiken in privaten Haushalten. Zum anderen die Frage, wie sich die Strukturentwicklung digitaler Märkte mittels qualitativer Methoden empirisch erschließen und analysieren lässt. Für den ersten Problemkomplex wurden folgende Methoden trianguliert (vgl. ausführlicher dazu Lamla 2007, 786-790):

- Online-Fragebogen, der zur Vorselektion des Samples, zur Erhebung von objektiven Daten und zur Vorbereitung eines Interviews anhand erster Angaben zum Internetnutzungsverhalten diente;
- narratives Interview zur (Internet-)Biografie, um die sinnstrukturellen Zusammenhänge zwischen Internetnutzungs- und Konsumverhalten einerseits und lebensgeschichtlich erworbenen kulturellen oder habituellen Dispositionen andererseits herauszuarbeiten;

- Leitfadeninterview zu Alltags- und Konsumpraktiken, welches zunächst unabhängig von der Internetnutzung nach fallspezifischen Relevanzen sucht, die im Spektrum konsumbezogener Internetanwendungen mehr oder weniger konsistent wiederkehren können;
- Gespräch am heimischen PC zur Erhebung von Surfgewohnheiten, da Alltagsroutinen nur begrenzt sprachlich repräsentiert und darstellbar sind;
- Argumentations- und Reflexionsfragen zur Erhebung von Deutungsmustern zum gesellschaftlichen Wandel im Internetzeitalter, von Selbstkonzepten, ethischen Vorstellungen und Kriterien der sozialen Anerkennung;
- ethnographische Beobachtungen im privaten Haushalt, wobei insbesondere die räumliche Konstellation des Internetzugangs für spätere Auswertungen fotografisch fixiert wurde;
- Website-Analysen von Favoritenseiten, um Abweichungen der Konsumpraktiken von Typisierungen feststellen zu können, wie sie - etwa durch das Design der Websites - seitens der Anbieter implizit oder explizit vorgenommen werden.

Für die Auswertung wurden insbesondere Verfahren der sequenzanalytischen Interpretation sowie der Codierung (mittels der Software MaxQDA2) eingesetzt. Die Analyse des Interviewmaterials erfolgte in mehreren Schritten. Zunächst wurde anhand der Ersterzählung und des obligatorischen immanenten Nachfrageteils zur (Internet) Biografie rekonstruiert, was [das] Internet aus der Perspektive der Lebensführung der Befragten bedeutet. Denn der Möglichkeitsraum Internet muss aufgrund seiner offenen Struktur zunächst pragmatisch geschlossen werden, wofür die Nutzerinnen und Nutzer auf verfügbares kulturelles Handlungs- und Hintergrundwissen zurückgreifen, in dem sich über die Biografie hinaus familien-, generationen-, gruppen- oder auch organisationsspezifische Erfahrungen, Traditionen, Routinen und Interessen sedimentiert haben. Anhand der episodischen Erzählungen zur Alltagsorganisation und zu ökonomischen Praktiken der Haushaltsführung und des Konsums wurden die im ersten Schritt generierten Hypothesen zum einen überprüft und verfeinert. Zum anderen ließen sich weiterführende Hypothesen darüber bilden, in welcher Hinsicht insbesondere der Konsumalltag und die Konsumgewohnheiten das für die soziale Konstruktion des neuen Kommunikationsraums maßgebliche Handlungswissen bereitstellen. In einem dritten Schritt wurde dann anhand der episodischen Erzählungen zur Internetnutzung sowie der Präsentation am heimischen PC (Surfgewohnheiten) untersucht, inwiefern sich dieses Wissen pragmatisch bewährt, wenn es auf die Strukturen und Dynamiken des digitalen Kommunikationsraums trifft. Dieser Schritt war für die Fallkontrastierung und Typenbildung entscheidend, insofern sich hierbei Fragen nach der lebenspraktischen Autonomiesicherung bzw. Anfälligkeit für Verstrickungen, d.h. nach fallspezifischen

Passungsverhältnissen und Verlaufskurven alltagsökonomischer Praxis und Internetnutzung untersuchen ließen.[1]

Konnten die Einzelfallanalysen und Fallkontrastierungen auf etablierte Methoden der qualitativen Sozialforschung zurückgreifen, so änderte sich dies mit dem Wechsel von der offline- zur online-ethnographischen Perspektive. Eine Ethnographie [des] Internets *im* Internet ist unverzichtbar, weil sich nur so die dynamischen Strukturentwicklungen des neuen Kommunikationsraums und seiner Marktplätze, Geldformen und Zahlungssysteme dokumentieren und in die Analyse einbeziehen lassen.[2] Entscheidend für die Kombination von Online- und Offline-Ethnographie (vgl. Miller/Slater 2001) ist dabei, von welchen *Kulturraum*-Konzepten diese Methoden-Triangulation ausgeht. So ließen sich diese Perspektiven einerseits so miteinander verknüpfen, als handelte es sich beim Internet um einen zweiten, eigenständigen Kulturraum, der mit dem ersten, ebenfalls eigenständigen Kulturraum vielfältig interferiert. Andererseits könnte die Verschränkung von Online- und Offline-Ethnographie auch als „multi-sited-ethnography" (Marcus 1995) gefasst werden, die Strukturen des Kulturraums (und Marktplatzes) nicht auf zwei Seiten fixiert, sondern ausgehend von den Konsumpraktiken den zunächst unbestimmten, hybriden Bezugsraum rekonstruiert (vgl. Lamla 2009 i.E.). Die empirische Einsicht, dass die zweite Auffassung dem Gegenstand angemessen ist, hat im Projekt zu einer Konzeption des Wechselverhältnisses zwischen Konsumpraktiken und Marktdynamiken im Internet geführt, die das von Anselm Strauss und Mitarbeitern schon in den 1970er Jahren für die Computerforschung empfohlene Theorem „sozialer Welten und Arenen" aufgreift (vgl. Strauss 1993; Kling/Gerson 1978; Clarke 2005): Die über Kernaktivitäten definierten sozialen Welten entsprechen den über Kommunikationstechnologien des Internets (insbesondere im Web 2.0-Zeitalter) konstituierten Kultur- und Handlungsräumen recht genau. Denn das Internet wird damit als offener Prozess sozialer Ordnungs- und Grenzbildung begriffen, an dem eine Vielzahl sozialer Welten (und Praktiken) durch Segmentierung, Intersektion und Aushandlung beteiligt ist. Zudem ist das Konzept anschlussfähig an neuere technik- (Latour 1995) und wirtschaftssoziologische (Fligstein 1996) Theorie- und Forschungsansätze und ihre Fragestellungen.[3]

1 Die (fallunabhängige) Strukturanalyse ausgewählter Websites dient hierbei komplementär dazu, Kongruenzen bzw. Inkongruenzen in den Konsumpraktiken aufzudecken und auf ihre sinnstrukturellen und habituellen Hintergründe sowie lebenspraktischen Konsequenzen zu befragen.

2 Beispielhaft sei auf jene Innovationen verwiesen, die mit dem Stichwort „Web 2.0" verbunden werden und die das Internet als (politischen) Bildungsraum in vieler Hinsicht verändern.

3 Für zukünftige Forschungen ist geplant, die digitale Evolution von Märkten und sozio-ökonomischen Ordnungen mit dieser Meso-Perspektive genauer zu analysieren. Ein erstes Lehrforschungsprojekt ist dazu im SoSe 2008 und WS 2008/09 an der Justus-Liebig-Universität Gießen durchgeführt worden. Für ihren theoretischen und methodologischen Input hierzu während zweier Workshops dankt der Verfasser Winfried Marotzki, Benjamin Jörissen und Jörg Strübing.

Zur Typologisierung der Online-Praktiken von Verbrauchern

Typen können in der qualitativen Sozialforschung in vielerlei Hinsicht aus empirischem Material gewonnen werden. Entscheidend ist der theoretische Ertrag, der sich aus den Abgrenzungen und Unterscheidungen gewinnen lässt. Hintergrund der folgenden Typologisierung ist das Interesse an Erkenntnissen über die „Verbraucherdemokratie" und ihre Potenziale im Internetzeitalter, wobei das Zusammenspiel von Konsumpraktiken und Marktdynamiken hierfür als empirischer Ausgangs- oder Zugangspunkt gewählt wird. Demokratieforschung wird dabei in einem sehr weiten, an John Deweys (1996) Pragmatismus angelehnten Sinne verstanden: Es soll untersucht werden, inwiefern sich in Kontexten des Marktes aus den Interaktionen und Interdependenzen beteiligter Akteure und Welten soziale Arenen formieren, in denen (sub)politische Aushandlungsprozesse über Aspekte der sozial-ökonomischen Ordnung vonstatten gehen. Im Projekt sind hierzu aus ca. 100 per Online-Fragebogen erfassten Personen 19 Fälle gemäß „theoretical sampling" ausgewählt und ausführlich untersucht worden. Diese Fälle lassen sich typologisch in folgende drei Prozessformen eingruppieren, wobei zum Verständnis der jeweiligen Spezifika die Dezentrierung der Kultur- und Interaktionsräume über den Konsumalltag im privaten Haushalt hinaus (und damit die Betrachtung von Interaktionspartnern wie technischen Agenten, ökonomischen Anbietern usw.) von Schritt zu Schritt immer wichtiger werden.

Die lebenspraktische Autonomie der Alltagsökonomie

In unserem Sample findet sich eine Reihe von Fällen, die belegen, dass die Routinen des Alltagslebens und die biografischen Dispositionen der Nutzer maßgeblich die Aneignung und Konstruktion des Internets – hier verstanden als „Konsummittel" (Ritzer 1999) – bestimmen. Beispielhaft hierfür kann der virtuelle Gang durch den Online-Supermarkt von Liselotte Arenowitz angeführt werden, die als Pendlerin zwischen dem Arbeitsort in der Schweiz und ihrer Familie und Partnerschaft in Deutschland die Vorteile der Onlinebestellung bei der schweizerischen Migros schätzen gelernt hat. Pragmatische Anforderungen der Alltagsorganisation werden hier zum bestimmenden Faktor der digitalen Transformation von Konsumgewohnheiten. Das Internet und sein Konsumangebot werden vollständig nach solchen Gesichtspunkten gefiltert. Dies macht Frau Arenowitz im Interview und bei der Vorführung ihrer Favoritenseiten am Bildschirm eindrucksvoll dadurch deutlich, dass sie ihren Online-Einkauf wie den gewohnten Gang durch die Regalreihen gestaltet. Sie hat ihren Einkaufszettel im Kopf und weiß längst genau, wo sie was findet. Welche Produkte und Offerten es rechts und links davon gibt, ist ihr gleichgültig. *Transformationen* der Alltagsökonomie finden daher kaum statt und verdanken sich – wenn überhaupt – pragmatischen Kompromissen, die ihr das digitale Kommunikationsmedium abverlangen: So gibt es für den Online-Einkauf abweichend vom gewohnten Supermarkteinkauf eine Mindestbestellsumme von 100 Franken, was aber kaum stört, da Frau Arenowitz ohnehin für längere Zeitabschnitte plant.

Für den Zusammenhang von Konsumpraktiken und Marktdynamiken wesentlich ist bei diesem *Typus* die Limitierung möglichen Markthandelns durch historisch-biografisch aufgeschichtete kulturelle und ökonomische Relevanzen des Alltagslebens. Dabei wäre die alltagsökonomische Internetnutzung als *Typik* eines rationalen, sparsam-kontrollierten Konsumentenverhaltens missverstanden. Denn die Fallstruktur bietet auch Raum für Verführungen durch Internetangebote, wenn es etwa um die Suche nach Geschenken für Bekannte und Verwandte geht. Aus biografieanalytischer Perspektive wird aber deutlich, dass sich dahinter nicht Inkonsequenz oder medial verselbständigte Konsumdynamik verbirgt. Vielmehr wird einfach eine ganze Bandbreite an Konsumpraktiken ins Internet verlagert, was im Falle von Frau Arenowitz auch mit Ausgrenzungs- und Stigmatisierungserfahrungen im „realen Leben" zusammenhängen könnte. Denn sie hatte in ihrer Berufsbiografie wiederholt mit Mobbing zu kämpfen, worauf sie nicht nur passiv mit Exit-Strategien reagiert, sondern mit aktiver Suche nach Kontexten, in denen eine berufliche Selbstverwirklichung unter Vermeidung solcher Schwierigkeiten möglich ist. So wechselt sie in der Situation von Arbeitslosigkeit etwa zu einem autonomen Radiosender, der im Beruf ähnlich von körperlicher Begegnung befreit wie das Internet im Konsumalltag. Deshalb verwundert es nicht, dass das Internet hier zum *uni*versellen Konsummittel wird, obgleich es die Relevanzen des Alltags und der privaten Lebensführung keineswegs bestimmt.

Wilhelm Urbig, dessen Internetkenntnisse sich weitgehend auf drei Konsum-Websites beschränken – eBay[4], Amazon[5] und ZVAB (Verzeichnis antiquarischer Bücher)[6] – bildet dazu einen minimalen Kontrast. Diese drei Seiten ermöglichen ihm, umfänglicher als über lokale Antiquariate sein Hobby auszuüben, klassische Literatur – vor allem die Bücher des Manesse-Verlags – zu sammeln. Und ihre Nutzung beschränkt sich auch konsequent hierauf. Beeindruckend ist dabei vor allem, wie die Ausweitung des Marktplatzes – Herr Urbig bestellt Bücher und CDs nun vielfach aus dem Ausland – mit einem rigiden Minimalismus sonstiger Kenntnisse rund um das Internet einhergeht. Beispielsweise ist Herr Urbig nur sehr wenig mit der Nutzung von Browsern vertraut und muss, um auf seine Seiten zu kommen, stets einen komplizierten Weg über die Suchmaschine Google gehen, in dessen Suchmaske er die Anfangsbuchstaben seiner Zielseite tippt, um durch die Speicherfunktion dann zu den von Google bereitgestellten Links zu kommen. Von einer Abspeicherung als Favoriten oder der Nutzung der Ad-

4 http://www.ebay.de
5 http://www.amazon.de
6 http://www.zvab.com

resszeile des Browsers hatte Herr Urbig bis zum Zeitpunkt des Interviews noch nichts gehört. Google und der Browser sind in der fallspezifischen Internetkonstruktion überhaupt nicht getrennt.

Dieser Fall macht deutlich, dass die Autonomie alltäglicher Lebenspraxis die Internetnutzung kehrseitig auch stark beschränken kann. Während Wilhelm Urbig seinen Handlungsraum gezielt erweitert und sich hierfür die nötigen Tipps von seinem Bruder holt, finden sich andere Fälle im Sample, bei denen die Alltagsroutinen verhindern, dass innovative Potenziale der digitalen Technologie, die für die eigene Lebenspraxis Entlastung bringen könnten, überhaupt in den Blick kommen. Wenn etwa die biografische Aneignungsgeschichte ein allzu diffuses, unzureichendes Wissen vom Internet vermittelt und eine veränderte Nutzung im Alltag hohe Transaktionskosten beinhalten würde, für die in den aktuellen Lebensentwürfen die zeitlichen Ressourcen fehlen, bleiben die digitalen Konsumwelten weitgehend verschlossen. Im Falle von Herrn Rieger etwa, für den es im Interviewgespräch schwer vorstellbar erschien, dass die hin und wieder für Präsentationen konsultierte Online-Enzyklopädie „Wikipedia" nicht von einem professionellen Unternehmen produziert werde, bleibt das Internet eine fremde Region. Und das obwohl der Finanzmanager im beruflichen Alltag routinemäßig mit komplexer Computer- und Intranet-Technologie operiert und sich die Herausforderungen an die Alltagsorganisation nach der Scheidung von der Mutter seiner Kinder mehren.

Im Fall von Heidemarie Hohenbichler zeigt sich dagegen, wie ein ausgeprägt bildungsbürgerlicher Habitus in Kombination mit der Erziehung von Kindern im Alter von Teenagern zum schrittweisen und gezielten Abbau der generationenspezifischen Fremdheit gegenüber dem neuen Medium führen kann. Auch bei ihr überwiegt – wie in den vorhergehenden Fällen – die Autonomie einer privaten Lebensführung, die sich in Alltagsgewohnheiten manifestiert, die durch das Konsummittel „Internet" vielleicht modifiziert, nicht aber in ihrer Relevanz-Struktur verändert werden.[7] Zugleich kann ihr Fall diese Relevanz-Struktur näher qualifizieren: So behalten Marktpraktiken bei diesem ersten Typus abgeleiteten Status in der Alltagsökonomie und die Hierarchisierung von ethischen Gesichtspunkten eines guten Lebens über deren Konkretisierung in biografischen Lebensplänen bis hin zu alltäglichen Mitteln des Konsums stellt selbst ein schützenswertes Gut dar. Bei Frau Hohenbichler wird dieser Zusammenhang sehr anschaulich, wenn sie sich über die maschinell generierten Buchvorschläge von Amazon aufregt und solche übergriffigen Werbeformen mit dem Hinweis auf die eigenen Autonomie- und Individualitätsansprüche streng zurückweist:

7 Marktdynamiken, die strukturell zu diesem Typus passen, ordnen sich diesen Relevanzen nach und stellen ein Internetangebot bereit, das z.B. hohe Anschlussfähigkeiten durch Ähnlichkeiten zum gewohnten Katalogeinkauf, durch Bereitstellung transparenter Produkt- und Preisinformationen und die Verwendung herkömmlicher Zahlungsmethoden (Rechnung, Vorkasse, Nachnahme, Bankeinzug) anstelle netzspezifischer Währungen usw. aufweist.

H: „Was Sie vielleicht interessiert äh die Amazonn (.) Seite hat ja so einen Dienst äh mhh (1) indem sie (.) sich mein Kaufverhalten und sich da rein schleicht in mein Gehirn und mir dann alles Mögliche vorschlägt (1) des ärgert mich (2) dann denk ich wieso jetz hab ich einmal en en Krimi mir gekauft wo halt äh zufällich kommt da vor des Wort Blut ja jetz (.) schlagen sie mir alles vor wo Blut vorkommt (.) des is ja doch wohl ätzend oder Käufer die dieses Buch gekauft haben haben auch jenes Buch gekauft da hab ich gedacht s s ne Frechheit ich weiß doch selber was ich kaufen will (.) also ich finde des bevormundend und schau des nie an (.) ne? (1) (I: hmhm) da stell'n sich mir die Haare auf weil (.) des kommt ma n bisschen zu big brother watching you (1) das des (.) ma weiß natürlich dass ma Spuren lässt mit jedem Klick ne des weiß man (.) aber das die jetz da gleich n Profil erstellen und jetzt Glauben ich bin eine Vampir (.) äh Freundin weil einma da in dem Titel des Wort Blut vorkam (.) also wirklich nee."

(Post)Soziale Transformation alltagsökonomischer Muster im Internetzeitalter

Einen maximalen Kontrast hierzu repräsentieren solche Fälle, in denen die Relevanzhierarchien im Rahmen internetvermittelter Konsumpraktiken modifiziert werden oder aus dem Gleichgewicht kommen. Auch bei diesem zweiten Typus haben die biografischen, generationenspezifischen und soziokulturellen Dispositionen einen wichtigen Einfluss, der das Wechselspiel von Konsumpraktiken und Marktstrukturen aber unzureichend erklärt. Während sich das Internetangebot dem ersten Typus anpassen muss, ist das Wechselspiel hier deutlich offener und unbestimmter. Wenn sich etwa das Bedürfnis nach sozialer Anerkennung mit Konsum- und/oder Internetsurfpraktiken vermischt und darin verselbständigt, hängt es stärker von der Internetbiografie, Online-Routinen und Angeboten ab, wohin sich die alltagsökonomischen Relevanzen entwickeln. Transformationspfade sind dann in größerem Maße kontingent, weil ethische Orientierungen der Lebenspraxis nicht mehr traditional verankert oder innengeleitet auftreten, sondern – im Wunsch nach Anerkennung – an außenleitende Instanzen delegiert werden (vgl. Riesman et al. 1958).

Bei Elke Bertram (vgl. Lamla 2007) lässt sich dieses Strukturmuster gut herausarbeiten. Nachdem ihre Berufsbiografie mit der Geburt ihres ersten Kindes einen scharfen Karriereknick erfährt, den sie als Personalmanagerin eines mittelgroßen Unternehmens als Missachtung und Degradierung erlebt, und ihr Familienalltag weitgehend durch Abwesenheit des Ehemannes gekennzeichnet ist, wird das Internet – nicht zuletzt aufgrund seiner Vorzüge, das Einkaufen und Organisieren des Alltags raum-zeitlich unabhängiger zu machen – zu einem immer wichtigeren Interaktionspartner. So stellt sich bei Frau Bertram die Gewohnheit ein, anstelle einsamer Abende vor dem Fernseher lieber „eBay-Abende" zu verbringen und das ein oder andere „Teil" zu ersteigern, von dem sie ihrem Mann besser nichts erzählt. Dabei ist das Anerkennungsmotiv mit dem beruflichen Selbstbild so tief verwoben, dass auch diese Surf- und Kaufpraktiken zunächst beruflich gerahmt und gerechtfertigt werden, nämlich als Produktrecherche für die Geschenk-Agentur, die sie parallel zum Familienalltag online aufbauen und betreiben will. Doch löst sich das „Stöbern" zunehmend aus dem beruflichen Kontext, in dem Suchen und Recherchieren stets relevante Internetpraktiken waren. In zunehmendem Maße täuscht sich Frau Bertram diesen Rahmen nur noch vor und fällt in einen „imaginativen Hedonismus" (Campbell 1987), den sie sich aufgrund ihres Selbstbildes als sparsam lebender Person allerdings nicht eingesteht. So wird das Blättern in Modezeitschriften und Katalogen zum Modell für die alltägliche Internetnutzung, auch wenn dies noch als produktive Tätigkeit einer professionellen Marktanalyse dargestellt wird. Und Konsumangebote, bei denen das Kaufen selbst zum Beleg für die eigene Sparsamkeit werden kann, wie etwa im Falle der Schnäppchenjagd bei eBay oder beim Punktesammeln mittels Payback-Karte, ermöglichen ebenfalls einen pragmatischen Kompromiss zwischen widerstreitenden Motiven.[8]

Eine ähnliche Sogwirkung hat eBay auf die leidenschaftliche Flohmarktgängerin Hanne Baumert, mit dem wichtigen Unterschied, dass Frau Baumert bereits vor dem Internetzeitalter Schwierigkeiten hatte, sich den Kauf schöner Dinge zu verkneifen. Eine Transformation ihrer alltagsökonomischen Praktiken findet somit eigentlich nicht statt. Aber die stark erweiterte Verfügbarkeit von Gebrauchtwaren und Sammlerstücken durch das Internet wird unter dieser Konsumdisposition zu einem Problem, weil das Fehlen von Stoppregeln nun dazu führt, dass der Ehemann von Frau Baumert immer wieder durch die Republik fahren muss, um alte Wohnanhänger, Wendeltreppen oder auch ein altes Boot abzuholen, dass zudem die Sammlung von Hüten und alten Masken seiner Frau immer größer wird und die angehäuften Schulden sich auf diese Weise jedenfalls nicht verringern. Hanne Baumert weiß um die „Suchtgefahren" des neuen Mediums, da sie diese an ihrem online-spielenden Sohn beobachten kann, der sich mit physisch Anwesenden nur noch auf LAN-Partys zu unterhalten scheint. Und sie verabredet mit ihm auch Maßnahmen zur Begrenzung seines Internetkonsums. Aber ihr selbst fällt dies noch schwer: Ihr auf die Nutzung von eBay weitgehend beschränktes Konsummuster schwankt zwischen exzessiver Nutzung und Phasen völliger Abstinenz, wobei den Projekten künstlerischer Selbstverwirklichung im Zuge der themenbezogenen Einrichtung von kleinen Wohneinheiten zur Vermietung die Rolle eines Taktgebers

8 Ausgehend von Georg Simmels Philosophie des Geldes rekonstruiert Christoph Deutschmann (2000) Praktiken wie den übersteigerten Geiz oder die exzessive Verschwendung und Verschuldung gleichermaßen als pathologische Folgen des Geldgebrauchs, die mit dem religiösen Verheißungscharakter dieses „absoluten Mittels" zusammenhingen. Dies ist ein anderer Fall von ökonomischer Praxis, bei dem das Medium die Führung übernimmt.

zukommt. Nachfolgende Interviewsequenz aus dem Surf-Abschnitt bringt dies am Beispiel „Afrika-Zimmer" zum Ausdruck:

> B: […] also ich hab ma in Afrika jetz kommen dann schon wieder neue das's gefährlich ne (.) jetz hab ich grad gesehn oh da war was [surft] (.) jetz kommt's [stöhnt] da muss man dann gucken (.) oder schnell weggucken @3@
> I: no- @.@ noch mal noch ma (.) also
> B: ja da kommt do immer was Neues (.) un manchmal seh ich so aus m Augenwinkel grad noch [atmet schockiert ein] da konnte was Gudes gewesen sein un dann geh ich manchma no zurück um die neuen Bildchen zu sehn die woll'n (.) ja klar die turnen einen an ne (1) @un dann muss ich gucken @1@
> I: okeh das sind (Artikel die kürzlich (.) beendet)
> B: neee die kommen neu (.) dann hat die ham jetz gesehn (.) also Ebay macht ja so Querverbin-
> B: ja ja
> H: dungen die ham gesehn (.) ich hab so was beobachtet hab's nit ersteigert oder bin überboten worden (I: ja) (.) das registrieren die dann ja un dann geben die einen zum Anlocken dann das was demnächst kommt was so ähnlich is (.) das @funktioniert ja@ @1@

Bei Vorliegen entsprechender biografischer Dispositionen kann also die dynamische Ausweitung von Optionen durch das Internet zur Transformation alltagsökonomischer Muster führen. Das Internet gewinnt in diesen Fällen über den instrumentellen Aspekt eines Konsummittels hinaus die Qualität eines Interaktionspartners, der in die Bildung von Erwartungen aktiv eingreift. Diese Qualitäten erinnern an das Theorem der „Post-Sozialität" von Karin Knorr-Cetina (1998). Es postuliert nicht das Ende von Sozialität, sondern deren Ausweitung auf Beziehungen zu Objekten. In dem Maße, wie komplexe technische oder Wissens-Objekte in spätmodernen Gesellschaften den Alltag prägen, entwickeln sich – teils kompensatorisch – soziale Bindungen zu diesen Artefakten. Ein besonders interessantes, extremes Beispiel hierfür liefert der Fall Jens Treichel, dessen exzessive Nutzung von Internetangeboten wie Paid-Mails[9] oder Web-Miles[10] im Interview auffiel. Erklärungsbedürftig daran erschien vor allem, dass ökonomische Motive für die Aufrechterhaltung dieser Praktiken allein keinesfalls ausreichend erschienen, weil sich Herr Treichel über die verschwindend geringen Verdienstmöglichkeiten einer Freizeit-Arbeit wie „Werbebanner-Klicken" oder „Testberichte-Schreiben" sehr im Klaren war. Damit stellte sich die Frage, welche anderen Motivkonstellationen hier vorliegen könnten. Ein Antwortversuch liegt in der Adaption der These von Karin Knorr-Cetina – allerdings mit einer kritischen Nuancierung: Die Formen der Reziprozität,

9 Bei Paidmails erhält der Nutzer eine Vergütung für das Lesen von Werbeemails.
10 Webmiles stellen ein Bonusprogramm im Internet dar. URL: http://www.webmiles.de/

die sich in Objekt- oder Artefaktbeziehungen entwickeln, bleiben im kommerziellen Internet mit seinen ökonomisch-technischen Agenten sehr häufig hinter den Erwartungen einer emotionalen ebenso wie ethisch-kognitiven Stabilisierung des Selbstbildes weit zurück.[11]

Auch aus diesem Grund dürfte die Suche nach Anerkennung bei vielen KonsumentInnen mit der Disposition zu außengeleitetem Handeln zur Nutzung von genuin *sozialen* Vernetzungsangeboten führen – seien dies nun Multi-User-Online-Games oder aber Foren und Communities, die unterschiedlichsten Zwecken eines sozialen Austausches dienen können. Auch Jens Treichel kann durch das Ansammeln von Web-Miles und andere Punktestände seine familienbiografisch bedingten Beziehungsdefizite nicht nachhaltig kompensieren und verlagert seine Aktivität letztlich auf die Teilnahme an Verbraucher-Communities, in denen das Schreiben minimal entlohnter Produkt-Erfahrungsberichte mit einem regen sozialen Austausch unter den Peers verknüpft wird. Während in seinem Falle die Hoffnungen auf soziale Anerkennung und Wertschätzung auch hier eher enttäuscht werden, lässt sich in minimalem Kontrast dazu am Fall Lena Pelzer zeigen, wie die Nutzung desselben Portals (Ciao[12]) biografische Transformationen begünstigen und zur Entwicklung neuer sozialer Kompetenzen führen kann, die das Repertoire der Problembewältigung alltäglicher Lebensführung durch soziales Networking erweitern.

Die ausgedehnte Nutzung von eBay – auch für Verkäufe – erklärt sich alltagsökonomisch bei Frau Pelzer zunächst aus Sparzwängen der jungen Familie mit zwei Kindern und geringem Einkommen. Erst allmählich transformiert sich das Internet zu einem Raum der Kommunikation und des sozialen Miteinander. Es ist die genannte Verbraucher-Community Ciao, in der sich Frau Pelzer ebenso wie Jens Treichel viele Stunden in der Woche aufhält, um kreativ und z.T. subversiv die Möglichkeiten der Meinungsbekundung und sozialen Vernetzung, die diese Plattform bietet, zu nutzen. Interessant am medien-biografischen Pfadverlauf von Frau Pelzer ist im Kontrast zu den vorangehenden Fällen vor allem, dass sie sich weniger in Abhängigkeiten verstrickt und das Internet bloß kompensatorisch für fehlende Unterstützung im sozialen Umfeld gebraucht. Vielmehr hat sie in ihrem Ehemann, von dem sie inzwischen getrennt lebt, das Negativbeispiel einer Online-Spielsucht direkt vor Augen und macht dessen Internetverhalten auch maßgeblich für die spätere Trennung verantwortlich. Hatte sie sich mit der Alleinverantwortung für die Familie fast schon abgefunden, an der Beziehung festgehalten und den Interneteinsatz – anders als ihr Ehemann – den Erfordernissen

11 Interessant ist es, diesen Ansatz anerkennungstheoretisch auszuweiten und die Frage zu stellen, welche Formen der Reziprozität sich in solchen Beziehungen reproduzieren können und unter welchen Umständen verdinglichende Effekte eintreten (vgl. Honneth 2005), insofern die anspruchsvolle Gabe der interpersonellen Anerkennung nurmehr simuliert wird.

12 http://www.ciaio.de

der Alltagsorganisation untergeordnet, so hilft ihr der soziale Austausch und die Erfahrung von Anerkennung über Online-Freundschaften, sich aus dieser Lage zu befreien und die privaten Abhängigkeiten aufzukündigen. Soziales Networking – online und offline – wird zum Modell einer Lebenspraxis, in der schließlich auch der Beruf als Anwältin mit der Rolle der Alleinerziehenden zweier Kinder vereinbar wird.[13]

„Strategischer Konventionalismus" – Märkte als subpolitische Arenen

Soziale Aktivitäten im Netz implizieren nicht notwendig auch Konflikte, die den ordnenden Rahmen, d.h. die geltenden Regeln und Normen des Austauschs von symbolischen Gaben und kommerziellen Gütern tangieren. Insbesondere ist dies dann nicht zu erwarten, wenn das Internet als Plattform für Kommunikationen genutzt wird, die sich weitgehend auf Selbstverständigung einer lange etablierten sozialen Welt beschränken. Viele thematisch gebundene Foren und Kommunikationsräume haben diesen Charakter und fungieren (vielleicht leicht modifiziert) als Fortsetzung kultureller Praktiken im neuen Medium. Mit der Zunahme an Komplexität und insbesondere an Intersektionen verschiedener sozialer Welten und Akteure dürfte sich dies allerdings ändern – insbesondere dort, wo innovative Praktiken entstehen. Dann werden soziale Ordnungen ausgehandelt, wobei verschiedene Prinzipien und Reziprozitätsformen zum Tragen kommen, angefangen von Solidarbeziehungen (insbesondere über die symbolischen Gaben von Anerkennung, Freundschaft usw.) über den ökonomischen Tausch von Äquivalenten mittels Geld bis hin zu einseitiger Instrumentalisierung und Ausbeutung (Sahlins 1965; Caillé 2008). Ansatzweise und im Kleinen finden sich subpolitische Aus-

---

13 Auch wenn sie ebenso wie ihr Ex-Mann große Teile der Lebensführung in digitale Räume verlagert, so unterscheidet sich das Muster doch – zumindest auf den ersten Blick – von dessen virtuellen Kriegszügen, die auf einer kommerziell produzierten Erlebniswelt basieren. Auf den zweiten Blick gilt es allerdings zu sehen, dass auch die offenere, freiere Praxis des sozialen Networking von Kommerzialisierung keineswegs frei bleibt: Die sozialen Aktivitäten von Lena Pelzer oder Jens Treichel werden durch den Betreiber der Plattform in mehrfacher Hinsicht kommerziell überformt, indem dieser den Meinungsaustausch und das Emergieren einer Online-Community systematisch als kulturelle Wertschöpfung (für die Werbung, das Marketing und die kommerzielle Marktforschung) ausnutzt, was den Verbrauchern selten voll bewusst wird (Lamla 2008b). Es gehört zu den unternehmerischen Leistungen im Kapitalismus, sich in einer dynamisch wandelnden Gesellschaft zu behaupten und kulturelle Trends – wie das Social Networking – aufzugreifen, um ihnen frühzeitig eine ökonomische Form zu geben (Schumpeter 1950). Dies gilt es zu berücksichtigen, wenn der Bildungswert solcher Plattformen für die Generierung von „user-generated content" eingeschätzt werden soll. Von einer Demokratisierung der Märkte durch soziale Produktion (Benkler 2006) sollte deshalb nicht vorschnell gesprochen werden, da Produktionsmittel im Internetzeitalter zwar sozialisiert werden, nicht aber die Verfügung über Möglichkeiten, ökonomischen Mehrwert daraus zu schöpfen. Diese hängen weiterhin von ungleich verteilter Macht ab, von der Unternehmen wie Google oder Amazon offensichtlich mehr besitzen als Produzenten eines YouTube-Videos. In den Sozialwissenschaften werden diese Entwicklungen unter dem Begriff „Prosumerism" gegenwärtig breit und kontrovers diskutiert (vgl. etwa Voß/Rieder 2005; Reichwald/Piller 2006; Bruns 2008).

einandersetzungen in den meisten Feldern, so etwa, wenn Lena Pelzer durch subversive Praktiken des Berichteschreibens eine Form des Protests gegen die technischen Vorgaben und Restriktionen des Plattformbetreibers ausübt. Ein anderer, extremerer Fall liegt vor, wenn die Online-Praktiken Auseinandersetzungen über die geltende Eigentumsordnung unseres Wirtschaftssystems implizieren oder anstoßen. Dies ist vor allem beim Vervielfältigen und Verbreiten digitaler Waren mit geschütztem Inhalt, etwa von Musik, Filmen oder auch Programmen, gegeben.

Insbesondere die männlichen Befragten haben im Interview bereitwillig von Down- und Upload-Praktiken mittels Peer-to-Peer-Programmen berichtet, die vom Stadium der frühen Napster-Zeit bis zu den aktuell verbreiteten Torrent-Clients reichen. Gemeinsam ist den Online-Konsumpraktiken dieses dritten Typus, dass sie Distanz zu jenen normativen Codes erzeugen, die in den digitalen Handlungsräumen durch geltendes Recht, durch Allgemeine Geschäftsbedingungen (AGB) sowie durch technische Standardisierung oder informelle Konventionalisierung verankert sind. In dieser Distanzierung liegen Chancen der politischen Verbraucherbildung. Allerdings kommt es in diesem Zusammenhang sehr darauf an, die verschiedenen Ausprägungen dieses Musters zu berücksichtigen, die einer „kreativen" Haltung gegenüber den Ordnungen des Marktes im Internet zugrunde liegen.

Ein erster Subtypus dieser Praktiken wird von Markus Dietze repräsentiert, der in den 1960er Jahren in der DDR geboren wurde und sich – ausgehend von seinen frühen Programmierkenntnissen und dem spielerischen Umgang mit einem aus dem Westen angeschafften Atari 130XE – die Weiten der Welt des Internets nach der Wende erschließt. Dabei führen ihn sein Technikinteresse und die Haltung spielerischer Exploration auch zur Nutzung der Musiktauschbörse Napster, wobei die Phase aber biografisch und sozial-räumlich begrenzt ist. So wie es in der DDR einen informellen Tauschsektor und Schwarzmarkt gegeben hat, der neben der offiziellen ökonomischen Ordnung existierte, wird auch die Nutzung von Napster nicht als Kampfansage an die Musikindustrie und Eigentumsordnung verstanden, obgleich Herr Dietze darin sehr wohl eine illegale Handlung sieht. Die Praktiken werden vielmehr pragmatisch re-normalisiert: Sie sind weitgehend ökonomisch motiviert gewesen, weshalb sie mit steigendem Einkommen wieder verschwanden, und werden mit der Innovationsfeindlichkeit einer Musikindustrie erklärt, die sich mit Kopierschutz und Digital Rights Management an überholte Ordnungen hefte, anstatt zeitgemäße, unkomplizierte Vertriebsformen für den MP3-Download zu schaffen. Obgleich Herr Dietze also ein recht differenziertes Verständnis von der Arena des digitalen Marktes hat, in der unterschiedliche Ökonomien gegenwärtig im Zustand einer vorübergehenden Anomie koexistieren, wobei die Strategien und Entscheidungen verschiedener „Player" Folgen für die jeweils anderen haben, positioniert er sich selbst nicht politisch dazu, sondern als Privatsubjekt, das um die Unschärfe legalen Handelns weiß, diese für sich ausnutzt und die eigene Abweichung von der gültigen und anerkannten Eigentumsordnung als jugendliches Ausprobieren des in der rechtlichen Grauzone Machbaren rechtfertigt. Diese *strategische Konventionalität* zeigt sich schließlich auch in der nachfolgenden Interviewsequenz, die das Verletzen der Reziprozitätsnorm in der anonymen Tauschgemeinschaft ironisiert und dadurch den brisanten Schritt in die Illegalität für sich vermeidet:

> D: „... was ich mir runtergeladen hab sind meistens auch nur Sachen die ich auf Kassette hatte und einfach nur noch mal in besserer Form haben wollte (I: hmhm) (1) das ist eigentlich der sonst hab ich die Tauschbörsen wenig genutzt und vor allen Dingen zähl ich zu den Parasiten die's meistens auch nur im Download nutzen und nicht im Upload (.) was bereitstellen (.) na ja (I: @.@) @.@."

In der jüngeren Generation der in den 1980er Jahren Geborenen lässt sich dieses Muster durchaus wiederfinden. Martin Hellwig ist allerdings nicht mehr in der komfortablen Lage, nur downloaden zu können, weil ihm das Programm eDonkey abverlangt, auch seinerseits Dateiordner seiner Festplatte freizugeben. Er ist dabei allerdings vorsichtig und darauf bedacht, seine Anonymität zu bewahren, um einer Strafverfolgung zu entgehen. Obwohl er vom Gefühl her etwas Illegales macht, rechtfertigt auch er seine Downloadaktivität einerseits mit der rechtlichen Grauzone, andererseits pragmatisch dadurch, dass seine Nutzung der Downloadmöglichkeiten – obgleich sein Rechner 24 Stunden am Tag läuft – sich in Grenzen halte. Das Ganze sei mehr eine Art ausgiebiges Testen von Filmen und Musik vor dem Kauf jener digitalen Kulturwaren, die ihn überzeugen und deren Besitz dann irgendwie materialisiert werden soll (was dazu führt, dass die „Verpackungen" digitaler Waren, deren eigene Qualität durch den Kauf von „Originalen" in keiner Weise verändert wird, diesen Wert symbolisieren müssen). Die paradoxe Verschmelzung von Konventionalität und strategischer Interessenverfolgung äußert sich hier in der Vorgabe, erst im Kauf käme die Wertschätzung zum Ausdruck, und dem gleichzeitigen Eingeständnis Herrn Hellwigs, dass „meistens äh such ich dann, ob ich's @runterladen@ kann @.@".

Die Motivkonstellation strategischer Konventionalität ist offenbar nicht ganz widerspruchsfrei zu haben und es stellt sich die Frage, welchen Wandel diese Online-Praktiken in biografischer Hinsicht erfahren. Wie schon bei Markus Dietze angedeutet, findet sich ein Transformationspfad, der zum Pol der Konventionalität führt. Im Sample repräsentiert Oliver Wagner diesen Subtyp in der Generation der in den 1980er Jahren Geborenen. Hat er anfangs die Musiktauschbörsen nachgiebig genutzt, so präsentiert er sich im Interview heute als „großer Verfechter *des Urheberrechts*", weil er selber Filme macht und später professionell machen möchte und um die Verdienstschwierigkeiten von Künstlern weiß. Für Herrn Wagner, der im Interview seinen Vater als starke moralische Autorität schildert, haben normative Selbstbindungen und Konsistenzpflichten größeres Gewicht. Er schert allerdings aus dieser Konstellation nicht vollends aus, weil einerseits Angst vor Strafverfolgung ihren Anteil hat und andererseits die eigene Tugendhaftigkeit mit strategischem Kalkül der Distinktion vorgetragen wird:

> W: „Ich bin wahrscheinlich einer der wenigen der durch diese Musiktauschbörsen sich im Endeffekt mehr CD's gekauft hat als er's ohne getan hätte (.) also das hab ich wirklich ganz konsequent gemacht immer rein- (.) -gehört äh gemerkt okeh da is ein Lied nur auf diesem Album dann war das Ganze überhaupt nich mehr relevant für mich hab ich auch sofort gelöscht (.) und sobald halt zwei drei Lieder relevant waren dann äh musste dieses Album sofort her und dann hab ich mir das (1) es ging dann auch im selben Zug los dass ich dann bei Amazon gekauft habe".

Allerdings geht diese Haltung von Oliver Wagner nicht so weit, andere Studierende zu missionieren zu versuchen oder in Urheberrechtsfragen politisch aktiv zu werden. Sein Engagement bleibt privat und spricht andere nur im Modus moralisierender Abgrenzung an. Zwar verlangt die offene Situation der Auseinandersetzung zwischen Musikindustrie, Künstlern, Hackern, der sozialen Welt des Open-Source und der Instanzen des Staates, dass die Nutzer der Tauschbörsen eine Position zu Fragen des Eigentumsrechts und der Ordnung von digitalen Märkten einnehmen und auch zu artikulieren lernen. Aber sie sehen sich nicht als „Market-Makers", nicht als Bestandteil kollektiver Akteure, sondern als individuelle Verbraucher, die sich in den bislang vorliegenden Fällen an den geltenden Konventionen orientieren. Auch das Handeln von Dominik Stein verbleibt in einem privaten, individuellen Rahmen, obgleich es sich dadurch unterscheidet, dass er die Kontingenz der ökonomisch-rechtlichen Ordnung eher als Freiraum für strategisches Handeln interpretiert, also zu den Konventionen und Rechtsregeln eine größere und bewusstere Distanz entwickelt. Bei ihm bildet also das subversive Moment des File-Sharing die dominante Orientierung, hinter die das konventionelle zurücktritt. Märkte erscheinen hier zwar nicht als normfreie Zonen, aber doch als Felder eines allgemeinen Interessenkampfes, an dem unterschiedliche Akteure mit unterschiedlichen Machteinsätzen teilnehmen. Als individueller Nutzer muss man sehen, wo man in diesem Kampffeld bleibt, wobei die Faktizität geltenden Rechts als relevante Randbedingung Berücksichtigung finden muss. Dies wird etwa an den vorbeugenden Maßnahmen gegen Strafverfolgung sichtbar:

> S: […] ich hab aber nich den normalen (.) Esel ich hab da ne etwas abge- abgeänderte Version von (I: hmhm) (1) die mir nämlich äh erlaubt (1) ähm (3) meine Einstellungen so zu tätigen dass ich nicht beschränkt werde. also normalerweise wenn man nicht n gewisses Pensum an Daten (1) selbst zur Verfügung stellt wird man ja beschränkt in der Bandbreite (I: hmhm) die man (.) saugen darf (I: hmhm) und da hab ich halt n anderes Programm (.) mir mal gesucht (1) ähm was
> I: das umgeht

S: (1) genau (I: hmhm) [...]

S: [...] aber wenn ich (1) eh nichts mache dann geb ich auch (1) die Geschwindichkeit frei dann hab ich dann (.) auch kein Problem mit (I: hmhm) (2) da gibt's natürlich auch Mittel und Wege und Tricks (1) ähm weillll das ja auch immer zunehmend (1) äh verfolgter wird (1) ähm (2) der Download is ja nich unter Strafe gestellt (1) es is ja (.) das Anbieten (1) von Ware und die gehn ja auch alle davon aus wenn ich so eine Tauschbörse nutze dass ich das auch anbiete (.) aber da gibt es auch Tricks (1) indem ich zum Beispiel in meinem (.) Download-Ordner (1) ganz viele andere Dateien habe (.) die (.) frei zugänglich sind also irgendwelche (1) freie Musik gibt's ja auch oder (1) Fernsehsendungen oder mhh was weiß ich irgendwelche (.) selbst gemachten Bilder (2) ähm (.) die setz ich auch bei mir in den Ordner setze da die Priorität (.) auf (.) ganz hoch und auf die anderen Sachen die eben illegal sind kann ich die Priorität auch ganz runter setzten (2) und wenn ich jetzt au noch beschränke okeh es dürfen maximal soundso viel Leute (1) irgendwie sich bei mir in die Warteliste stellen (.) ähhm dann kommen die quasi nie dazu (.) die illegalen Downloade überhaupt (1) äh dranzukommen beziehungsweise (.) nur sehr (.) sehr wenich

I: hmhm (.) damit sind Sie auf der sicheren Seite

S: na sicher nich aber etwas sicherer ja (I: hmhm) (.) da musste ich mir früher gar keine Gedanken drüber machen früher hatte ich n n meinen Vertag bei Arcor (.) und Arcor gibt keine äh (.) persönlichen Daten von über IP-Adressen weiter (1) kann ich mir auch sehr sicher sein weil der (1) äh Vorstandsvorsitzende von Arcor is nämlich auch gleichzeitich der Vorsitzende des äh (.) Verbraucherschutzbundes (1) (I: hmhm) gewesen und (.) ich (.) vertrau dem dann einfach weil sacht wenn der sacht nee (.) machen wir nich un Datenschutz un haste nich gesehn (.) dass der das dann auch wirklich nicht (.) weitergibt.

Dominik Stein entwickelt Taktiken, um den konsumistischen Hedonismus mitleben zu können, ohne dafür (viel) Geld ausgeben zu müssen. Biografisch spielt dabei sicherlich eine Rolle, dass er in prekären Verhältnissen aufgewachsen ist und nach Konflikten mit seinem Stiefvater noch in seiner Oberstufenzeit in eine eigene Wohnung gezogen ist, also die Familienkontakte abgebrochen und sich früh selbst durchgeschlagen hat. Da er bislang seine Bildungsabschlüsse (Abitur, begonnenes FH-Studium) nicht erworben hat, sondern Ausbildungen wiederkehrend abbricht, scheint sich daran in nächster Zeit auch wenig zu ändern. Herr Stein bewahrt sich unter diesen Bedingungen Autonomie dadurch, dass er sich neben Gelegenheitsjobs in kreativer Weise die im Internet gegebenen Gewinn- und Sparmöglichkeiten aneignet. Erinnert dieses Muster in mancher Hinsicht an Jens Treichel, so ist die Haltung gegenüber der politisch-rechtlichen Ordnung hier doch eine andere, erfindungsreichere. Statt für Cent-Beträge Click-Work zu betreiben oder ellenlange Verbraucherberichte zu schreiben, versucht Dominik Stein lieber seine Computerspielfähigkeiten (Autorennen) zu barer Münze zu machen oder nutzt die zur Kundenbindung oder Marktforschung gedachten Gutscheine und Rabatte beim Online-Kauf, freilich ohne sich zu binden, sondern so, dass die Registrierung als Neukunde mehrfach Vergünstigungen bringt. Allerdings birgt dieser „abenteurerkapitalistische" Habitus auch Risiken, wie Dominik Stein beim Online-Pokern erfahren musste, das seine Schulden kräftig wachsen ließ. Und es gehört für ihn zur Normalität, mit Vertragspartnern in Konflikt zu geraten, etwa mit dem bislang einzigen langjährigen Arbeitgeber – einem großen Online-Versandhaus für Computerbedarf und Elektronik – weil er die Waren parallel in großem Stil bei eBay umgesetzt hat.[14] Er geht aber nicht so weit wie andere aus dem weiteren Sample, defekte Waren ohne entsprechende Kennzeichnung über eBay zu verkaufen. Insofern haben auch für ihn grundlegende Konventionen des Markthandelns durchaus noch Gültigkeit, jedoch nicht unhinterfragt. Er beurteilt diese Normen weniger idealistisch als verpflichtendes Sollen, sondern realistisch entlang differenzierter Informationen über gängige Online-Marktpraktiken. Das Wissen über den alltagsökonomischen Handlungsraum gewinnt auf diese Weise enorm an Komplexität, bleibt in seiner Handlungsrelevanz aber primär auf die Realisierung privat-ökonomischer Eigeninteressen bezogen.

Fazit: Politische Bildungsräume?

Werden Bildungsprozesse vom Verbraucher zum Bürger als „Shifting Involvements" vorgestellt, die ihren Ausgang bei den Enttäuschungen im privaten Konsumalltag nehmen und über den Wandel von Metapräferenzen der Lebensführung in die politische Handlungsarena führen (vgl. Hirschman 1984), dann fungieren digitale Konsumwelten wohl nicht als politische Bildungsräume. Zwar behaupten die hier rekonstruierten Typen von Online-Praxis in unterschiedlichem Maße ihre Autonomie gegenüber expansiven Marktentwicklungen im Internet, aber sie verbleiben weitgehend im privaten Rahmen und partizipieren nicht an öffentlichen Kämpfen oder Prozeduren eines de-

14 S: „ähm irgendwie hat mir aber mein Arbeitgeber da einen Strich durch die Rechnung gemacht weil (.) der dann gesagt hat nein ich durfte das nich aufgrund (1) meines Arbeitsvertrages und ich würde ja (1) wenn ich ein leuchtendes Kabel verkaufe übers Internet würd ich ja (2) meinem Arbeitgeber die Kundschaft wegnehmen (.) und die da auch wohl vielleicht die Angst hatten ich könnte (.) einem Kunden sagen hier nee kaufen Se das nicht da und ne (.) ich geb Ihnen mal (.) ne Adresse (.) wo Se das irgendwie anders her beziehen deswegen haben die mir das auch unterbunden (2) ja und so ist das Ganze wieder (.) auf Eis gegangen (I: hmhm) weil (.) ich da auch mxx schon etwas Hemmungen hatte das dann wirklich auch (.) durchzuziehen weil (1) wenn man das dann wirklich (.) richtig offiziell macht dann (.) muss man das auf Gewerbeschein machen muss das ganze versteuern dann bleiben ja nicht (nur) die achthundert Euro netto hängen sondern (.) man muss sich versichern und den ganzen Kram man (1) muss zwei Jahre Gewährleistung anbieten und (.) deswegen hab ich das dann gelassen (I: hmhm) (1)."

mokratischen Kollektivs, um die Bedingungen dieser Autonomiesicherung auf höherer Ebene zum Verhandlungsgegenstand zu machen. Insofern bleibt die Arbeitsteilung zwischen offizieller Politik – auch: Verbraucherpolitik – und bürgerlichen Privatsubjekten auch in den Konsumwelten des Internetzeitalters die dominante Form. Allerdings könnte ein partizipatorisches Demokratieverständnis auch zu hoch angesetzt sein, um jene Bildungsprozesse zu erkennen, die im Rahmen dieser Arbeitsteilung gleichwohl von großer Bedeutung sind. Das wird sichtbar, wenn die Perspektive präziser auf die Arenen und ihre Akteure gerichtet werden, von denen die Ordnungen der Märkte im Internetzeitalter ausgehandelt werden. Neben staatlichen und wirtschaftlichen Akteuren im engeren Sinne findet sich hier eine Reihe von intermediären Instanzen der Verbraucherpolitik, wie Verbände, NGOs, aber auch Selbsthilfegruppen und Repräsentanten unterschiedlicher sozialer Konsumwelten, etwa von Brand Communities, der Open Source Bewegung, von Hackern und Befürwortern des File-Sharing usw. Es kommt für die weitere Forschung zur Verbraucherdemokratie darauf an, zu rekonstruieren, wie die gefundenen Konsum- und Verbrauchertypen sich zu solchen Aushandlungsprozessen verhalten und umgekehrt, wie die vielfältigen politischen Akteure auf die Verbraucherinnen und Verbraucher Bezug nehmen, welche(s) Verbraucherbild(er) sie dabei offenbaren und in welche Richtung sie die Verbraucherschaft ggf. verführen, umwerben, instrumentalisieren, informieren oder auch politisieren wollen (vgl. hierzu auch Gabriel/Lang 1995).

Hinter der Rede vom Consumer Citizen und der bürgerschaftlichen Mobilisierung von Verbrauchern verbergen sich in erster Linie Diskursphänomene, in denen sich die verschiedenen konkurrierenden oder kooperierenden Akteure dieser Arenen auf Verbraucher beziehen und diese in unterschiedliche Richtung zu aktivieren versuchen, sei es für nachhaltigen Konsum, das Vorziehen des Neuwagenkaufs in der Wirtschaftskrise, einen coolen Lifestyle usw. Hinter dem Appell an die Macht der Verbraucher verbirgt sich oftmals der Kampf um die Verfügung über diese „Ressource", darüber, ihren kollektiven Willen auslegen und vertreten zu dürfen, aber auch darüber, ihr Handeln im Sinne der eigenen Ziele zu beeinflussen, seien diese nun ökonomisch motiviert, staatliche Lenkung beabsichtigend oder an ethischen bzw. ästhetischen Kriterien betroffener sozialer Welten ausgerichtet. Man denke z.B. an die Kampagnen, die Millionen User überzeugen wollen, den Firefox-Browser zu installieren, um dem Microsoft-Konzern Marktanteile abzujagen, um zu erkennen, wie verschiedene dieser Ziele auch ineinander greifen können. Für das Thema Verbraucherdemokratie und die bildungstheoretischen Fragen ist hierbei von Interesse, wie der durch die Konsumpraktiken (und ihrer verschiedenen Typen) konstituierte Resonanzboden dabei in Schwingung versetzt wird, ob politische Bildungsprozesse eher befördert oder gehemmt werden.

Unter Aspekten der politischen Aushandlung von Marktordnungen im Internetzeitalter haben die alltäglichen Entscheidungen von Verbrauchern des *ersten Typus* nach eigenen ökonomischen und kulturellen Relevanzen ihrer Lebenspraxis zwar auch am historischen Wandel Anteil, der die Kriterien für Märkte aber in langen Wellen über den Wechsel von Generationen verändert und auf technische Innovationen oder neue Herausforderungen eher träge reagiert. Entweder sind die politischen Codes bereits Bestandteil dieser Relevanzen, dann müssen diese Verbraucher nicht mehr überzeugt werden und sind leicht ansprechbar – so wie Frau Arenowitz etwa aus ökologischer Überzeugung regionale Produkte beim Lebensmitteleinkauf bevorzugt, aber nicht auf Biolebensmittel festgelegt ist. Oder die Konsumgewohnheiten liegen quer dazu, dann wird sich daran über Diskurse, die am individuellen Konsumverhalten ansetzen, wenig ändern lassen. Die Räume und Welten des Internets haben darauf keinen Einfluss, weil auf sie ohnehin selektiv nach den jeweiligen Relevanzen zugegriffen wird.

Anders dagegen die Verbraucher des *zweiten Typs*, die zur Bestätigung ihres Selbstbildes auf die Anerkennung von anderen angewiesen sind und in stärkerem Maße auf von außen, sei es technisch, sozial oder auch kommerziell vorgegebene Relevanzen reagieren. Dieser Typus steht im Fokus der Verbrauchermobilisierung unterschiedlichster Akteure in den Aushandlungsarenen der Märkte. Ihre Einbindung für unterschiedliche Ziele durch das Bereitstellen von artifiziellen Online-Communities, wie die Verbraucherplattformen vom liberalen Ciao bis hin zum ökologischen Pendant Utopia[15] zeigen, ist unter bildungstheoretischen Gesichtspunkten wiederum fragwürdig, weil die Abhängigkeit der Außengeleiteten hier eher strategisch ausgenutzt wird, anstatt sie zum Ausgangspunkt für die Stärkung individueller und kollektiver (demokratischer) Autonomiepotenziale zu nehmen. Politische Bildungsprozesse könnten und müssten hier an der moralischen Grammatik ansetzen, die im Kampf um Anerkennung eingelassen ist (vgl. Honneth 1992; Ricœur 2006) und dadurch Anschlussfähigkeit in dieser Verbraucherschaft besitzen. Sie freizusetzen dürfte unter Bedingungen einer fragmentierten Öffentlichkeit und einem dementsprechend segmentierten Internet aber enorm erschwert sein, wodurch die Koexistenz verschiedener manipulierender Zugriffsweisen (durch Werbung, Kampagnen, Mainstreaming usw.) wahrscheinlich wird.

Davor gefeit ist wiederum der *dritte Typus*. Hier überwiegen Cleverness und ein Marktwissen, so dass diese Verbraucher strategische Absichten des Marketing oder anderer Akteure zu entlarven und auch taktisch zu unterlaufen wissen. Mit ihrer Distanz zu den normativen Ordnungen der Märkte haben diese Verbraucher ein Gespür für den politischen Aushandlungscharakter dieser Ökonomien. Für sie fungiert das Internet als ein Raum, an dem der fluide Charakter digitaler Märkte unmittelbar beobachtbar und nachvollziehbar wird, wobei sie diese Erkenntnis auch über den Bereich der Online-Praktiken hinaus zu generalisieren wissen. Damit bilden sie eine Basis für die kritische Öffentlichkeit der Verbraucherdemokratie, insofern ihre strategische Haltung zu mög-

15 http://www.utopia.de

lichen Marktpraktiken und zu den Grenzen ihrer Legalität auch auf die Kontingenz der Konventionen, die Machtungleichheiten im ökonomischen Feld und daraus resultierende Herausforderungen für die Einhegung von Konflikten, d. h. für die rechtliche und lebensweltliche Institutionalisierung der Märkte hinweisen. Und solange sie sich aus dem Horizont der normativen Begründungspflichten ihres Markthandelns nicht völlig herauslösen, positionieren sie sich auch zu den Argumenten der Konfliktparteien in der öffentlichen Arena, wie das Beispiel des File-Sharing gezeigt hat. Gleichwohl folgt daraus noch kein politisches Engagement für diese Verbraucheröffentlichkeit. Vielmehr bleibt der Handlungsrahmen der hier untersuchten Verbraucher auf die private Interessenverfolgung weitgehend beschränkt. Politisch wird diese Arena daher erst, wenn durch weitere Akteure, z.B. zivilgesellschaftliche Instanzen wie NGOs, Verbraucherverbände oder auch Parteien, Regierungen, EU-Kommissionäre, PR-Manager der Konzerne, Selbsthilfegruppen (z.B. Patientenvereinigungen) usw. öffentliche Diskurse über Markt-Praktiken in Gang gebracht werden (vgl. Baringhorst 2009 i.E.). Und politische „Bildungsprozesse" – mit dem Ziel der Steigerung kollektiver Autonomie durch Verfahren demokratischer Willensbildung und moralischer Normbegründung – können in diesen Arenen nur entstehen, wenn die Diskurse auch Standards einer deliberierenden Öffentlichkeit erreichen (vgl. Habermas 1992). Als digitaler Basar ist das Internet viel zu fragmentiert und weit davon entfernt, solche Standards von selbst zu generieren. Der politische Bildungsraum der Verbraucherdemokratie bleibt folglich darauf angewiesen, dass eine kritische Öffentlichkeit lernt, ihre kommunikative Macht in die Aushandlungsarenen digitaler Märkte und Konsumwelten wirksamer als bislang einzuschleusen und dort zu verankern.

Literatur

Adloff, Frank/Mau, Steffen (Hrsg.) (2005): Vom Geben und Nehmen. Zur Soziologie der Reziprozität. Frankfurt/New York: Campus, S. 73-91.

Baringhorst, Sigrid (2007): Konsumenten als Netizens. Das Internet als ambivalentes Medium für ein Empowerment von Verbrauchern. In: Baringhorst/Kneip/März/Niesyto 2007, 81-108.

Baringhorst, Sigrid/Kneip, Veronika/März, Annegret/Niesyto, Johanna (Hrsg.) (2007) Politik mit dem Einkaufswagen. Unternehmen und Konsumenten als Bürger in der globalen Mediengesellschaft. Bielefeld: transkript.

Baringhorst, Sigrid (2009): Politischer Konsumerismus im Netz – Chancen und Probleme demokratischer Protestpolitik. Revitalisierung demokratischer Bürgerbeteiligung im Web 2.0? In: Bieber/Eifert/Groß/Lamla i.E.

Benkler, Yochai (2006): The Wealth of Networks. How Social Production Transforms Markets and Freedom. New Haven/London: Yale University Press.

Bieber, Christoph/Eifert, Martin/Groß, Thomas/Lamla, Jörn (Hrsg.) (i.E.): Soziale Netzwerke in der digitalen Welt. Frankfurt am Main/New York: Campus.

Buber, Renate/Holzmüller, Hartmut H. (Hrsg.) (2007): Qualitative Marktforschung. Konzepte - Methoden - Analysen. Wiesbaden: Gabler.

Bruns, Axel (2008): Blogs, Wikipedia, Second Life, and Beyond: From Production to Produsage. New York et al.: Peter Lang.

Caillé, Alain (2008): Anthropologie der Gabe. Frankfurt am Main/New York: Campus.

Campbell, Colin (1987): The Romantic Ethic and the Spirit of Modern Consumerism. Oxford: Blackwell.

Clarke, Adele E. (2005): Situational Analysis. Grounded Theory after the Postmodern Turn. Thousand Oaks, CA: Sage.

Dahrendorf, Ralf (1994): Der moderne soziale Konflikt. Essay zur Politik der Freiheit. München: dtv.

de Certeau, Michel (1988): Kunst des Handelns. Berlin: Merve.

Deutschmann, Christoph (2000): Geld als "absolutes Mittel". Zur Aktualität von Simmels Geldtheorie. In: Berliner Journal für Soziologie, Nr. 3/2000, 301–313.

Dewey, John (1996): Die Öffentlichkeit und ihre Probleme. Bodenheim: Philo.

Fligstein, Neil (1996): Markets as politics. A political-cultural approach to market-institutions. In: American Sociological Review, Vol. 61, 656-673.

Gabriel, Yiannis/Lang, Tim (1995): The unmangeable consumer. Contemporary consumption and its fragmentations. London: Sage.

Giddens, Anthony (1991): Modernity and Self-Identity. Self and Society in the Late Modern Age. Cambridge: Polity.

Habermas, Jürgen (1992): Faktizität und Geltung. Beiträge zur Diskurstheorie des Rechts und des demokratischen Rechtsstaats. Frankfurt am Main: Suhrkamp.

Heinzel , Friederike/Thole, Werner/Cloos, Peter/Köngeter, Stefan (Hrsg.) (i.E.): „Auf unsicherem Terrain". Ethnographische Forschung im Kontext des Bildungs- und Sozialwesens. Wiesbaden: VS Verlag.

Hirschman, Albert O. (1984): Engagement und Enttäuschung. Über das Schwanken der Bürger zwischen Privatwohl und Gemeinwohl. Frankfurt a. M.: Suhrkamp.

Hitzler, Ronald/Honer, Anne/Pfadenhauer, Michaela (Hrsg.) (2008): Posttraditionale Gemeinschaften. Theoretische und ethnographische Erkundungen. Wiesbaden: VS Verlag.

Honneth, Axel (1992): Kampf um Anerkennung. Zur moralischen Grammatik sozialer Konflikte. Frankfurt am Main: Suhrkamp.

Honneth, Axel (2005): Verdinglichung. Eine anerkennungstheoretische Studie. Frankfurt am Main: Suhrkamp.

Kling, Rob/Gerson, Elihu M. (1978): Patterns of Segmentation and Intersection in the Computing World. In: Symbolic Interaction, Vol. 1, No. 2, 24-43.

Knorr-Cetina, Karin (1998): Sozialität mit Objekten. Soziale Beziehungen in post-traditionalen Wissensgesellschaften. In: Rammert 1998, 83-120.

Lamla, Jörn (2007): Konsumpraktiken in der virtuellen Alltagsökonomie. Forschungsdesign und exemplarische Fallskizze. In Buber/Holzmüller 2007, 779-803.

Lamla, Jörn (2008a): Consumer Citizen: The Constitution of Consumer Democracy in Sociological Perspective. In: Re-Shaping Consumer Policy in Europe? Special Issue of German Policy Studies, ed. by Ch. Strünck, Vol. 4, no. 1. Online: http://www.spaef.com/article.php?id=909 [16.06.2009]

Lamla, Jörn (2008b): Markt-Vergemeinschaftung im Internet. Das Fallbeispiel einer Shopping- und Meinungsplattform. In: Hitzler/Honer/Pfadenhauer 2008, 170 - 185.

Lamla, Jörn (2009): Zugänge zur virtuellen Konsumwelt. Abgrenzungsprobleme und Revisionsstufen der Ethnografie. In: Heinzel/Thole/Cloos/Köngeter i.E..

Latour, Bruno (1995): Wir sind nie modern gewesen. Versuch einer symmetrischen Anthropologie. Berlin: Akad.-Verl.

Marcus, George E. (1995): Ethnography in/of the World System: The Emergence of Multi-Sited Ethnography. In: Annual Reviews Anthropology Jg. 24, 95-117.

Miller, Daniel/Slater, Don (2001): The Internet. An Ethnographic Approach. Oxford/New York: Berg.

Rammert, Werner (Hrsg.) (1998): Technik und Sozialtheorie. Frankfurt am Main/New York: Campus.

Reichwald, Ralf/Piller, Frank Thomas (2006): Interaktive Wertschöpfung: Open Innovation, Individualisierung und neue Formen der Arbeitsteilung. Wiesbaden: Gabler.

Ricœur, Paul (2006): Wege der Anerkennung. Erkennen, Wiedererkennen, Anerkanntsein. Frankfurt am Main: Suhrkamp.

Riesman, David/Denney, Reuel/Glazer, Nathan (1958): Die einsame Masse. Eine Untersuchung der Wandlungen des amerikanischen Charakters. Reinbek: Rowohlt.

Ritzer, George (1999): Enchanting a Disenchanted World: Revolutionizing the Means of Consumption, London: Pine Forge Press.

Sahlins, Marshall (1965): Zur Soziologie des primitiven Tauschs. In: Adloff/Mau 2005, 73-91.

Scammell, Margaret (2000): The Internet and Civic Engagement: The Age of the Citizen-consumer. In: Political Communication, Vol. 17, 351-355.

Schumpeter, Joseph A. (1950): Kapitalismus, Sozialismus und Demokratie. 6. Aufl. 1987. Tübingen: Francke.

Strauss, Anselm L. (1993): Continual Permutations of Action. New York: Aldine de Gruyter.

Strauss, Anselm/Corbin, Juliet (1996): Grounded Theory. Grundlagen Qualitativer Sozialforschung. Weinheim: Juventa.

Voß, Günter/Rieder, Kerstin (2005): Der arbeitende Kunde. Wenn Konsumenten zu unbezahlten Mitarbeitern werden. Frankfurt am Main/New York: Campus.

Zelizer, Viviana A. (1994): The social meaning of money. Princeton, NJ: Princeton Univ. Press.

Medienkunst als Medienbildungsraum an der Schnittstelle von Wissenschaft und Öffentlichkeit

von Daniela Küllertz

Das Leben in modernen Gesellschaften ist von einer Vielzahl entscheidungsoffener, aber zum Teil existenziell folgenreicher Handlungsmöglichkeiten bestimmt. So kann man sich etwa vor einer Geburt entscheiden, ob die Stammzellen aus dem Blut der Nabelschnur entnommen werden sollen, um sie entweder für Forschungszwecke zur Verfügung zu stellen oder einfrieren zu lassen, damit zu einem unbestimmten Zeitpunkt unter veränderten biotechnologischen Bedingungen darauf zurückgegriffen werden kann. Die gesamte Biografie des Menschen ist in der Moderne von zahlreichen (teilweise stellvertretenden) Entscheidungssituationen geprägt, von Fragen medizinischer Behandlung wie etwa Impfung im Säuglingsalter bis hin zur Entscheidung für eine Patientenverfügung und Vorsorgevollmacht oder Fragen lebensverlängernder medizinischer Maßnahmen im höheren Alter. Wissenschaftliches Wissen – sei es naturwissenschaftlich-technisches oder geistes- und sozialwissenschaftliches Wissen – spielt für solche Entscheidungssituationen zunehmend eine relevante Rolle. Wissenschaft geht konstitutiv in Entscheidungssituationen ein, wie etwa im Bereich der Politikberatung, in Form von Begleitforschung etwa im pädagogischen Bereich, in medizinischen Handlungskontexten, ebenso in den öffentlichen Diskurs um biotechnologisch erzeugte ethische Konfliktlagen, um nur einige der vielen Handlungskontexte zu nennen, in denen wissenschaftliches Wissen und Methoden der Wissensproduktion eine tragende Rolle spielen. Über wissenschaftliche Fachkreise hinaus ist in den Feuilletons und der institutionalisierten Politik die Rede von umfassenden Verwissenschaftlichungsprozessen, sogar von der Wissen(schaft)sgesellschaft[1], einer schillernden Zeitdiagnose mit zahlreichen Bedeutungsfacetten.

Leben mit dem Wissen der Wissenschaften

Unter Verwissenschaftlichung stellte man sich in der frühen Soziologie einen linearen Prozess gesteigerter Rationalisierung als auch der zunehmenden Kontrollmöglichkeit durch angehäuftes Wissen vor (vgl. Bonß 2002; Schelsky 1961). Mit der „tatsächlichen Umstellung auf wissenschaftliches Wissen als programmatisch gesellschaftskonstitutives und faktisch gesellschaftssteuerndes Moment" (Bonß 2002, I) wich diese Vorstellung der Einsicht in die Uneindeutigkeit, Bedeutungsoffenheit und Unabgeschlos-

1 Vgl. etwa Kübler (2008), Held (2009) Weingart (2008), Carrier/Roggenhofer (2007), Müller/Stravoravdis (2007) Unger (2009) und Seifert (2008).

senheit (Wengart 2001; Wehling 2002, 119f) hier und die Riskanz wissenschaftlichen Wissens (Bonß 2002: I) dort.

Die zeitgenössische Bedeutung wissenschaftlichen Wissens kann, wie es der Wissenschaftssoziologe Peter Weingart (2005, 50) tut, in einer „umfassenden Therapeutisierung der Gesellschaft" gesehen werden: „Alle suchen Beistand für Entscheidungen unter Ungewissheit in Gestalt eines fremden Gegenüber". Andererseits kann Wissenschaft jedoch selbst, wie im Fall der Humangenetik, zu neuen Entscheidungssituationen führen, für die die „Spezifikation unserer Werte noch fehlt" (Joas 2002, 74) und die mit Blick auf das Problematischwerden kulturspezifischer und selbst- und weltkonstitutiver Sinngefüge wie das der Natur des Menschen oder die Dichotomie von Kultur und Natur auch nicht so einfach sein dürfte. Hinzu kommt, dass tradierte Wertorientierungen miteinander in Konflikt geraten: so steht beispielsweise dem Wert von Selbstverwirklichung und Selbstbestimmung der ethisch begründete Wunsch nach Kontrolle biotechnischer Forschung entgegen. Der Einsatz von Bioethikkommissionen kann, so Weingart (2005,45f), kein probates Mittel zur Problemlösung sein, da die Schwierigkeit kultureller Einbettung biomedizinischer Techniken in einen Diskurs verlagert würde, der keine substanziellen Lösungen liefern könne. Es bedarf letztlich einer öffentlichen Verständigung über neue biotechnische und wissenschaftlich geschaffene Möglichkeiten, die gesellschaftliche Werte zu wissenschaftlichem Wissen und zu den mit diesem verbundenen Handlungsmöglichkeiten in Beziehung setzt und neu abstimmt (vgl. Weingart 2005, 46), wobei „nach dem Wegfall der Selbstverständlichkeit des Menschen" (Schrage 2000,64)[2] der Offenheit und Ambivalenz der Situation Rechnung getragen werden muss.

Die Unsicherheit und Vorläufigkeit wissenschaftlichen Wissens ist im Hinblick auf die zunehmende Angewiesenheit auf wissenschaftliches Wissen einerseits und die mit gesellschaftlichen Demokratisierungsprozessen einhergehenden Ansprüche an öffentliche Kontrolle von Wissenschaft und Forschung andererseits problematisch. Hinzu kommt, dass die Produktion wissenschaftlichen Wissens ebenso unkontrollierbar ist wie dessen Verbreitung (vgl. Weingart 2005, 41)[3] – insbesondere den Neuen Medien und hier dem Internet kommt dabei eine konstitutive Bedeutung zu. Die mit Digitalisierung und Vernetzung ermöglichte breite Teilhabe sowohl der Fach- als auch Laienöffentlichkeit an wissenschaftlichen Diskursen bringt jedoch vor allem für letztere die Notwendigkeit mit sich, unabgeschlossenes, teilweise widersprüchliches und bedeutungsoffenes Wissen interpretieren, meint verstehen und bewerten, zu können. Hier

2 Der Wegfall des Menschen meint die Loslösung des wissenschaftlichen Machbarkeits- und Gestaltungshorizontes von der Gattung und dem Einzelwesen Mensch. Biotechnologie bezieht sich nicht mehr auf den Menschen, sondern auf Erbinformationen jeglicher Lebewesen und die Herstellung von Leben. Juristisch korreliert das Auseinanderfallen von Rechtsperson und die Manipulation genetischer Identitäten (vgl. Schrage 2000, 56).

3 vgl. ebenso Schrage (2000, 55), der von einer „partiellen Autonomisierung einer objektiven, rationalen und überparteilichen, den Weltanschauungsdebatten enthobenen Sphäre des Technischen" spricht.

spielen verschiedene Faktoren eine wichtige Rolle, angefangen bei den unterschiedlichen Darstellungsformaten und deren Reflexionsoptionen (vgl. Jörissen/Marotzki 2009, 43ff), da nun zu Wissenschaftsmagazinen im Print- und massenmedialen Bereich, zu Kriminaltechnikserien und Wissenschaftsdokumentationen im Fernsehen oder wissenschaftlichen Radiofeatures jede Menge Wissenschaftskommunikationsplattformen im Netz hinzukommen. Zu nennen sind beispielsweise öffentliche Bibliografien, Wissenschaftsblogs, Online-Vorlesungen wie das World-Lecture-Project[4], wissenschaftliche Audiotheken[5] als auch Präsentationstauschplattformen wie Slideshare[6], wissenschaftliche (Video-)Suchmaschinen wie beispielsweise Yovisto[7] oder Google Scholar[8], Internetforen und Mailinglisten als auch die Open Access Bewegung (vgl. Hagenhoff et. al. 2007). Neben Fragen zu kognitiven Prozessen hinsichtlich dieser neueren Darstellungsformate und ihrer Eigenschaften (vgl. Stadtler 2006; Bromme 2005) auf Seiten des Laien selbst, treten Fragen nach den lern- und bildungsrelevanten Möglichkeiten der Darstellung und ausdrucksmäßigen Interpretation wissenschaftlichen Wissens und wissenschaftlicher Methoden der Wissensproduktion in den Vordergrund. Medienbildungstheoretisch ist vor allem deren Bedeutung für die öffentliche Auseinandersetzung mit und die Bewertung von wissenschaftlichem Wissen im Hinblick auf dessen Öffnung für neue Sinnbezüge und die Entstehung neuer Zonen bedeutungsvoller Unbestimmtheit relevant. Hier ist die Möglichkeit zur Veränderung existenziell bedeutsamer Sinnbezüge als einer den veränderten Lebenslagen angemesseneren Neuorientierung durch die Schaffung einer auf den medienspezifischen Ausdrucksmöglichkeiten beruhenden subtileren Sprache gegeben. Diese medienspezifische Möglichkeit der Herstellung neuer Sinnbezüge, die Offenheit und Ambivalenz artikulieren, kann als Medienbildungsraum verstanden werden. Die öffentliche und über medienspezifische Ausdrucksformate mitbestimmte Auseinandersetzung mit wissenschaftlichem Wissen ist in diesem Sinne ein genuines Arbeitsfeld der Medienbildungsforschung und der Medienpädagogik.

Es ist jedoch erstaunlich, dass der Stellenwert medienspezifischer Darstellungsformate für Wissenschaftspräsentation und –interpretation sowohl kaum ein Forschungsthema in der Medienbildungsforschung als auch ein eher randständiges Thema in der Medienpädagogik ist[9]. Dies erstaunt aus einer praktischen Perspektive umso mehr,

4 http://www.world-lecture-project.org

5 Bspw. http://audiothek.philo.at

6 http://www.slideshare.net

7 http://www.yovisto.com

8 http://scholar.google.de

9 Eine Ausnahme bildet hier die internationale Konferenz über „Künstler in der Gesellschaft" in Venedig im Juli 2009. Es handelt sich um eine medienpädagogische Initiative des Leonardo Education Forums. Das Thema medienkünstlerische Wissenschaftskommunikation wird hier aber von der Frage überlagert, wie in einer verantwortungsvollen Ausbildung von Medienkünstlern eine Kultur der Gestaltung und Reflexion von

wenn man sich die Veränderung der Berufsfelder (medien-)pädagogischer Praktiker vor Augen führt, die nunmehr als Wissensarbeiter im Kontext neuer Kommunikationstechnologien, insbesondere dem Internet tätig werden (vgl. Bittkau-Schmidt 2008). Vor dem Hintergrund des zunehmenden Stellenwertes der über Medien getragenen öffentlichen Auseinandersetzung um Bedeutung und Legitimation von unsicherem und vorläufigen wissenschaftlichen Wissen ist es zudem bemerkenswert, dass die Öffnung des deutschsprachigen medienpädagogischen Mainstreams für die kulturtheoretische Integration von Mediengebrauch (Paus-Hasebrink/Hipfl 2005) nicht zu einer substanziellen Auseinandersetzung mit dem Stellenwert medienspezifischer Darstellungsformate für die öffentliche Interpretation und Bewertung wissenschaftlichen Wissens geführt hat. Zwar gab es im Kontext der Infotainment-Debatte eine Reihe von Untersuchungen im Bereich der Medienpädagogik, die sich mit der Verknüpfung von Information und Unterhaltung auseinandergesetzt hat (vgl. Reinmann-Rothmeier/Mandl 1997a; 1997b), eine systematische Fortführung dieser Perspektive auf andere Formate und mit Blick auf digital-vernetzte Medien hat es jedoch nicht gegeben. Ein Grund für diese Zurückhaltung mag darin liegen, dass die starke Konzentration auf die aktiven Medienrezipienten[10] in der Medienbildungsforschung mit einigen Ausnahmen (vgl. etwa Marotzki 2007; Godina 2007) und in der Medienpädagogik zu einer tendenziellen Vernachlässigung der Medienproduktionsseite geführt hat (vgl. Paus-Hasebrink/Hipfl 2005, 17) bzw. umfassende Perspektivverschränkungen durch die Dichotomie von Produktions- und Rezeptionsforschung nur langsam initiiert werden.

Ich möchte im Folgenden am Beispiel der Medienkunst zeigen, dass der kreative Umgang mit Medien, deren technische Basis auf Digitalisierung und Vernetzung beruht, Medienbildungsräume an der Schnittstelle zwischen Wissenschaft und Öffentlichkeit im Hinblick auf medienspezifische Ausdrucks- und Reflexionsoptionen[11] eröffnet. Mein Hauptargument für den medienbildungsrelevanten Charakter des hier

Medientechnologien befördert werden kann. Auch im Sammelband „Bildung im Neuen Medium. Education Within A New Medium. Wissensformation und digitale Infrastruktur", herausgegeben von Torsten Meyer (2007, 120-134), ist das Thema präsent. Das Projekt „PID- Perspektiven im Diskurs" sollte im Zeitraum 2007 - 2008 unter der Leitung von Bernd Schorb als themenzentrierte aktive Medienarbeit tschechische und deutsche Heranwachsende dazu befähigen, sich mit dem Thema Präimplantationsdiagnostik in Form von schulischen Praxisprojekten, gemeinsamen Workshops, Expertenvorträgen und Onlinediskussionen kritisch auseinanderzusetzen und eigene Positionen zu beziehen (vgl. Schorb u.a. 2008). Bereits im Vorgängerprojekt „informieren – reflektieren – partizipieren" wurden Mädchen und Jungen unter Leitung von Schorb in Gruppenprojekten angeregt, sich mit dem Thema moderne Medizin und Biotechnologie auseinanderzusetzen, eine qualifizierte Meinung dazu zu entwickeln und sich mittels eines Medienproduktes zu positionieren (vgl. Schorb et. al. 2006).

10 Berücksichtigt man die Erosion der Grenze zwischen Rezipienten und Produzenten in zeitgenössischen Medienpraxen hinlänglich, so muss prägnanter von der professionellen Produktionsseite im Vergleich zur Laien-Produktionsseite gesprochen werden.

11 Vgl. zum Terminus Reflexionsoptionen Jörissen/Marotzki (2009)

vorgestellten medienkünstlerischen Umgangs mit wissenschaftlichem Wissen, der als Dramatisierung wissenschaftlichen Wissens und wissenschaftlicher Methoden der Wissensproduktion angesehen werden kann (vgl. Shusterman 2005, 111ff), ist dabei folgendes: Gerade weil Wissenschaft hier nicht wie beispielsweise in Wissenschaftsmuseen durch narrativ-anschauliche Rahmungen präsentiert wird, sondern wesentlich einer dialogischen Thematisierungsweise folgt, kann der unsichere, normativ ambivalente und vorläufige Charakter wissenschaftlichen Wissens zum Ausdruck gebracht und damit erfahren werden. Anknüpfend an skizzierte Beispiele medienkünstlerischer Dramatisierung von Wissenschaft werde ich auf medientheoretische Arbeiten von Flusser und Manovich zum Stellenwert von Dialogizität auf medientechnischer Ebene von Digitalisierung und Vernetzung eingehen, um diese Überlegungen auf die von Bollnow sprachanalytisch begründete pädagogische Bedeutung des Dialoges für die Entstehung neuer Sinnbezüge zu beziehen. Diese Theoriebezüge werde ich in Rekurs auf (medien-)bildungstheoretische Überlegungen Marotzkis aufgreifen, um die medienkünstlerische Auseinandersetzung mit wissenschaftlichem Wissen als Medienbildungsraum zu konturieren.

Medienkunst als öffentlicher Dialog mit Wissenschaft

Bereits in traditionellen Formen künstlerischer Wissenschaftskommunikation wie den Gedächtnistheatern ging es um das Auffinden einer Ordnung der Wissenspräsentation, die den „Geist aufmerksam hält und das Gedächtnis erschüttert" (Matussek 2004, 3). Damit ist bereits angedeutet, dass es in künstlerischer Darstellung von Wissenschaft um neue Einsichten in Zusammenhänge und Ähnlichkeitsbeziehungen hinsichtlich wissenschaftlichen Wissens und wissenschaftlicher Methoden der Wissensproduktion geht, die unsere vormaligen, kulturell tradierten und ansozialisierten Sinnbezüge erschüttern. In der Medienkunst kommt zu dieser Charakteristik künstlerischer Darstellung wissenschaftlichen Wissens (meist) der symbol- und medienreflexive Umgang mit Medien hinzu und das ist aus medienbildungstheoretischer Perspektive äußerst interessant.

Unter Medienkunst wird im mittlerweile breiteren Sinne Kunst verstanden, die sich mit der „medialen Verfasstheit unserer Welt" (Arns 2008) auseinandersetzt, welche die Aufmerksamkeit auf die teilweise nicht mehr sichtbare Präsenz und Ausweitung von Medien und Technologien in viele Lebensbereiche richtet und deren Wirkungsweisen auf menschliches Verhalten reflektiert (vgl. Arns 2008). Dabei findet die Auseinandersetzung mit einer selbstverständlich gewordenen medialisierten Welt nicht unbedingt in digitalen und vernetzten Medien statt, so die künstlerische Leiterin des Hartware Medienkunstvereins Dortmund Inke Arns:

„Die Medienkunst beginnt so, sich vom Zwang der Verwendung neuer Medien und neuer Technologien zu emanzipieren. Die Kunst unter postmedialen Bedingungen [...] loest sich von der Beschaeftigung mit ihrer eigenen Materialitaet und wendet sich den vielfaeltigen Formen von gegenwaertiger, ubiquitaerer Medialitaet zu."

Im englischsprachigen Raum wird Medienkunst jedoch häufig synonym mit der Begrifflichkeit „new media art" verwendet. Wenngleich ich die Erweiterung des Medienkunstbegriffes im Hinblick auf den Stellenwert der Medien- und Symbolreflexivität dieser Kunstform aus kunsttheoretischer Perspektive sinnvoll finde, geht es mir im Folgenden aus einer medienbildungstheoretischen Betrachtung um jene Medienkunst, die wissenschaftliches Wissen und Methoden der Wissensproduktion in Medien präsentiert und umwertet, deren technische Basis auf Digitalisierung und Vernetzung beruht.

Ich möchte an dieser Stelle zwischen Bio Art, Nanomandala und Six Appartements Beispiele medienkünstlerischen Umgangs mit wissenschaftlichem Wissen skizzieren, die die Problematik naturwissenschaftlich gesteigerter Kontingenz (vgl. Joas 2002) als Zunahme entscheidungsoffener Handlungsmöglichkeiten mit existenzieller Bedeutung aufgreifen und eine medienbildungsrelevante Schnittstelle zwischen Wissenschaft und Öffentlichkeit markieren.

Genesis – biotechnische Transformation ins Unbekannte

Ein bekanntes Beispiel ist das seit nunmehr 10 Jahren in verschiedenen europäischen Ausstellungskontexten gezeigte BioArt-Projekt Genesis[12] von Eduardo Kac. Kac ist für seine transgene Kunst[13], die er in den 90er Jahren des vergangenen Jahrtausends entwickelte, einem internationalen Publikum und im akademischen Kontext recht bekann geworden (vgl. Reichle 2005). In der transgenen Kunst werden biotechnologische Verfahren etwa der Genmanipulation verwendet, um deren kulturelle Bedeutung aufzuführen. Das Schlüsselelement von Genesis ist ein Künstlergen, das von Kac durch verschiedene Transformationstechniken als synthetisches, in der Natur nicht vorkommendes Gen entwickelt wurde. Ein Satz aus der biblischen Genesis[14] wurde ins Morsealphabet, weches symbolisch für den medientechnisch durch Telemedien evozierten soziokulturellen Wandel steht, übersetzt. Besagter Satz selbst zitiert den Glauben an einen Schöpfergott, welcher den Kosmos aus dem Nichts erschuf und dem Menschen die

12 Eine Projektdokumentation findet sich auf der Website von Eduardo Kac unter http://www.ekac.org/geninfo2.html

13 In transgener Kunst geht es um die technische Manipulation von Organismen, wobei sich der Begriff transgen auf Organismen bezieht, die fremde DNA in sich tragen. Ausgangspunkt für Kac sind transgene Lebewesen, wobei es ihm um Verhältnis von Technologien und Glaubenssystemen geht.

14 „Macht Euch die Erde untertan und herrscht über die Fische im Meer und die Vögel unter dem Himmel und über das Vieh und über alles Getier, das auf Erden kriecht" (1 Mose 28).

Herrschaft über die Natur zuwies. Die zu Grunde liegende Vorstellung einer Objekt-Natur (vgl. Weber 2001) wird in der Dramatisierung naturwissenschaftlichen Wissens mit der biotechnologischen Operationalisierung von Natur in Verbindung gebracht.

Der in den Binärcode des Morsealphabetes übersetzte Genesis-Satz wurde dann in eine DNA-Sequenz transformiert. Das synthetisch erzeugte DNA-Fragment wurde durch enzymatische Präparation in die DNA von E.-coli-Bakterien eingeschleust. Durch verschiedene biologische Prozesse innerhalb der Bakterien entstand schließlich ein neues künstlerisches Eiweißmolekül. Über das Internet und eine Schnittstelle im Ausstellungsraum konnte die Mutation der Bakterien durch die Regulierung des UV-Lichtes beeinflusst werden.

Durch diese verschiedenen biotechnologischen und teleaktiven Prozesse manipulierter beschleunigter Mutation wurde der biblische Satz im Bakterium durch Rücktransformationen über die jeweiligen Technologien geändert. Komplexe Transformationsprozesse führen also zu einer (kaum lesbaren) Veränderung von Bedeutungen und Glaubenssystemen, so scheint das Werk transgener Medienkunst nahezulegen, wobei diese Überzeugungen und Glaubenssysteme (Genesis-Satz) selbst die Art der biotechnisch und medienspezifischen (Binärcode) Transformationsprozesse mitbestimmen. Es entsteht ein komplexes Wechselverhältnis, wobei die Elemente des Transformationsprozesses nicht selbstständig sind. Dabei bleibt offen, was genau neue biotechnologische Möglichkeiten für die menschliche Lebensführung und Kultur bedeuten, wie sie zu bewerten sind.

Der Bedeutungskontext für die Interpretation und Bewertung dieser naturwissenschaftlichen Prozesse und Wissensformen ist nicht mehr das Labor, sondern die Lebenswelt des Betrachters. Biotechnologische Verfahren und Optionen werden, wie Kac sich in einem Interview[15] selbst ausdrückt, „nach Hause geholt". Während in den Laboratorien Handlungsorientierungen der Wahrheitsfindung und Nutzbarmachung Priorität haben, ist der lebensweltliche Bedeutungshorizont im Wesentlichen durch die am guten Leben orientierte Perspektivität betroffener Lebensführung gekennzeichnet, wodurch sich neue Sinnbezüge ergeben können.

Auf die vielschichtigen Bedeutungszusammenhänge der hier kurz vorgestellten Arbeit aus dem Bereich der Bio-Kunst kann ich an dieser Stelle nicht weiter eingehen, das würde den Rahmen des vorliegenden Beitrages sprengen. Wichtig für den hier verfolgten medienbildungstheoretischen Zusammenhang ist die spezifische medienkünstlerische Dramatisierung von naturwissenschaftlichem Wissen als bedeutungsoffen und ambivalent. Kac bringt in Genesis naturwissenschaftliche Verfahren und damit verbundene epistemologische Grundannahmen wie etwa die der Objekt-Natur auf die Bühne,

15 Interview auf One on One (23.2.2008), Verfügbar über: http://www.youtube.com/watch?v=evxlR3zJ11o

wodurch jene Verfahren und Grundannahmen nicht nur als bedeutsam markiert[16], sondern umgewertet werden. Verschiedene Lebensbereiche pluralistischer Gesellschaften werden in einer dialogischen Thematisierungsstruktur durch die metadiskursive Praxis jener künstlerischen Aufführung wissenschaftlichen Wissens zusammengeführt. Dabei ist Metadiskursivität nicht auf Argumentation und wörtliche Sprachlichkeit angewiesen – hier wird vielmehr etwas über kulturspezifisch-naturwissenschaftliche Diskurse gesagt, indem es parodierend aufgeführt wird. In Genesis werden Verfahren der Naturwissenschaften nachgeahmt, charakteristische Züge naturwissenschaftlicher Praxis werden auf die Bühne lebensweltlicher Öffentlichkeit gebracht und zugleich einer Neubewertung unterzogen, wodurch eine neue (jedoch keine beliebige) Wirklichkeit entsteht. Existenziell bedeutsame kulturelle Selbst- und Weltbezüge wie etwa die Schöpfungsgeschichte, die Vorstellung einer Objekt-Natur und die Dichotomie von Natur und Kultur (ja sogar die Verquickung von religiösen und naturwissenschaftlichen Weltverständnissen) treten in ein kaum zu überschauendes und nur bedingt kontrollierbares Wechselverhältnis mit wesentlichen Kulturtechniken des 21. Jahrhunderts, wie die Dechiffrierung der DNA, biotechnisch ermöglichte Manipulation biologischer Prozesse und teleaktive Medien. Prägnanzbildende Unbestimmtheit[17], die Bildungsprozessen als Veränderung existenziell bedeutsamer Selbst- und Weltverhältnisse (Marotzki 1990) vorausgeht, entsteht in dieser Dramatisierung wissenschaftlichen Wissens dadurch, dass naturwissenschaftliches Wissen hin zu multiplen Bedeutungsmöglichkeiten durch dialogische, nicht narrative Rahmung geöffnet wird.

Dadurch, dass Kacs Genesis keine Geschichte erzählt, sondern vielmehr beständiger Transformationsprozess dialogisch verflochtener Elemente ist, dass es weder Anfang noch Ende und auch keine Entwicklung mit Höhepunkten usw. gibt, kann wissenschaftliches Wissen als Bestandteil eines komplexen, immerwährenden und offenen Transformationsprozesses unselbstständiger Teilaspekte dramatisiert werden. Dialogisch ist diese medienkünstlerische Form der Bedeutungskonstitution in verschiedener Hinsicht. Zum einen in Bezug auf die Parodie als symbolische Form selbst. Parodien sind insofern dialogisch, weil sie durch den Differenz konstituierenden Bezug auf ein Original charakterisiert sind. Diese dialogische Form bringt aus einer übergeordneten Perspektive auf kulturspezifische Deutungsfiguren problematische Implikationen von kulturellen Erzählungen und Darstellungen zum Ausdruck. Diese Dialogizität über die Form ist metadiskursiv, sie entfaltet eine der alltäglichen und konkreten praktischen Lebensführung übergeordnete (distanzierend-reflexive, nicht außen stehende) Perspektive auf kulturell bedeutsame Diskurse und eine Differenz zu tradierten Deutungsformen. Metadiskursivität bedeutet hier zudem Metareflexivität als gesteigerte Assimilation von

---

16 Vgl. zur Vorstellung von Dramatisierung als Bedeutsamkeitsmarkierung und Intensivierung der Handlung Shusterman (2005,102ff)

17 Vgl. zum Terminus die Begrifflichkeit der postsemantischen Unbestimmtheit bei Jung (2009)

innerer und äußerer Perspektive (vgl. Jung 2005) - verstanden als eine gesteigerte wechselseitige Anpassung der Perspektive betroffener Lebensführung und der distanzierenden Perspektive des Beobachters. Dabei spielen Digitalisierung und Vernetzung eine wichtige Rolle, denn die numerische Präsentation und die modulare Struktur digitaler Medienobjekte (Manovich 2002) und die durch Vernetzung ermöglichte Wechselseitigkeit (Flusser 2005; 2007) eignen sich für parodierende Ausdrucksformen in besonderem Maße. Darauf werde ich an anderer Stelle näher eingehen.

Des Weiteren sind die verschiedenen Transformationsprozesse, die scheinbar unendlich und in Bezug auf ihre Ergebnisse als tendenziell offen aufgeführt werden, wesentlich dialogisch: Alphabet, genetischer Code, biologische Prozesse und menschliche Manipulation dieser treten in einen komplexen Dialog, der Kultur und Leben verändert. Dabei spielt Vernetzung und Digitalisierung als dialogisches Moment eine konstitutive Rolle. Während ein Computer die Fernanfragen der Internetakteure steuerte, war der andere Computer für die DNA-synthetisierte Musik, deren Parameter von den bakteriellen Vermehrungs- und Veränderungsalgorithmen abgeleitet wurden, zuständig. Für Kac sind Ende des 20. Jahrhunderts die Sprache, der DNA-Code und die binäre Logik die basalen Elemente der Schöpfung: dem Prinzip der Digitalrechner ähnlich, sind biologische Prozesse nun programmierbar und zur Verarbeitung und Speicherung von Daten fähig. Damit würde die Grenze zwischen dem Leben und den digitalen Daten brüchig (vgl. Kac 1999).

Die parodierende Dramatisierung wissenschaftlichen Wissens in Kacs Genesis führt auf, wie Biotechnologie auf verschiedenen Bedeutungsebenen und in vielerlei, jedoch nicht beliebigen Bedeutungsweisen verstanden werden kann, jedoch ohne die Schaffung eines in sich geschlossenen Sinnes, sondern als Öffnung zu einem dialogischen Weltverhältnis und damit zum Unbekannten, normativ Ambivalenten und Unsicheren hin. Diese Öffnung bzw. Schaffung prägnanzbildender Unbestimmtheit als einem Bezeichnen dessen, was nicht gesagt werden kann, aber bedeutsam ist, wird durch die Form der Parodie, die Aufführung von Partizipation verschiedener Kulturen als auch durch die Aufführung der Möglichkeiten (kaum überschaubarer) Manipulation und der Komplexität und Offenheit von Transformationsprozessen in einer dialogischen Thematisierungsstruktur erzeugt, wobei Digitalisierung und Vernetzung ausdruckstragende Elemente sind.

Die dialogisch aufgeführte Offenheit biotechnologischer Möglichkeiten wird bei Kac als entscheidungsoffene Freiheit und als existenzieller Zwang thematisch, in dem Teilhabe und Verantwortlichkeit als relevante implizit angesprochene Wertbezüge an Bedeutung für Handlungsvollzug und Lebensführung gewinnen. Teilhabe und Verantwortlichkeit gehen als kontingenzangemessene Wertorientierungen (Joas 2001)[18] in

18 Den Hintergrund für die Bezeichnung „kontingenzangemessene Wertorientierung" bildet die zeitgenössische sozialwissenschaftliche Diskussion um den Zusammenhang gestiegener Kontingenz, gestiegener Des-

die ästhetisch erzeugte prägnanzbildende Unbestimmtheit als subtilerer Ausdruck des Stellenwertes gestiegener Kontingenz durch Biotechnologie ein. Diese selbstkonstitutiven Wertorientierungen können als wertbezogenes abstrakteres Gemeinsamkeitsverständnis verstanden werden, dass in Kulturen gestiegener entscheidungsoffener Handlungsmöglichkeiten partikulare Ideale und Werte unberührt lässt und wesentlich dazu motiviert, andere Perspektiven imaginativ zu übernehmen (Empathie) und sich mit verschiedenen Auffassungen vom Guten als für ein erfülltes Leben Wünschenswertem auseinanderzusetzen (vgl. Joas 2001).

Nanomandala – Nanowissenschaft und die Größe im Kleinen

Perspektivität und Annäherung in der Begegnung religiöser und wissenschaftlicher Kulturen ist auch wesentlicher Gegenstand des Medienkunstprojektes Nanomandala. Nanomandala[19] wurde von der Medienkünstlerin Victoria Vesna und dem Biochemie-Professor James K. Gimzewski von der University of California in Los Angeles (UCLA) gemeinsam mit Mönchen eines Klosters im indischen Gaden Lhopa entwickelt. Ausgangspunkt von Nanomandala ist die Schaffung einer Ähnlichkeitsbeziehung zwischen Nanoforschung und den Methoden, die Mönche anwenden, wenn sie mühsam ihre Sand-Mandalas Partikel für Partikel zusammensetzen.

Mandalas sind buddhistische und hinduistische religiöse Symbole des Universums. Sie sind meist kreisförmig oder quadratisch und haben ein Zentrum. Während der

integration und des Verlustes verbindlicher Werte in pluralistischen Gesellschaften. Hans Joas kritisiert, dass mit der Desintegrationsthese Prozesse der Wertbindung kognitivistisch verkürzt würden, denn die alleinige Kenntnis von Handlungsalternativen führe nicht zum Wert- und Bedeutungsverlust bestimmter Handlungsmöglichkeiten. Für eine solche Erschütterung alter Werte bzw. die Entstehung neuer Wertbindungen, und das ist bildungstheoretisch enorm wichtig, bedarf es Erfahrungen der Selbsttranszendenz und Selbstbildung, nicht der rational-argumentativen Rechtfertigung (vgl. Joas 2001, 7). In pluralistischen Gesellschaften sind die Akteure hinsichtlich eigener und der Spielräume anderer mit einer größeren Ungewissheit und mit Deutungsproblemen konfrontiert, die „kontingenzangemessene" Formen der Wertbindung notwendig machen (vgl. Joas 2001, 7ff). Solche Wertbindungen weisen „ein höheres Maß an Freiheit in der Bindung " auf (Joas 2001, 9) die darin besteht, so Joas, dass die Einwilligung in die Bindung immer wieder neu gefordert ist, da die Konfrontation mit Alternativen häufiger ist. Joas ist nun der Ansicht, dass Wertbindungen die im Zeitalter gestiegener Kontingenz überlebensfähig sind, drei miteinander verbundene Momente aufweisen: Werteprozessualisierung, Wertegeneralisierung und Empathie. Empathie bezeichnet die einfühlende Fähigkeit, die Welt mit den Augen anderer zu sehen, welche im Umgang mit einer wachsenden Zahl Fremder in pluralistischen, medial-globalisierten Interaktionsgemeinschaften zunehmend an Bedeutung gewinnt. Werteprozessualisierung ist die Einigung auf Prozeduren des Umgangs und die Bereitschaft, sich an diese zu halten. Wertegeneralisierung als basale Ebene kontingenzangemessener Wertbindung meint hier die Ausbildung eines (abstrakteren) Gemeinsamkeitsverständnisses differenter Wert-Kulturen, die die partikulare Bindungskraft konkreter Ideale und Werte unberührt lässt (vgl. Joas 2001, 7ff).

19 Eine ausführliche Projektdokumentation findet sich hier: http://nano.arts.ucla.edu/mandala/process.php, eine Videoaufzeichnung der Besucherinteraktion findet sich hier http://nano.arts.ucla.edu/mandala/video/mandala.mov

äußere Bereich symbolisch die Vorstellung des Universums evoziert, deutet das Zentrum auf das Heilige, auf höchste Göttlichkeit. Mandalas haben kartenähnliche Eigenschaften und sind durch ihre anschaulichen Strukturen bis hin zu kleinen symbolischen Details charakterisiert. Sie stellen im Buddhismus und Hinduismus eine Übung eingehender geistiger Versenkung dar. Von Indien und Tibet aus verbreitete sich das Mandala als Meditationsobjekt und als zweidimensionale symbolische Darstellung eines dreidimensionalen geistigen Objekts in ganz Ostasien. Oft arbeiten mehrere Mönche wochenlang konzentriert an der Herstellung eines Mandalas, wobei im Fall von Sandmandalas[20] das Wegwischen dieser mühsamen Arbeit am Ende charakteristisch ist. Die Selbsttranszendenz in jener Arbeit als Überschreitung der Grenze zwischen Körper-Identifikation und Raumerfahrung soll nach buddhistischer Lehre die Anhaftung an ein dauerhaftes Selbst überwinden und zur meditativen Einsicht in die kontinuierliche Veränderung des Lebens und somit zur Weisheit verhelfen. Der Bezug der Mandalas zu extremer Genauigkeit und imposanten kosmologischen Strukturen war der Grund für die Anwesenheit einer Gruppe tibetanischer Mönche in einem nanotechnologischen Labor (vgl. Kemp 2007).

Zunächst arbeiteten vier Mönche einen Monat lang acht Stunden pro Tag im Los Angeles County Museum of Art an einem Sandmandala für die Tantragöttin Chakrasamvara. Dieses Mandala umkreist den prachtvollen Wohnsitz der Gottheit Heruka Chakrasamvara und wird auch als „Rad der höchsten Glückseligkeit" (Kemp 2007) bezeichnet. Es symbolisiert das weibliche Ideal der Klugheit. Das knapp 2,5 m große Mandala wurde mit Hilfe eines Kranes, der am Ende seines Armes eine Digitalkamera installiert hatte, abfotografiert. Das Mandala wurde in ungefähr 500 Schüssen in jeweils zehn verschiedenen Abstandsintervallen mit dem Weitwinkelobjektiv fotografiert, zu dem ein Makroobjektiv dazu geschaltet wurde. In einer zweiten Stufe wurde die Mitte des Mandalas, die in Gimzewski`s Pico-Labor im UCLA neu hergestellt wurde, fotografiert und in einer nächsten Stufe wurden die Sandkörner fotografiert, die im PICO-Labor für die Mikroskopaufnahmen genutzt werden sollten.

Zwei Mönche reproduzierten das Zentrum des Mandalas später im PICO-Labor am UCLA, was von einem Studenten vor Ort zuerst mit einem optischen Mikroskop visualisiert und dann mit einem höher auflösenden Elektronenmikroskop gescannt wurde. Sodann wurden einhundert der besten hoch aufgelösten Fotografien und mikroskopische Aufnahmen ineinander gebettet, um die Auflösung zu verbessern und ein einziges großes Bild des Mandalas zu schaffen, das bis in den Nanobereich[21] skaliert war.

20 Sandmandalas werden aus farbigen Sandkörnern losen Sandes hergestellt.

21 Der Nanobereich bezeichnet eine Größenordnung vom Einzelatom bis zu einer Strukturgröße von 100 Nanometern (nm), wobei Nano als Maßeinheit den milliardsten (10^{-9}) Teil meint, ein Nanometer ein Milliardstel Meter (10^{-9} m) misst. Im engeren Sinn meint Nanotechnologie die Veränderung von Materialien im atomaren bzw. molekularen Bereich. In dieser Größenordnung werden die Oberflächeneigenschaften ge-

Abb. 1: Tibetanische Mönche und der Nanowissenschaftler Jim Gimzewski im PICO-Labor

Durch die Beschränkung der Bildbearbeitungssoftware Photoshop und After-Effects musste das Bild in neun Abschnitte geteilt werden. Die Abschnitte wurden dann hoch auflösend in zehn verschiedenen Stufen gezoomt und jeweils in eine hoch aufgelöste Videoanimation transformiert. Um den Eindruck von Bewegung zu erzeugen, wurden die Videos digital skaliert und schließlich zu einem fünfzehnminütigen Video für die Installation komponiert. Für die Produktion dieses Videos wurden 36 Computer gleichzeitig benötigt, mit Hilfe derer die Filme über zwei Tage gerendert wurden. Zur Installation wurde ein Mandala-Soundtrack komponiert, dessen erster Teil aus Aufnahmen vom Malibu-Beach bestanden, dem Ort an dem die Akteure verschiedener Disziplinen und Kulturen zusammentrafen. Ein weiterer Teil wurde aus Aufnahmen während der Arbeit der Mönche im PICO-Labor komponiert und besteht weitestgehend aus dem verkratzenden Ton des Mandala-Werkzeugs und Gebetsglocken. Der dritte Teil des Soundtracks besteht aus dem Gesang der buddhistischen Mönche vom Gaden Lhopa Khangtsen Kloster.

Das Mandala-Video wurde als AVI-Datei über einen PC abgespielt und mit Hilfe eines Projektors und eines reflektierenden Spiegels in der Installation in verschiedenen Museen seit 2003 auf einen mit weißem Sand bedeckten Tisch von etwa 2,5 m Durchmesser projektiert[22]. Die Bilder variierten sanft von einer Gesamtansicht bis hin

genüber den Volumeneigenschaften der Materialien zunehmend wichtiger und quantenphysikalische Effekte müssen berücksichtigt werden. Zugleich besteht die Möglichkeit, im atomaren Bereich Eigenschaften zu beeinflussen und schöpferisch zu gestalten. Vgl. ausführlicher Gazsó et. al. (2007) sowie Euler (2006).

22 Zunächst wurde die Installation im Rahmen der Ausstellung "nano - a Media Arts & Science Exhibition" im Los Angeles County Museum of Art - LACMA, Los Angeles, CA gezeigt.

zu mikroskopischen Ansichten der Oberfläche eines Sandkorns. Das Video wurde in Endlosschleife abgespielt, um ein sich beständig änderndes Bild zu erzeugen. Besucher sahen, wie eine sich langsam entfaltende Skalierung von der molekularen Struktur eines einzelnen Sandkornes zum erkennbaren Mandala in einen Sandhaufen projektiert wurde und konnten selbst jene Skalierung beeinflussen.

Für Kemp hat die Dialogizität jener medienkünstlerischen Thematisierung von Nanowissenschaft als Verbindung von auf minuziöser Sorgfalt und unermüdlicher Wiederholung gegründeter buddhistisch-spiritueller Geduld mit den gottlosen Prozessen der Wiederholung, zu denen Computer fähig sind, etwas sehr Bewegendes und löst das Empfinden tiefer Schönheit aus. Für ihn teilen buddhistische Mönche und Nanowissenschaftler das Wunder der Skalierung, das in der ergreifenden Komposition eines geordneten Ganzen aus unzähligen Teilen liegt. Sowohl traditionelle religiöse Kontemplation als auch moderne technologische Wissenschaft reichen auf jeweils unterschiedliche Weise in die Gebiete der Unendlichkeit, so Kemp. Für den Kunsthistoriker liegt hier das „ästhetische Reich des Erhabenen“ (Kemp 2007), das von all denen bewohnt würde, die ehrfürchtig vor den Wundern des Universums und vor den vielfältigen geistigen Möglichkeiten stehen, die wir nutzen, um dem, was wir sehen und fühlen, Bedeutung zu verleihen.

Nanowissenschaft wird in Nanomandala nicht als Erkundung einer objektiven Ordnung thematisch, sondern als Schöpfung kulturspezifischer Wirklichkeit und als Werterfahrung. Wissenschaft ist zwar auf einen uns überschreitenden Bedeutungshorizont wie etwa die Struktur des Universums in der Nanotechnologie und Quantenphysik bezogen, dieser Bezug ist jedoch eine kulturspezifische Art der Wirklichkeitskonstitution, hier über wissenschaftliches Wissen als spezifische Schöpfung von Welt und Selbst. Über die dialogische Verschränkung verschiedener kultureller Deutungskontexte und innewohnender Wertbezüge als auch verschiedener kultureller Praktiken wird in Nanomandala die schöpferische Dimension wissenschaftlicher Erkenntnis thematisch. Aufgeführt wird eine Wissenschaft und deren Technologie als Methode der Wissensproduktion, die zwar gottlos, doch zugleich ergreifend ist und Gefühle des Erhabenen zu evozieren vermag. Nanomandala erzählt keine Geschichte der Entstehung wissenschaftlicher Erkenntnis und darüber, wie es dazu kam, dass wir heute wissen, was wir wissen. Wesentliches Ausdruckselement ist Dialogizität, auf visueller und akustischer Ebene durch die Technik digitaler Bildbearbeitung und mit Hilfe von Animationssoftware, auf der Ebene von wissenskonstitutiven Kulturtechniken wie der Schaffung von Mandalas und mikroskopischer Aufnahmen von Gegenständen als auch auf der Ebene von Symbolizität und Sinngefügen (Buddhismus und Naturwissenschaft). Aufgeführt wird nicht ein Werden von Etwas, sondern unablässige Wiederholung von Skalierung zwischen Partikel und Ganzem und die mit dieser verbundene symbolische Schöpfung von Welt. Dialogisch wird die intelligente (Mandalas als Technik zur Erlangung von Weisheit, Nanotechnologie als wissenschaftliche Erkenntnis) Schaffung von etwas Neuem, das – insofern es den Schaffenden zugleich überschreitet – mit Gefühlen der Präsenz von Größe und Heiligkeit einhergeht und zugleich Erstaunen und Erfurcht erzeugt.

Six Appartements – Klimaforschung und die Transformation zwischen Leben und Tod

In dem Medienkunstprojekt "Six Appartements" ist diese Präsenz eines das Subjekt überschreitenden Bedeutungshorizontes stärker mit dem Gefühl des Erschauderns verbunden, was ein Stück weit am Bezugsrahmen der Klimaforschung und der kulturellen Bedeutung globaler Erderwärmung liegen mag. Für seinen Beitrag "Six Appartements" erhielt der Filmemacher und Medienkünstler Reynold Reynolds auf dem Berliner Medienkunstfestival transmediale 2009, das sich mit dem Thema Klimawandel und dessen kultureller Bedeutung unter dem Titel „deep north" beschäftigt hat, den Distinction Award[23]. Six Appartements ist eine zwölfminütige Zwei-Screen-Video-Projektion, die als Loop aufgeführt wird. Poetisch wird das Leben von sechs Menschen, das sich ausschließlich in deren Appartements abspielt, portraitiert.

Durch die Splitscreen-Technik werden inszenierte Auszüge aus dem isolierten Leben der Mieter von sechs Appartements eines Hauses und deren triste Lebensabläufe zwischen schlafen, essen, fernsehen und Radio hören auf visueller und akustischer Ebene nebeneinandergestellt. Thematisiert wird ein Leben ohne Drama, das durch die massenmedial entworfenen Probleme der Welt und die aufkommende ökologische Krise via Fernsehen und Radio überschattet wird, von diesen Problemlagen jedoch eigenartig unberührt bleibt. Isolation und Verbindung bestehen auf verschiedenen Ebenen nebeneinander. Durch Bildkomposition, räumliche Montage[24], durchdachte Kamerafahrten und wirkungsvolle Schnitttechnik beziehen die Bilder auf den zwei Leinwandhälften die jeweils dargestellten einsamen Leben für den Betrachter aufeinander: nur die Protagonisten existieren unbemerkt voneinander und bis auf den Empfang von Radio- und Fernsehsendern abgeschnitten von der Außenwelt in ihren Appartements. Urban-isoliert leben die sechs Bewohner ein in seinen tagtäglichen Routinen und Handlungsabfolgen unterschiedliches, in seiner Passivität und Ereignisarmut jedoch gleiches Leben, das - durch Verfall bestimmt - auf den Tod zusteuert. In der Projektbeschrei-

23 Eine Dokumentation der Preisverleihung und ein Auszug der Videoprojektion findet sich hier: http://www.transmediale.de/de/reynold-reynolds-accepts-distinction-award-09-six-

24 Lev Manovich (2002) konstatiert, die Ein-Bildschirm/Ein-Bild-Logik des Kinos sei als der Bildschirm zu einem punktgrafischen Computerdisplay wurde durchbrochen worden und es etablierte sich die räumliche Montage, die gewissermaßen gegen die Kinotechnologie zeitlicher Montage verlief.

bung auf der Website des Künstlers heißt es, die Verbindung zur Welt liegt nicht in teilhabender Sorge um massenmedial thematisierte Krisen, sondern vielmehr in den mikroskopischen Prozessen der langsamen Zersetzung des eigenen Körpers, der Nahrungsmittel und Lebensräume. Sie liege in der passiven Konsumhaltung, welche die Menschen mit jedem Moment näher zu ihrem Tod führt. Die Inszenierung jener teilnahmslosen, lethargischen und dem Verfall in gleichem Maße ausgesetzten, doch mit Blick auf Gewohnheiten und Lebensstil sehr unterschiedlichen Lebensformen ist durch Reynolds metaphorische Ikonografie des unkontrollierbaren und vergänglichen Lebens, in vielen Kritiken als starke Vanitas-Thematik beschrieben, jenseits narrativer Darstellung charakterisiert.

Die Portraitierung von Handlungsabläufen der Appartement-Bewohner wird immer wieder durch Zeitverschiebungen (über Zeitraffer-Elemente und fantastische Verläufe überzeichnet), unwirkliche Ereignisse und Verfremdung von Elementen wie Nahrungsmittel und deren Verwesung, die zugleich neues Leben entstehen lässt, gebrochen. Stark im Zentrum steht das Thema der Transformation, das selbst den Tod noch zum Motor des Lebens macht. Im passiven Verharren steckt Tod und Leben zugleich: die stete und unabänderliche Transformation des Lebens einschließlich des natürlichen Wechselspiels von Verfall und Leben sind wesentliches Bedeutungselement dieser Video-Projektion, wobei Sinn durch das Nebeneinanderstellen verschiedener symbolischer Verweise entsteht. Der medienkünstlerische (mittelbare) Umgang mit wissenschaftlichem Wissen etwa aus dem Bereich der Klimaforschung zur globalen Erderwärmung, dem anthropogenen Treibhauseffekt (vgl. Intergovernmental Panel on Climate Change 2007; Oreskes 2004) und den damit verbundenen gesellschaftlichen Diskussionen um die Folgen des Klimawandels und Fragen des Klimaschutzes, symbolisiert durch die Radio- und Fernsehbeiträge im Splittscreen-Video, ist hier jenseits eines rezeptiven Standpunktes schöpferisch umwertend. Die naturwissenschaftlich unter verschiedenen Unsicherheiten (Wirtschaftswachstum der kommenden Jahre, Energiebedarf usw.) prognostizierten Veränderungen unserer klimatischen Lebensbedingungen werden medien- und symbolreflexiv kontextualisiert und somit neu verstanden und bewertet. Zugleich wird die massenmediale Auseinandersetzung mit diesem Wissen und anknüpfenden Fragen als Gegenstand einer äußerlich bleibenden Welt für die zum Tod hin Lebenden angedeutet. Kriegs- und Katastrophenberichte als auch Fakten über die globale Erderwärmung werden über Fernsehen und Radio konsumiert. Das unausweichliche Bedrohungsszenario ökologischer Krisis ist Hintergrundrauschen in einem Prozess beständiger Transformation, die Leben heißt und an denen, die es zu haben glauben, vorbeizieht und doch zugleich seine Spuren hinterlässt:

> “Yet whilst it may appear that nothing is happening here, the apartment building and its inhabitants‘ bodies are aging, giving way to bacteria, larva, and finally trans-

formation. Televisions and radios tell them about the destruction of the whole planet but it does not effect their lives. Everything is in a state of resolute conversion.“ (Reynolds 2009, project description)

Reglose, gewissermaßen tote Gesichter, ungestörte Routinen einer passiven Lebensweise stehen neben massenmedial aufbereiteten Hiobsbotschaften und Wohnräumen, die die laufende Umwandlung des Lebens (teilweise grotesk überzeichnet) symbolisieren. Fast scheint es, so eine Besucherin der transmediale in einem Blog, als würden die Krisenmeldungen den Bewohnern den Aufenthalt in ihren stillen und leeren Räumen behaglicher machen (Stefanie 2009). Eine andere Besucherin schreibt in ihrem Blog: „Selten habe ich eine so beklemmende Darstellung des Lebens in urbaner Isolation gesehen“ (Hoffmann 2009).

Für die Betrachter scheint eine Spannung zwischen ganz individueller, Gefühle des Schauderns auslösender Lebensführung und deren Degradierung zur Bedeutungslosigkeit aus der Perspektive des diese Individualität übersteigenden Prozesses von Werden und Vergehen, von fortwährender Transformation – aus der für die Naturwissenschaften erkenntniskonstitutiven Perspektive des außen stehenden Beobachters – zu entstehen. Diese Spannung ist eigentümliches Element jener Ambivalenz, die sich in der lebendigen Produktivität des Todes und der vernichtenden Wirkung von Veränderungsprozessen wiederum zeigt. Zentrales Ausdruckselement dieser Ambivalenz, die immer nur angedeutet wird, ist dialogische Splitscreentechnik und Manipulation durch digitale Bildkomposition für Verfremdungseffekte auf der Basis digitaler Medien.

Dialogizität als Medienbildungsraum – Umdeutung auf der „Höhe der Sprachlichkeit“ und der kommunikationstechnologischen Infrastruktur

Anhand der geschilderten medienkünstlerischen Umgangsweisen mit wissenschaftlichem Wissen und damit verbundenen gestiegenen Handlungsoptionen wurde knapp dargestellt, dass hier weniger im Modus narrativ-anschaulicher Rahmung von Wissenschaft verfahren, denn vielmehr eine dialogische Aufführung jenes Wissens und verbundener Kontingenz unternommen wird. Medientechnische Eigenschaften gehen hier konstitutiv in den Ausdrucks- (Interpretations- und Umwertungs-)akt ein. In Genesis spielen computergenerierte Manipulation und Transformation als auch teleaktive Beeinflussung eine konstitutive Rolle, die auf medientechnischer Digitalisierung und Vernetzung beruht. Die Bildkomposition und Skalierungseffekte in Nanomandala sind ebenfalls computergeneriert und basieren damit auf Digitalisierung. In „Six Apartments“ wurde der 16 mm Film in ein digital dateibasiertes Videoformat transformiert, das die Nachbearbeitung durch die Möglichkeit des nicht-linearen Schnitts erheblich erleichtert und digitale Bildkomposition für Verfremdungseffekte in der Post-Produktion ermöglicht. Auf medientechnischer Ebene spielen also Computerisierung, insbesondere Digitalisierung und Vernetzung eine ausdruckskonstitutive Rolle, die medienspezifische Reflexionsoptionen (Jörissen/Marotzki 2009) unter Bedingungen konkreten Medienhandelns eröffnet. Der Blick auf Flussers medienwissenschaftliche Unterscheidung von dialogischen und diskursiven Medien[25] informiert hinsichtlich medienbildungstheoretisch relevanter medientechnischer Eigenschaften digital-vernetzter Medien ebenso wie Manovichs formalanalytische Bezeichnung des Stellenwertes der digitalen Basis von Neuen Medien und der modularen Struktur von Medienobjekten (Manovich 2002).

Medientechnische Dialogizität bei Flusser

Was Flussers Medienanalyse aus der Perspektive der Medienbildungsforschung interessant macht, ist der Stellenwert den Flusser dialogischer Kommunikation einräumt und dessen darauf referierende medienanalytische Differenz zwischen einkanaligen und zweikanaligen Medien. Wichtig ist seine Unterscheidung zwischen Verbündelung und Vernetzung (vgl. Flusser 2005, 143ff): einkanalige Medien (Massenmedien) folgen einem „Bündelschaltplan", in welchem „Sender bündelartig Informationen an zu jeder Antwort unfähige, also verantwortungslose und unmündige Empfänger ausstrahlen" (Flusser 2005, 147f). Dem entgegen folgen zweikanalige Medien einem „Netzschaltplan", die wechselseitiges Senden und Empfangen von Botschaften ermöglichen. Sie basieren auf „Vorrichtungen zum Vernetzen" (Flusser 2005, 147) und bilden neben einkanaligen Medien die Informationsinfrastruktur zeitgenössischer Gesellschaften.

> „Sollte jedoch die Vernetzung die Massenmedien durchdringen und durch sie hindurchdringen, und sollten die vernetzenden Inseln wie Computerterminals, Video-Circuits oder Hypertexte die Bündelung zerreißen können, dann wäre die utopische Informationsgesellschaft, worin wir einander verwirklichen können, technisch und von daher auch existentiell in den Bereich des Machbaren vorgedrungen" (Flusser 2005,148f).

Flusser (2005, 143) nennt diese utopische (demokratischere) Gesellschaft „telematische Informationsgesellschaft". Der Begriff Telematik, auf welchen Flusser referiert, wurde 1978 von Nora und Minc geprägt und beschreibt die „wachsende Verflechtung von Rechnern und Telekommunikationsmittel[n]", die vernetzend „Bild, Ton und Informationsinhalte in eine vielschichtige Wechselbeziehung treten lässt" (Krüger/Reschke

25 Wobei hier die Unterscheidung von dialogischen und monologischen Medien prägnanter wäre. Vgl. Flusser (2005, 2007), ebenso argumentiert Bertold Brecht (1989, orig. 1932/1933) in seiner Radiotheorie, vgl. auch Scheibel (2008, 19ff)

2004). Kommunikation hat für Flusser eine politische Funktion, die in der gemeinsamen Suche nach Wahrheit im Dialog besteht (vgl. Flusser 2005, 137; Heibach 2001). Medienschaltungen, also die medienspezifische Infrastruktur gesellschaftlicher Kommunikationsverhältnisse, spielen hier eine konstruktive oder destruktive Rolle. Kommunikation hat zudem auch eine ethische Bedeutung: Kommunikation erzeugt (nur) im Dialog Verantwortung für den anderen, so Flusser. Betrachtet man also die Bedingungen von Datenübertragung und Datenspeicherung in jeweiligen medienspezifischen Kommunikationszusammenhängen, wird deutlich, so der Tenor Flussers, dass Kommunikation als Dialog nur in vernetzten Medien ermöglicht wird[26] (vgl. Flusser 2005, 137; Heibach 2001). Neben diesem medienbildungstheoretisch wichtigen Aspekt der Vernetzung Neuer Medien, welche Dialogizität auf der Ebene medialer Kommunikationsbedingungen anlegt, spielt ein weiterer Aspekt eine konstitutive Rolle, den Flusser angedeutet und Manovich detaillierter ausgearbeitet hat: Computerisierung und Digitalisierung.

> „Die Schnellrechenmaschinen [...] rechnen mit zwei Fingern [...], aber dies so schnell, daß sie besser rechnen können als die größten Mathematiker. [...] Die zweite hier hervorzuhebende Eigenschaft der Schnellrechenmaschine ist die Tatsache, daß sie überraschenderweise nicht nur kalkulieren, sondern auch komputieren kann, das heißt, sie vermag [...] auch [...] Zahlen zu Gestalten zu synthetisieren" (Flusser 2005, 210).

Diese Eigenschaften (vernetzter) Computer als Schnellrechenmaschinen verbindet Flusser mit einer spezifischen Denk- und Wahrnehmungsform, dem nulldimensionalen, kalkulatorischen Bewusstsein, von welchem er das lineare Bewusstsein unterscheidet (vgl. Flusser 2005, 207). Während im linearen Bewusstsein kausal, narrativ literarisch und buchstäblich gedacht werde, sei letzteres kalkulierend und strukturanalytisch (vgl. Flusser 2005, 209). Das kalkulatorische Denken zersetzt die Welt in Partikel und kann diese wiederum variabel wieder zusammensetzen (vgl. Flusser 2005, 210). Aus Symbolen des kalkulatorischen Denkens (Algorithmen) können Alternativen synthetisiert und projiziert werden (einschließlich das Selbst), die die Konkretisierung der uns umgebenden Umwelt haben können (vgl. Flusser 2005, 211). Unabhängig von den Differenzen einer pragmatistisch-kulturanthropologischen Medienbildungstheorie, wie sie hier verfolgt wird, zu den Paradigmen von Flussers Medientheorie ist für den hier verfolgten Zusammenhang Flussers Einsicht in die Bedeutung medientechnischer Eigenschaften für menschliche Kommunikation, für Wahrnehmung und Denken und in diesem Sinne für Reflexivität wichtig. Damit ist nicht nur der Stellenwert von Vernetzung für Partizipation und verantwortungsvoll orientierende Dialogizität gemeint, sondern auch die

26 Dialog in diesem verstandenen Sinne hat allerdings zur Voraussetzung, dass Informationen mehr sind als Informationen – nämlich Artikulationen gelebten Lebens (vgl. Jung 2005).

spezifische Dialogizität des Digitalen, die im Wesentlichen auf Beeinflussung (meist als Manipulation bezeichnet) beruht.

Die Sprache Neuer Medien bei Manovich als medientechnische Dialogizität

Bei Manovich werden die von Flusser skizzierten Aspekte von Digitalisierung etwas genauer in den Blick genommen. Manovich (2002, 49ff) beschreibt fünf Prinzipien, die digitale Medien von anderen Medien unterscheiden und welche die kulturelle Bedeutung von Computerisierung bezeichnen. Zwei dieser Prinzipien sind für Manovich grundlegend: der Umstand, dass Medienobjekte in digitalen Medien numerische Repräsentationen und programmierbar sind und zweitens die nicht-hierarchische Organisation aller Medienobjekte als Folge ihrer modularen Struktur. Modularität bezeichnet hier den Umstand, dass Medienobjekte ihre Selbstständigkeit auch dann behalten, wenn sie modifiziert, zugänglich gemacht oder ersetzt werden:

> "Media elements, be it images, sounds, shapes, or behaviors, are represented as collections of discrete samples (pixels, polygons, voxels, characters, scripts). These elements are assembled into larger-scale objects but they continue to maintain their separate identity." (Manovich 2002, 51)

Diese modulare Struktur digitaler Medien macht deren Manipulation sehr einfach, teilweise können Teile mit wenigen Mausklicken gelöscht oder ersetzt bzw. hinzugefügt werden. Auf den Prinzipen der numerischen Präsentation von Medienobjekten und deren modularer Struktur in digitalen Medien beruhen drei weitere Prinzipien, die Manovich als Automation, Variabilität und Transcoding beschreibt (vgl. Manovich 2002, 53ff). Die Automation von Operationen im Umgang mit digitalen Medien wird durch die modulare Struktur und die Programmierbarkeit von Medienobjekten ermöglicht. Sie führe dazu, dass menschliche Intentionalität, jedenfalls teilweise, vom produktiven Prozess gelöst würde. Beispiele für niedere Stufen der Automation seien jene Umgangsformen mit digitalen Medien, in denen modifiziert und produziert würde, indem Vorlagen oder einfache Algorithmen Verwendung finden, wie beispielsweise Filter oder Farbskalierungen in Bildbearbeitungssoftware. Höhere Automationsebenen seien dort zu finden, wo Automation sich (bis zu einem bestimmten Punkt) auf die in Objekten angelegte Bedeutung (Semantik) bezieht, wie beispielsweise im Kontext Künstlicher Intelligenz. Mit Automation eng verbunden und ebenfalls auf den Prinzipien der Modularität und der numerischen Repräsentation basierend ist das Prinzip der Variabilität (vgl. Manovich 2002, 56). Ein Objekt in den Neuen Medien kann in sehr verschiedenen, teilweise unendlichen Versionen existieren, die durchaus automatisch durch den Computer zusammengestellt werden können. Weil Objekte in Neuen Medien als digitale Daten repräsentiert sind, die ihre eigene Identität in jeweiligen Zusammenstellungen behalten, können sie spontan verändert (produziert, angepasst) werden. Als Beispiele für dieses Variabilitätsprinzip nennt Manovich etwa Datenbanken, die Endnutzer-Objekte generieren, die in Auflösung, Form und Inhalt variieren. Weil es durch Digitalisierung möglich wird, Daten (Inhalt) vom Interface (Schnittstelle) zu trennen, können – als weiteres Beispiel für Variabilität in den neuen Medien – sehr verschiedene Schnittstellen zu denselben Daten führen. Transcoding als fünftes Prinzip digitaler Medien ist für Manovich die wesentlichste Konsequenz der kulturellen Computerisierung (vgl. Manovich 2002, 63). In der Sprache Neuer (digitaler) Medien meint Transcoding die Übersetzung von etwas in ein anderes Format (vgl. Manovich 2002, 64). Der wichtigste Aspekt dieses Prinzips sei der Umstand, dass die Struktur computerisierter Medien den etablierten Konventionen der Datenorganisation durch den Computer folgt. Strukturbezogen sind Medienobjekte hier kompatibel zu und transcodierbar in andere Computerdatenformate. Wichtig für den hier verfolgten Zusammenhang ist, dass Transcoding auf mehreren Ebenen stattfindet, wobei eine allgemeinere Ebene die der kulturellen Transcodierung ist. Ein Beispiel hierfür seien Datenbanken (im metaphorischen Sinne) (vgl. Manovich 2002, 94, sowie Arns 2002, 2) als neue symbolische Form, die im Computerzeitalter Erfahrungen als auch die Sicht auf Selbst und Welt strukturiert und alte Formen narrativer Darstellung durch andere Formen der Bedeutungskonstitution ersetze[27].

> "Many new media objects do not tell stories; they don't have beginning or end; in fact, they don't have any development, thematically, formally or otherwise which would organize their elements into a sequence. Instead, they are collections of individual items, where every item has the same significance as any other." (Manovich, 2002, 194)

27 Manovich versteht unter Datenbanken im weiteren Sinne Sammlungen von Gegenständen, mit welchen der Nutzer in verschiedenen Operationen umgehen kann. Manovich macht anhand verschiedener Beispiele wie Multimedia-Enzyklopädien deutlich, dass Datenbanken die dominierende Form innerhalb digitaler Medien seien (vgl. Manovich 2002, 195ff). Ein Charakteristikum von Datenbanken ist, dass immer wieder Elemente hinzukommen. Datenbanken repräsentieren die Welt als Listen von Elementen und verweigern die Ordnung dieser Listen. Erzählungen schaffen im Gegensatz dazu einen Ursache-Wirkungs-Zugang zu scheinbar ungeordneten Elementen (vgl. Manovich 2002,199). Datenbanken und Erzählungen sind natürliche Feinde, so Manovich: sie konkurrieren um dasselbe Territorium menschlicher Kultur, wobei jeder das exklusive Recht beansprucht, dieser Welt Bedeutung zu verleihen. Trotz dieser Differenz können Datenbanken, die ihrer Logik nach in Widerspruch zur materiellen Form der Datenbank stehenden Narrationen unterstützen. Während klassische lineare Narrationen für Manovich einer von vielen möglichen Zugängen zu Datenbanken darstellen, begreift er in Anlehnung an Mieke Bals erzähltheoretische Bestimmung des Narrativen Hypernarration als Summe aller multiplen Zugänge zu einer Datenbank „The `user` of a narrative is traversing a database, following links between its records as established by the database's creator. An interactive narrative (which can be also called `hypernarrative` in an analogy with hypertext) can then be understood as the sum of multiple trajectories through a database" (Manovich 2002, 200).

Unabhängig von der problematischen kinematografischen Interpretation in Manovichs Analyse der Sprache Neuer Medien (vgl. Arns 2008) sind die von ihm beschriebenen Prinzipien digitaler Medien medienbildungstheoretisch relevant und anschlussfähig. Die Prinzipien der numerischen Repräsentation und der Modularität digitaler Medienobjekte bezeichnen zusammen mit dem Aspekt der Vernetzung als auch den Prinzipien der Automation (automatisierte Manipulation von Medienobjekten), Variabilität (Offenheit der Manipulation/Beeinflussung) und des Transcoding (schöpferische Manipulation/Beeinflussung) die medientechnisch eröffneten Möglichkeiten vereinfachter Manipulation von Medieninhalten und bedeutungskonstitutiver kommunikativer Teilhabe. Dialogizität findet bereits auf der Ebene der Datenstruktur bzw. der Ebene der Trennung von Daten und deren Anwendung, die diese Daten selbst immer wieder neu (als bedeutungsvolle) schafft, statt. Dialogizität findet sich also schon auf der medientechnischen Ebene der modularen und numerisch repräsentierten Medienobjekte, ebenso in Automationsprozessen (bspw. Bild und Filter), im Hinblick auf die Variabilität von Medienobjekten (Verhältnis von Software zu Upgrade etwa) und in Bezug auf Transcodierungsmöglichkeiten (Umformatierung). Ebenso ist Vernetzung, wie Flusser betont, wesentlich dialogisch. Diese medientechnische Dialogizität weist wiederum mehr Freiheitsgrade für dialogische Kommunikation und Artikulation[28] auf.

Für die Medienbildungsforschung und das Arbeitsgebiet der Medienpädagogik muss unter dialogischer Kommunikation jedoch mehr verstanden werden, als wechselseitige Beeinflussung. Hier geht es dann nicht mehr nur um die auf Digitalisierung und Vernetzung beruhende dialogische Artikulationsfreiheit als Abwesenheit medientechnischer Beschränkung von Wechselseitigkeit und damit um negative Freiheit[29]. Vielmehr wird danach gefragt, inwieweit der konkrete Umgang mit Medien, die auf technischer Ebene vergleichsweise verstärkt dialogische Möglichkeiten für Kommunikation und Artikulation bereitstellen, zur Entstehung neuer existenziell bedeutsamer Sinnbezüge führen kann. Hier ist eine Perspektivverschränkung notwendig, die die Wirklichkeit kultureller Kommunikation nicht vorschnell unter medientechnische Eigenschaften subsumiert. So gibt es beispielsweise empirisch begründeten Anlass zur Verschränkung der Analyse medientechnischer Artikulations- und Kommunikationsbedingungen mit einer strukturellen Analyse von medienspezifischen Darstellungsformaten und innewohnen-

28 Die Bezeichnung Artikulation zielt bei Jung entgegen dem „kognitionslastigen Begriff der Repräsentation" auf das verstehende und auslegende Realitätsverhältnis des Menschen aus der Perspektive der ersten und zweiten Person Singular und Plural. Anders als beim repräsentationalen Beobachterstandpunkt der dritten Person sei der Wirklichkeitsbezug aus der Perspektive betroffener Lebensführung wesentlich artikulatorisch, d.h., gelebtes Leben wird hier für bestimmte kulturhistorische Subjekte durch Ausdrucksgestalten erschlossen, die die Bedeutung jenes gelebten Lebens so weit „stilisieren, konventionalisieren und fixieren, dass sie verstanden werden kann." (Jung 2002, 148).

29 Vgl. zur Differenz negativer (Abwesenheit äußerer Zwänge) und positiver (verwirklichter) Freiheit Taylor (1992).

den Reflexionsoptionen, die an den konkreten Umgang mit Medien in verschiedenen Handlungskontexten rückgebunden wird. Die Sinnhaftigkeit einer perspektivenverschränkenden Medienbildungsforschung wird im Hinblick auf Studien deutlich, die die Problematik der starken Orientierung jugendlichen Medienhandelns an standardisierten und konfektionierten Angebotsstrukturen in digital-vernetzten Medien in das Blickfeld medienpädagogischer Forschung rücken (vgl. etwa Hartung/Brüggen 2007).

Eine medienbildungstheoretische Untersuchung des Verhältnisses von Medien und der Veränderung existenziell bedeutsamer Sinnbezüge (vgl. Marotzki 1990), die entsprechend integrativ verfährt, bedarf eines theoretisch stringenten und empirisch tragfähigen Konzeptes medienspezifischer Sprache und Symbolismen hinsichtlich der Konstitution von Selbst und Welt. Hier sehe ich die Fruchtbarkeit einer Verknüpfung von Bollnows Sprachanalyse mit bildungstheoretischen Annahmen von Winfried Marotzki als auch mit Blick auf eine hinlängliche Berücksichtigung medientechnischer Artikulations- und Kommunikationsbedingungen.

Dialog als „Höhe der Sprachlichkeit" bei Bollnow

Für Bollnow (1966; 1968; 1979) ist Sprache als Verständigungsmedium nur im Gespräch verwirklicht, wobei die Unterscheidung zwischen monologischen und dialogischen Formen der Kommunikation wichtig ist (vgl. Bollnow 1986, 3). Monologische Kommunikationsweisen wie etwa der argumentative Sprechmodus seien, so Bollnow, gerade nicht verständigungsorientiert, weil es hier im schwächsten Sinne um die Begründung der eigenen (gesicherten) Position bzw. Perspektive geht:

> „In der Begründung führe ich Gründe an, die für meine Anschauung sprechen. Aber das Heranziehen von Gründen ist immer etwas Nachträgliches, mit dem ich eine Auffassung, darin ich selbst auch ohnehin sicher bin, einem anderen überzeugend machen will" (Bollnow 1968, 3).

Monologische Sprech- und damit Denkformen von der Begründung (Argumentation) bis zum (mathematisch-naturwissenschaftlichen) Beweis seien zwar grundsätzlich unentbehrlich für menschliche Lebensführung, so sie jedoch zur dominanten Form des Sprechens und in diesem Sinne des Denkens würden, handele es sich um Sprechen als Machtanwendung. Sprache wird dann zum Mittel und hört auf „Sprache im vollen menschlichen Sinne" (Bollnow 1968, 4) – in der Weise Ausdrucksmedium und Medium der (Selbst-)Verständigung – zu sein. Sprache ist in diesem Sinne nur in dialogischer Kommunikation und besonders im Gespräch verwirklicht. Im Gespräch geht es um die Suche nach Wahrheit[30] und um tiefe Lebensfragen, die keinem anderen Zweck, wie etwa

30 Zwar war die Vorstellung einer geteilten Orientierung an Wahrheitsfragen auch konstitutiv für Habermas' Vorstellung verständigungsorientierten Handelns, sein von Motiven und Werten bereinigter Diskursbegriff

dem Erreichen eines bestimmten Zieles im Fall der Beratung oder dem Interessensausgleich bei Verhandlungen, untergeordnet ist (vgl. Bollnow 1979, 1f; Bollnow 1968, 7). Das Gespräch ist durch seine Offenheit charakterisiert, womit freie Fügung von Rede und Gegenrede, die Abwesenheit eines Gesprächszieles oder Ergebnisses als auch eines vorgegebenen Themas gemeint sind (vgl. Bollnow 1964, 51ff). Anders als in der Unterhaltung oder der Konversation ist das Gespräch durch seine Gegenstandsorientierung ausgezeichnet: hier geht es um tiefe (letzte) Lebensfragen, was bei den Beteiligten zu erhöhter Anspannung und Engagement führt und dem Gespräch einen anderen Tiefgang verleiht, als dies in Unterhaltungskontexten und in der Konversation der Fall ist. Zwar nähere sich die Gesprächsführung oft der Diskussion, sei jedoch in Anlehnung an Jaspers als „liebender Kampf" zu verstehen:

> „Der Einwand ist kein Angriff, und er wird nicht als Bestreitung, sondern als Bereicherung der eigenen Meinung aufgenommen. Es geht ja nicht um Positionen, die der eine dem anderen streitig macht, sondern um sich wechselseitig ergänzende Aspekte einer gemeinsamen Sache. [...] Das Aussprechen und für sich beanspruchen eines Unbedingten bedeutet eine Grenze des Gesprächs (z.B. als Überzeugung oder Bekenntnis), die das Gespräch beenden muss" (Bollnow 1966, 52-53).

Der Mensch gewinnt sich erst als Person, die sich zu sich verhalten kann, durch Sprache (vgl. Bollnow 1966, 184). Sprache kann– und das ist medienbildungstheoretisch von höchster Bedeutung – ihren anthropologisch-kulturellen Stellenwert der (Selbst-) Verständigung und –konstitution nur haben, wenn sie angemessen gebraucht wird. Im Gespräch sei Sprache mit ihrer vollen Macht zur Verwandelung ausgestattet.

> „Der Sprechende verwandelt sich, indem er am verantworteten Wort sich selbst, sein eigentliches Selbst gewinnt. [...] Aber auch der, dem sich beschwörend das Wort zuwendet, verwandelt sich, wenn er unter die Macht des Worts gerät" (Bollnow 1964, 29).

Medienbildungstheoretisch relevant ist die Vorstellung Bollnows, der Mensch würde sein Selbst nur im Medium der Sprache (der verwirklichten Sprache des Gespräches) bilden. Sprache ist dabei zwar Macht, aber Ermächtigung zugleich: das Selbst ist der „existenziell zu verstehende [...] Kern, in dem der Mensch sich in einer nie geschenkten, sondern erst in ausdrücklicher Anstrengung erworbenen Festigkeit allem Wandel des Lebens und der Umstände gegenüberstellt." (Bollnow 1966, 194, 187). Diese ausdrückliche Anstrengung im Gespräch, dessen Offenheit und die Orientierung des ar-

---

verkürzte jene im Medium des Symbolischen stattfindende (Selbst-)Verständigung auf den Kampf der besseren Argumente. Bei Bollnow ist jedoch wertbasiertes Engagement konstitutiv für angemessene (Selbst-) Verständigung, insbesondere die Wertschätzung des Gesprächspartners und dessen Perspektive als auch des Gespräches selbst.

tikulierenden Mühens am Gegenstand sei verantwortlicher und angemessener Sprachgebrauch. Angemessenheit bezieht sich dabei auf das Erleben von Sprechenden und Hörenden, die im Hinblick auf die qualitative Vielfalt erlebter und sich immer wieder verändernder Lebensbedingungen zu einem kreativen Umgang mit Sprache führen muss:

> „Die beiden Kennzeichen des richtig gebrauchten Worts, die Angemessenheit an die Situation und die schöpferisch gestaltende Artikulation, widersprechen einander nicht, sondern nur, wo sie sich in einer Art beständiger Resonanz vereinigen, kann die Sprache ihr eigenstes Wesen erfüllen. Nur da offenbart sich die wahre Macht des Worts" (Bollnow 1964, 29).

In anderen Worten: die Freiheit des Menschen ist nicht Negation der Bestimmung durch künstliche Offenheit (Unbestimmtheit als Haltung[31]), sondern (durch die Lebensbedingungen als Bedeutungshorizonte bedingte) Freiheit zur kreativen Selbstbestimmung. In Bollnows Kritik an Jaspers` negativer Methode der Existenzerhellung (vgl. Bollnow 1938, 28ff) wird Unbestimmtheit ähnlich wie in den bildungstheoretischen Überlegungen Marotzkis (Marotzki 1990) als substanzieller Hintergrund für die Entstehung von Neuem betont. Unbestimmtheit sei aber kein Selbstzweck, sondern vielmehr eine als Unruhe erfahrene schöpferische Unbestimmtheit, die über sich selbst – nämlich zur Prägnanzbildung – hinaustreibt. (Medien-)Bildung im Sinne eines Wandels existenziell bedeutsamer Selbst- und Weltbezüge vollzieht sich nur im (er-)mächtigenden Medium des Symbolischen und zwar nur außerhalb des Bereiches einer selbstverständlich verstandenen Welt, nämlich dort, wo der Mensch in „neue, noch unentschiedene Situationen eintritt" (Bollnow 1966, 101). Gesprächsbedarf als Voraussetzung selbst- und weltkonstitutiven Artikulierens und als Bedingung eines Umgangs mit Kommunikationstechnologien im Sinne eines Verständigungsmediums entwickelt sich offenbar erst auf dem konstitutiven Boden einer als offen wahrgenommenen Situation.

Medienkunst als Medienbildungsraum

Hier liegt der medienbildungstheoretische Stellenwert von Medienkunst. Die hier skizzierte Medienkunst bezeichnet erfahrungsbasierte, unbestimmtheitskonstitutive und zugleich prägnanzbildende Artikulations- und Verstehenshandlungen teilweise inkorporierter Akteure, die in einem vortypisierten kulturhistorischen Kontext unter sich verändernden Lebensbedingungen die Unsicherheit, normative Ambivalenz und Unabgeschlossenheit wissenschaftlichen Wissens und damit verbundener entscheidungsoffener Handlungsmöglichkeiten artikulierbar und somit erfahrbar macht Sie öffnet

31 Ähnlich ist auch Rortys Ironieverständnis zu deuten (1992, engl. Ausgabe 1989) als auch das Freiheits- und Sprachverständnis des Poststrukturalismus bei Foucault und Derrida.

die Situation öffentlicher Wahrnehmung wissenschaftlichen Wissens, wissenschaftlicher Methoden der Wissensproduktion und verbundener Handlungsoptionen zum Unbekannten und Ungewissen hin. Durch die Schaffung medienspezifischer prägnanzbildender Unbestimmtheit schafft sie die Grundlage für einen öffentlichen Dialog in und um die Wissen(schaft)sgesellschaft. Medienkunst wird zum Medium der (Selbst-)Verständigung in einer Gesellschaft, in der wissenschaftliches Wissen und wissenschaftliche Methoden der Wissensproduktion von unhintergehbarer selbst- und weltkonstitutiver Bedeutung sind. Die dialogische Dramatisierung von Wissenschaft in der Medienkunst schafft eine vage Differenz[32] zu tradierten selbst- und weltkonstitutiven Sinnbezügen, die im Hinblick auf Sozialisationsprozesse individuiert[33], in Bezug auf sich verändernde Lebensbedingungen dann befähigt, wenn durch dem Erleben angemessenere Symbolismen Erfahrungen tiefgreifender Art, in der Rede Bildungserfahrungen, für Bildungssubjekte ermöglicht werden, die zu einer umfassenden Veränderung existenzieller Sinnbezüge führen können (vgl. Marotzki 1990)[34]. Die Konvergenz von Medien, Computer und Telekommunikation zu einem Hypermedium ermöglicht in der Medienkunst als symbol- und medienreflexivem Medienhandeln die kreative Schaffung neuer symbolischer Formen zur angemessenen Artikulation neuer Erfahrungen gestiegener Kontingenz im Hinblick auf den hohen kulturellen und subjektiven Stellenwert wissenschaftliches Wissens. Diese Medienbildungserfahrungen bezeichnen selbst- und weltkonstitutive Werterfahrungen.

Während Bollnow vor nun mehr als 40 Jahren zu der Einschätzung gelangte, der Mensch habe vor den Möglichkeiten des Gespräches versagt (vgl. Bollnow 1968, 7), konstatiert der Kommunikationswissenschaftler Jo Reichertz in einer aktuellen Zeitdiagnose, die globalisierende Welt habe sich zu einer Kommunikationsgesellschaft gewandelt, in der mit oder ohne Medien mehr und folgenreicher kommuniziert würde und in welcher Kommunikation immer wichtiger werde (vgl. Reichertz 2007, 189). Medienbildungstheoretisch bleibt vor diesem Hintergrund zu fragen, welche (neuen) Möglichkeiten die Wissen(schaft)s- und Kommunikationsgesellschaft für ihre Mitglieder eröffnet, die dazu befähigen, sich auf der „Höhe der Sprachlichkeit" (Bollnow 1968, 7), aber auch auf der Höhe kommunikationstechnologischer Infrastruktur zu verständigen. Medienkunst kann als eine dieser neuen Möglichkeiten angesehen werden, in der medienspezifische Symbolismen und eine multimodale Sprache Medium der öffentlichen Verständigung über die Bedeutung wissenschaftlichen Wissens und mit diesem verbundener Handlungsoptionen und Lebensmöglichkeiten werden. Medienkunst ist dann ein digital-vernetzter Medienbildungsraum – auch für die Entstehung kontin-

32 Auch Alfred Schäfer (2008) verwendet den Begriff der artikulierten Differenz, allerdings in einem anderen Theorierahmen, als das hier der Fall ist.

33 Vgl. zum Verständnis von Bildung als individuierende Selbstbefähigung Schäfer (2004).

genzangemessener Formen der Wertebildung –, wenn sie eine subtilere Sprache unter kreativer Auslotung der auf Digitalisierung und Vernetzung beruhenden Ausdrucksmöglichkeiten entfaltet, welche in Bezug auf das Erleben der Mitglieder dieser sprachhandelnden Interaktionsgemeinschaft angemessener erscheint, als tradierte Sinngefüge und Konventionen der Bedeutungskonstitution.

Literatur

Arns, Inke (2008): Und es gibt sie doch. Ueber die Zeitgenossenschaft der medialen Kuenste. In: HMKV, Hartware, Medienkunstverein, 1996-2008, Dortmund. Vorabveröffentlichung in der Mailingliste Rohrpost (15.3.2008). Online: http://www.mail-archive.com/rohrpost@mikrolisten.de/msg02238.html [8.4.2009]

Arns, Inke (2002): Metonymical Mov(i)es. Lev Manovich's „The Language of New Media". In: dichtung-digital (27.7.2002). Online: http://www.brown.edu/Research/dichtung-digital/2002/07-27-Arns.htm [8.4.2009]

Bittkau-Schmidt, Susan (2008): Wissen und Handeln in virtuellen sozialen Welten. Neue berufliche Handlungs- und Gestaltungsspielräume von PädagogInnen. Wiesbaden: VS Verlag.

BMBF (2008): Deutschlands Rolle in der globalen Wissensgesellschaft stärken. Strategie der Bundesregierung zur Internationalisierung von Wissenschaft und Forschung. Online: http://www.bmbf.de/pub/Internationalisierungsstrategie.pdf [8.4.2009]

Bollnow, Otto Friedrich (1964) Die Macht des Worts. Sprachphilosophische Überlegungen aus pädagogischer Perspektive. In: „neue pädagogische bemühungen" (Nr. 17/18). Online: http://www.otto-friedrich-bollnow.de/doc/MachtdesWorts.pdf [15.05.2008]

Bollnow, Otto Friedrich (1966) Sprache und Erziehung. 2. Auflage, Stuttgart: Kohlhammer.

Bollnow, Otto Friedrich (1968): Erziehung zum Gespräch. In: Zeitschrift für Pädagogik, 7. Beiheft: Sprache und Erziehung, 217-229, 5-7, 231-240. Online: http://www.otto-friedrich-bollnow.de/doc/ErzzumGespraech.pdf [15.05.2008]

Bollnow, Otto Friedrich (1979): Das Gespräch. In: Die Ehrfurcht vor dem Leben, erläutert von K. Suzuki, Asahi Verlag Tokyo 1979, 45-51. Online: http://www.otto-friedrich-bollnow.de/doc/Gespraech.pdf [15.05.2008]

Bonß, Wolfgang (2002): Riskantes Wissen? Zur Rolle der Wissenschaft in der Risikogesellschaft. Beitrag zum Kongress „Gut zu Wissen". In: Heinrich-Böll-Stiftung 2002.

Brecht, Bertold (1989): Der Rundfunk als Kommunikationsapparat. Rede über die Funktion des Rundfunks;-Vorschläge für den Intendanten des Rundfunks; Radio - eine vorsintflutliche Erfindung? In: Werke, Bd. 21, Schriften I, Berlin u.a.

Bromme, Rainer/Jucks, Regina/Wagner, Thomas (2005): How to refer to „diabetes"? Language in online health advice. In: Applied Cognitive Psychology, 19, 569-586. Online: http://wwwpsy.uni-muenster.de/inst3/AEbromme/web/veroef/2005/BroJuWaApplied.pdf [8.4.2009]

Carrier, Martin/Roggenhofer, Johannes (2007): Wandel oder Niedergang?. Die Rolle der Intellektuellen in der Wissensgesellschaft. Bielefeld: Transcript.

Dalferth, Ingolf U./Stoellger, Philipp/Hunziker, Andreas (Hrsg.) (2009): Unmöglichkeiten. Zur Phänomenologie und Hermeneutik eines modalen Grenzbegriffs. München: Mohr Siebeck.

Gazsó, Andrè/Schiemer, Fritz/Greßler, Sabine (Hrsg.) (2007): nano: Chancen und Risiken aktueller Technologien. Wien: Springer.

Godina, Bojan (2007): Unsichtbare Religion des Subliminalen Marketings in den Medien: ein epochaltypischer Beitrag zur Medienbildung bei Kindern und Jugendlichen. Berlin: Pro Business.

Höfling, Siegfried/Mandl, Heinz (Hrsg.) (1997): Lernen für die Zukunft - Lernen in der Zukunft. Wissensmanagement in der Bildung. Berichte und Studien der Hanns-Seidel-Stiftung, Bd. 74. München: Hanns-Seidel-Stiftung e.V.

Elias, Norbert (1980): Die Fischer im Mahlstrom. In: Elias 1983, 73-183.

Elias, Norbert (1983): Engagement und Distanzierung. Frankfurt am Main: Suhrkamp.

Euler, Manfred (2006) Wege in die Nanowelt. In Euler/Forchel 2006, 533 - 554.

Euler, Manfred/Forchel, Alfred (Hrsg.) (2006): Physikdidaktik. Theorie und Praxis. Berlin, Heidelberg: Springer.

Flessner, Bernd (Hrsg.) (2000): Nach dem Menschen. Der Mythos einer zweiten Schöpfung und das Entstehen einer posthumanen Kultur. Freiburg: Rombach. Flusser, Vilèm (2007): Kommunikologie. 4. Auflage. Frankfurt am Main: Fischer Taschenbuch Verlag.

Flusser, Vilèm (2005): Medienkultur. 4. Auflage, Frankfurt am Main: Fischer Taschenbuch Verlag.

Fromme, Johannes/Schäffer, Burkhard (Hrsg.) (2007): Medien, Macht, Gesellschaft. Wiesbaden: VS Verlag.

Hagenhoff, Svenja/Seidenfaden, Lutz/Ortelbach, Björn/Schumann, Matthias (2007): Neue Formen der Wissenschaftskommunikation: Eine Fallstudienuntersuchung. Göttingen: Niedersächsische Staats- und Universitätsbibliothek.

Hartung, Anja/Brüggen, Nils (2007): Selbstinszenierung Jugendlicher in (virtuellen) Kontaktbörsen. In: Neuß/Große-Loheide 2007, 143-152.

Heibach, Christiane (2001): Vom Nutzen und Nachteil der Medientheorien für die Erwachsenenbildung. Vortrag am Deutschen Institut für Erwachsenenbildung. (15.11.2000), Online: http://www.die-frankfurt.de/esprid/dokumente/doc-2001/heibach01_01.htm [6.03.2008]

Heinrich-Böll-Stiftung (Hrsg.) (2002): Gut zu Wissen. Münster: Westfälisches Dampfboot.

Held, Martin (2009): Bildungsökonomie in der Wissensgesellschaft. Marburg: Metropolis-Verlag.

Hoffmann, Jennifer (2009): Transmediale 09: Gefühlskälte im tiefen Norden? (2.3.2009) Online: http://www.jenniferhoffmann.com/2009/02/03/transmediale-09-gefuehlskaelte-im-tiefen-norden/ [8.4.2009]

IPCC/Intergovernmental Panel on Climate Change (2007): IPCC Fourth Assessment Report - Working Group I Report on „The Physical Science Basis". Online: http://www.ipcc.ch/ipccreports/ar4-wg1.htm [9.4.2009]

Krüger, Gerhard/Reschke, Dietrich (2004): Lehr- und Übungsbuch Telematik: Netze, Dienste, Protokolle. Mit Website. München: Hanser Fachbuchverlag.

Kübler, Hans-Dieter (2008): Mythos Wissensgesellschaft. Wiesbaden: VS Verlag.

Joas, Hans (2002): Wertevermittlung in einer fragmentierten Gesellschaft. Zu Chancen und Problemen erhöhter Kontingenz. In: Die Politische Meinung. Monatszeitschrift zu Fragen der Zeit. Megathema Familie (9/2002) 394. Online: http://www.kas.de/wf/de/33.752/ [7. 4.2009]

Joas, Hans (2001): Wertevermittlung in einer fragmentierten Gesellschaft. Vortrag von Prof. Dr. Hans Joas anlässlich des vierten Werkstattgespräches der Initiative McKinsey bildet. im Schloss Tegel, Berlin, am 3.12.2001. Online: http://www.mckinsey-bildet.de/downloads/02_idee/w4_vortrag_joas.pdf [7. 4.2009]

Jörissen, Benjamin / Marotzki, Winfried (2009): Medienbildung - eine Einführung. Theorie - Methoden - Analysen. Stuttgart: UTB.

Jung, Matthias (2002): Hermeneutik zur Einführung. 2. Auflage, Hamburg: Junius.

Jung, Matthias (2005): „Making us explicit": Artikulation als Organisationsprinzip von Erfahrung. In: Schlette/Junge (2005), 103 - 142.

Jung, Matthias (2009) „Leaving it implicit" – Zur anthropologischen Prägnanz von Unbestimmtheit. In: Dalferth/Stoellger/Hinzinker 2009.

Kac, Eduardo (1999): DETAILED DESCRIPTION OF GENESIS. Online: http://www.ekac.org/geninfo.html [9.4.2009]

Kemp, Martin (2007): Science in culture: Heaven in grains of sand. Nanoscientists and Tibetan monks unite to explore the mysteries of the mandala. (12.9.2007). In: Nature 449, 146 (13 September 2007) | doi:10.1038/449146a

Manovich, Lev (2002): The Language of New Media. Cambridge: MIT Press. Online: http://www.manovich.net/LNM/Manovich.pdf [15.09.2008]

Marotzki, Winfried (2007): Die Macht der Erinnerung: Involvement und Reflexion; Aspekte einer strukturalen Medienbildung am Beispiel Film. In: Fromme/Schäffer (2007), 77-100.

Marotzki, Winfried (1990): Entwurf einer strukturalen Bildungstheorie. Weinheim: Deutscher Studien-Verlag.

Matussek, Peter (2004): Der Performative Turn: Wissen als Schauspiel. In: Digitale Transformationen. Erstveröffentlichung in: Fleischmann, Monika/Reinhard, Ulrike (Hrsg.): Digitale Transformationen. Medienkunst als Schnittstelle von Kunst, Wissenschaft, Wirtschaft und Gesellschaft. Heidelberg. Online: http://netzspannung.org/positions/digital-transformations (02. Dezember 2004)

Meyer, Torsten (Hrsg.) (2007): Bildung im Neuen Medium. Education Within A New Medium. Wissensformation und digitale Infrastruktur. Knowledge Formation and Digital Infrastructure. Münster: Waxmann.

Müller, Hans-Rüdiger/Stravoravdis, Wassilios (2007): Bildung im Horizont der Wissensgesellschaft. Wiesbaden: VS Verlag.

Neuß, Norbert/Große-Loheide, Mike (Hrsg.) (2007): Körper. Kult. Medien: Inszenierungen im Alltag und in der Medienbildung. Bielefeld: GMK

Oreskes, Naomi (2004): The Scientific Consensus on Climate Change. In: Science Vol. 306 (4. 12.2004; korrigiert: 21. Januar 2005). Online: http://www.sciencemag.org/cgi/reprint/306/5702/1686.pdf [8.4.2009]

Paus-Hasebrink, Ingrid/Hipfl, Brigitte (2005): Medienpädagogik in Österreich: Perspektiven, Potenziale und Probleme – Ein Kaleidoskop in acht Bildern. In: Medienpädagogik – Zeitschrift für Theorie und Praxis der Medienbildung, 11 Media Education. Online: http://www.medienpaed.com/05-1/paus-hasebrink_hipfl05-1.pdf [15.09.2008]

Reichertz, Jo (2007): Die Macht der Worte und der Medien. Wiesbaden: VS Verlag.

Reichle, Ingeborg (2005): Kunst aus dem Labor. Wien/New York: Springer.

Reinmann-Rothmeier, Gabi/Mandl, Heinz (1997a): Wissensmanagement in der Bildung. In: Höfling/Mandl 1997, 56-66.

Reinmann-Rothmeier, Gabi/Mandl, Heinz (1997b): Wissensmanagement: eine Antwort auf Informationsflut und Wissensexplosion. In: Höfling/Mandl 1997, 12-23.

Schäfer, Alfred (2004): Über Schwierigkeiten beim Versuch, die Welt zu moralisieren. Zur Perspektive eines christlichen Dogon auf die magische Macht der Schreine. In: Schäfer/Wimmer 2004, 155-167.

Schäfer, Alfred (2008): Kulturelle Fremdheit und artikulierte Differenz. Überlegungen zum gegenwärtigen Ort der Bildungstheorie. Vortrag auf dem 21. Kongress der Deutschen Gesellschaft für Erziehungswissenschaft (DGfE) „Kulturen der Bildung" in Dresden am 19.3.2008. Unveröffentlichtes Vortragsmanuskript.

Schäfer, Alfred/Wimmer, Michael (Hrsg.) (2004): Tradition und Kontingenz. Münster: Waxmann.

Scheibel, Michael (2008): Architektur des Wissens. Bildungsräume im Informationszeitalter. München: kopaed.

Scgelsky, Helmut (1961): Der Mensch in der wissenschaftlichen Zivilisation. Köln: Westdeutscher Verlag.

Schlette, Magnus / Jung, Matthias (Hrsg.) (2005): Anthropologie der Artikulation. Begriffliche Grundlagen und transdisziplinäre Perspektiven. Würzburg: Königshausen & Neumann.

Schorb, Bernd / von Holten, Susanne / Würfel, Maren / Keilhauer, Jan (2006) Modelle & pädagogische Hinweise für themenzentrierte aktive Medienarbeit zum Thema Gentests. Leipzig. Online: http://www.uni-leipzig.de/~mepaed/sites/default/files/dok/Themenzentrierte%20aktive%20Medienarbeit%20zum%20Thema%20Gentests.pdf [19.4.2009]

Schorb, Bernd/Keilhauer, Jan/Weißflog, Gregor (2008): PID – Perspektiven im Diskurs. Tschechische und deutsche Jugendliche mit Medien aktiv im Diskurs zur Präimplantationsdiagnostik. Projektinformationen. Online: http://www.uni-leipzig.de/~mepaed/projekt/pid-perspektiven-im-diskurs [19.4.2009]

Schrage, Dominik (2000): Selbstentfaltung und künstliche Verwandtschaft. Vermenschlichung und Therapeutik in den Diskursen des Posthumanen In: Flessner 2000, 43-65.

Schulz-Schaeffer, Ingo/Böschen, Stefan (Hrsg.) (2002): Wissenschaft in der Wissensgesellschaft. Wiesbaden: VS Verlag.

Seifert, Herbert (2008): In den Kraftwerken der Wissensgesellschaft. Berufliche Schulen - vom Ausland bewundert, in Deutschland unterschätzt. Politisches Feuilleton. Deutschlandradio Kultur. (30.05.2008) Online: http://www.dradio.de/dkultur/sendungen/politischesfeuilleton/793049/ [8.4.2009]

Shusterman, Richard (2005): Leibliche Erfahrung in Kunst und Lebensstil. Berlin: Akademie Verlag.

Stadtler, Marc (2006): Auf der Suche nach medizinischen Fachinformationen. Metakognitionen bei der Internetrecherche von Laien. Münster: Waxmann.

Stefanie (2009): My trip to the :: Transmediale :: in Berlin. The Humlab Blog. Online: http://blog.humlab.umu.se/?cat=143 [8.4.2009]

Taylor, Charles (1992): Negative Freiheit?: Zur Kritik des neuzeitlichen Individualismus. Frankfurt am Main: Suhrkamp.

Unger, Alexander (2009): Zur Hybridisierung der Lernkultur in der Wissensgesellschaft: virtuelle Lernumgebungen und die neue Kultur des Lernens. Münster: LIT.

Weber, Jutta (2001): Umkämpfte Bedeutungen. Natur im Zeitalter der Technoscience. E-Dissertation. Online: http://elib.suub.uni-bremen.de/diss/docs/E-Diss228_webersec.pdf [8.4.2009]

Wehling, Peter (2002): Die Schattenseiten der Verwissenschaftlichung In: Schulz-Schaeffer/Böschen 2002, 119-142.

Weingart, Peter (2008): Die Stunde der Wahrheit?: zum Verhältnis der Wissenschaft zu Politik, Wirtschaft und Medien in der Wissensgesellschaft. 2. Auflage. Weilerswist: Velbrück Wissenschaft.

Weingart, Peter (2005): Die Wissenschaft der Öffentlichkeit. Essays zum Verhältnis von Wissenschaft, Medien und Öffentlichkeit. Birkach: Velbrück Wissenschaft.

Autorenverzeichnis

Grell, Petra, Dr., Juniorprofessur für Medien und lebenslanges Lernen an der Universität Potsdam. *Arbeitsschwerpunkte:* Medienpädagogik/Mediendidaktik, Erwachsenenbildung, Hochschuldidaktik.

Hugger, Kai-Uwe, Dr., Univ. Professor für Medienpädagogik und Mediendidaktik an der Universität zu Köln. *Arbeitsschwerpunkte:* Erforschung digitaler Kindheit und Jugend, Medienkompetenzforschung, Erforschung medienpädagogischer Professionalität.

Jörissen, Benjamin, Dr., vertritt z. Zt. die Professur für Angewandte Medienwissenschaft an der Fakultät für Pädagogik an der Universität der Bundeswehr München. *Arbeitsschwerpunkte:* Medienbildung, Pädagogische Anthropologie, qualitativ-empirische Bildungsforschung.

Küllertz, Daniela, M.A., Doktorandin für Medienbildungsforschung an der Otto-von-Guericke-Universität, Magdeburg. *Arbeitsschwerpunkte:* kulturanthropologisch-pragmatistische Medienbildungstheorie, Medienbildungsforschung und Diskurstheorie.

Lamla, Jörn, Dr., vertritt z. Zt. die Professur für Allgemeine Soziologie an der Justus-Liebig-Universität Gießen. *Arbeitsschwerpunkte*: soziologische Theorie, Politische Soziologie und Wirtschafts-/ Konsumsoziologie.

Marotzki, Winfried, Dr., Univ. Professor für Allgemeine Pädagogik an der Otto-von-Guericke-Universität, Magdeburg. Arbeitsschwerpunkte: Bildungstheorie, Medienbildung, Qualitative Sozialforschung.

Meyer, Torsten, Dr., Juniorprofessor für „Erziehungswissenschaft unter besonderer Berücksichtigung der Forschung und Lehre im Bereich Multimedia" am Fachbereich Erziehungswissenschaft an der Universität Hamburg. *Arbeitsschwerpunkte:* Bildung im Neuen Medium, Medieninduzierte Wissensformationen und –formatierungen, Schul- und Hochschulentwicklung.

Schachtner, Christina, DDr., Univ. Professorin für für Medien- und Kommunikationswissenschaft an der Alpen-Adria-Universität Klagenfurt. *Arbeitsschwerpunkte:* Digitale Medien und Bildung, Subjektkonstruktionen und digitale Kultur, Transkulturalität in virtuellen Netzwerken.

Schelhowe, Heidi, Dr., Univ. Professorin für Digitale Medien in der Bildung, Informatik an der Universität Bremen. *Arbeitsschwerpunkte:* Softwareentwicklung für Bildungskontexte, Gestaltung von Lernumgebungen, empirische Forschung und Evaluation.

Schwalbe, Christina, Dipl. Ing, M.A., wissenschaftliche Mitarbeiterin am Fachbereich Erziehungswissenschaft an der Universität Hamburg. *Arbeitsschwerpunkte:* Kommunikationsstrukturen in Bildungsprozessen, Medien & Bildung aus kulturwissenschaftlicher Perspektive, kulturelle Übermittlung.

Selwyn, Neil, Dr., Senior Lecturer, Institute of Education - University of London, UK. His *research and teaching focuses* on the place of digital media in everyday life, and the sociology of technology (non)use in educational settings.

Thiedeke, Udo, Dr., Privatdozent am Institut für Soziologie an der Johannes-Gutenberg Universität Mainz. *Arbeitsschwerpunkte:* Soziologie der Medien und der virtualisierten Vergesellschaftung, allgemeine Soziologie und soziologische Theorien, Soziologie der Bildung.

Unger, Alexander, Dr., wissenschaftlicher Mitarbeiter an der Otto-von-Guericke-Universität Magdeburg. *Arbeitsschwerpunkte:* Neue Medien und mediale Umgebungen in pädagogischen Kontexten, Raum als pädagogische Kategorie, Sozialisation- und Handlungstheorie unter medialisierten Bedingungen.

GPSR Compliance

The European Union's (EU) General Product Safety Regulation (GPSR) is a set of rules that requires consumer products to be safe and our obligations to ensure this.

If you have any concerns about our products, you can contact us on ProductSafety@springernature.com

In case Publisher is established outside the EU, the EU authorized representative is:

Springer Nature Customer Service Center GmbH
Europaplatz 3
69115 Heidelberg, Germany

Batch number: 10809466

Printed by Printforce, the Netherlands